D1191784

NOVA

1965-1975

NOVA 1965-1975

Compiled by David Hillman & Harri Peccinotti
Edited by David Gibbs

Left
April 1967
Photograph by
Harri Peccinotti.

BATSFORD

First published in the United Kingdom in 1993
by Pavilion Books Limited

This revised edition first published by Batsford,
an imprint of Pavilion Books Limited
43 Great Ormond Street
London WC1N 3HZ

Designed by David Hillman
and Karin Beck

A CIP catalogue record of this book is
available from the British Library.

ISBN 9781849944786

Printed and bound by Leo Paper Products Ltd, China

2 4 6 8 10 9 7 5 3 1

This book may be ordered direct from
the publisher at the website:
www.pavilionbooks.com,
or try your local bookshop.

Contents

6 Introduction to the revised edition
Yet the light still shines

14 **The covers**

36 Chapter 1
All shook up
1954-1964

46 Chapter 2
All you need is love
1965-1968

86 Chapter 3
Stairway to heaven
1969-1972

168 Chapter 4
Candle in the wind
1973-1975

216 Appendix
Who did what when

230 Index

YET THE LIGHT STILL SHINES

This is the story of the magazine called *Nova*, its brief brilliance and lasting legacy. It was a creation of extraordinary vigour and style, very much a product and a mirror of the brash and joyful period that had begun in the optimistic and affluent mid-Sixties, the heyday of The Beatles, The Rolling Stones and Mary Quant. It lit up the lives of the fashionable set – and of those who would be part of it – before it flickered and died in the back-biting, hyper-inflationary mid-Seventies when heroes such as David Bowie embodied the escapism that dealt with a world dominated by sour politics and the Vietnam War. It had lasted just eleven years.

The story had actually started earlier in the Sixties. Newspaper magnate Cecil Harmsworth King, who owned the then-mighty *Daily Mirror*, had created a press leviathan over the Fifties and early Sixties by gobbling up many smaller and rival fish in the sea. One of these was George Newnes, a leading magazine publisher in London, which was bought by King in 1963.

By 1965, King's empire consisted of The Mirror Group's two national daily and two national Sunday newspapers, nearly 100 consumer magazines, more than 200 trade and technical journals and various book publishing interests. King renamed this great organisation International Publishing Corporation (IPC) and the somewhat unwieldy grouping began to rationalise its titles and holdings to eliminate unhelpful competition between its various subsidiaries and titles in the same markets.

A crucial role was played in all this by Hugh Cudlipp, Editorial Director of Mirror Group Newspapers. He was King's right-hand man, eventually taking over the reins of the whole empire when King stepped down, after some manoeuvrings, in 1968. Cudlipp was ambitious and had been credited with the creation of the modern British tabloid as evinced by the *Daily Mirror* (to be followed by the *Sun*), introducing new ideas and an approachable editorial and visual character that gave the papers a more populist appeal. To bolster and feed Cudlipp's openness to new ideas and freedoms, he hired as his PA Harry Fieldhouse, who had been editor of *Tatler.*

Fieldhouse was a kindred spirit. He had proved himself as an innovator on *Tatler* and it was he who devised the first plan for *Nova*. With Cudlipp's sanction, he developed it and became its first editor in 1965. He had shown at *Tatler* his ability to create a thoroughly up-to-date tone, depth and accessibility. He had also cultivated a loyal band of contributors there, some of whom were to remain important to him and to *Nova*. These included Angela Ince, Penny Vincenzi and cookery writer Elizabeth David, who all became *Nova* regulars.

Fieldhouse must have been prescient with his title for the new magazine. '*Nova*' is the feminine form of the Latin *novus* meaning 'new'. Indeed, early covers carried the line 'A new kind of magazine for the new kind of woman'. But, more tellingly, 'nova' is the astronomical name for a star that suddenly increases its light output tremendously and then fades away to its former obscurity in a few months or years. Did he know something?

Nova had such a radical, even experimental, approach that sales were initially disappointing. Although this was to be expected, it meant that Cudlipp became worried and Fieldhouse left after just seven months.

The first issues were certainly wobbly but could be considered work in progress for a magazine that was well in advance of its time. But the energy from the backdrop of the mid-Sixties soon began to charge its pages. It was a time of extraordinary creative output in fashion, design and music, especially in London, and the press was fast catching up.

Nova's offices were in Covent Garden, which was still operating in its original form as the central fruit and vegetable market for the trade. It was a 24-hour world of life and character, and this rubbed off on the small creative businesses in the area. There was even a pub or two that remained open all night in a time when 'Last orders!'

was still set at 10.50pm for the rest of the country. Where it was 'happening' was undoubtedly Britain, London in particular, where Covent Garden was one of the principal creative hubs.

The man who became the new editor and who rode the Sixties whirlwind, putting *Nova* firmly on its feet, was Dennis Hackett. For all its early uncertainty, a magazine was soon to emerge that came to epitomise the mood of the times. Hackett was recruited from *Queen* magazine and took over the editorship in September. Working hand in glove with art director Harri Peccinotti, the two soon established what became the recognisable *Nova* style, a combination of brilliant writing displayed with photography, graphics, illustration and typography of prodigious originality and impact.

Peccinotti had been with the magazine since day one and was more than anyone responsible for originating and developing the *Nova* 'look'. The famous NOVA typeface, first used on the cover of the January 1966 issue, was taken from old wood type blocks collected by illustrator and cartoonist Ralph Steadman and stored at the back of his garage. He knew Peccinotti, who recognised the value of the old wooden pieces and put four of them in particular to very good use. After relinquishing his role as art director in 1967, Peccinotti remained a regular photographer for the life of the magazine.

Just as his predecessor had done, the new editor drew on his own network of talent to add them to *Nova*'s writers. These included painter Molly Parkin as fashion editor, the American Irma Kurtz, Arthur Hopcraft on sports and film and the flamboyant astrologer Patric Walker, whose work for some reason was initially presented with no by-line. Brigid Keenan was sometime assistant editor to Dennis

Hackett and remembers: 'He had huge charisma; he always thought outside the box: he [even] once wanted to print *Nova* back-to-front because he noticed that women started reading the magazine at the end.' Hackett was only editor for four years but in that time he captured and fired the imagination as he set the magazine on course for fame and notoriety.

Nova had begun its life as a member of the George Newnes stable, which was carrying on under its own name as part of IPC, publishing a wide range of worthy titles from *Woman's Own*, *Rave* and *Flair* to *Practical Mechanics.* Meanwhile the so-called rationalisation of IPC continued until finally six divisions emerged from the clean-up. One of the last to be created was IPC Magazines, formed in 1968 out of the group's many consumer titles including those of George Newnes. In this great melee of publications, it was perhaps not so surprising that something original and unconventional could be generated before anyone higher up in the organisation really took notice.

Nova's conception was to provide an alternative to traditional women's magazines. But it soon developed into something more, and something that had never been seen before, a mixture of daring and artistic imagery with unconstrained writing that were always at the edge of current taste and acceptability. The issues and causes of gender, race, sexuality and individual rights, so familiar today but then just whispered, were blazed and table-thumped by *Nova* with wit, boldness and panache.

Like many original creations, *Nova*'s success was not so much planned, modelled and developed, but rather the result of coincidences of timing, place and the coming together of a particular band of talented people. Today, the kind of data gathering and analysis, circulation forecasts and the application of economic and social metrics needed to prove that a new idea for a magazine would stand a chance of success in the market would certainly have put the kibosh on such a radical and chancy enterprise as *Nova*.

Nova's readers half a century ago would not have comprehended our modern individualism, successor to their own newer freedoms. Daily life and behaviour may be conducted nowadays according to contemporary idealism and enlightenment, but they are also shaped and tempered by others' approval and disapproval, by burgeoning rules and regulations and even laws. All the paraphernalia of modern technology: social media, personal computers, smart phones and the rest, which have given our 'swipe-click' lives so much efficiency and convenience, are meant to be liberating. But in their own ways they are also quite the opposite.

Yet the preoccupations of the Sixties were not very different from our own. And they were the meat and drink of *Nova*, which was well into its stride by the time Hackett departed in 1969. IPC Magazines then turned to the *Sunday Times Magazine* for new blood. Peter Crookston was appointed editor while the art director's baton was taken on ably by David Hillman, who was to stay with the magazine until it closed in 1975.

Hillman had worked with art director Michael Rand at the *Sunday Times Magazine* when its reputation was at its most formidable. At *Nova* he sustained the magazine's visual impact and influence, adding his own brand of style and wit to proceedings and as well as to the galaxy of star contributors. Hillman was one of those band of graphic designers that had emerged in the Fifties and Sixties as successors to the more lowly commercial artist. The luminaries of the craft included Derek Birdsall, who had also been art editor at *Nova* for a few issues after Peccinotti left. Other notable exponents of the day, and occasional contributors to *Nova*, included Alan Fletcher and Colin Forbes who went on to found the extraordinary design group Pentagram towards the end of the Seventies. They were joined later by John McConnell, who incidentally had also had an office near *Nova*'s in Covent Garden. Hillman, too, was eventually to join this remarkable partnership, where in the Eighties he was to carry out one of his greatest commissions – the radical redesign of the *Guardian*.

Crookston had been features editor at the *Sunday Times Magazine* and, as an admirer of the *New Yorker,* he was inclined to give *Nova* an American feel. But the editorial style he applied was a fraction off what the magazine's reputation had been built on. And so Gillian Cooke succeeded him as editor in 1970, with Hillman installed as deputy editor as well as art director in 1971.

Many of the original writers and editors continued to contribute their spark. Penny Vincenzi, who had worked on the very first issue, was there as beauty editor. Fashion editor Caroline Baker had also joined the magazine in the early days as a receptionist, became Molly Parkin's assistant and then fashion editor in 1967 when Parkin relinquished her full-time role.

As the Seventies progressed, IPC Magazines became gradually more technocratic with an increasingly firm and realistic grip on the statistics of survival. The economy hit the rocks, costs rose, advertising fell and the magazine shrunk. Life was a good deal gloomier than in the previous decade and *Nova*'s readers were no longer in the mood for its carefree conceits, even if they were themselves diminished. Increasing competition, led by of Helen Gurley Brown's massively resourced *Cosmopolitan* from America, which began publishing a UK edition in 1972 with its own take on liberated feminism, also started nicking *Nova*'s readers. By 1975, circulation figures were half those of ten years earlier. The end was inevitable; *Nova* closed.

This book, first published in November 1993, is a chronicle of a magical story characterised by an invigorating freedom and breaking of establishment rules. It tracks the rapid changes society was undergoing at the time and how these were also being fomented in the magazine's pages. But, above all, the book records and reproduces *Nova*'s special kind of visual brilliance, which has hardly been matched since. It showcases the work of leading photographers such as Terence Donovan, Helmut Newton, Diane Arbus, Hans Feurer, Sarah Moon and many others who were regular contributors. New and established illustrators and artists were also recruited to give *Nova* its special visual edge, including Alan Aldridge, Peter Blake, Mike McInnerney, Roger Law and Celestino Valenti.

Fashion is flighty and impermanent by definition; here today then gone, not just tomorrow but the next day and the next. But for *Nova*, tomorrow is now, it continues to be with us in spirit and influence. So it was something much more than fashion. Profound changes in the detail of style and of technique that have occurred between the 1960s and now may be interesting. But the new attitudes and aspirations that *Nova* nurtured and championed, sometimes even created, represent something that hasn't changed, just grown and become taken for granted. They are all the more enthralling for that. Where and how did all this start? This book has your answer.

David Gibbs, September 2019

Editors

Harry Fieldhouse
March 1965 – August 1965

Dennis Hackett
September 1965 – December 1967

Bill Smithies
January 1968 – June 1968

Dennis Hackett
July 1968 – April 1969

Peter Crookston
May 1969 – November 1970

Gillian Cooke
December 1970 – October 1975

Art Directors

Harri Peccinotti
March 1965 – November 1966

Derek Birdsall
December 1966

John Blackburn
January 1967 – April 1967

Bill Fallover
May 1967 – February 1968

Derek Birdsall
April 1968 – January 1969

David Hillman
June 1969 – October 1975

The covers

JUNE 3s
Nova
A NEW KIND OF MAGAZINE FOR THE NEW KIND OF WOMAN
Is this culture? Your character in colour/Charity now/
Alarming girl graduates/Peter Hall interviewed/Space is
kids' stuff/Holiday clothes. That can't be culture-it's fun

NOVA
MARCH 3s
A NEW KIND OF MAGAZINE FOR THE NEW KIND OF WOMAN
This is No. 1 of the British monthly with the 1965 approach. What's the isometric system? Mary Rand figures it out. What does Christopher Booker say about Miss Cardinale? (That's her above.) Who's Mr. Blond? Pages & pages of answers, plus Jill Butterfield, Robert Robinson, Elizabeth David, Irwin Shaw and Paris fashion. And where's 'Terra Nova'? Explore inside

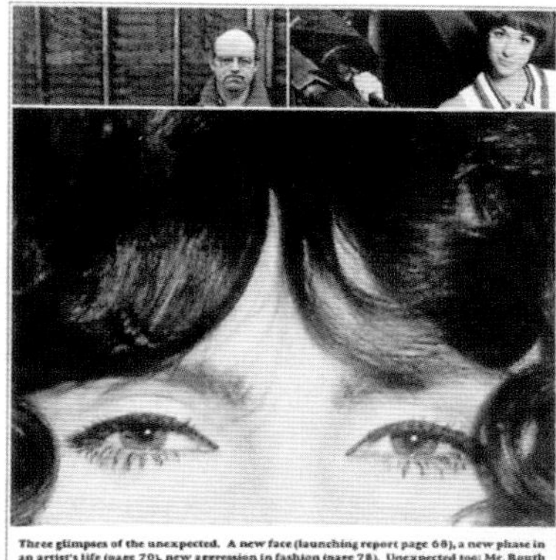
NOVA
Three glimpses of the unexpected. A new face (launching report page 68), a new phase in an artist's life (page 70), new aggression in fashion (page 78). Unexpected too: Mr. Routh offers his excuses. No excuses, though, for Laurie Lee or the James Gould Cozzens story

NOVA
MAY 3s
A NEW KIND OF MAGAZINE FOR THE NEW KIND OF WOMAN
Now hear this!
If you've ever thought of emigrating consult Nova's report
on a girl who upped and went to New York
If you nearly married a G P find out what you
missed and feel better about it. If you like fish, hate children,
can't fathom abstracts, go for Richard Harris
...it's all here.

NOVA
JULY 3s
A NEW KIND OF MAGAZINE FOR THE NEW KIND OF WOMAN
Say what you like, and Jeanne Moreau does, where else would you find the gen on chirology, portrait painters, and acupuncture? If you wouldn't want to, then try choosing a school, or marrying under duress, or looking a million for much less. You'd have to be dead not to care. (There's a piece on being dead too)

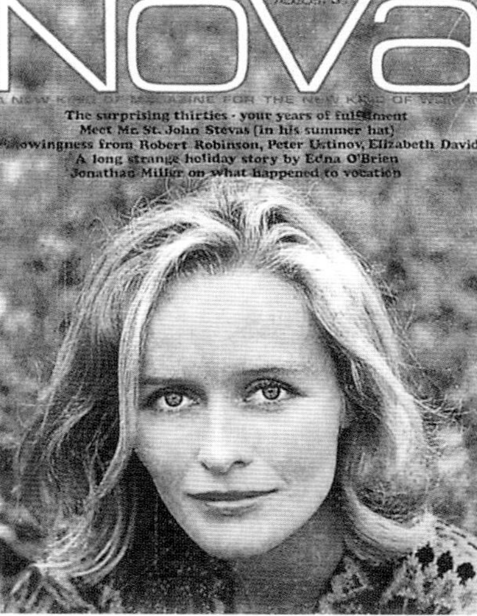
NOVA
The surprising thirties - your years of fulfilment
Meet Mr. St. John Stevas (in his summer hat)
Knowingness from Robert Robinson, Peter Ustinov, Elizabeth David
A long strange holiday story by Edna O'Brien
Jonathan Miller on what happened to vocation

NOVA
SEPTEMBER 3s
FOR WOMEN WHO THINK MAGAZINES DON'T UNDERSTAND
What Jeeves wouldn't dream of telling about the rich
Those literary furies by Ruth Inglis
Introducing Astra Nova
What to wear this autumn
The problems of living with a successful husband

NOVA
FOR WOMEN WHO THINK MAGAZINES DON'T UNDERSTAND
TWO EXPERIMENTS IN ROYAL MARRIAGE
GRETA GARBO AT 60 • CHILDBIRTH CAN BE FUN • PICTURES

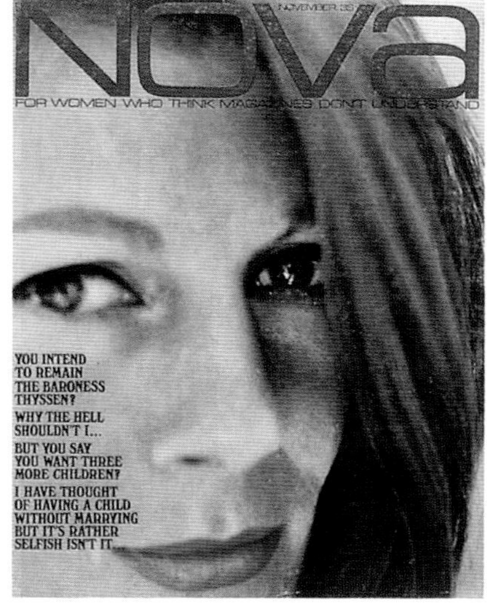
NOVA
FOR WOMEN WHO THINK MAGAZINES DON'T UNDERSTAND
YOU INTEND TO REMAIN THE BARONESS THYSSEN?
WHY THE HELL SHOULDN'T I...
BUT YOU SAY YOU WANT THREE MORE CHILDREN?
I HAVE THOUGHT OF HAVING A CHILD WITHOUT MARRYING BUT IT'S RATHER SELFISH ISN'T IT...

NOVA
Read your children's hands/Pick your Christmas clothes, presents, food/
And the mail train robbery?-Spare a thought for the wives
Find out who Alfie is and think...Whatever's happening to Christianity?

JANUARY 1966 THREE SHILLINGS
NOVA

NOVA
WE REGRET TO ANNOUNCE THAT IT IS POSSIBLE THAT 1.8 OF OUR READERS WILL BE MURDERED THIS YEAR
THESE, OF COURSE, ARE ONLY THE ONES WHO WILL BE DISCOVERED. SEE PAGE 20

YOU MAY THINK I LOOK CUTE
BUT WOULD YOU LIVE NEXT DOOR
TO MY MUMMY AND DADDY?
Start reading on page 14

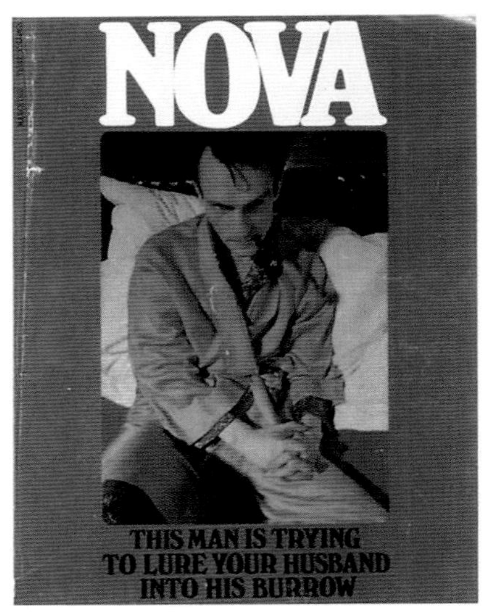
NOVA
THIS MAN IS TRYING
TO LURE YOUR HUSBAND
INTO HIS BURROW

NOVA
THE QUEEN AT 40.....DOES SHE
EXPECT TOO MUCH? (DO WE?)

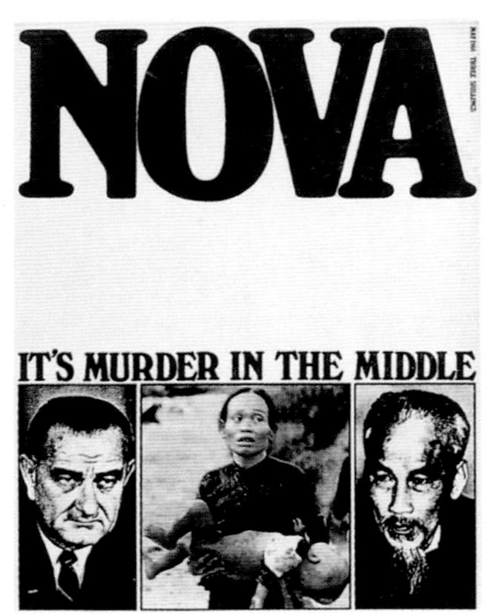
NOVA
IT'S MURDER IN THE MIDDLE

NOVA
WILL ANYONE WITH
ANY INFORMATION ABOUT
THIS MAN PLEASE CONTACT
THE RUSSIAN EMBASSY

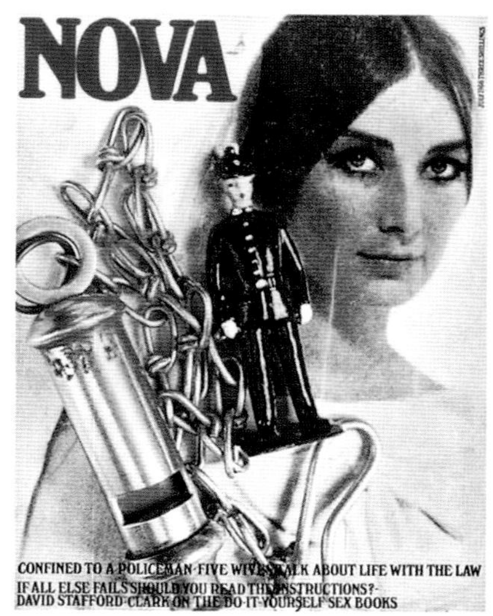
NOVA
CONFINED TO A POLICEMAN-FIVE WIVES TALK ABOUT LIFE WITH THE LAW
IF ALL ELSE FAILS SHOULD YOU READ THE INSTRUCTIONS?-
DAVID STAFFORD-CLARK ON THE DO-IT-YOURSELF SEX BOOKS

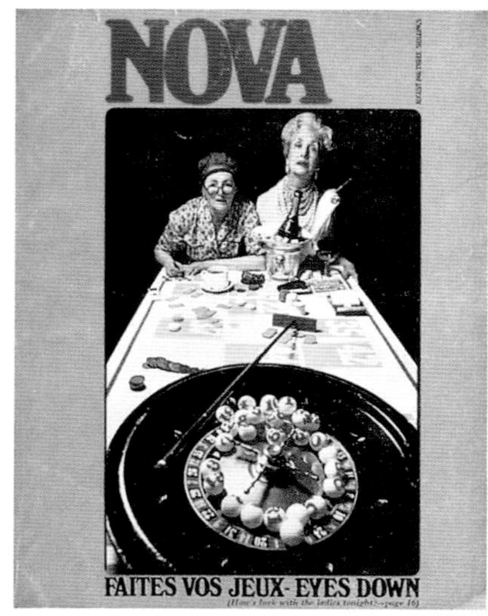
NOVA
FAITES VOS JEUX-EYES DOWN

NOVA
❛THERE ARE MANY ROADS TO PERFECTION... I HAVE TRIED TO EXPLAIN THE WAY IT IS FOR THE AVOWED VIRGIN❜
DIALOGUE WITH A NOVICE MISTRESS-PAGE 52

NOVA
THE SECRET OF SSH...YOU KNOW WHO...SEE PAGE 62

NOVA

IF YOU'RE A HOUSEWIFE (AND BORED BY IT)
OR AN OLDER WOMAN (AND FEELING IT) OR A
UNIVERSITY WIFE (AND HATING IT)-PAY UP.
THIS ISSUE IS FOR YOU.
AND AS FOR THAT CHARACTER ABOVE...
COME BACK HANCOCK ALL IS FORGIVEN-AGAIN

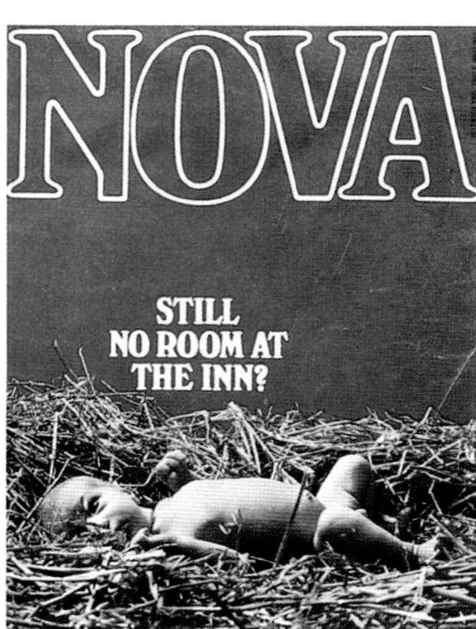
NOVA
STILL NO ROOM AT THE INN?

NOVA
HOW
TO SPEND THE
FREEZE:
HIBERNATE

NOVA
Yes, we're living in sin
No, we're not getting married
Why? It's out of date

NOVA
Clore Cadbury Flower
Curzon Isaacs d'Abreu
Keith Butter Edmonstone
These girls are expecting millions-but what else?

NOVA
FEBRUARY 1967 THREE SHILLINGS
THEY CONSENT
IN PRIVATE

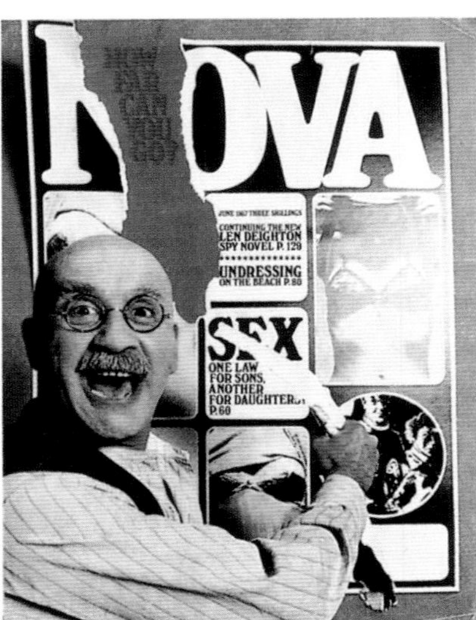
NOVA
CONTINUING THE NEW
LEN DEIGHTON
SPY NOVEL P. 129
UNDRESSING
ON THE BEACH P. 80
SEX
ONE LAW
FOR SONS,
ANOTHER
FOR DAUGHTERS
P. 60

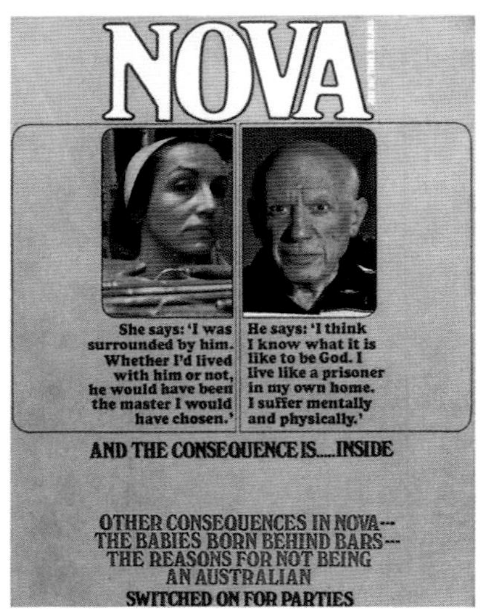
NOVA
She says: 'I was
surrounded by him.
Whether I'd lived
with him or not,
he would have been
the master I would
have chosen.'
He says: 'I think
I know what it is
like to be God. I
live like a prisoner
in my own home.
I suffer mentally
and physically.'
AND THE CONSEQUENCE IS.....INSIDE
OTHER CONSEQUENCES IN NOVA---
THE BABIES BORN BEHIND BARS---
THE REASONS FOR NOT BEING
AN AUSTRALIAN
SWITCHED ON FOR PARTIES

MAY 1967 THREE SHILLINGS
NOVA
STARTING
LEN DEIGHTON'S
NEW SPY BOOK.
ALSO DAVID FROST,
MOREAU, BROPHY,
SHRIMPTON, PROOPS,
LADY CHICHESTER
WHY DO
WOMEN
HAVE BABIES?

NOVA
SEX: I HAVE NEVER HAD
THE OPPORTUNITY TO FIGHT
FOR MY HONOUR YET
COLOUR: I WOULD NOT
WANT TO ASSOCIATE WITH
PEOPLE OF SUCH LOW MENTAL
CALIBRE THAT THEY WOULD
CREATE THIS KIND OF BAR
STARVATION: THANK GOD
I'M NOT IN THEIR SITUATION.
THERE IS NO POINT IN
TALKING ABOUT IT
AND TO THINK THAT
MISS WORLDS USUALLY TALK
WITH THEIR SWIMSUITS

NOVA
CAMBRIDGE CLASS OF '67:
THE BOY MOST LIKELY TO SUCCEED.

NOVA
Adam and Eve: the first love-in

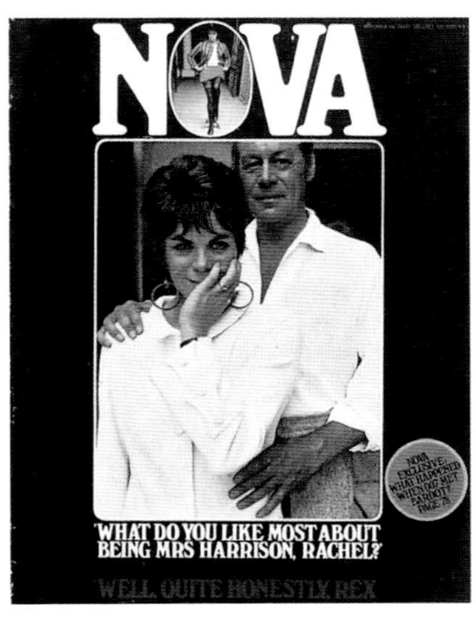
NOVA
'WHAT DO YOU LIKE MOST ABOUT
BEING MRS HARRISON, RACHEL?'
WELL, QUITE HONESTLY, REX

NOVA
MEDITATE
SALIVATE

'I HAVE A CERTAIN VULGAR NOTORIETY. HERE IS A WAY THAT NOTORIETY CAN BE PUT TO A BETTER USE'
AT 42, MARLON BRANDO FINDS HIS CAUSE IN STARVING CHILDREN.
NOVA

NOVA
50 YEARS AFTER THE VOTE:
ONLY THE CHAINS HAVE CHANGED

NOVA
Where may you touch?
Mother, father, boy-friend, girl-friend, turn to page 60

NOVA
APRIL 1968 THREE SHILLINGS AND SIXPENCE
THE SEE-THROUGH DRESS IS A SYMPTOM NOT AN EPIDEMIC
FASHION AND DIAGNOSIS PAGE 64
Also see-through husbands page 86

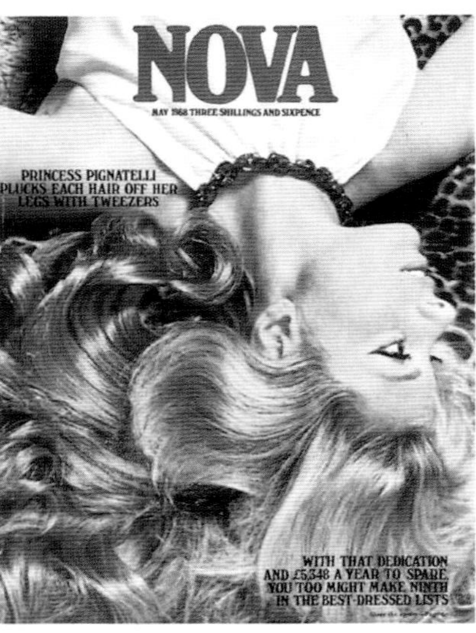
NOVA
MAY 1968 THREE SHILLINGS AND SIXPENCE
PRINCESS PIGNATELLI PLUCKS EACH HAIR OFF HER LEGS WITH TWEEZERS
WITH THAT DEDICATION AND £5,348 A YEAR TO SPARE, YOU TOO MIGHT MAKE NINTH IN THE BEST-DRESSED LISTS

NOVA
'BEING A FILM STAR IS A BORE. IT IS BETTER TO KEEP ONE MAN WARM ALL YOUR LIFETIME.'
-AVA GARDNER, NOW 45, WHO WENT COOL ON MICKEY ROONEY, ARTIE SHAW AND FRANK SINATRA

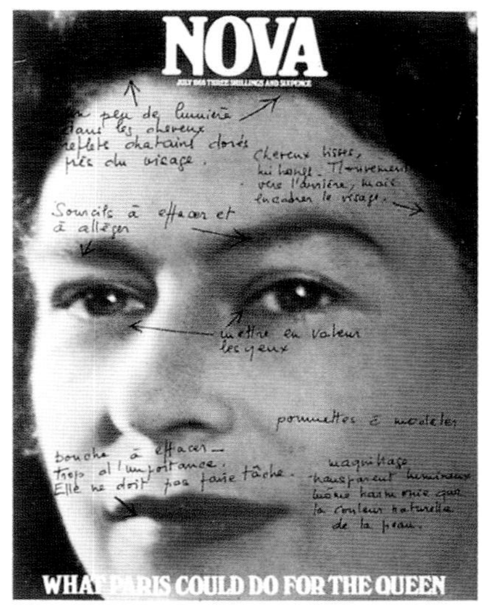
NOVA
WHAT PARIS COULD DO FOR THE QUEEN

NOVA

WHY CAN'T THEY STAY AT HOME?

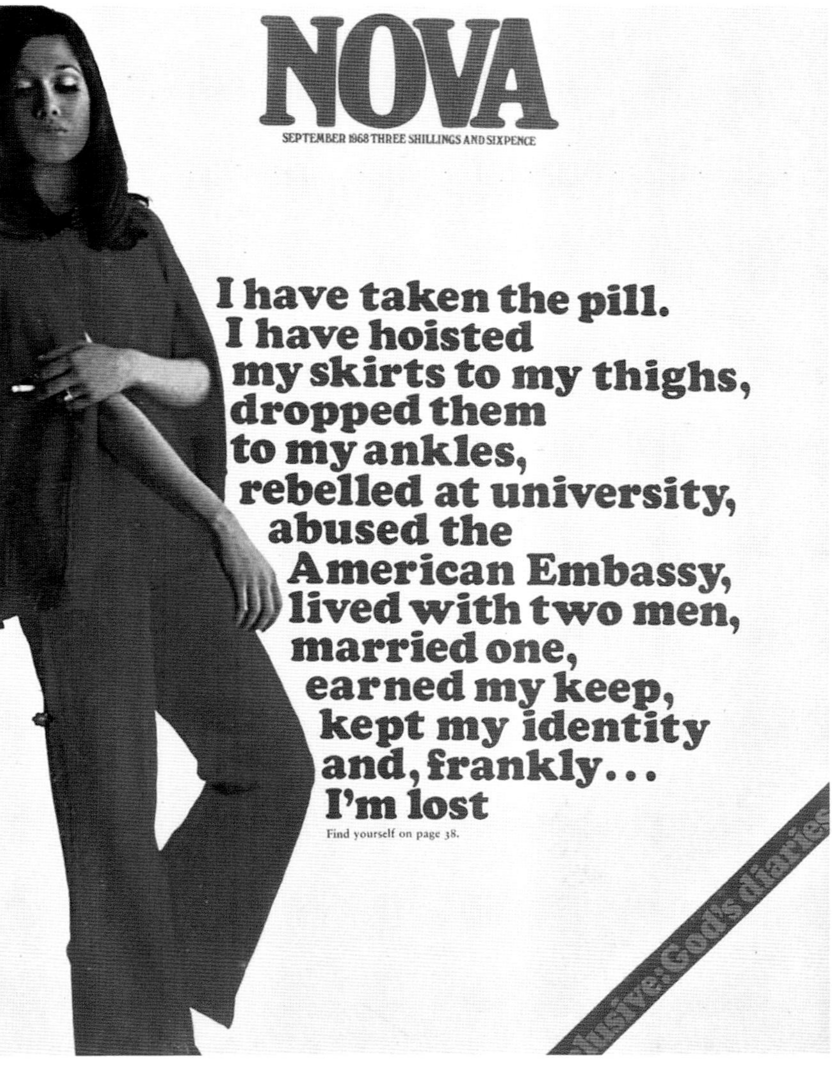
NOVA
SEPTEMBER 1968 THREE SHILLINGS AND SIXPENCE
I have taken the pill.
I have hoisted
my skirts to my thighs,
dropped them
to my ankles,
rebelled at university,
abused the
American Embassy,
lived with two men,
married one,
earned my keep,
kept my identity
and, frankly...
I'm lost
Find yourself on page 38.

NOVA
PRIVATE FACES
TWIGGY, THE QUEEN, PRINCE PHILIP,
THE POPE, FROST ETC...PAGE 60

NOVA
Muggeridge: is he Britain's biggest bore?
Jane Fonda: men I'd like to have babies by if...
Veruschka: who's zoo in modelling!

NOVA
What makes children revolt, take pot, drop out, love in
and not understand their parents

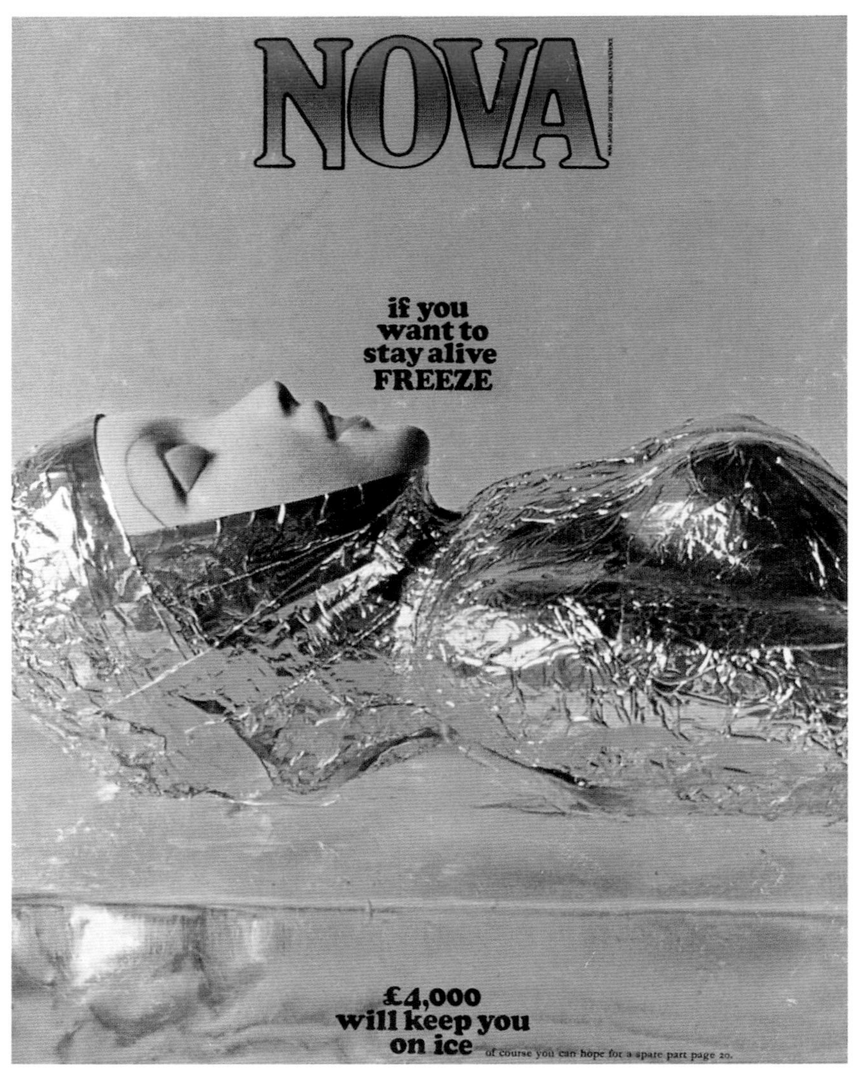

NOVA

Dear Madam,
At the close of business last night
your account was overdrawn £25.5s.8d.
I should be glad if you would take
steps to remedy this situation immediately and in any case telephone me
today as I should like to discuss the
future conduct of your account.

Yours faithfully,

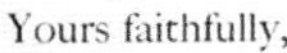

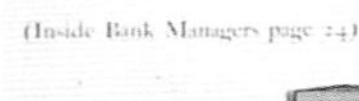

(Inside Bank Managers page 24)

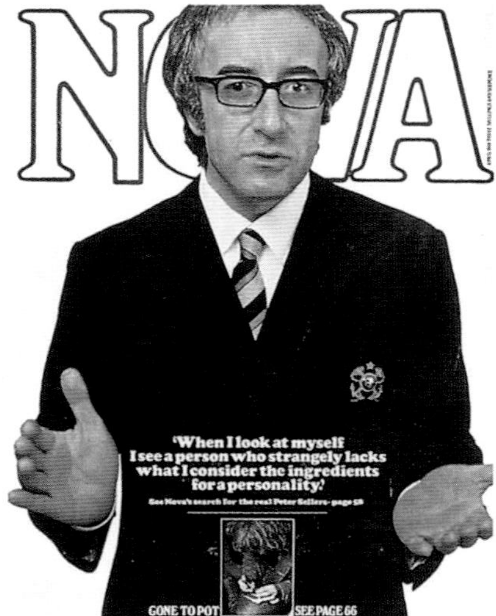

The month David Hillman joined *Nova*, the printers went on strike and the May and June issues were combined.

NOVA
Michael Halsey and Geoffrey Hull think their wives have suffered enough anxiety over birth control. So they've done something positive about it. They've had themselves sterilised

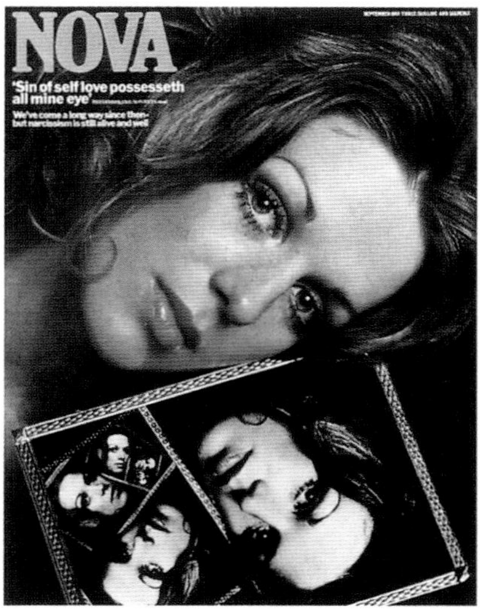
NOVA
'Sin of self love possesseth all mine eye'

NOVA
We're all for equality of the sexes
–but this is too much!

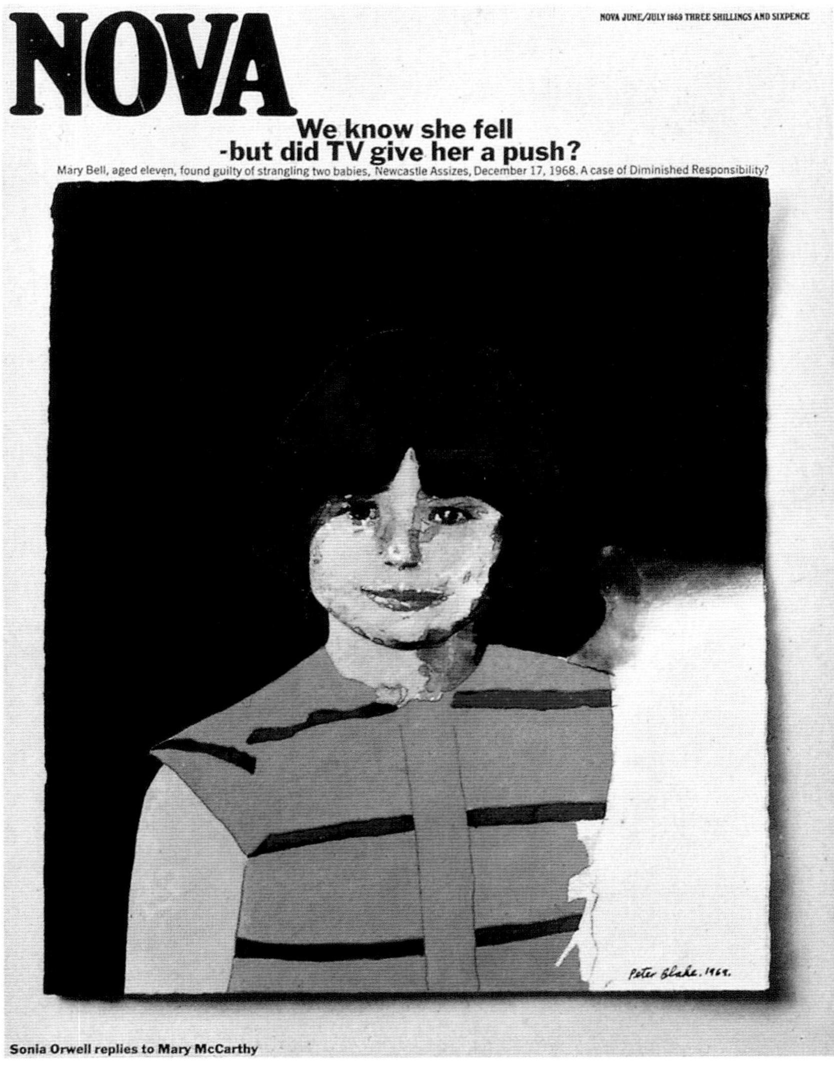
NOVA
NOVA JUNE/JULY 1969 THREE SHILLINGS AND SIXPENCE
We know she fell
-but did TV give her a push?
Mary Bell, aged eleven, found guilty of strangling two babies, Newcastle Assizes, December 17, 1968. A case of Diminished Responsibility?
Peter Blake. 1969.
Sonia Orwell replies to Mary McCarthy

NOVA
RICH WOMEN
ARE PIERRE'S LIFE
-LUCKY PIERRE?
THE MARGARET
AND
TOWNSEND ERA
ENOCH POWELL
AS P.M.
HOW TO GROW
YOUNG AFTER 30

NOVA
LAUGHTER:
THE GREAT
CHARACTER
GIVEAWAY
ANDY WARHOL'S
NEW
SUPERSTARS
MEN WITHOUT
WOMEN
LORD HILL:
WHAT MAKES
CHARLIE RUN?

NOVA
INSIDE EVERY WOMAN THERE'S A STRIPPER LONGING TO GET OUT
MORDECAI RICHLER DEBUNKS IAN FLEMING
BRILLIANT TRAVEL IDEAS
FANTASTIC FAKE FURS

NOVA
How to package a Prime Minister
The man who invented pop art
George Formby is still with us
A. S. Byatt in praise of Monica Dickens

NOVA
BARDOT: 'WHY I LOOK BETTER AT 35'

NOVA
FEBRUARY 1970 THREE SHILLINGS AND SIXPENCE
FASHION NEEDS RE-THINKING. START HERE...
SPAN-LAND ANALYSED
WHAT'S SO SPECIAL ABOUT JOHN CASSAVETES' GIRLS?
PEOPLE WHO ADVERTISE FOR SOULMATES
SHORT STORY BY NADINE GORDIMER

NOVA
3/6
NOW HEAR THIS... WHEN I'M RUNNING THIS COUNTRY THINGS WILL BE VERY DIFFERENT
(See how different on page 44)
The great executive wife myth
Susan Wilding Five husbands later
What men hate about home
The continuing story of Tinderbox Green
Girl's eye-view of a playboy's lair
John Mortimer fights censorship

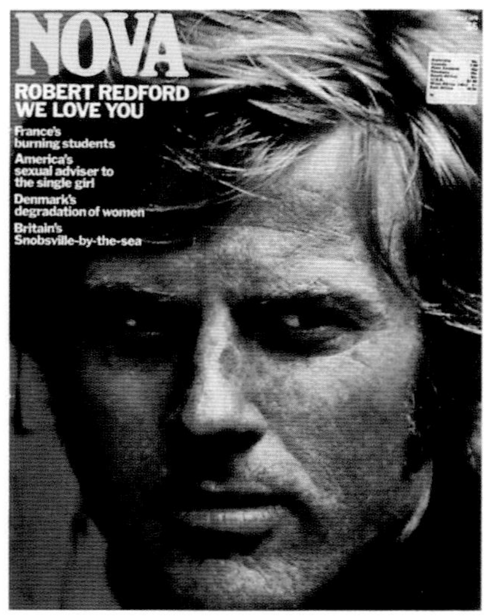
NOVA
ROBERT REDFORD WE LOVE YOU
France's burning students
America's sexual adviser to the single girl
Denmark's degradation of women
Britain's Snobsville-by-the-sea

NOVA
3/6
MAY 1970
THE DARING DUDS OF MAY
Are middle-class women mean?
Farewell (and good riddance) to the big-time surgeon
LONSDALE

NOVA
3/6
WOULD YOU BELIEVE I ONCE HAD A FLAT CHEST, GREY TEETH AND A POT BELLY? FOR THE SECRET OF MY SUCCESS SEE INSIDE
Your friendly neighbourhood witch
Helen Lawrenson's underground diary
At 30 the world is full of married men

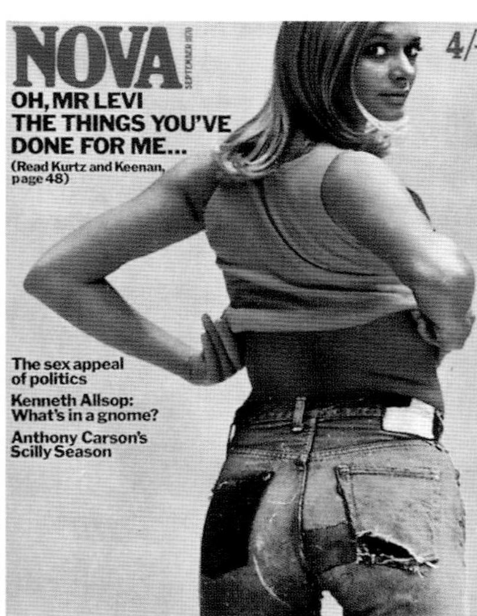
NOVA
4/-
OH, MR LEVI THE THINGS YOU'VE DONE FOR ME...
(Read Kurtz and Keenan, page 48)
The sex appeal of politics
Kenneth Allsop: What's in a gnome?
Anthony Carson's Scilly Season

NOVA
OCTOBER 1970
4/-
How three wives chose their lovers
Girls in their student bliss
Rugby's touchline widows
The bigamist's victim
Some men think that plump is pretty
Every girl a gaucho

NOVA
4/-
20 NP
Stop twitching– you're a big girl now (see page 70)
It's tough being

NOVA
4/-
20 NP
The dressing-up game only grown-up girls can play
'People are daft' says Ernie. He should know... he makes a living stealing from them
Jealousy makes murderers of us all

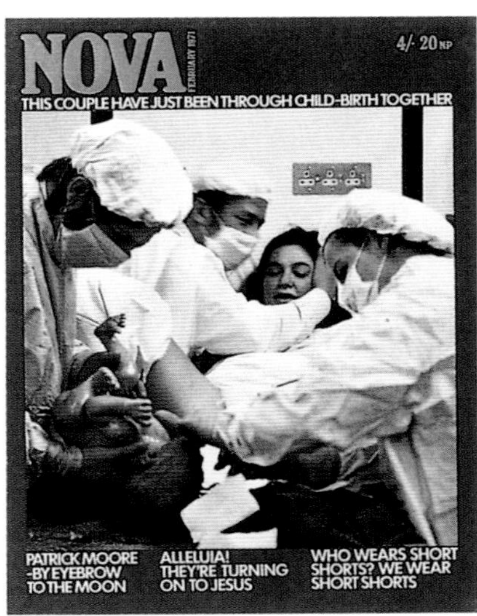
NOVA
FEBRUARY 1971
4/- 20NP
THIS COUPLE HAVE JUST BEEN THROUGH CHILD-BIRTH TOGETHER
PATRICK MOORE -BY EYEBROW TO THE MOON
ALLELUIA! THEY'RE TURNING ON TO JESUS
WHO WEARS SHORT SHORTS? WE WEAR SHORT SHORTS

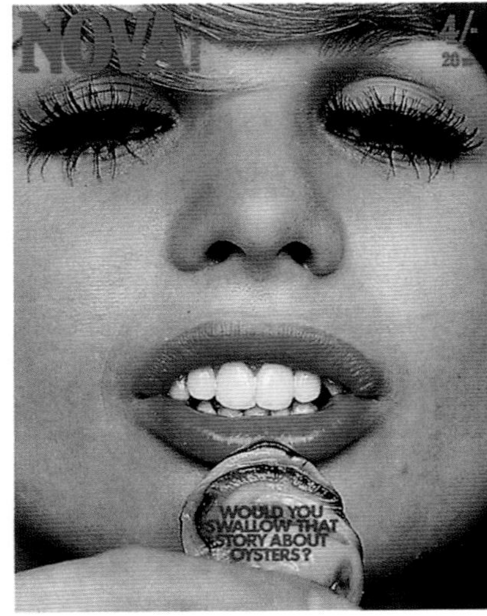
NOVA
WOULD YOU SWALLOW THAT STORY ABOUT OYSTERS?

NOVA
MARCH 1971
4/- 20NP
DARKLY, DEEPLY, BEAUTIFULLY BLUE
Good on you
IS OLD AGE A PUNISHABLE OFFENCE?
CAN A WOMAN LOVE TWO MEN AT ONCE?
THE GOSPEL ACCORDING TO A HOMOSEXUAL PRIEST

NOVA
MAY 1971 20 PENCE
How to undress in front of your husband
and a flick-book to amuse him while he waits
POLANSKI HIGH ON POLANSKI
MOROCCAN FASHION
GARDEN STATUES COME INDOORS
IS YOUR CHILD INHERITING YOUR HANG-UPS?
FIRST LOVE REMEMBERED

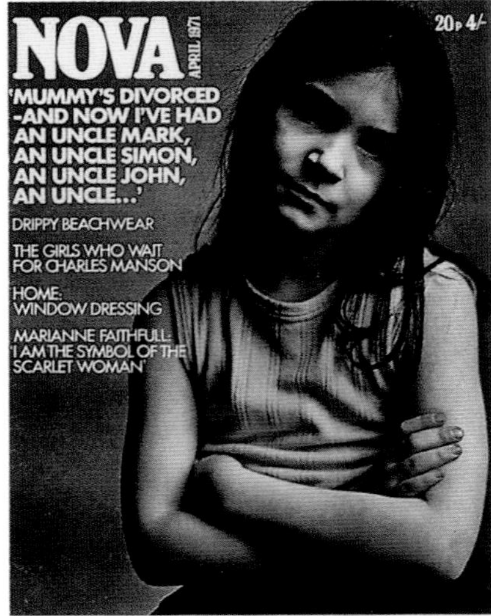
NOVA
APRIL 1971
20p 4/-
'MUMMY'S DIVORCED -AND NOW I'VE HAD AN UNCLE MARK, AN UNCLE SIMON, AN UNCLE JOHN, AN UNCLE...'
DRIPPY BEACHWEAR
THE GIRLS WHO WAIT FOR CHARLES MANSON
HOME: WINDOW DRESSING
MARIANNE FAITHFULL: 'I AM THE SYMBOL OF THE SCARLET WOMAN'

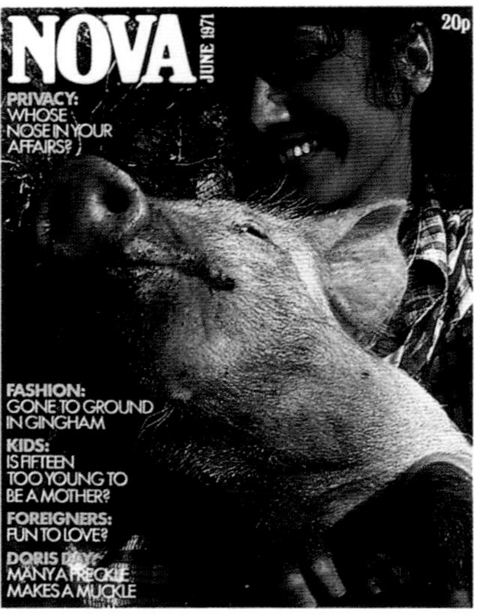
NOVA
JUNE 1971
20p
PRIVACY: WHOSE NOSE IN YOUR AFFAIRS?
FASHION: GONE TO GROUND IN GINGHAM
KIDS: IS FIFTEEN TOO YOUNG TO BE A MOTHER?
FOREIGNERS: FUN TO LOVE?
MANY A FRECKLE MAKES A MUCKLE

NOVA
IT'S AN UGLY BUSINESS BEING BEAUTIFUL
A FATHER'S RIGHT TO BE LEFT HOLDING THE BABY

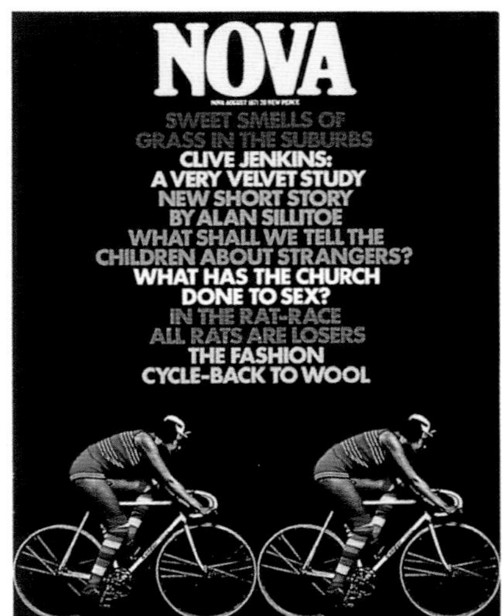
NOVA
SWEET SMELLS OF GRASS IN THE SUBURBS
CLIVE JENKINS: A VERY VELVET STUDY
NEW SHORT STORY BY ALAN SILLITOE
WHAT SHALL WE TELL THE CHILDREN ABOUT STRANGERS?
WHAT HAS THE CHURCH DONE TO SEX?
IN THE RAT-RACE ALL RATS ARE LOSERS
THE FASHION CYCLE-BACK TO WOOL

NOVA
SEPTEMBER 1971
20p
ONE MAN'S MEAT IS ANOTHER MAN'S GLUCONO-D-LACTONE
DRESSED TO KILL
PETER WALKER, CABINET SUPERSTAR
FIND THE FACE THAT FITS YOU
MISSIONARIES IN THE MELTING POT

NOVA
OCTOBER 1971
20p
WARNING
THIS ISSUE MAY BE HAZARDOUS TO MEN'S HEALTH

NOVA
20p
TAKE YOUR PARTNERS FOR THAT OLD-TIME SPECTACULAR-MONOGAMY
ALSO: INSIDE BRITAIN'S GHETTO

NOVA
20p
'ADULTERY, RAPE, EROTICISM, EXTORTION -ANOTHER JOLLY CHRISTMAS ISSUE!'

NOVA
JANUARY 1972
20p
NOW
WE KNOW
WHAT
THE COMMITTEE'S
BEEN UP TO
SECRET

NOVA
20p
WOMEN AND MONEY
MARRIAGE;
WHAT HOLDS IT
TOGETHER?
THE NEW
UPDIKE
JAPAN:
SCHIZOPHRENIC
SUPERSTATE

NOVA
20p
SO YOU
THINK
THIS PICTURE
EXPLOITS
WOMEN
Don't you know it also
exploits men?
REMEMBER:
your overweight,
overstressed,
sexually oppressed,
economically
enslaved man needs
liberating too!
On the other hand,
being exploited has its
lighter side
SPECIAL
PULL-OUT

NOVA
20p
SELF-LOVE IS NEVER HAVING
TO SAY YOU CAN'T AFFORD IT
SEEN AND NOW HEARD;
CHILDREN SPEAK UP AND YOU'D
BETTER BE LISTENING
ARE YOU SURE
YOU'RE GOOD IN BED?

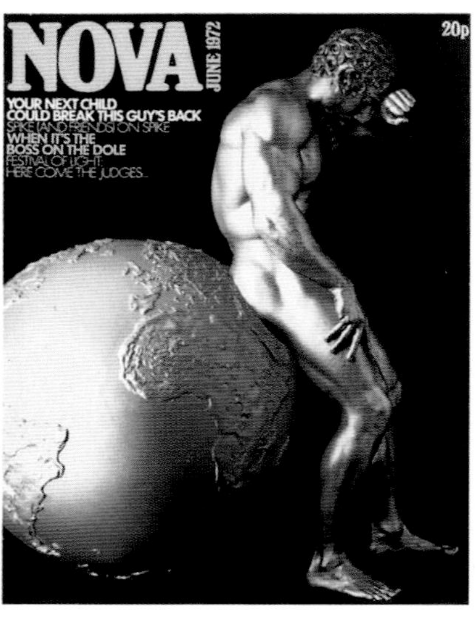
NOVA
JUNE 1972
20p
YOUR NEXT CHILD
COULD BREAK THIS GUY'S BACK
SPIKE (AND FRIENDS) ON SPIKE
WHEN IT'S THE
BOSS ON THE DOLE
FESTIVAL OF LIGHT:
HERE COME THE JUDGES...

NOVA
20p
TAKE OFF THE BOIL
AND SIMMER GENTLY
FAMILIES AT WAR:
REPORT FROM BELFAST
WILL YOU STILL
LOVE ME WHEN I'M 50?
LITTLE STARS OF STAGE
AND CLASSROOM
THE BATTLE AGAINST
MIGHTY MOUSE

NOVA
20p
THE SNARES OF FREEDOM: TWO WEEKS IN THE LIFE OF AN EX-PRISONER
PEOPLE WHO DISLIKE THEIR CHILDREN

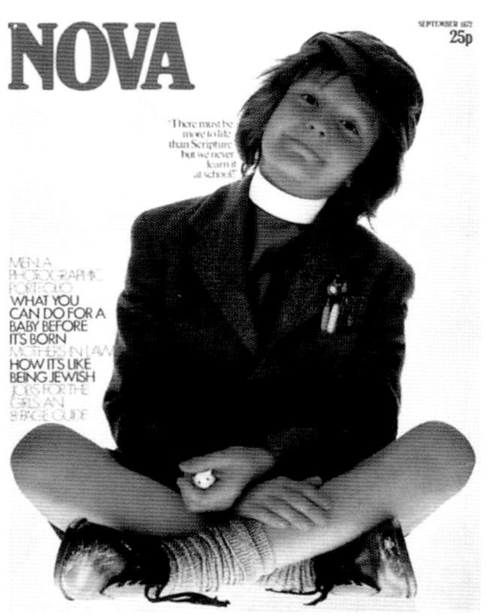
NOVA
25p
WHAT YOU CAN DO FOR A BABY BEFORE IT'S BORN
HOW IT'S LIKE BEING JEWISH

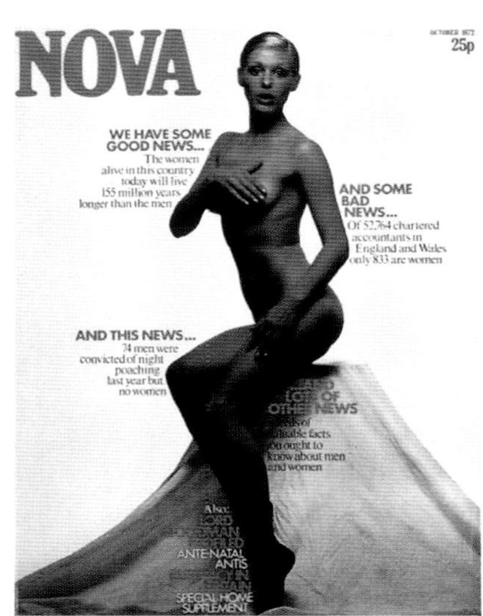
NOVA
25p
WE HAVE SOME GOOD NEWS...
The women alive in this country today will live 155 million years longer than the men
AND SOME BAD NEWS...
Of 52,764 chartered accountants in England and Wales only 833 are women
AND THIS NEWS...
74 men were convicted of night poaching last year but no women
ANTE-NATAL ANTIS

NOVA
MAY 1972
20p
PERFECT
THE PERFECT BABY OR THE BIGGEST THREAT SINCE THE ATOM BOMB?
Dare we leave it to the scientists?
MY MEMORY AND I BY PENELOPE MORTIMER
GHASTLY GOOD TASTE IN FASHION
HOUSEWIVES' FANTASIES, DREAMS AMONG THE DISH-CLOTHS
MARGARET THATCHER: MIDDLE CLASS OF '72

SUPERSTAR SPECTACULAR ONE NIGHT ONLY
GLAMOROUS STARS! AMAZING TRICKS! STUNNING TURNS! FANTASTIC DISCOVERIES!

NOVA
25p
PLAY LADY PLAY
THE DRINKER'S GUIDE TO WINE
THE BARMAN'S GUIDE TO

NOVA
COULD YOU BELIEVE THAT FISH AND CHIPS CONTAINED...
SO WHO NEEDS HEALTH FOOD?
Also: WHAT ARE FATHERS FOR?
THE CREATOR OF CHARLIE BROWN

NOVA
25p
YOUR BREASTS

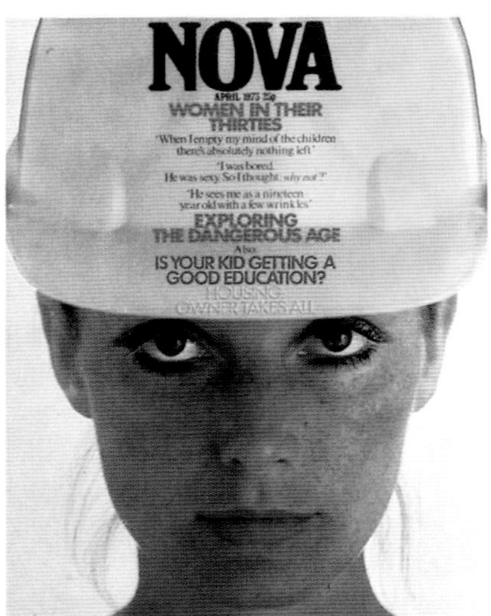
NOVA
WOMEN IN THEIR THIRTIES
EXPLORING THE DANGEROUS AGE
IS YOUR KID GETTING A GOOD EDUCATION?

NOVA
25p
'...to love and to cherish as long as both of us keep this agreement'
BRITAIN'S FIRST MARRIAGE CONTRACT
GETTING TO KNOW YOUR SEX POTENTIAL
LIARS TURN TO PAGE 66

NOVA
PORTRAIT OF A CRIMINAL FAMILY
WHEN PRIESTS GO RADICAL... WHAT NEXT?

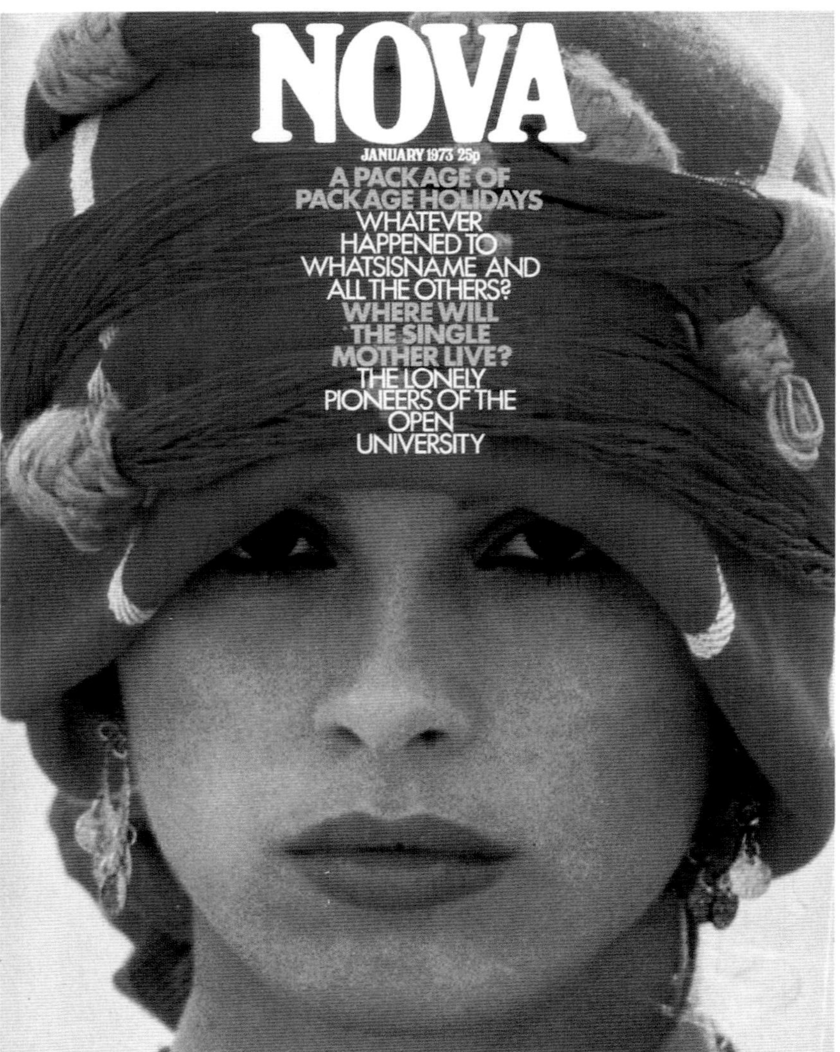
NOVA
JANUARY 1973 25p
A PACKAGE OF PACKAGE HOLIDAYS
WHATEVER HAPPENED TO WHATSISNAME AND ALL THE OTHERS?
WHERE WILL THE SINGLE MOTHER LIVE?
THE LONELY PIONEERS OF THE OPEN UNIVERSITY

NOVA
25p
DON'T
LAUGH IT'S
JACQUES
SHOPS
WITH
A FOREIG
FLAVOUR
NOVA'S
100TH ISS
THE INSID
STORY
OF THE
OTHER 99

NOVA
OCTOBER 1973
25p
LUCKY YOU-NOW YOU CAN OGLE ME
That's what I call liberation... ...do you?
HOW TO KEEP YOUR COOL WHEN YOU LOSE IT
BARBARA WINDSOR'S, AHEM, ASSETS
AROMATIC FACTS ABOUT HERBAL REMEDIES
COMPLETE SIX-MONTH BEAUTY

NOVA
25p
Looks clean, feels clean, but by golly she's filthy! (See why cleanliness is next to impossible on page 41)
THE BACHELOR LIFE FOR BETTER AND FOR WORSE
GIRLS IN MORAL DANGER -BUT FROM WHOM?

NOVA
25p
IF SHE GIVES UP, WHAT HOPE IS THERE FOR THE REST OF US?
AGE IS WHAT WE ALL DO

NOVA
what inflation could mean by 1976
Shetland wool Fairisle pullover at Scottish Merchant, £1130 John Craig cotton shirt, £475; Levi's button fly jeans, £440 Argyll wool socks, from £60 at Take Six; Sandals, £250; Mary Quant Choosy Cherry lipstick, £55. If you think we're joking, see p.127
Also, friends who give a little help to your sex life. The cures you buy over the counter-do they really work? House-husbands take over the kitchen sink-and all about rabbits (yes, rabbits...)

NOVA
ZENA, AGED 10
Monday and Wednesday I go to the disco. My dad collects me at quarter past nine Mondays and twenty to ten Wednesdays. I only dance for half an hour. Rest of the time I put on make-up and nail varnish
WHO STOLE THIS CHILDHOOD?

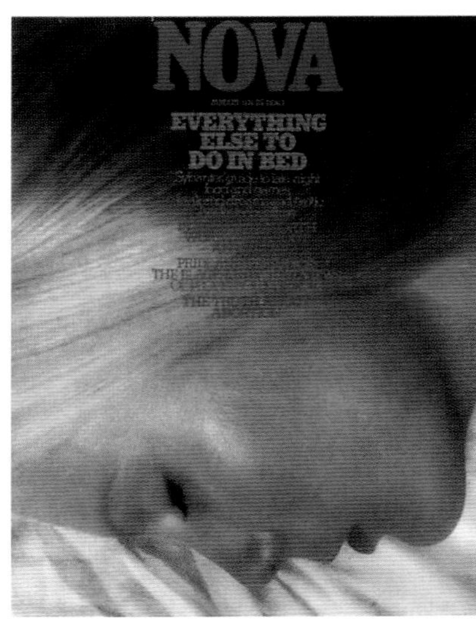
NOVA
EVERYTHING ELSE TO DO IN BED

NOVA
25p
'If I lived in a society where it was considered OK to go on having children, I would quite happily belt out one a year'
ALL YOU WANT TO KNOW ABOUT NOT HAVING BABIES

NOVA
INSIDE: THE TRUTH ABOUT PRUDE POWER
June 74
30p.
ENTS
31 A summer season
Photographs, Aurora
Sports day, fun fairs, cricket matches: all the summer-scented events happen on your doorstep
43 All in good time
By Judith Froshaug
Photographs, Graham Hughes
When should a woman decide to be a mother?
48 Prude Power
By Maggy Meade-King, Hilary Macaskill, Betka Zamoyska
These people have decided what will shock you. But did they ever ask you?
52 'I'm jacking Britain'
By Hilary Macaskill
Photographs, Shaun Skelly
better life for the kids
hairdressing
88 Poems
By Erica Jong
92 Tarzan's mighty leap to fame
Return of the king of the comic-strips
CENSORED

NOVA
DOING HER BIT... ARE YOU DOING YOURS?
Inside: Making out by making do or how to tighten your belt and keep smiling through

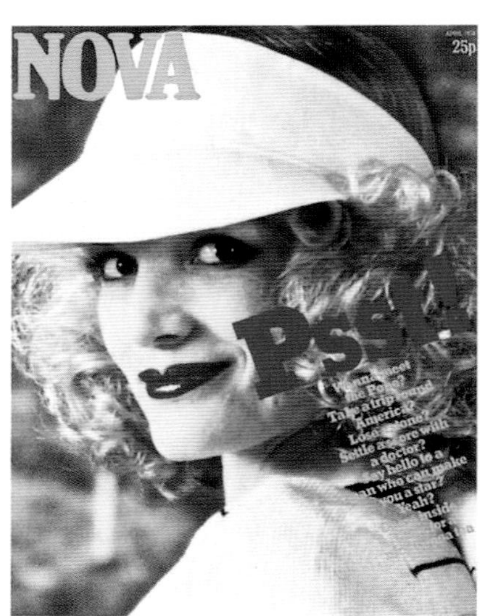
NOVA
25p

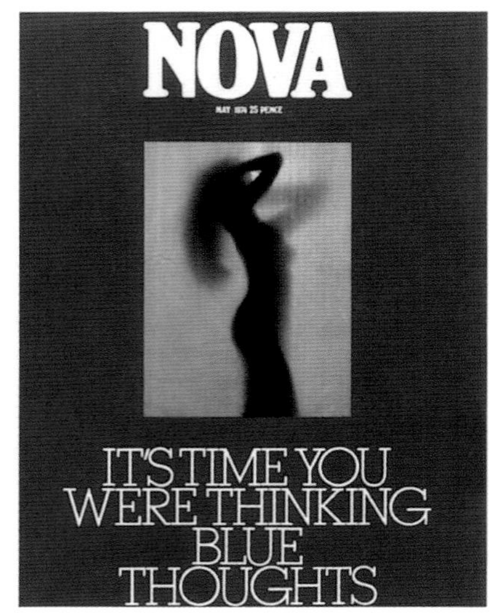
NOVA
IT'S TIME YOU WERE THINKING BLUE THOUGHTS

NOVA
CARE FOR US?
WHY NICE
GIRLS THROW
BOMBS
NEW SHORT STORY
10 PAGES OF
LOOSE LIVING

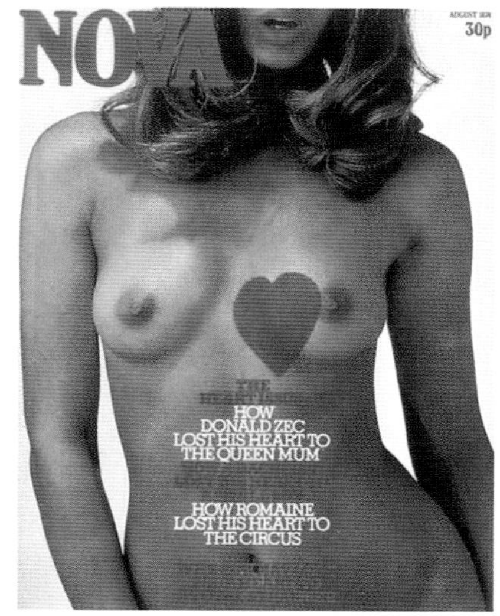
30p
HOW
DONALD ZEC
LOST HIS HEART TO
THE QUEEN MUM
HOW ROMAINE
LOST HIS HEART TO
THE CIRCUS

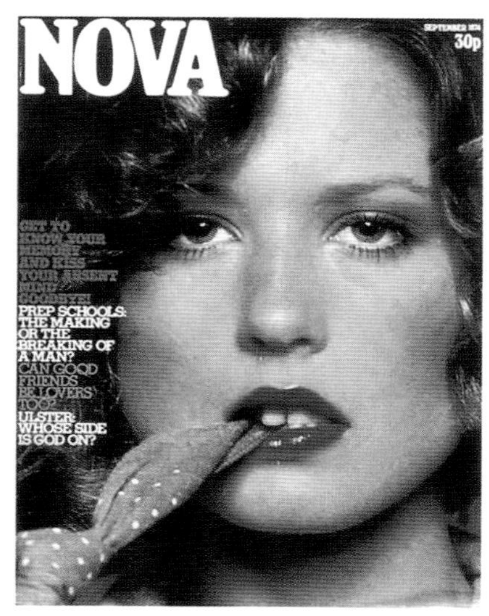
NOVA
30p
PREP SCHOOLS:
THE MAKING
OR THE
BREAKING OF
A MAN?
CAN GOOD
FRIENDS
BE LOVERS
TOO?
ULSTER:
WHOSE SIDE
IS GOD ON?

NOVA
OCTOBER 1974 30 PENCE
WHAT A HINT OF
MASCARA
COULD DO FOR
HAROLD WILSON
WHAT A YOUNG
DOCTOR WOULD DO FOR
A NIGHT'S SLEEP
WHAT A BIT OF THE
OLD RAZZAMATAZZ
WOULD DO
FOR SHOW-JUMPING
WHAT AN
UNMARRIED FATHER
WOULD LOVE
TO DO FOR HIS BABY
WHAT THE
SEVENTIES HAVE
DONE FOR SEX...
TOO MUCH!
OH, AND BY THE WAY,
HAPPY BIRTHDAY PG WODEHOUSE

NOVA

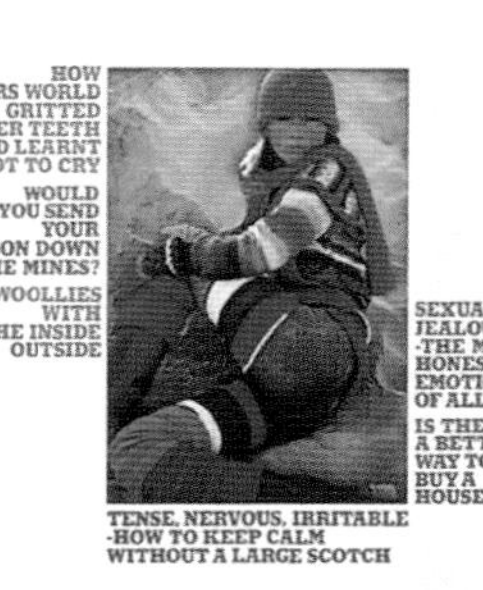
HOW
MRS WORLD
GRITTED
HER TEETH
AND LEARNT
NOT TO CRY
WOULD
YOU SEND
YOUR
SON DOWN
THE MINES?
WOOLLIES
WITH
THE INSIDE
OUTSIDE
SEXUAL
JEALOUSY
-THE MOST
HONEST
EMOTION
OF ALL?
IS THERE
A BETTER
WAY TO
BUY A
HOUSE?
TENSE, NERVOUS, IRRITABLE
-HOW TO KEEP CALM
WITHOUT A LARGE SCOTCH

NOVA

JANUARY 1975 30p

'The time has come,' the housewives said,
'To talk of many things:
Of pay-and hours-and nursery schools-
Of cabbages-and
AND ABOUT TIME TOO!'

NOVA

FEBRUARY 1975 30p

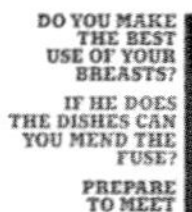

DO YOU MAKE THE BEST USE OF YOUR BREASTS?

IF HE DOES THE DISHES CAN YOU MEND THE FUSE?

PREPARE TO MEET THINE ARMAGEDDON?

IF YOU WANT TO BUY A HOUSE BUY IT NOW

IS JOE GORMLEY THE LIGHT OF YOUR LIFE?

THINK PINK AND THE WORLD WILL LOOK ROSY

NOVA

MARCH 1975 35 PENCE

COULD YOU BE THE MOST INTERESTING PERSON YOU KNOW?

A LOVE STORY BY PENELOPE MORTIMER

WHAT MAKES A NICE YOUNG MAN SWAP BEER, CARS AND GIRLS FOR A CASSOCK AND CROSS?

STOP THE CLOCK, YOU TOO CAN STAY YOUNG

HOW TO BUY THE BEST OF BLANKETS—EXTRA SPECIAL NOVA OFFER

THE FINAL SOLUTION FOR PEOPLE WHO REALLY CAN'T STICK TO A DIET

SLIP INTO SOMETHING SKIN TIGHT

NOVA

APRIL 1975 35 PENCE

WHY EVERYTHING IN YOUR WARDROBE'S STILL LOVELY

WHAT CAN THE FRENCH TEACH US ABOUT WOMEN?

MARTIAL ARTS: BUILDING UP THE INNER WOMAN

HOW TO BE A TWO-PARENT FAMILY EVEN AFTER DIVORCE

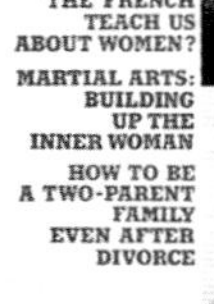

BOYS WILL BE BOYS AND GIRLS WILL BE GIRLS BUT HOW DO THEY SEE EACH OTHER?

WHAT TENNESSEE WILLIAMS TOLD IRMA KURTZ

CAN YOUR HEADACHE PILL HURT YOUR BABY?

WHATEVER'S HAPPENED TO PIGTAILS?

NOVA

Summer Special

MAY 1975 35p

Bobby Fischer: Chess is better than girls

Glasshouses -and the people who live in them

John Updike: A month of Sundays

How to live within your means

What happens to sex after marriage?

What kids get up to at school

Change the direction of your life-an important Nova series

NOVA

JUNE 1975 35p

Russell Harty: can six million viewers be right?

How to get a job abroad

Fashion and the well kept woman

Romance is living happily ever after

Dig your own gold

Do men make better secretaries?

The world economy: death rattle or birth pangs? Read Alvin Toffler

NOVA
JULY 1975 35p
WHAT WOMEN WILL DO TO BE BEAUTIFUL
IS MARRIAGE A MEAL TICKET?

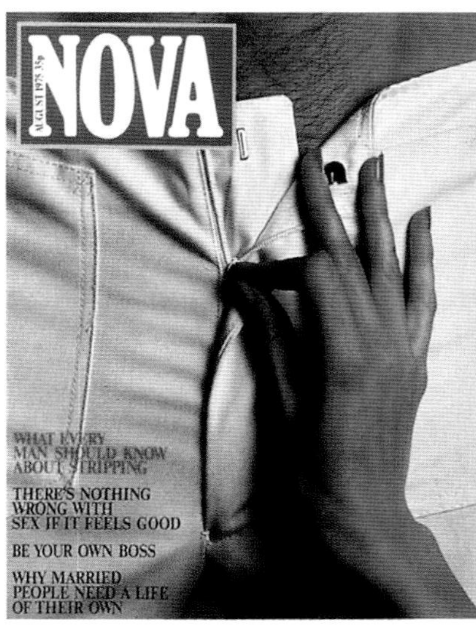

NOVA
AUGUST 1975 35p
WHAT EVERY MAN SHOULD KNOW ABOUT STRIPPING
THERE'S NOTHING WRONG WITH SEX IF IT FEELS GOOD
BE YOUR OWN BOSS
WHY MARRIED PEOPLE NEED A LIFE OF THEIR OWN

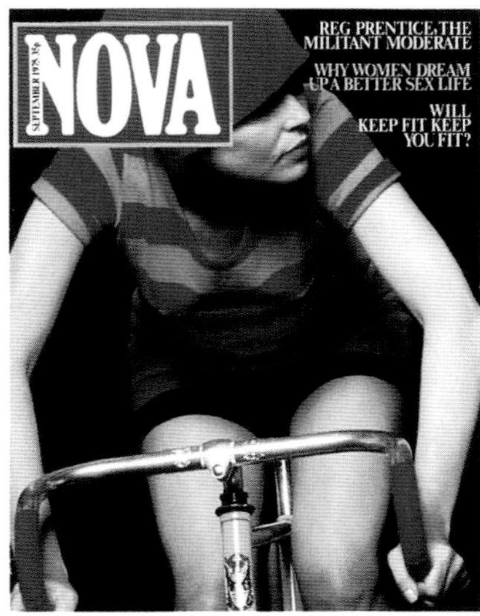

NOVA
SEPTEMBER 1975 35p
REG PRENTICE: THE MILITANT MODERATE
WHY WOMEN DREAM UP A BETTER SEX LIFE
WILL KEEP FIT KEEP YOU FIT?

SOMETHING BREWING IN THE SUBURBS
WILL YOUR DOGGY HAVE A WHITE WEDDING?
HAVE THE MODERATES GONE TOO FAR?
'One thing you can say for baldness, it's neat'

Chapter 1

All shook up 1954-1964

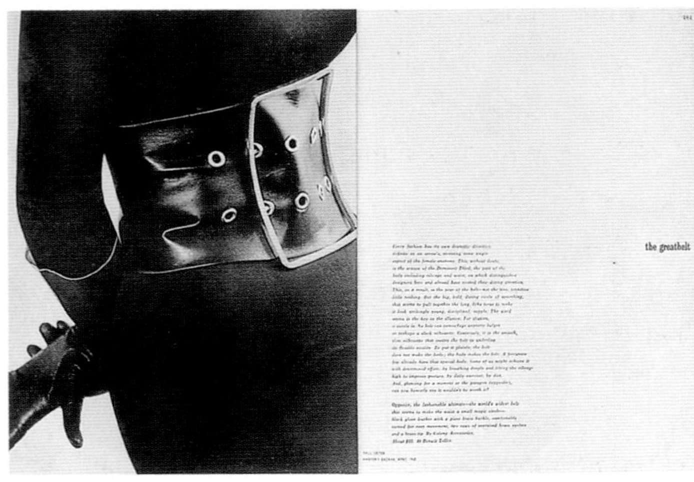

Harper's Bazaar in April 1962. Close-up photography working with imaginative typography also became one of *Nova*'s hallmarks. The art director was Marvin Israel and the photographer Saul Leiter, who later became a regular at *Nova*.

Nova's history spanned just eleven years, a bright star that flared and quite suddenly faded. The cultural and artistic streams that coincided to ignite *Nova*'s brief brilliance were produced by nothing less than the redefinition of culture and society that began in post-war Europe and America.

By 1954 the threat of nuclear obliteration had gradually replaced the collective peace of mind with a kind of angry helplessness. Radical politics in Britain, on the crest of a wave after the war, began to lose credibility, while esteem for what was derisively called the establishment also went into decline. The senile imperialism of the Suez adventure in 1956 added to the conviction that the old ways were irrelevant. For many, especially the young, the future had to be in the hands of new kinds of people with new ways of thinking.

And there they were. The Angry Young Men such as John Osborne, Kingsley Amis and Keith Waterhouse wrote anti-establishment plays, books and films. From across the water came the 'beat' writing of Jack Kerouac and William Burroughs and the music of Thelonius Monk, Miles Davis and Charlie Parker. While Jackson Pollock dripped paint on to the canvas and Francis Bacon evoked darkness and death, the Modern movement had emerged in art and architecture to change the way people lived.

The older generation became increasingly disapproving of what was going on, which was the whole idea. If Marilyn Monroe's sexuality raised eyebrows, then Brigitte Bardot's raised out-and-out protest. Marlon Brando and James Dean were labelled as subversive as they lounged and brooded in anti-theatrical movies, and Elvis Presley invented a new way of singing and moving which upset people (even the spelling of Rock 'n' Roll gave two fingers to convention). These were the popular icons of the post-war cultural revolution's first wave.

There was a pause. In 1959 Harold Macmillan told affluent Britain 'You never had it so good' and in 1960 Americans elected as President, John F Kennedy – brilliant, young and handsome. A little hope was emanating from the established order, and people acquiesced for a while. But with Macmillan's resignation and Kennedy's assassination in 1963, the second wave of post-war cultural revolution began in earnest. In America the protest movement started to find its voice; in Britain the Beatles arrived, and pop would never be the same.

Television had an increasing role to play in all this. It was by definition populist. Incessant middlebrow programming fostered liberal attitudes by devaluing the proprietorial skew on printed information. Magazines had been the main servants of popular culture since the last century, and even into the Seventies it was believed that the role of the magazine would be supplanted by television. America's *Life* magazine was a case in point. It had created a different genre, combining often brilliant news photography with disciplined graphic design. Its success was based on bringing the images behind the news into the home. This, however, was done even better by television and the magazine succumbed in the Seventies.

Life came from a golden era for magazine art in pre-war America. For many magazines how they looked was as important as what they said. And how they looked was due to the talents of people who combined planned photography, typography and layout into a beautiful whole. These were the art directors – T M Cleland and Eleanor Treacy on *Fortune*, M F Agha on *Vanity Fair* and Alexey Brodovitch who spanned the war years on *Harper's Bazaar*. Their influence into the post-war period was to help define the magazines of the burgeoning television age. In aiding as well as serving post-war cultural liberalisation, television in fact created new opportunities for magazines. It may have killed the few in direct competition but it could not match the kind of depth and artistry that magazines were able to achieve for special interests. Old titles adapted and many new titles prospered in the liberal atmosphere television helped to create.

New York was the powerhouse of magazine design in the Forties and Fifties. Taking up the legacy of the great pre-war art directors were men such as Otto Storch on *McCall's*, Henry Wolf on *Esquire, Harper's Bazaar and Show*, Art Paul on *Playboy* and Alexander Liberman on *Vogue*. It was no coincidence that they were working on magazines that were serving the cultural revolution – the arts, entertainment, sex and the new role of women. By this time, American and European magazine design were increasingly feeding off each other. American freshness and vigour were tempered by the European rationalism of the Bauhaus tradition. European magazines learned from the exuberance of American magazines in the Fifties and began to produce the direct precursors of *Nova*.

In Europe the appeal of the Fifties and Sixties avant-garde had attracted a great amount of talent into the world of commercial art. Publishers recognised the power of those who could manipulate imagery, so commercial artists emerged as art directors in the American tradition or as the more typographically disposed graphic designers. Two in particular began to change the conventions of how magazines should look: Tom Wolsey on *Town* magazine and then on *Queen* (where Dennis Hackett, later to be *Nova*'s editor, was deputy editor), and the Swiss photographer and artist Peter Knapp on *Elle*. Michael Rand on the *Sunday Times Magazine*, where David Hillman was an art editor, also began to broaden the editorial scope of design in a way that was to be adopted by *Nova*.

But perhaps the most intimate influence on *Nova* came from Germany. This was *Twen*, universally admired by the vigorously aesthetic sub-culture of designers and photographers emerging in the Sixties. *Twen* had been a student project of Christa Peters, who later became a photographer for *Nova*. The format and the name was taken on by a publisher, and Willy Fleckhaus became art director. Such was the force of his talent that he soon became *de facto* editor. He used to invite visiting designers to take over his job while he was on holiday. One of these was Harri Peccinotti, who in 1965 became *Nova*'s founding designer and art director.

Harper's Bazaar
Art Director, Henry Wolf

Harper's Bazaar had the good fortune or good judgement to employ two of the most outstanding magazine designers of the century – one after the other. The first, Alexey Brodovitch, is regarded as no less than the father of modern magazine design. He joined *Harper*'s in 1934 and stayed for twenty-four years. He was an innovative and intuitive designer whose breadth of visual ideas, great wit and sense of space created the look of contemporary magazines. Brodovitch's typography was always elegant and resourceful and he pioneered photography that was deliberately shot to the design of a page. Henry Wolf who had made his reputation at *Esquire* magazine took over at Harper's in 1958 and proceeded to match his predecessor's virtuosity while imbuing the magazine with more overt graphic artfulness.

Above
December 1959.

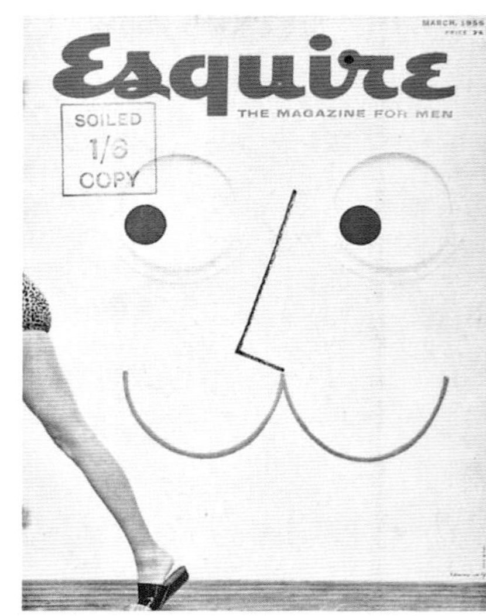

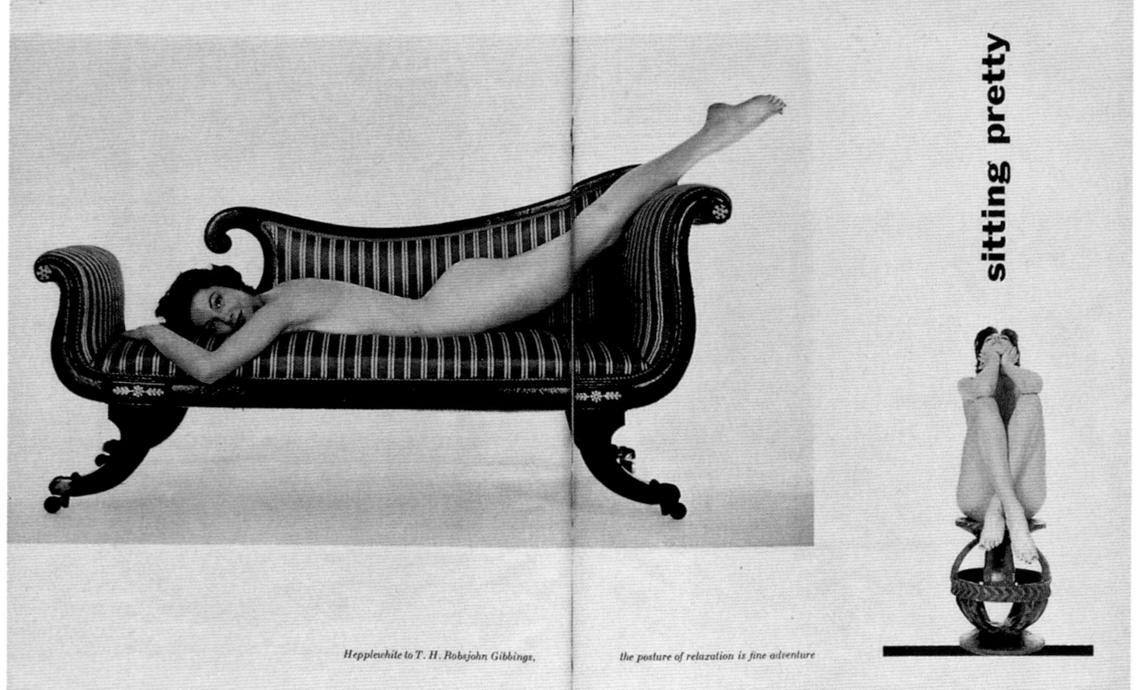

Esquire
Art director, Henry Wolf

Henry Wolf worked on *Esquire* magazine between 1952 and 1958. He used his covers especially as a canvas for arresting and improbable juxtapositions of imagery which were always expressive and never simply decorative. The surrealistic tendency of his design work was supported by canny art direction and tight typography in the European tradition.

Above left
July 1958.
Above right
March 1955.
Left
December 1954.
Photographs by Fernand Fonssagrives.

WHO ISN'T AFRAID OF EDWARD ALBEE?

A complex young playwright says "boo" to Broadway and the world

by Mary Lukas

When Edward Albee was just past 20 and enjoying the exquisitely novel sensation of being down-and-out in Greenwich Village, he used to play a game in which he speculated on the murder of his friends. He was living in a grimy walk-up where the talk went on all night. Just before dawn, as the unnatural light began to define the clutter of old newspapers, beer cans, records and books on which he sat, a glaze would come into his look, and a peculiar drift to his right eye. In a slow, precise voice he would select his imaginary victims: one must go because he was a private nuisance; another, because he was a public bore; a third, out of a kind of friendly feeling to spare him an inevitably hot and lonely summer in New York.

Edward Albee, now 34 and the most discussed figure of the current Broadway season, is still inclined to mayhem of the mind. His "Who's Afraid of Virginia Woolf?", the meticulously detailed account of a night-long, bloodletting battle between a college professor and his wife, has raised the hackles on the necks of New York audiences as perhaps no other play has since Tennessee Williams set a bunch of Spanish-speaking urchins on one of his protagonists and had them eat him alive in "Suddenly Last Summer." Although the violence in Albee's play is mostly psychological, its cumulative impact is something like having watched an automobile accident in three-hour slow motion. The man and woman circle each other in different postures and on different grounds, lashing out with jokes and jibes as lacking in content and as cruel as those that occur in real life. Relentlessly they accelerate the attack as though searching for some kind of black consummation until they reach that point of hurt beyond which lies nothing but despair. When the curtain falls, they are murmuring like children and collapse in ruins in each other's arms.

While carnage accumulates onstage, offstage Mr. Albee himself is busy refining a personal style persistently more formal and reserved. He has become a responsible member of the intellectual community; he participates in learned panels* and lectures in half a dozen schools. He lives on a tree-lined street in a highly respectable section off lower Fifth Avenue, in an old-fashioned building with long windows and a fanlight door. The apartment is spare and striking—like his plays. Sunlight articulates the colors of theareboned Swedish furniture. A glass lantern hanging in the window catches and bends back the light. Chagall and Picasso lithographs stare from the walls. Cats (he has three) prowl the parquet floors.

He is practiced and easy with interviewers. He talks about works in progress: a dramatization of Carson McCullers' "The Ballad of the Sad Café" ("The problem will be to put it into dialogue and keep it McCullers'; there is almost no dialogue in the book."): a novel, the whole of which takes place as a man walks from the door to the window of his room; and a charade play called "The Substitute Speaker." Albee talks concisely, smiles wickedly when amused, from under his dark lashes. He maintains a deeply listening attitude, and if the stranger has from time to time the feeling that in facing Albee he is staring into a kind of glass, whose polished surface flatteringly reflects the interviewer's own persuasions, he is simultaneously aware that the attitude may be as much the mark of courtesy as of contrivance.

At intervals the phone rings. Albee answers, dispatches the caller skillfully, returns. For one who has carried his celebrity so short a time, he has an extraordinary ease of manner. There is no trace of the breathlessness of the long-distance runner who has finally hit the tape, none of the exuberance one would expect of the longtime anonymous friend of the accomplished who has finally made it on his own. "I was never competitive," Albee replies to a question about his Village years. "I always knew someday I would do something. Immodest as it sounds, it seemed inevitable when it came."

To Albee's friends, his steep, swift and apparently effortless rise to fame is more surprising. "A few years ago," said one, "it was impossible to imagine him as anything but the side-kick of [composer] William Flanagan: now it is impossible to imagine him as anything but what he is." "But Edward has always had a charmed life," another mused, and then went on to expatiate poetically on how Fortune, helpless as she might be to romance him in certain areas, was always eager as a girl to woo him in others.

Albee's earliest years read like a chapter from "The Lucky Orphan." Adopted when he was two weeks old by Frances and Reed Albee (the Keith-Albee theater chain), he was whisked off to a sprawling Tudor stucco house in Westchester; to a world of servants, tutors, riding lessons; winters in Miami, summers sailing on the Sound. There was a Rolls to bring him, snuggled in lap robes, to matinees in the city; an inexhaustible wardrobe housed in a closet big as an ordinary room; a profusion of toys; numberless pets, ranging from a St. Bernard to pull his sleigh in the wintertime to a penful of guinea pigs.

But in the casting of the Albee family circle, Fortune—to carry on his friend's metaphor—proved less adept. Cyril Connolly has remarked that "the childhoods of the clever are invariably unpleasant, a record of grievances and snubs, of too brutal perceptions and too smart replies." In Edward's case the problem was compounded; the Albee child-parent relationship was as spectacular a mismating of temperaments as can be imagined. Mr. Albee was a man habitually in agreement with his wife, whose taciturnity led him to announce (Continued on page 112)

*SHOW's Inter-American symposium among them.

Irving Penn

SHOW: FEBRUARY 1963 83

Show
Art director, Henry Wolf

Henry Wolf moved from *Harper's Bazaar to Show* in 1961. *Show* was an arts magazine and Wolf was at pains to respect the dignity as well as the creativity of its subject matter. Continuing to indulge his love for the unexpected, he added greater refinement to his picture play and typography, striving to make the whole magazine a visual feast in its own right. At *Show*, Wolf's work sometimes reached the sublime, crowning his achievements and confirming his place as the greatest of the post-war magazine designers.

Top
February 1963. Photograph by Irving Penn.
Above
June 1962.
Above right
October 1961.
Right
August 1962. Photograph by Mel Sokolsky.

Curtain Lines

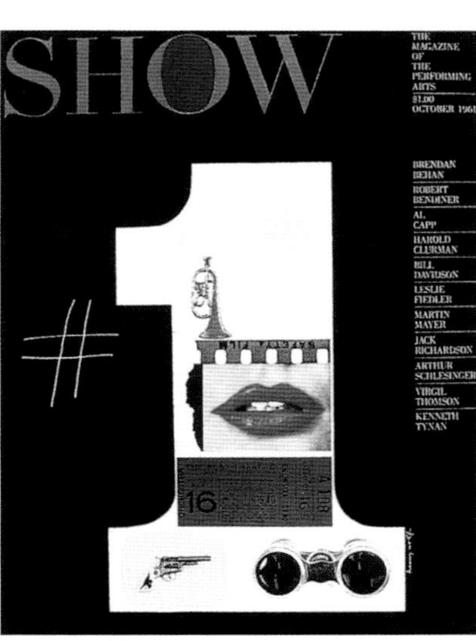

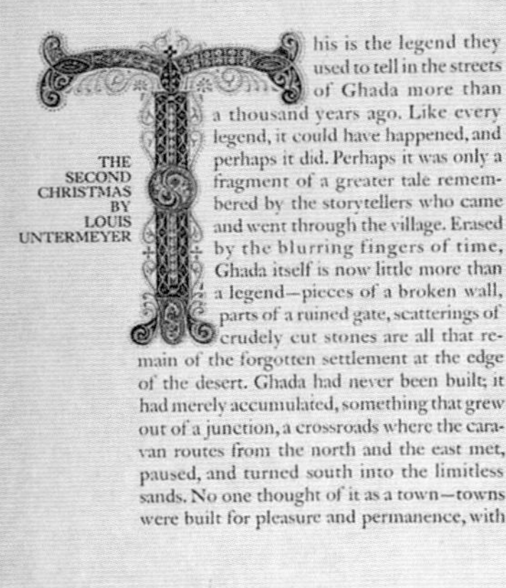

THE SECOND CHRISTMAS BY LOUIS UNTERMEYER

This is the legend they used to tell in the streets of Ghada more than a thousand years ago. Like every legend, it could have happened, and perhaps it did. Perhaps it was only a fragment of a greater tale remembered by the storytellers who came and went through the village. Erased by the blurring fingers of time, Ghada itself is now little more than a legend—pieces of a broken wall, parts of a ruined gate, scatterings of crudely cut stones are all that remain of the forgotten settlement at the edge of the desert. Ghada had never been built; it had merely accumulated, something that grew out of a junction, a crossroads where the caravan routes from the north and the east met, paused, and turned south into the limitless sands. No one thought of it as a town—towns were built for pleasure and permanence, with stout houses and bright shops and places of entertainment and a palace set in a park—but Ghada was a clutter of nondescript shelters raised on rocks and held together with rushes and caked mud. Those who lived there numbered fewer than two hundred. □ The story begins before dusk of a certain day. It begins with a man leading a donkey, carrying a woman and a child. The woman was young and beautiful, and she held the child in her arms, for he was still a baby, and his face was covered with a veil against the blowing sand. The man was not old, but older than the woman; he was grizzled, heavy-set; the tools of his trade hung from a rope knotted about his waist. The donkey was feeble and footsore. They had come a long way. □ "Look," said the man, pointing toward the sunset, which colored the drab earth with transient loveliness. "Ghada. We can rest there." □ It was farther than he thought. The weight of the air did not lessen; eddies/*continued on page 148*

McCall's
Art director, Otto Storch

Otto Storch was one of the clutch of great New York post-war magazine designers. On *McCall's* he established such rigid discipline in planning typography, photography and illustration that he became probably more influential than the editor himself in the magazine's appeal. But in contrast to Willy Fleckhaus on *Twen* who also took control of the whole magazine, Storch had an abiding respect for what the words of his magazine said. His work epitomised the new ethos of the art director: that all the elements of a page should be components of a single image.

Above left
December 1961.
Photograph by Bert Stern.
Above right
December 1961.

Eros
Art director, Herb Lubalin

Eros was an extraordinary hardback magazine that only lasted four issues. It bravely showed how to handle sex without exploitation and with a great deal of artistic flair and refinement. Herb Lubalin had made his mark in the redesign of the *Saturday Evening Post* at the start of the Sixties. He later developed into a typographic specialist, often called in on the design of new magazines and other publications. At *Eros* he used his considerable typographic repertoire as a framework for powerful and poignant imagery. The magazine went under when its editor Ralph Ginzburg was sent to jail for obscenity – the last thing the magazine was about.

Far right
Autumn 1962.
Photographs by Bert Stern of Marilyn Monroe six weeks before she died.
Right
Winter 1962. Photograph by Ralph M Hattersley Jr.

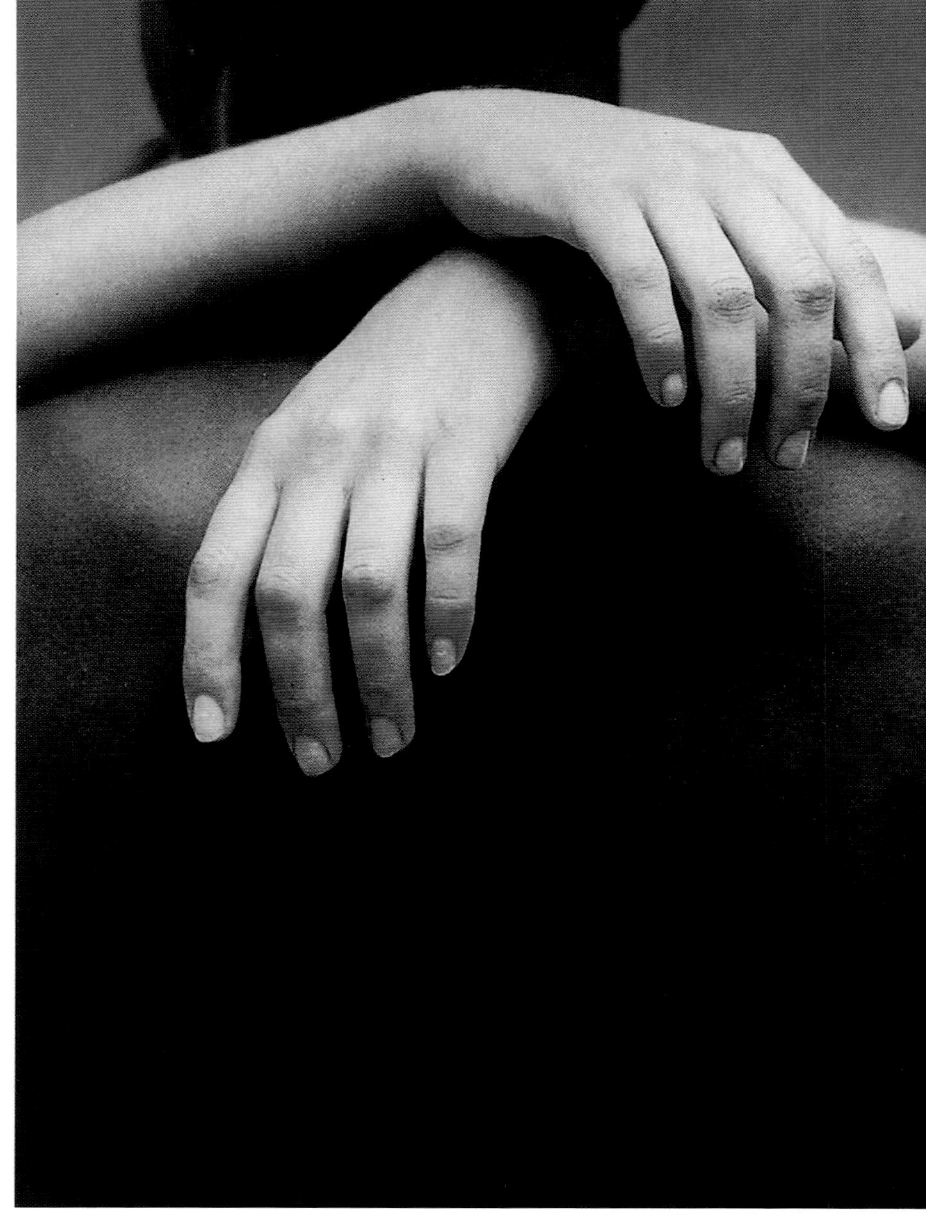

"The passing of time is making it clear that the peak of Marilyn Monroe's tragedy was that she never knew how much people everywhere loved her." Richard Watts Jr., critic.

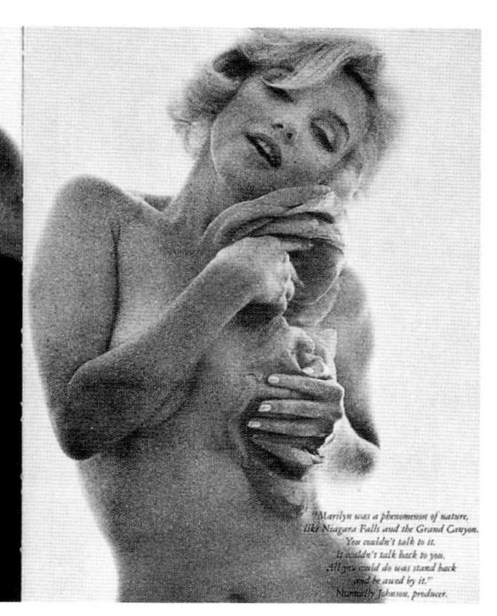
"Marilyn was a phenomenon of nature,
like Niagara Falls and the Grand Canyon.
You couldn't talk to it.
It couldn't talk back to you.
All you could do was stand back
and be awed by it."
Nunnally Johnson, producer.

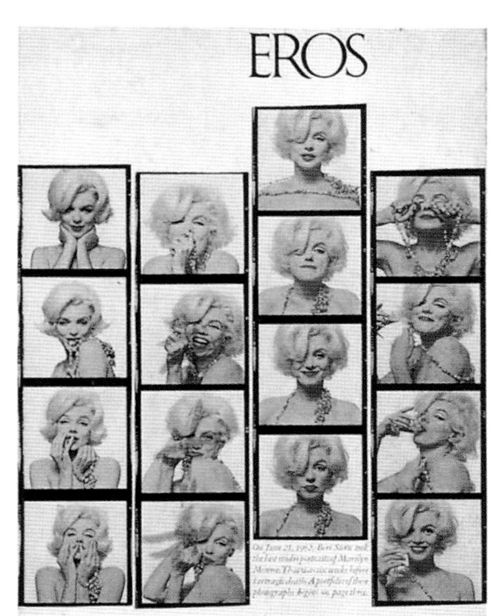
EROS

Pelisse super-lisse :
c'est du satin de Nylon noir,
c'est de la loutre,
c'est un imperméable-pardessus
par-dessus une robe de crêpe.
Laroche.

PETER KNAPP

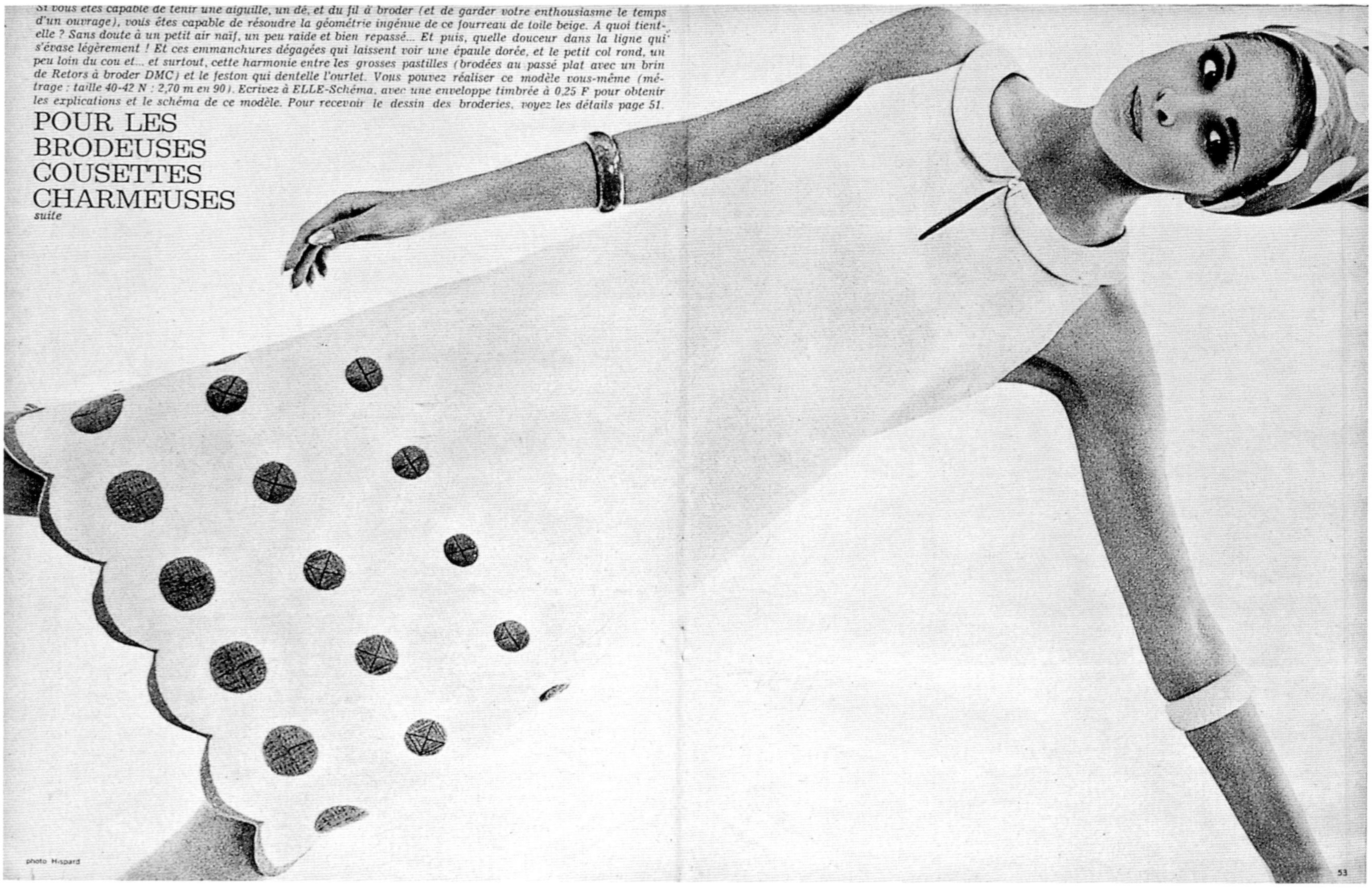

Si vous êtes capable de tenir une aiguille, un dé, et du fil à broder (et de garder votre enthousiasme le temps d'un ouvrage), vous êtes capable de résoudre la géométrie ingénue de ce fourreau de toile beige. A quoi tient-elle ? Sans doute à un petit air naïf, un peu raide et bien repassé... Et puis, quelle douceur dans la ligne qui s'évase légèrement ! Et ces emmanchures dégagées qui laissent voir une épaule dorée, et le petit col rond, un peu loin du cou et... et surtout, cette harmonie entre les grosses pastilles (brodées au passé plat avec un brin de Retors à broder DMC) et le feston qui dentelle l'ourlet. Vous pouvez réaliser ce modèle vous-même (métrage : taille 40-42 N : 2,70 m en 90). Ecrivez à ELLE-Schéma, avec une enveloppe timbrée à 0,25 F pour obtenir les explications et le schéma de ce modèle. Pour recevoir le dessin des broderies, voyez les détails page 51.

POUR LES BRODEUSES COUSETTES CHARMEUSES
suite

photo Hispard

53

Elle
Art director, Peter Knapp

Peter Knapp took over at *Elle* in 1959. The magazine had already established itself as elegantly designed in the French tradition. Knapp gave it startling vigour and life, propelling it into the future with anarchic layouts of angles and twists. He pioneered the free-form design that came of age in the Eighties – but with one huge difference: Knapp had no Mac to help him. Within this happy, liberated style Knapp's typography was always disciplined and the photography purposefully fresh and totally devoid of the porcelain posing of the established fashion genre. Knapp's work at *Elle* was particularly admired by David Hillman and his definitive influence was also carried over into the pages of *Nova* as a photographer.

Top left
July 1963.
Photograph by Marc Hispard.
Bottom left
September 1963.
Photograph by Peter Knapp.

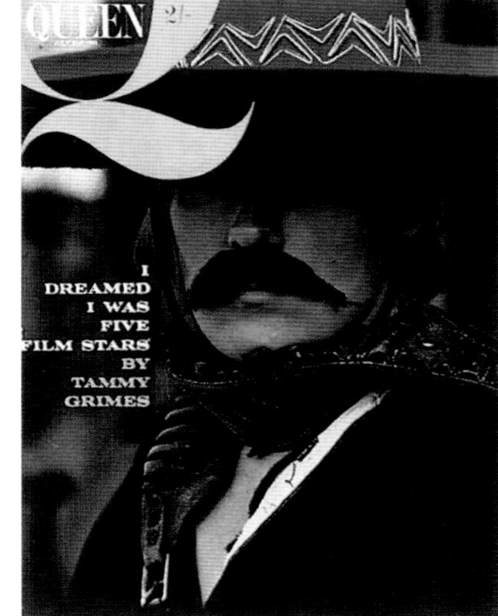

Queen
Art director, Max Maxwell

Before the arrival of *Nova*, *Queen* was the only women's magazine from Britain that had dared to break new ground in the presentation of fashion and style. It was David Hamilton whose carefully art-directed photography and unconventional typography gave a British dimension to the 'design of ideas' that had long been established in New York. Max Maxwell developed Hamilton's original work on *Queen* until 1963 when Tom Wolsey took over at the magazine after he left *Town*.

Top left and right
July 1962. Photographs by Saul Leiter.

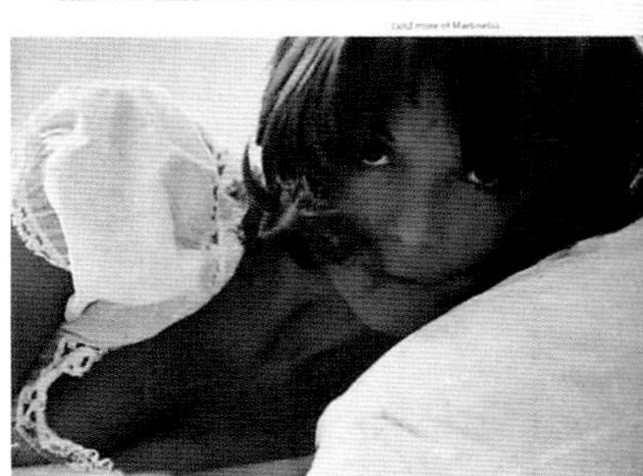

Town
Art director, Tom Wolsey

Tom Wolsey started to work at the somewhat prosaic *Man About Town* clothes magazine in 1961. He seized the opportunity to take the insipid traditions of British magazine design by the scruff of the neck and give them a good shaking. Stark, disciplined and geometric design replaced the lazy and unimaginative layout style that was still the rule for so many magazines. The title changed to *About Town* and then *Town*, as it developed into a highly fashionable and influential general-interest magazine, entertaining as much with its imagery as its editorial approach.

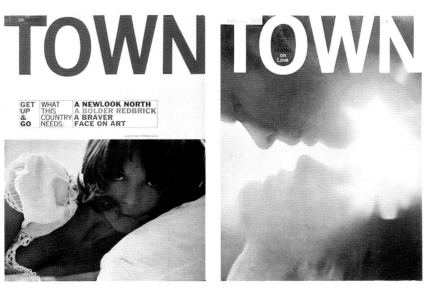

Above left
June 1963.
Photograph by Willy Rizzo.
Above right
February 1963.
Photograph by Art Kane.
Right
November 1961.
Photograph by John Bulmer.

Twen
Art director, Willy Fleckhaus

In terms of design *Twen* was the most admired magazine of the Sixties. It was as a struggling freelance journalist – with no reputation or formal design education – that Willy Fleckhaus landed the art director's job at *Twen*. The magazine had originated as a student publication which photographer Christa Peters took on at art college, named and managed to sell to a publisher friend in Cologne. *Twen* was originally designed by Max Bill, and Fleckhaus remained true to Bill's ideas and disciplines. Fleckhaus's formula was simple: large and small pictures juxtaposed, and bold headlines and copy used in blocks purely as design elements. But it was his utterly uncompromising attitude that allowed his outrageous and defiant vision to be translated into the most exciting bravura on the page. Photography was bold and often shocking; typography was simply design first, words second. In the face of this extraordinary force, none of the magazine's editors lasted long; *Twen* became Fleckhaus's magazine. No art director has had such power before or since.

Covers, top to bottom
April 1962,
December 1963,
March 1963.
Above and far right
1963. Month and photographer unknown.
Right
March 1965, the same month as the first issue of *Nova*. Photographs by Peter Beard.

PHILIP ROTH

Eli, der Fanatiker

HAUTNAH

und näher ist so manches in diesem Heft. In Roald Dahls seltsamer Kurzgeschichte wird auf Haut gemalt. Unter die Haut werden so manchem Literaten die Brecht-Erinnerungen von Hermann Kesten gehen, der lange Zeit Tuchfühlung mit dem Dichter hatte. Gerhard Zwerenz' Polemik zum zehnten 17. Juni geht ans dicke Fell des Bundesbürgers. Leichter abzuschürfen war Hans-Jürgen Uskos Haut, als er die Zentrifugalkraft per Go-Kart erprobte. Wie man die Haut am besten bedeckt, wo auch die schönste Sonne sie nicht bräunen darf, zeigt unser Bade-Bazar. Wo, wie bei Peter Neugebauer, Vivat Vampir gerufen wird, ist eine Gänsehaut wohl nicht weit. Katholische Bräute von heute begleitete Ann Thönnissen in den Ehe-Unterricht. Wie ein alleinstehendes Mädchen sich seiner Haut wehrt, schildert Helen Gurley Brown in unserem Großen Leitfaden für Ledige. Sie kämpfte siebzehn Jahre lang, ehe sie sich mit Haut und Haar in eine Ehe stürzte. Schlußtip fürs nächste Heft: im Juli druckt twen Materialien und Diskussionsbeiträge zum Paragraphen 175.

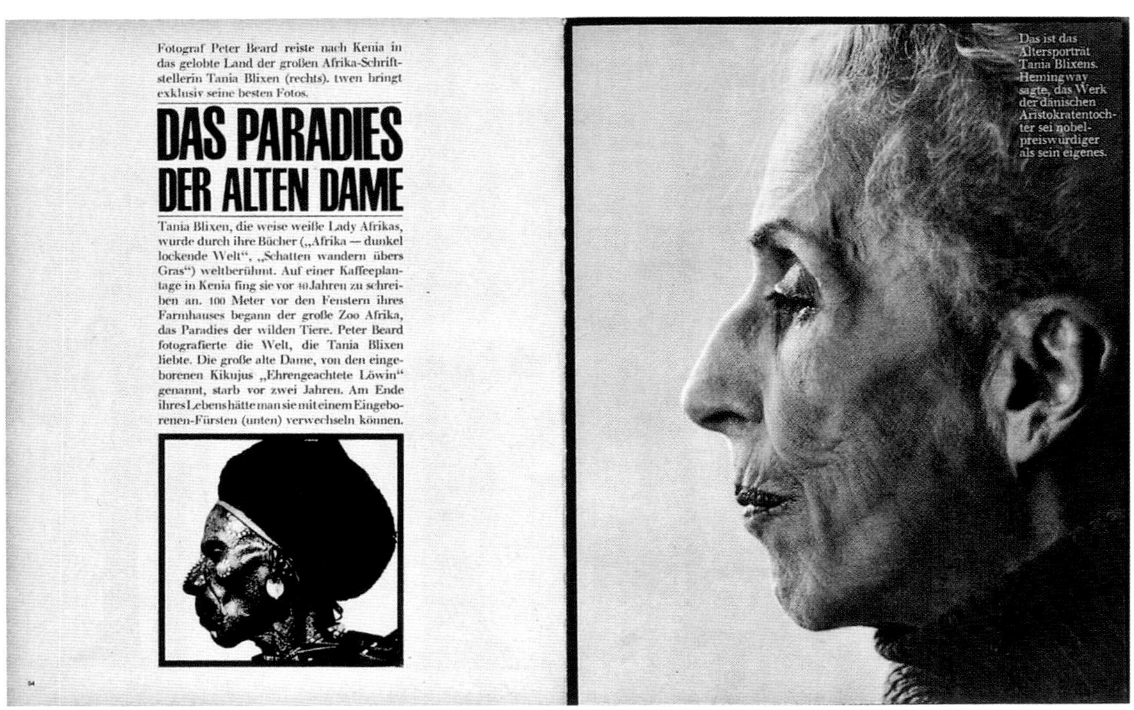

Fotograf Peter Beard reiste nach Kenia in das gelobte Land der großen Afrika-Schriftstellerin Tania Blixen (rechts). twen bringt exklusiv seine besten Fotos.

DAS PARADIES DER ALTEN DAME

Tania Blixen, die weise weiße Lady Afrikas, wurde durch ihre Bücher („Afrika — dunkel lockende Welt", „Schatten wandern übers Gras") weltberühmt. Auf einer Kaffeeplantage in Kenia fing sie vor 40 Jahren zu schreiben an. 100 Meter vor den Fenstern ihres Farmhauses begann der große Zoo Afrika, das Paradies der wilden Tiere. Peter Beard fotografierte die Welt, die Tania Blixen liebte. Die große alte Dame, von den eingeborenen Kikujus „Ehrengeachtete Löwin" genannt, starb vor zwei Jahren. Am Ende ihres Lebens hätte man sie mit einem Eingeborenen-Fürsten (unten) verwechseln können.

Das ist das Altersporträt Tania Blixens. Hemingway sagte, das Werk der dänischen Aristokratentochter sei nobelpreiswürdiger als sein eigenes.

Chapter 2

All you need is love 1965-1968

March 1966
Molly Parkin chose her own stars of Paris fashion. Paco Rabanne was one. Photograph by Jeanloup Sieff.

The Sixties era didn't really start until 1963 – the liberated Sixties, the Beatles Sixties, the mini-skirt Sixties, the flower-power Sixties. (Philip Larkin invoked his poet's licence and declared that 'Sexual intercourse began in 1963'.) By the same token it didn't end until well into the Seventies when surliness and introversion finally overtook the country. This was *Nova's* era too. It began with unprecedented personal wealth in Britain. This and the maturing of the new cultural strands, which included expressionist art, *cinéma vérité*, kitchen-sink drama, blues-based popular music and a separate identity for youth, had generated the confidence in people to create nothing short of a 'brave new world'. And one of the main items on the agenda for change was the role of and attitude towards women.

In 1964 the publishers George Newnes called a meeting to discuss proposals for a new magazine for women. The definition was rather imprecise, but it was not to be like other women's magazines. Amongst those present were Harry Fieldhouse and Harri Peccinotti, who were to become respectively the new magazine's first editor and art director. In March 1965 *Nova* was launched. Others were to take up the radical formula that Fieldhouse and Peccinotti created, and develop it, refine it and make it succeed. But it was these two who originally assembled the elements that were to distinguish *Nova* as the quintessential magazine of the Sixties era.

Nova showed how women could behave, how they could look – without being told. Dressing came to symbolise this liberation. Women looked for new ways to express their escape from preconceptions and preconditions. In the early part of the decade the trend had been for innocent, unfitted, little-girl dresses and hipster trousers. Then in 1964 André Courrèges introduced his seminal collection in Paris. Amongst the innovative, clean lines and colour of his space-age designs were short skirts – worn with boots. By that time British designers did have knees just peeping out in an après-swim look, but what Courrèges offered was uncompromising. It was the mini. Now women could show they meant business without equivocation. The hemline went higher and higher until in 1965 it was six inches above the knee. Along with Vidal Sassoon's free, clean-cut hairstyles, women had transformed themselves from Dusty Springfields into Sandie Shaws. By 1967 the trend had developed into an even greater earthiness as flower power and psychedelia began to represent the ever-more earnest reaction against convention.

Launched into these heady times the first few issues of *Nova* faltered. The parts were all there but not the greater whole. In September 1965 Dennis Hackett came from deputy editor of *Queen* to take over the editorship from Harry Fieldhouse. Hackett was the right man at the right time. He understood what *Nova* was and, importantly, what it could be. With relish he developed the freedoms that the magazine offered and handed them on to the art director, fashion and beauty editors, instructing them to be as irreverent and as radical as they dared. *Nova*'s editorial team was bulging with talent. It had Kenneth Allsop writing on music, Elizabeth David on food and Penny Vincenzi on fashion. Christopher Booker, Irma Kurtz and Robert Robinson were regulars and Patric Walker started doing the stars – but with no by-line to begin with. Writers were given unaccustomed scope to spread their wings. Four, five thousand-word articles appeared without any attention from the sub-editor's knife. Journalism was less affected by the public relations industry then, and the magazine's reputation and the talent of its writers brought access to the most curious situations and the most reclusive personalities.

Nova was created for women – 'intelligent' women as was proclaimed on its early covers. It was determined to raise women's occupational identity from the cooking, knitting, mothering and housewifeing stereotype to an altogether more worldly figure who did everything for herself and thought everything for herself on equal terms with men. Until *Nova*, women's magazines had traditionally been coy about one huge area of women's lives – sex. *Nova* was the first to cover the concerns that were also the issues of female liberation – orgasm, contraception, abortion, marriage, childbirth, parenthood, and how to get men, how to keep them and how to enjoy them. This, of course, all appealed to men's curiosity too and engendered a large male readership – not the least because the women in the magazine were beautiful and the photography of fashion was often anarchically erotic.

In 1968 George Newnes, and *Nova*, became part of IPC Magazines. Cecil King, head of IPC, cast a paternal eye on his new *enfant terrible* and sanctioned Hackett's radical editorship, which was certainly steering *Nova* onto a course that commanded increasing attention and circulation. Harri Peccinotti, whose design sense, typography and photography were the essential ingredients of the *Nova* look, left his full-time art director's post in 1966 but continued to influence the magazine with his characteristic layouts and photography. Between 1966 and 1969 the art director's chair was filled by Derek Birdsall (on and off), John Blackburn and Bill Fallover, who had been Peccinotti's assistant.

Hackett's inspired choice for a new fashion editor had been the painter Molly Parkin. A dynamic sense of colour and design was all she needed to guide her. Unfettered by the accepted wisdom of the fashion system, she introduced an unconventional and startling view of what women could wear. Always teasing the edges of taste, one day she went too far, even for her long-suffering editor. But she had set the standard. Caroline Baker who joined *Nova* as receptionist, and became Molly Parkin's assistant, took over the fashion editorship in 1967. She understood Parkin's success and built on it as she emerged as a creative force in her own right. If women's fashion has always been about sex, women's magazines had never said so. *Nova* did. The whole magazine, both visually and editorially, was creating a running portrait, a definition of the 'new' woman. What would be revealed in next month's issue? It was compulsive.

1965

Daily Mirror

HERE HE'LL LIE, WHERE HE WANTED TO BE

The Queen: Our survival is his memorial

Britain said goodbye to its man of the century.

The times they were a-changing.

The swinging Sixties translated to celluloid.

The year

Sir Winston Churchill died; the nation was genuinely moved. Kenneth Tynan said the first 'fuck' on TV; whatever else he said was soon forgotten. The Race Relations Act was passed. On TV Gerry Anderson's *Stingray* and *Thunderbirds* made their first appearances and Nell Dunne's play *Up the Junction* shocked people who didn't live in places like that. Ian Smith made his unilateral declaration of independence (UDI) for Rhodesia. Malcolm X was shot. Edward Heath took over the Tory leadership from Sir Douglas-Home. At the cinema, Rita Tushingham, Michael Crawford and Ray Brooks in *The Knack* summed up mid-sixties high spirits, Julie Christie and Omar Sharif were more circumspect in *Dr Zhivago* and, distinctly untrendy, *The Sound of Music* was one of the biggest hits ever. It also spawned one of the year's best-selling albums: amongst others were *The Freewheelin' Bob Dylan, Beatles for Sale* and *Rolling Stones Volume II*. The singles charts introduced a 17-year old, pre-nose-job Cher singing *I Got You Babe* with Sonny Bono. Other names making it big were The Who, Marianne Faithfull, the Supremes, Sandie Shaw, the Kinks, and a number of Dylan look/sound-alikes. On the crime front, Ronald Biggs, the Great Train Robber, escaped from Wandsworth prison and the death penalty was abolished in Britain. Billy Graham came from America to save London from its sins. And in December mini skirts six inches above the knee were spotted in the King's Road, Chelsea.

Right
April 1965
Setting the *Nova* style, an early fashion feature by Penny Vincenzi on black-and-white lingerie. Photograph by Gordon Carter.

June 1965
Harri Peccinotti characteristically used type and photography as one conception across a whole spread. The article on charities was by Mollie Barger.

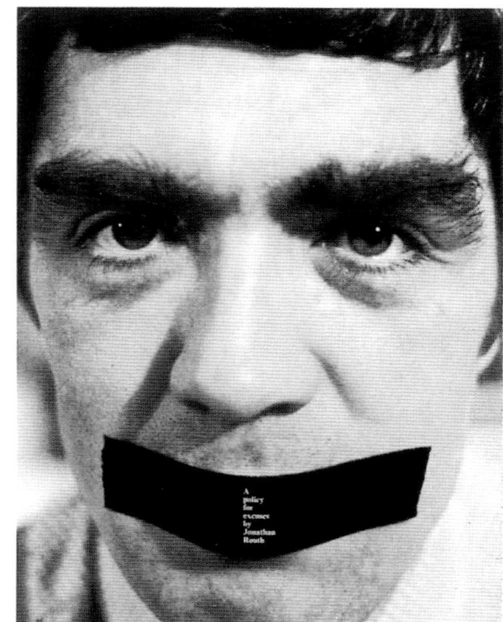
A
policy
for
excuses
by
Jonathan
Routh

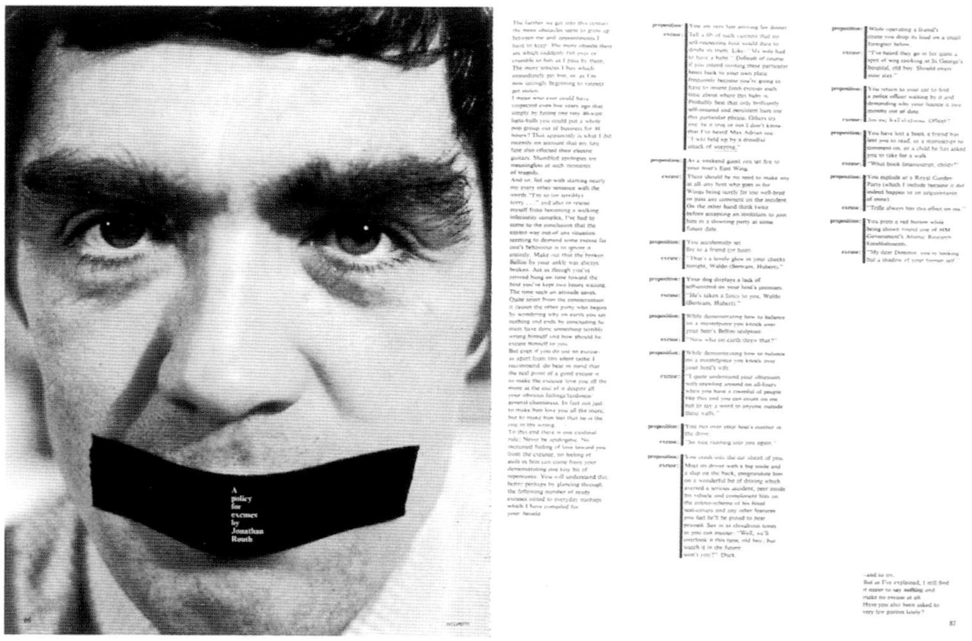

April 1965
Jonathan Routh, garrulous and inquisitive host of the British TV version of *Candid Camera*, created a series of good excuses for difficult situations. Photograph and layout by Harri Peccinotti.

Put out more flags

There was welfare long before there was a Welfare State, only it was called charity. Why does the collecting still go on, and should it? This survey examines some of the muddles left over from past collecting and points to important opportunities for charity in the future

by Mollie Barger

Not long ago the Roman Catholic Little Brothers of the Poor gladdened the hearts and bellies of several hundred indigent ancients with a dinner that began with hot rum punch and crescendoed via lobster salad to trimmed turkey and compôte de fruit flambé, accompanied by French champagne and a hundred dozen roses. This happened—need we say it?—in America. Nothing is too good, the Little Brothers declared, for those who have nothing. A Welfare State can provide life's necessities, but not the luxuries that give it joy and dignity.

It is easy to snipe at this novel view of charity, which bubbles champagne in America while Asia starves, but it represents a distinct advance on Victorian attitudes, when to be poor was to be morally deserving of reproach. Anyway, what *is* charity? St Paul had

CONTINUED ON PAGE 22

Photo: Peccinotti

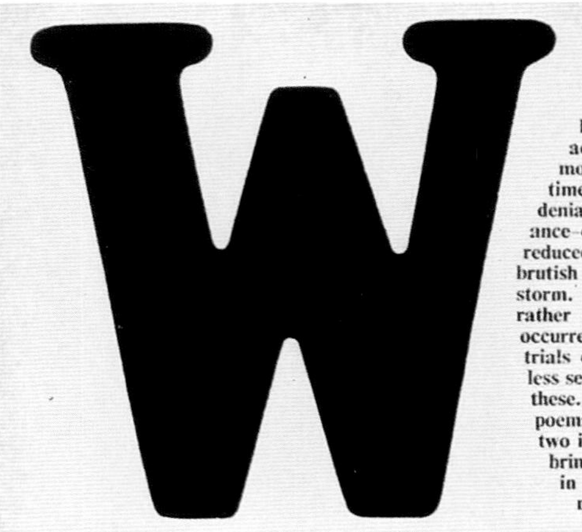

A human being of any sensitivity spends his life balancing a denial and an acceptance of life. The sour mood of these poems reflects a time in my life when emotional denial came uppermost and acceptance–openness, energy, hope–was reduced to a barely traceable vestige, a brutish stubbornness in the face of the storm. The subject is the pain of loss rather than the means by which loss occurred, whether illness, the simple trials of married love or some general, less self-centred *angst*, or a compound of these. The sequence opens with two poems of nightmare, continues with two in which the awakening into day brings little change, hesitates–in The Serving Maid–over a mode of false compromise, finishes with two poems of comfortless endurance.

Beloved,

A little of what we have found. . .

It is certain that maturity and peace are to be sought through ordeal after ordeal, and it seems that the search continues until we fail. We reach out after each new beginning, penetrating our context to know ourselves, and our knowledge increases until we recognize again (more profoundly each time) our pain, indignity and triviality. This bitter cup is offered, heaped with curses, and we must drink or die.

And even though we drink we may also die, if every drop of bitterness–that rots the flesh–is not transmuted. (Certainly the individual plight is hideous, each torturing each; but we are guilty, seeing this, to believe that our common plight is only hideous. Believing so we make it so: pigs in a slaughter-yard that turn and savage each other in a common desperation and disorder.) Death, either way, is guilt and failure. But if we drink the bitterness and can transmute it and continue, we resume in candour and doubt the only individual joy–there stored necessity to learn. Sensing a wider scope, a more penetrating harmony, we begin again in a light innocence to grow toward the next ordeal.

Love also, it seems, will continue until we fail: in the sensing of the wider scope, in the growth toward it, in the swallowing and absorption of the bitterness, in the resumed innocence . . .

Wormwood

I have dreamt it again: standing suddenly still
In a thicket, among wet trees, stunned, minutely
Shuddering, hearing a wooden echo escape.

A mossy floor, almost colourless, disappears
In depths of rain among the tree shapes.
I am straining, tasting that echo a second longer.

If I can hold it . . . familiar if I can hold it . . .
A black tree with a double trunk–two trees
Grown into one–throws up its blurred branches.

The two trunks in their infinitesimal dance of growth
Have turned completely about one another, their join
A slowly twisted scar . . . that I recognize . . .

A quick arc flashes sidewise in the air,
A heavy blade in flight. A wooden stroke:
Iron sinks in the gasping core.
I will dream it again.

Mask of Love

Mask of Love, staring
Aghast out of unreason,
Do you come to us for peace?
Me, flinching from your stare?
Her, whose face you bear?

Remember how we have come
To stand again and again
On peaks of stress, face
To face, wearied with horror,
Screaming in ecstasy
Across the narrow abyss.

Remember
That our very bodies lack peace:
In tiny darknesses,
In accustomed hideousness,
The skin angrily flames,
Nerve gropes for muscle
Across the silent abyss.

You have seen our nocturnal
Suicidal dance,
When the moon hung vast, and seemed
To wet our mocking mouths;
She, turning in despair
Round some tiny mote;
I, doubled in laughter,
Clasping my paunch in grief
For the world in a speck of dust;
Between us, the fuming abyss.

Dumb vapours pour
Where the mask of Love appears,
Reddening, and disappears.

First Light

A prone couple still sleeps
While a pale deadly light ascends
Out of the sea: dawn-
Light, reaching across the hill
To the dark garden. The grass
Emerges, soaking with grey dew.

In brutal silence an empty
Kitchen takes form, tidied and swept,
Blank with marriage–where shrill
Unreason and Jew-face Law have kept
Another vigil far
Into the night, and raved and wept.

Upstairs a whimper or sigh
Comes from an open bedroom door
–A child enduring a dream
That grows, at the [illegible]t touch of day,
Unendurable–
And lengthens to an ugly wail.

The Secret Garden

It stands in a tangled place. Flails of thorn
Crawl into the lawn; on every hand
Glittering, toughened branches drink their dew,
And I see with bitterness in every drop
The clumsy earth pivot on a coarse heel,
Repeating her dull demand:
Corrupt, corrupt, visible, invisible.

A child stands an instant at my knee.
His mouth smells of innocent energy, light
As light. Embrace him, and all his angel race!
I touch my hand to his pearl flesh, taking strength;
He stands still, absorbing in return
The first chill of the curse.
How sweet the kernel of his waiting brain. . .

Then set him free. Oh how, or why, prepare
A son for the sour encounter? A rasping boredom
Funnels into death! I see my hands
Reach out coldly–tending, as they rot,
A fragrant evanescent few. It seems
While any semblance remains
I'll cultivate my garden for the dew.

Thomas Kinsella, born 4 May 1928 in Dublin; married with three children. Recently resigned from the Irish Department of Finance. At present living by poetry in the United States, at Southern Illinois University. Principal books of poe

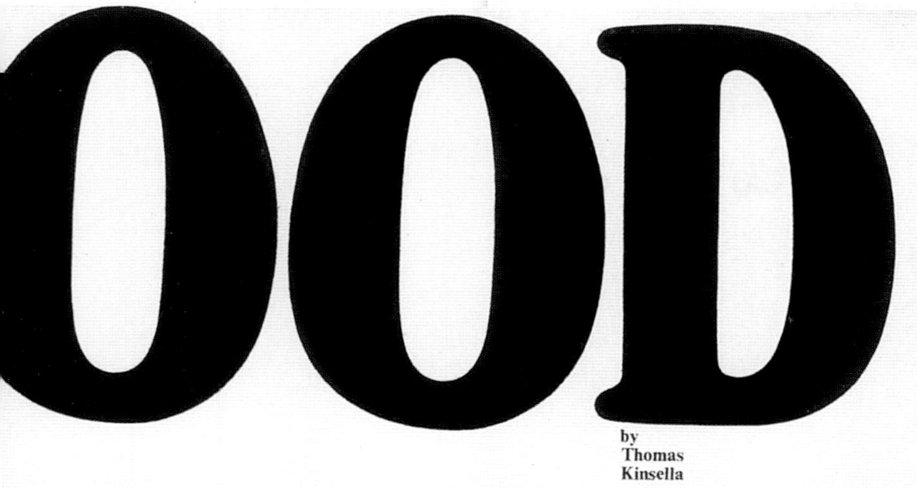

by
Thomas
Kinsella

December 1965
Seven poems by Thomas Kinsella – the first time the famous *Nova* headline typeface was used. Harri Peccinotti discovered a complete set of wood-block Windsor capitals while visiting Ralph Steadman's garage with Barry Fantoni. From it he later designed the lower-case set. The typeface was used for the cover logo from January 1966 onwards.

The Serving Maid

Mirror, though you show me my decay
So soon begun–yellowed skin and eyes,
And shadowed lips withering–while I stand
And drag my brush through hair that keeps no shape,
Mirror, mirror, I can laugh at you.
This squawking busybody almost thrives
On jeering at itself; it serves me well.

My eyes, too bright, half question. Too-bright eyes,
I answer with a raucous 'I reject!',
A cheerier glitter, swallowing back again
My childhood's wholesome fright, as when I found
Renunciation, with a first false cry
And heaviness of soul–then rushed to serve,
Chiding cheerily. To take that weight.

Soul-consuming Love lay waiting, blindly
Offering helplessness, angrily wasting.
I give God thanks I found her. Such a one . . .
Old feathery bones and flesh to tug and turn,
To lift and wipe, jingling the crumpled bed;
Every part, from heels to glistening chin,
A torment of demands. Guilt-eater!

I come, I come, in decent skirt and jumper
And flat-heeled shoes, with flowers and prayer book
All in order, to remember you;
To kneel by the grave's gravel and pluck the weeds.
Replace the withered things and, if I could,
Grope down at your bones and take away
Even death's eery filth, tidying your substance;

To whisper you my cry of false derision
With face grown pale in wholesome hopelessness;
To let the wretched gasp of self-regard
Tear happily, and service flood my veins.
Plot by plot, through shade of stone and yew,
The muddied paths lead to my buried health,
And I need not sicken of my endless cheer.

Remembering Old Wars

What clamped us together? When each night fell we lay down
In the smell of decay and slept, our bodies leaking,
Limp as the dead, breathing that smell all night.

Then light prodded us awake, and adversity
Flooded up from inside us as we laboured upright
Once more to face the hells of circumstance.

And so on, without hope of change or peace.
Each dawn, like lovers recollecting their purpose,
We would renew each other with a savage smile.

On a Gift in the Shape of a Heart

Open this and you will see
A waste, a nearly naked tree
That will not rest till it is bare.
It shivers, shivers in the air
Scraping at its yellow leaves
And suffers–when the tempest heaves–
In fierce relief, the Heaven-sent
Convulsions of self-punishment.

What cannot rest till it is bare,
Though branches crack and fibres tear.

and a great star fell from heaven, burning as it were a torch; and it fell on the third part of the rivers and upon the fountains of waters; and the name of the star is called Wormwood; and the third part of the waters became wormwood; and many men died of the waters, because they were made bitter.
–Apocalypse, ch. 8, verses 10 and 11.

These poems are from the book, Wormwood, shortly to be published in a limited edition by the Dolmen Press (Dublin) at 31s 6d, and distributed in London by Oxford University Press.

another September (1958) and Downstream (1962), both published by Dolmen Press (Dublin)/Oxford University Press (London)

39

A WOMAN AT THE SEASIDE

MORNING

August 1965
The story was by Edna O'Brien. The display type was made up by Harri Peccinotti using rubber-stamp characters. The illustration was by Alan Aldridge.

How they took the dread out of summer

A vivid reminder of the miracle we already take for granted: the rout of a crippling disease that menaced the swimming months in Britain less than a decade ago

A page of exciting contemporary history by **Alan Wykes**

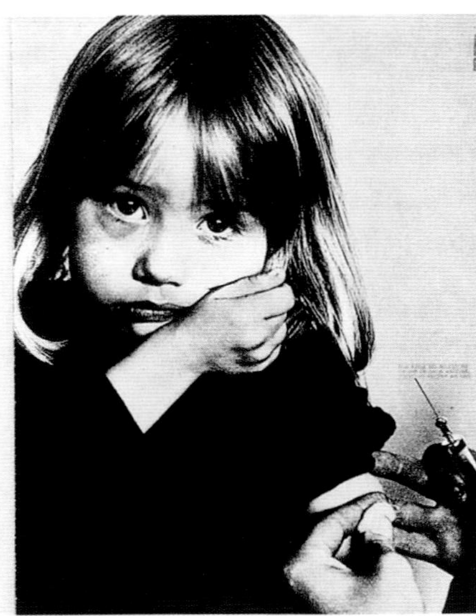

Ten summers ago a question alarming mothers all over Britain was "Should I let my child swim?" At that time every schoolchild was still a potential victim of the postwar upsurge of poliomyelitis. It is a crippling disease, occasionally even a killer. Distracted parents saw the rising numbers of its victims tabulated in the newspapers like road casualties ('Manchester: 147 last year, this year 223'). Some remembered Franklin D. Roosevelt, stricken lame for life. They pictured their own children in iron lungs or leg braces. The year's casualties could easily reach 8,000 cases, and the anxious peak was always in the swimming months. Polluted rivers and bathing pools were a known source of infection, though houseflies, food, and droplets sneezed by polio carriers could also spread it.

Alarm first shook the public in 1946, when it became clear that despite nearly half a century of research the disease was gaining the upper hand. Polio had become a notifiable infectious disease as recently as 1913, three years after it was established that a virus caused the infection, and cases had varied between 500 and 1,000 a year ever since. (Before 1900 the disease was too rare to be investigated at all.) Suddenly in the first year after World War II the number of notified cases in Britain alone soared to

August 1965
An article by Alan Wykes on the conquest of the paralysing disease poliomyelitis, which struck mainly in summer. (There were over 7,000 cases a year in the early Fifties, reducing to zero by the Sixties.) Photograph by Harri Peccinotti.

WHAT IS PSYCHO-PROPHYLAXIS

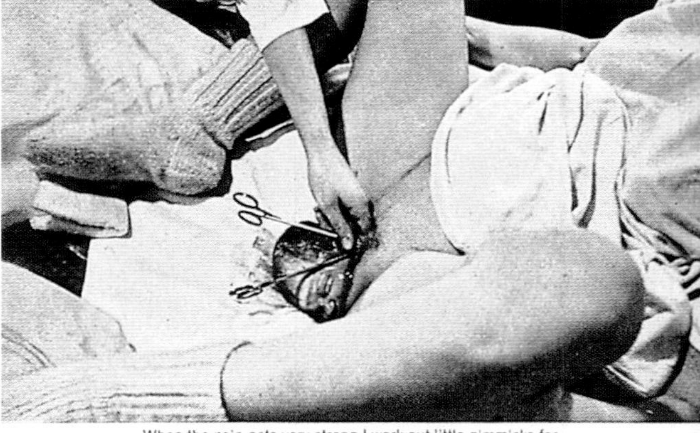

When the pain gets very strong I work out little gimmicks for disassociation, like fixing my eyes on a picture and seeing how slowly they can travel up it. If at any time you'd like to give the whole thing up and go home, please, it's just before the head is born when the pain really starts building up

54

December 1965
Peta Fordham's article on women with men doing time.

LITTLE WOMEN OUTSIDE

Crime has glamour, pound-note thin, quick vanishing. Two years after the mail train robbery, some still lingers in the public mind, some possibly in the minds of those who escaped. But to the women whose menfolk are now facing countless Christmases inside, the glamour went long ago. Notoriety is harder to live with. In many ways, wives and families share the sentence. In this article, **Peta Fordham,** author of The Robbers' Tale, reflects on the position of women in criminal society.

Opposite The iron gin that waits for sin – a contemporary version of Wilde's image is at Durham, a top-security prison which includes among its tenants some of the mail train men. This is the exercise yard, a patchwork of paths that spells privilege for thirty minutes in the early morning, an unexpanding freedom that knows no seasonal goodwill

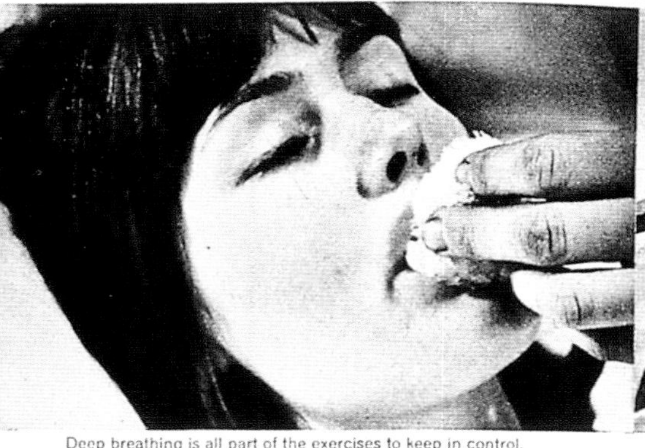

Deep breathing is all part of the exercises to keep in control. With the hard work of concentrating on my breathing I get very sticky, and Anthony wipes my face with a wet sponge now and then. They told us in class that when your face is wiped with a wet sponge you suck it like a baby, for comfort. It's true

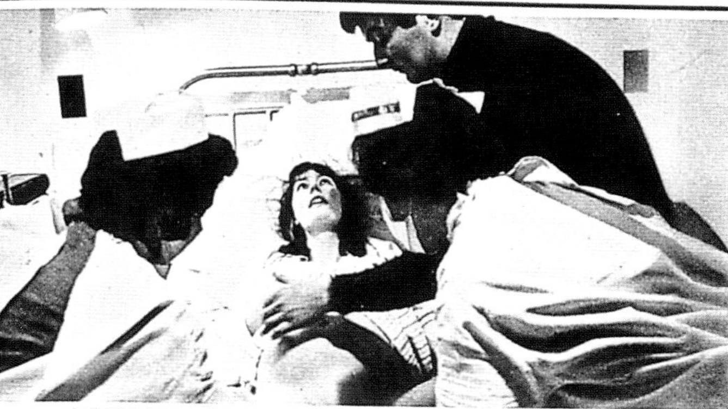

Anthony takes over the massage when I get tired. The very light fluttering, almost butterfly, strokes I learned in classes would probably tickle normally, but while you're having a contraction it gives you something to concentrate on, and it's very comforting. They offer me drugs, but I want to be conscious throughout

I'm pushing as they taught us—and obviously the head is showing, because Anthony looks so pleased. I can't see it because I've still got the bump. This is a difficult patch; very exhausting. I'm getting about thirty seconds' rest between contractions. I suppose the pain is acute, but if I concentrate it takes care of itself

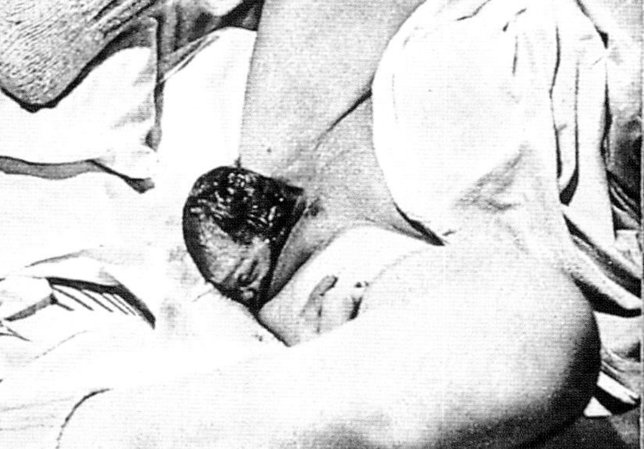

The nurse says 'I don't want you to push on the next contraction, because the cord is round its neck.' Then she cuts the cord and I hear the baby cry—and there's just this little head—it's marvellous! Then the head turns and I can see the face, and I put my hands down to feel it. Anthony says, 'Look, the eyes are open'

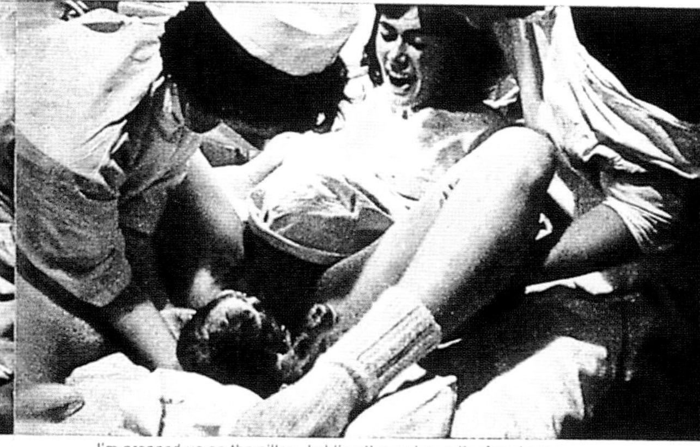

I'm propped up on the pillow, holding the underneath of my knees as we were taught, and Anthony is supporting one knee. Funnily enough I'm not at all curious about the sex yet, but I can't wait to hold it. Once the head is born, you're concentrating so hard on what you're doing that you have no sensation of pain

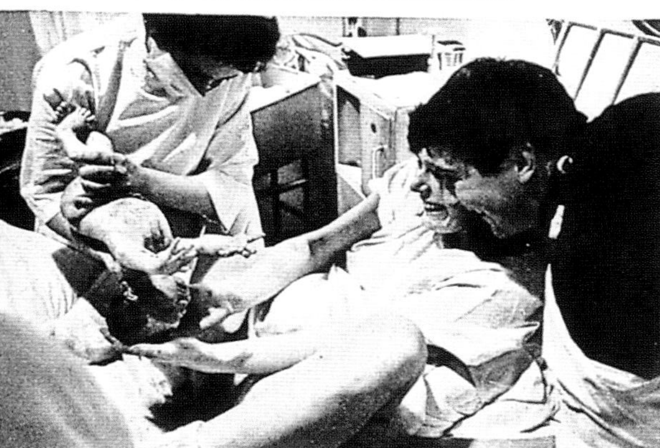

As I see her I shout 'Ooh, look!' and Anthony says 'Don't say that—you've got a roomful watching you already.' The funny thing is that you feel you're giving everyone a present by having a baby. During pregnancy I sometimes wondered what I'd look like in labour. In fact, when the time comes I feel quite beautiful

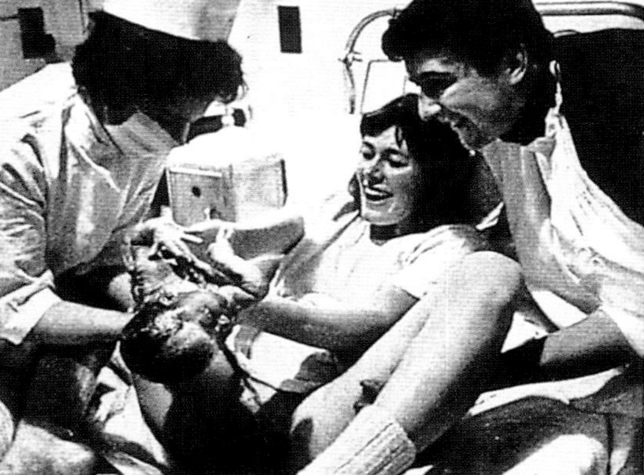

The nurse holds her out, lifts her legs and I put my hands under her arms. She feels heavy, much heavier than when I carried her around all these months. 'Doesn't she make a noise?' Anthony says as she starts to shriek. He keeps saying 'Oh look, she's got five fingers and toes!' as though he'd expected her not to

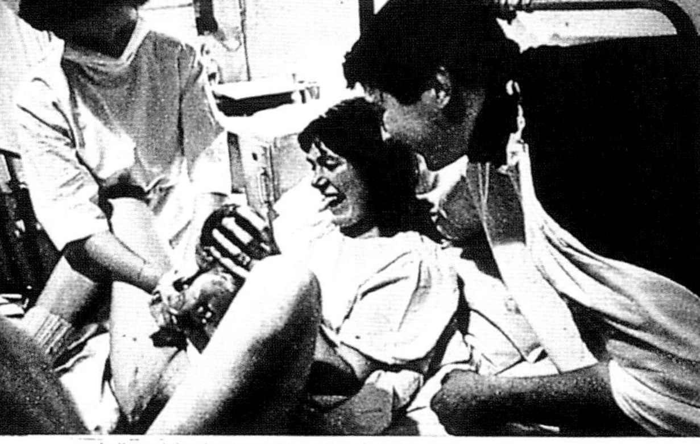

Anthony takes her while I have the afterbirth. I have a few stitches because I had a little tear in labour, but what with the deep breathing and the fact that I'm feeling so pleased with myself the stitches don't seem to matter. Anthony looks at his watch and tells his daughter what time she was born

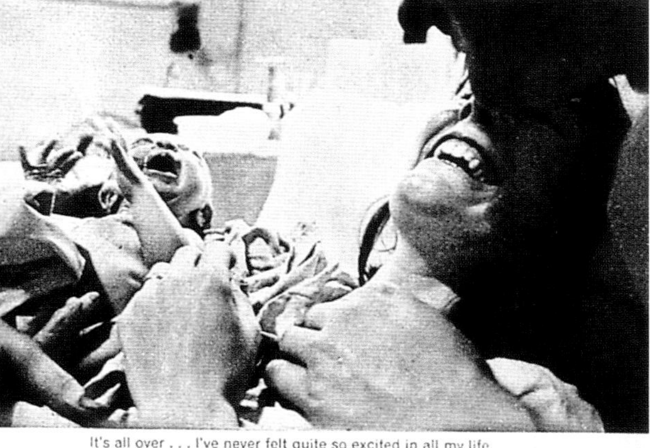

It's all over . . . I've never felt quite so excited in all my life. Between Anthony and me there is a most terrific sense of achievement; something we've shared because we've been through it together—it's almost as though he's had the baby, too. I just feel happy—the fact that women have had babies before doesn't mean a thing

PHOTOGRAPHS BY JOHN MINSHALL

October 1965
John Minshall turned up at *Nova* one day with these photographs and inspired an article by Lee Langley and Audrey Whiting on the novel idea that childbirth could actually be fun.

1966

Twiggy's was the face they all wanted to photograph.

Aberfan would never be the same again.

The Beatles became cartoons in the *Yellow Submarine* film.

The year

Everyone cheered and laughed as Bobby Moore's England beat Germany in the World Cup final at Wembley. Everyone grieved and cried over the Aberfan disaster which buried a school and 144 children under a coal slag slip. The prisons continued to leak, this time spy George Blake escaped from Wormwood Scrubbs. Having trouble with its slim Commons majority from 1964, Labour improved its position in another general election. Further away the Soviet's *Venera III* spacecraft was the first to land (crash, in fact) on another planet. Indira Ghandi became Prime Minister of India. The Red Guards ran amok in China purging revisionists. At the cinema Michael Caine kissed the girls and made them cry in *Alfie*. A year of classics in the charts had *Yellow Submarine* and *Eleanor Rigby* from the Beatles, *River Deep, Mountain High* from Ike and Tina Turner and *Good Vibrations* from the Beach Boys. The Monkees arrived on TV from Hollywood doing a Beatles rip-off every week, and doing it pretty well too. Also new on the small screen were Johnny Speight's beguiling bigot Alf Garnett in *Till Death Us Do Part*, and just the right mix of actors, graphics and tongue-in-cheek in *Batman*. *Cathy Come Home* continued the BBC's first-class reputation for working-class television drama. Carnaby Street vied with the King's Road as London's centre of pop fashion. And Twiggy became Woman of the Year, although not obviously qualifying yet.

Right
June 1966
'Prepare to face your figure' – on the beach bodies are as important as clothes. Photograph by Harri Peccinotti.

Nylon anorak by V de V at Aqua Sprite 20 gns. Silver PVC shoulder bag by Sally Jess 6½ gns. Glasses made to order from A M Sheridan 8 gns

36

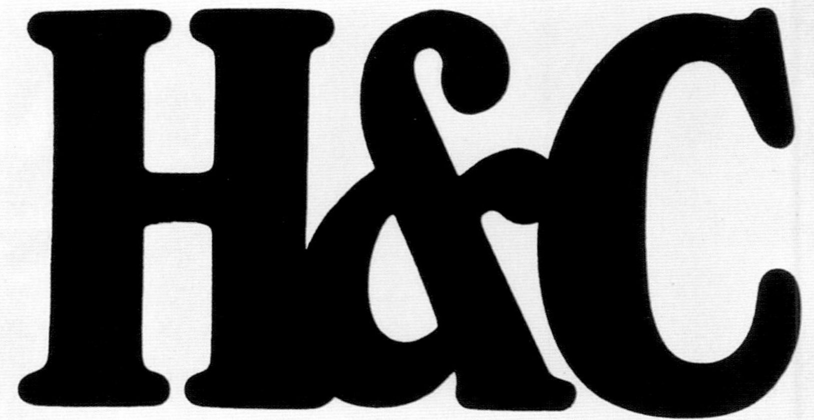

Shopping for winter holiday clothes in a grey-sky Britain which will survive the brilliance of a foreign sun can be disconcerting. Hot intense colours and vivid design can seem disturbingly bright, even garish, in our cold winter light. Picture them instead flattering a tan, glowing under a sizzling sun beating down on boat-deck or beach—pastels in these conditions would only keep you firmly in the fashion shade. So go for colours clear and strong.

Apply the same principle in choosing clothes for colder climates. Aim for intensity there, too. The success of Op Art design in clothes has proved convincingly the basic excellence of black and white—see for yourself how striking they can be against a snowy landscape. If your skiing is below standard, make sure your appearance is Gold Medal level. Since there's not much variation in basic ski outfits, excel individually with good definite colour and interesting texture. Sunglasses are an indispensable addition to your wardrobe for either sort of holiday. Superlative design in the past few seasons has made them as much a fashion item as a shield from the sun.

On pages 78-88 we give you a travel guide for the season 1966; on the opposite and following pages you can start choosing your winter holiday wardrobe now

37

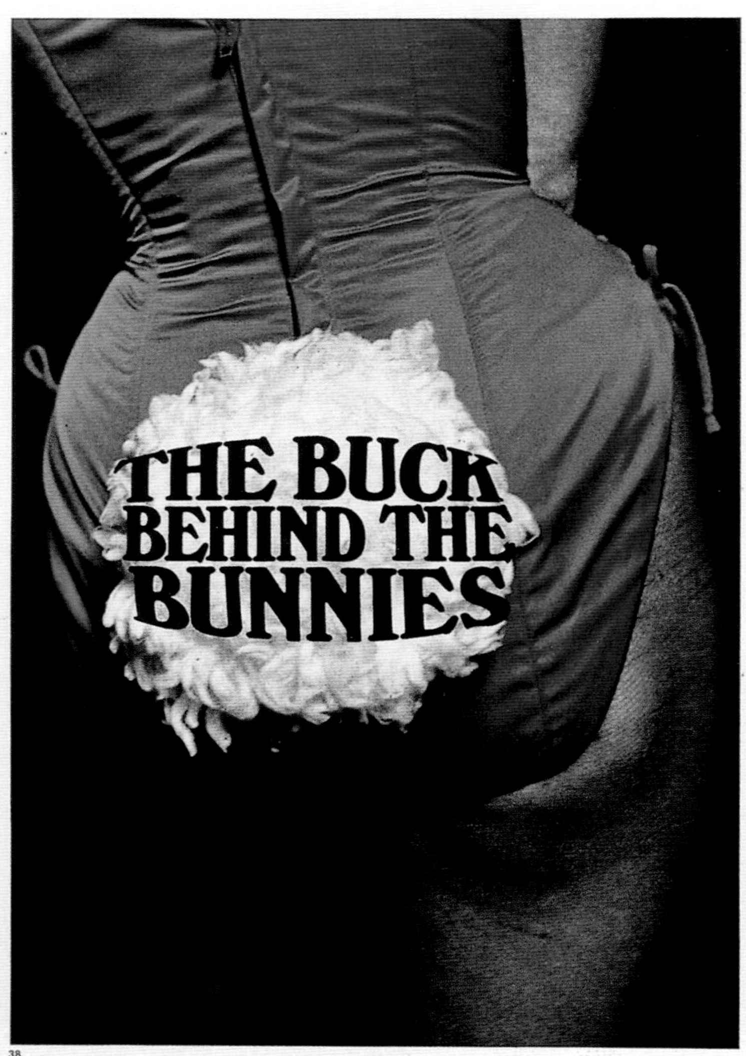

38

In Spring, it is confidently expected and certainly calculated in Chicago, the fancy of young and not-so-young men in Britain will be turning to Bunnies. And in the first wild days of March, Hugh Hefner's Playboy Organisation will be hoping to recoup some of their £1,500,000 investment in a Park Lane burrow. This is meant to be the first of the European sites and it is expected that Manchester will eventually have its own Bunny Club. The expected clientele of the London burrow will be 2,500. One hundred native bunnies will be on parade, probably less pneumatic than those fulsome nudes who suggest abandon without responsibility from the pages of Playboy, but probably nubile enough to pull in the customers. Drinks will lend enchantment to the eyes of beholders at the price of 10s each. There will be meals, entertainment, and the American-type status symbol of belonging for each member. The success of this look-at-but-don't-touch type of sex is undoubted in America. It will be interesting to see the effect here. Mr Hefner's hope is that men who go there will be sufficiently stimulated to go home and 'have good sex with their wives or girl friends.' It is to be hoped that the stimulus of the English bunnies will not make them less discriminating than that. To examine closely the proselytiser of sexual freedom and the Bunny philosophy, Nova sent Mary Holland to Chicago to see Mr Hefner who has such liberating intentions for your husbands and boy friends. Hefner is, just for an issue, for every rabbit must have his day, Nova's

playmate of the month

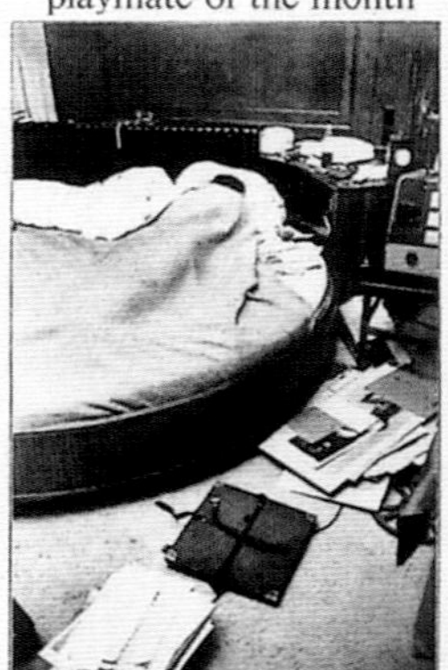

39

by Toni Del Renzio

There is just no substitute for real home-made ices. Indeed it is almost a universal rule that any ice made in large quantities is synthetic. The exception would be ices made by a large number of hands.

All that modern machinery and industrialism has done for ices is to complicate the formulae, demand ever more synthetics and emulsifying agents, and turn out in vast quantities a product that should never cross anyone's lips. Anyway, ices are easy to make by hand, as it were. Sugar, fruit and water suffice for granite or sherbets; and sugar, cream, eggs and fruit or other natural flavours are all that's needed for ice creams and mousses.

These are the two basic types of ices, and naturally, the one was already known to the ancient Romans – the emperor Nero having his made from that snow they stored in caves – and the other was known to the ancient Chinese and brought back to Europe, specifically to Venice, by Marco Polo. Henri II of France had Venetians in the royal kitchens to make his ices and tried to prevent their secrets from passing to other households. So did England's Charles I. In the middle of the seventeenth century the Italian Procopio Calpelli founded the Café Procope in Paris and launched the fashion for ices among less exalted personages. The fashion crossed not only the Channel but the Atlantic as well and by the early eighteenth century New York's first ice-cream parlours were being opened and the stately colonial houses of the Deep South had their freezers. George Washington had two at Mount Vernon. Cornets and cones were invented for the Louisiana Purchase Exhibition at St Louis in 1904

All types of ices can be made in the ice compartment of an ordinary refrigerator; but if the initial freezing is done in some sort of improvised freezer – a metal container placed in a bowl of crushed ice and salt, allowing for thorough stirring – a better result is obtained than when the mixture is occasionally taken out of the refrigerator to be stirred. Nevertheless with a bit of practice anyone can acquire enough know-how to make very acceptable ices by this latter method. Good granite can even be made without the stirring.

In the former method the first step is to take out the ice tray and turn the regulator to maximum freezing. In half an hour the refrigerator will be ready for use. Meanwhile crush the ice from the tray and pack it round the tin in which the ice cream is to be made, along with some gros sel (coarse sea salt); pour the cold prepared mixture into the tin and stir vigorously until it begins to take. Put the lid on the tin and place it in the freezing compartment of the refrigerator. After twenty minutes take it out, give it another vigorous stirring and replace. After a further twenty minutes repeat this operation. Care must now be taken to adjust the freezer to maintain the ice in its best condition and not to over-freeze it, though with a proper mould this is not necessary.

The freshly made ice, cream or otherwise, is called mantecato and is served by the spoonful with fruit, or different flavours and types of ices are combined. Prepared as it should be, not refrozen, the mantecato should be soft and melting and therefore no attempt should be made to give it a particular shape.

Shaped ices, when made in individual servings, are the bomba which is spherical, the parfait (cylindrical), and the stracchino (square). These moulds are increasingly difficult to find in ordinary shops and it is perhaps better to use larger ones or, in the absence of those made specifically for ices, jelly moulds, which work quite well.

The moulds should be left in the refrigerator for at least half an hour before being filled with the ice mixture, which must be packed in fairly tightly. If an authentic ice mould is used, smear the outer rim with butter before putting on the lid and leave in the ice compartment for an hour or so. If some other type of mould is employed, you should cover it with greaseproof paper carefully cut to the size and shape of the container, and then seal the join with butter.

Granita di caffè Make 1½ pints of strong black coffee and dissolve ½ lb of sugar in it. While this is cooling add a zest of lemon peel. When cold remove the lemon peel and if desired pour in 1 tablespoon of rum or brandy. Freeze as above. Granita di limone Squeeze 6-8 lemons to produce ½ pint of juice and mix this with 1 pint of water. Add ½ lb sugar and the peel of 2 lemons. Bring slowly to the boil and simmer for two or three minutes. Remove the peel before freezing. Granita di aranci Squeeze enough oranges to give ½ pint of juice. Proceed as in the previous recipe but adjust the quantity of sugar according to the sweetness of the oranges. Granita di fragole Pulp 2 lb strawberries through a sieve. Add the juice of 1 orange and a few crushed mint leaves. Dissolve ½ lb sugar in ½ pint of water and boil gently for five minutes. Allow to cool and then mix with the fruit pulp. Remove the mint leaves and freeze. These granite can be made with any fruit but when using peaches, apricots or cherries, add the cracked stones to the boiling water and sugar and strain before pouring over the fruit pulp. Gelato di crema This is really frozen custard, crema inglese. Beat the yolks of 4 eggs along with ½ pint of cream in a double boiler. (Alternatively 6 yolks and ½ pint of milk will do.) Add a paring of lemon peel and stir constantly until the mixture thickens. Take off the heat and continue to stir, adding 3 oz sugar and some flavouring such as vanilla. Allow to cool and then freeze. Gelato di crema al caffè Infuse 1 oz finely ground coffee in ½ pint of boiling milk. Leave to cool and then beat in the yolks of 6 eggs. Then proceed as in the previous recipe. Gelato di crema al cioccolato Dissolve 5 oz grated chocolate in ½ pint of milk that is not quite boiling. Cool the mixture, then proceed as before. Gelato di crema al tè Mix ¼ pint of strong tea with ¾ pint of milk and follow the method described in the previous recipes. Gelato di crema alle mandorle, nocciole or ai pistacchi. This is almond, hazelnut or pistachio ice cream. The procedure is the same as for crema inglese, but first the ground nuts are mixed with a little milk and then added to the boiling milk and left to infuse for a quarter of an hour or so. With pistachio it is usual to add a few drops of some vegetable green colouring. All three flavours are improved by a touch of vanilla. These are all mantecato and are normally served in a coppa or glass. Here are some of the ways they can be garnished and combined. Coppa costa d'oro Mix into the vanilla ice some small pieces of soft milk chocolate and toasted almonds. Three-quarters fill the glass with this mixture and then pile on some whole toasted almonds. At the moment of serving pour over a little rum-flavoured hot chocolate sauce. Coppa misurina Put a layer of wild strawberries or raspberries in the bottom of the glass. Cover with vanilla ice, add a few more strawberries or raspberries, and sprinkle with sugar and cinnamon. Coppa araba Soak some sultanas for an hour in rum and put 1 teaspoonful in each glass. Then fill the glass with coffee ice cream and decorate with two or three stoned dates. Mousse au café Beat together in a pan 6 egg yolks, 1 oz sugar, 1 tablespoon of very strong coffee and a little vanilla essence. Then over a low flame add the whipped white of an egg and whip the mixture. When it is warm take off the heat and whip until cold and like a stiff batter. Then carefully mix in ½ pint of cream, slightly sweetened and stiffly whipped. Put into a mould and freeze for some three hours. To make other mousses adapt the directions given above for the various gelati. To make ice cream for bombe, parfaits or stracchini, it is best to depart from the basic cream-ice recipe. Beat the egg yolks with ½ pint of water (in which ½ lb sugar has been dissolved) over a lively heat. When it thickens take off the stove and mix with an equal amount of whipped cream and the required flavouring. Bomba Aida Line the mould with mandarin or tangerine ice cream and fill the centre with vanilla ice to which has been added 1 teaspoon of kirsch. Bomba successo Line the mould with apricot ice cream and fill the centre with whipped cream in which have been mixed some fine slivers of apricot and a little kirsch. Bomba tutti frutti Line the mould with strawberry ice and fill the centre with vanilla ice cream mixed with chopped candied fruits soaked in rum. All these can also be made as parfaits or stracchini.

WHERE THE FUN IS

Don't just sit there, disorientate. React to environment with ears, eyes, hands and feet, react aesthetic, react sensual. If you don't know what this means have a look at a Keith Albarn fun palace. The one we show here is on the Wren development at Henley at present. Children living on the estate will be able to play there, but grown-ups can take it on a different level, perhaps several levels. This particular fun palace is an offshoot of a larger one because of restrictions of space and money, and consists of five basic cells in which the environment changes constantly, activated by movement of spectator. As you walk through, the lighting and background sound change pattern. If you can't afford £750 for the back garden, see if you can adapt some of the ideas for children's rooms and Christmas party decorations. Outside the palace on pages 72 and 73 are some of the brightest clothes yet designed for children, all by Carol Payne and available from Kids In Gear, Carnaby Street, London. Details on page 99.

Inside the palace on pages 74 and 75 the children dress up in beautifully designed paper hats by Brian Harris, more clothes by Gear, and coloured fur coats available for all ages and made to measure from Valerie and Geoffrey Goad. Further details on page 99.

If this is the thirtieth consecutive year that you have been giving, as an adult, Christmas presents to adult friends and family, then you may well be thinking that twenty-nine plus one equals frustration and a lack of fun. So bear in mind that since those long sunny days (in December?) when so many things were fun, the space age has caught up with children's toys, and the sophisticated shrugs with which a nine-year-old greets a walking, talking (literally) robot (pages 76 and 77) give no clue to the fun which a sophisticated adult will get from it. The noise some of them make is dreadful, but you can go even better and convert the parlour into a discotheque, with a juke-box or a pin-ball machine, or other barometers of sanity. Details on page 99, and don't take that bit about the thirtieth year too hard. A joke is a joke.

If automated action isn't enough you can always try the real thing. We took the photographs on pages 78 and 79 in Harrods' pet shop, which can produce anything from a deodorised skunk to a snake that lives on live mice. In between are budgerigars, bush babies, goldfish, toucans, rabbits, Peruvian long-haired guinea pigs and macaws. Even more frightening ideas, terrestrial and aquatic, on page 99.

❛I believe God has willed to call on women as much as on men, and we haven't the right to say: No, thanks, we're only women and can't accept such responsibilities❜

INGRID BJERKAAS
The first woman priest in Norway

CONTINUED OVERLEAF

Previous pages
January 1966
Molly Parkin's feature on colour dressing – hot for the beach and cold for the ski slopes. Photographs by Michel Certain.
March 1966
As the latest of Hugh Hefner's Playboy Clubs opened its doors in London, Mary Holland examined money and the Bunny.
August 1966
Toni del Renzio, an expert on the Dada movement, was the best cook Harri Peccinotti knew. So he was asked to describe how to make real Italian ice cream at home. The 'Neopolitan' typography on the right, made from roman, bold and italic, was all hand set by a bemused compositor under Harri Peccinotti's direction.
December 1966
The final page wrap-up of a picture feature on unusual Christmas ideas rudely faced the lead-off page of a sombre article on Ingrid Bjerkås, Norway's first woman priest.

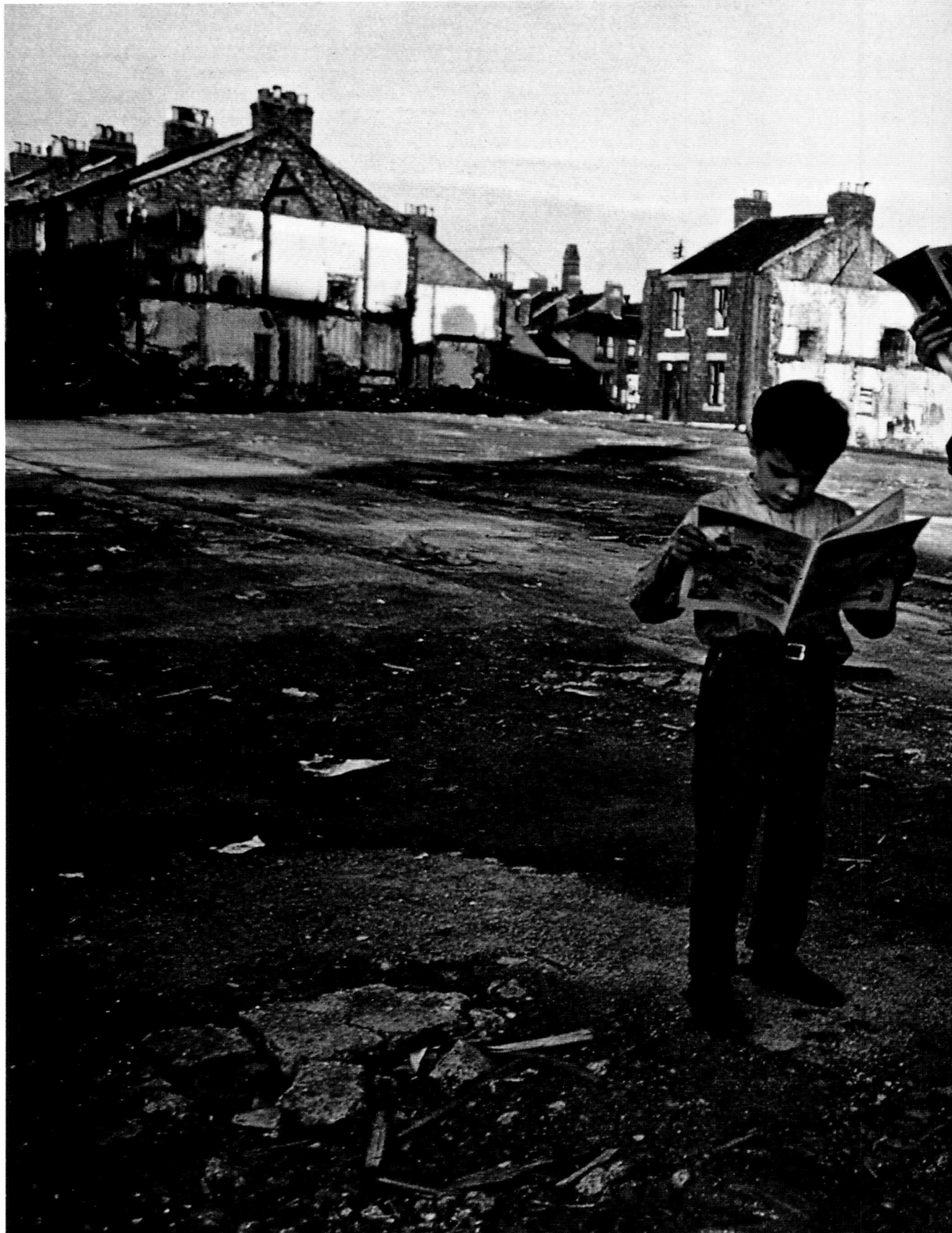

October 1966
'Swings and roundabouts' suggested that money saved on bargains should then be invested in extravagance. Photographs by Saul Leiter.

SWINGS & ROUNDABOUTS

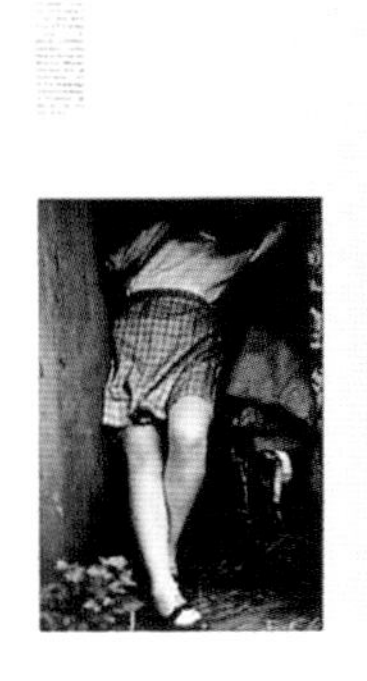

Right
August 1966
It was meant to be twelve pages of black girls in colour clothes. Harri Peccinotti shot the photographs as such, and went on holiday. Meanwhile the editor had some sort of a brainstorm and asked for the last six pages to include white girls in prim suits. The effect was more than anodyne: it killed the idea stone dead.

HOW PARIS SEES YOU THIS SPRING

February 1966
Nova was already questioning the relevance of *haute couture*, concentrating instead on the Paris designers moving to *prêt-à-porter*. Photographs by Harri Peccinotti.

Cotton hat, 6s 3d, racing vest, £2 16s 9d, both by Holdsworth. Cotton training vest, 18s 11d, by Holdsworthy; striped cotton hat, 6s 8d, by Holdsworth. Nylon striped racing vest, £2 16s 9d; cotton hat 6s 8d; embroidered cotton racing vest, £5; striped cotton hat, 6s 8d; all by Holdsworth

...P-P-P-PAGES TO MAKE YOU THINK ABOUT C-C-C-COLOUR BY MOLLY PARKIN

One of the comforts of growing up and older is that you at least learn which colours suit you best, not only by what you are told but, more important, by how you feel wearing them. A lot of women stubbornly continue to buy colours that they love on other people but in which they themselves look ghastly. On the other hand, if what you have on improves your own state of mind – go ahead and wear it. After all, Shirley MacLaine, who seems one of the happiest actresses to emerge from Hollywood, appears on lists of the world's worst dressed women, which must be proving something. It can take a long time and a lot of self-discipline to learn by your mistakes. Everyone's wardrobe bears dreadful evidence of impulse-buying – heaven knows what would be there if clothes were as cheap as chocolate. Subtle shades on the wrong person can be disastrous, a complete camouflage. Yet strong colours need living up to; they can easily dominate the woman inside unless she herself is as vivid in personality or colouring. For this reason we photographed the following sportswear on dark-skinned girls. The design and cost of these clothes are extremely good, but they are featured mainly as an exercise in exciting colour combinations. The subtle colours of the tweeds and suedes following them are just as good however. They complement and are improved by their British surroundings. It has taken a Frenchman, Daniel Hechter, to see this and to produce fresh, elegant fashion from traditional British dress. That is, tweeds coupled with immaculate tailoring. If your leg-length enables you to wear trousers successfully, and it does depend on this as much as on the size of your rump, trouser suits are very much the answer to winter warmth. The longer line jacket on page 45 is particularly flattering to all ages and sizes, but with both suits do make sure that your proportions look right without a high heel. It would seem madness, if your strongest asset were your ankles, to hide them in trousers and long boots. Boots too do need a good length of leg, especially with short skirts. Far better to wear warm tights or fine wool stockings with pretty shoes. The suedes are examples of rethinking. John Stephen in Carnaby Street is now turning his attention to women's clothes and has made a man's jacket on leaner lines to be worn with a skirt. Ossie Clark of Quorum has designed the other suit. Both are cut on good modern and economical lines. Stockists given on page 74.

Leather crash helmet by Holdsworthy, £2 6s. T-shirt by Ampro Sports, 11s 6d. Basketball shoes by Lonsdale Sports, £1 1s 6d.
Crash helmet by Holdsworth, £1 12s 6d. Nylon racing vest by Holdsworth, £3 10s. Boxing boots by Lonsdale Sports £2 7s 6d. Vinyl crash helmet by Holdsworth, £1 12s 6d.
Woollen leg warmers by Holdsworthy, £1 5s 9d a pair. Track shoes by Lonsdale Sports, £3 7s 6d. Crash helmet by Holdsworthy, £2 6s.
T-shirt by Ampro Sports, 10s 6d. Leather boxing boots by Lonsdale Sports, £3 10s

Embroidered racing vests, woollen shorts and cotton hats all by Condor Cycles, £4, £3 10s and 6s 6d each

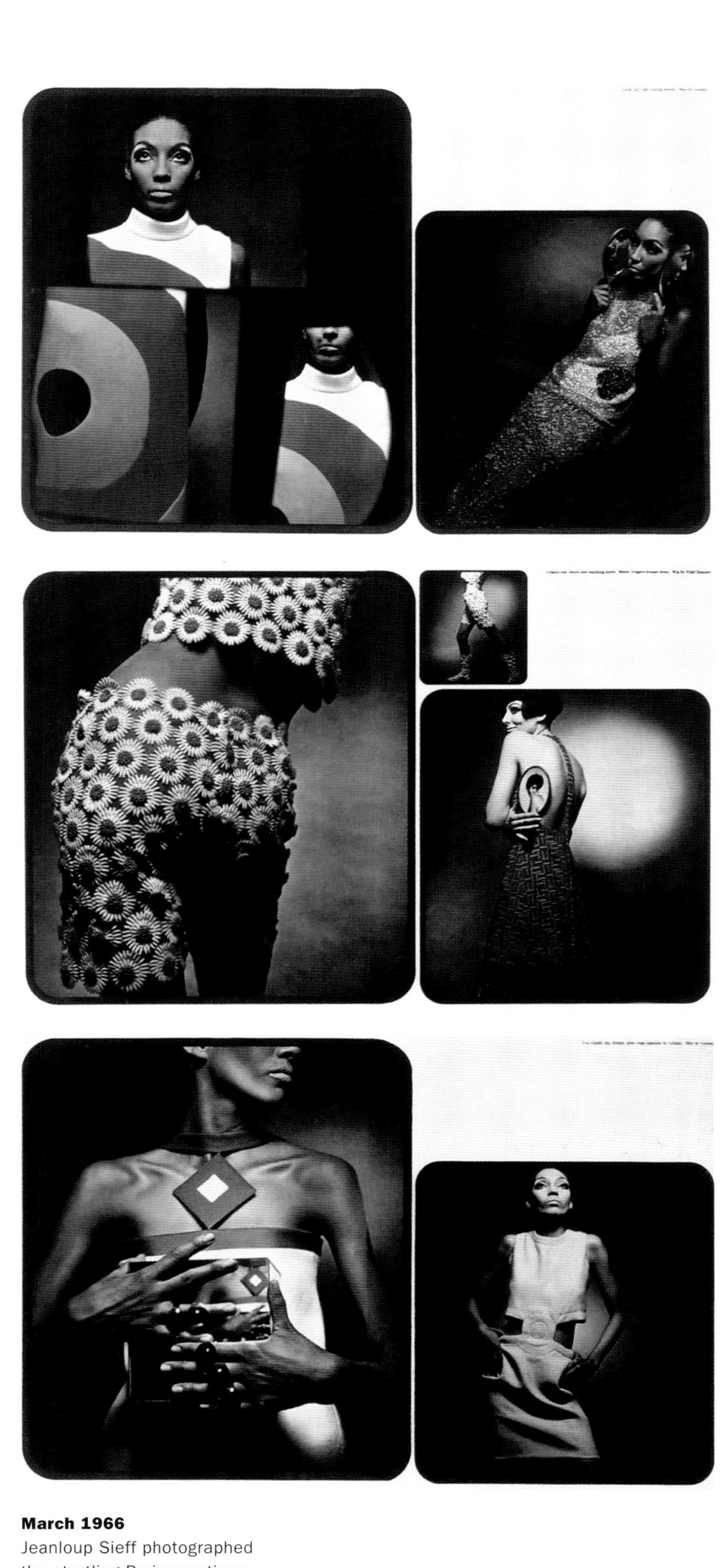

March 1966
Jeanloup Sieff photographed the startling Paris creations of Cardin, Ungaro and Paco Rabanne, picked as the year's stars by fashion editor Molly Parkin.

Right
March 1966
'Women in search', an article by Alma Birk on the new quest for fulfilment. Illustration by Edda Köchl.

July 1966
Alan Aldridge illustrated 'Cinderella gone to seed', a cartoon allegory written by Molly Parkin on how an overweight Cinders eventually found the right clothes and landed her prince.

ILLUSTRATION: EDDA KÖCHL

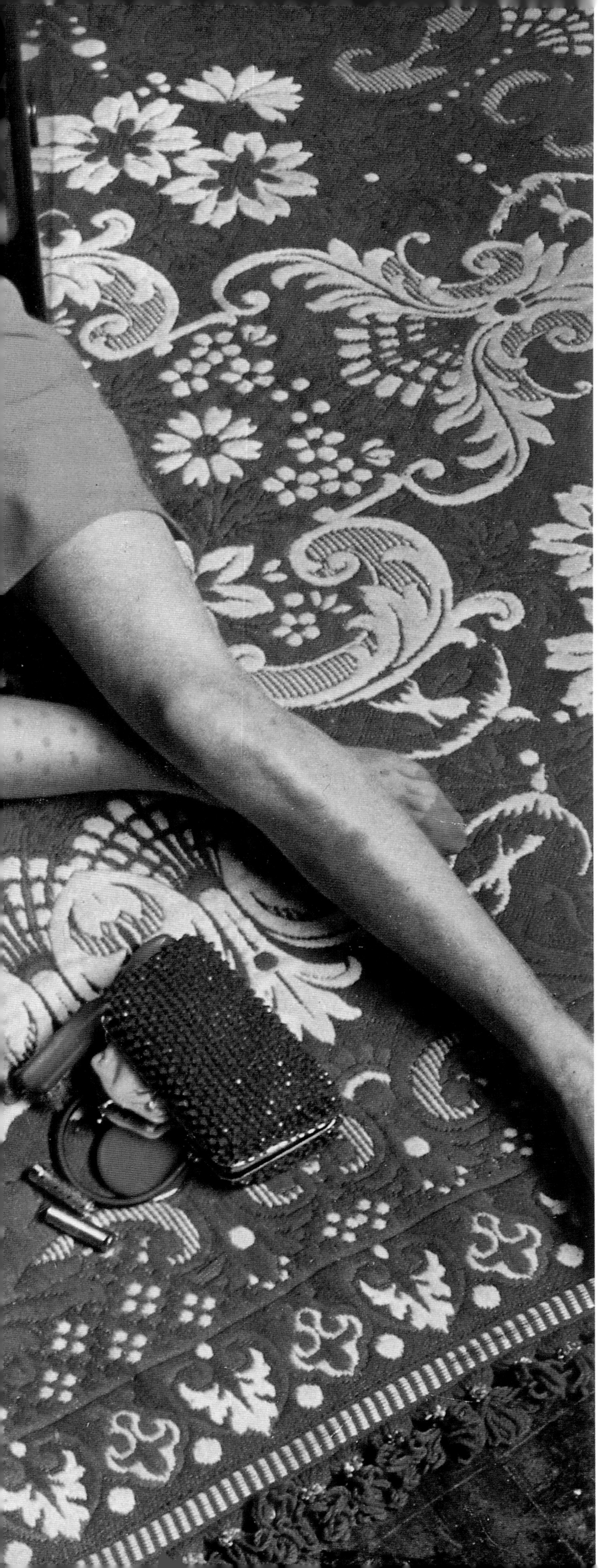

November 1966
'Prepare to meet thy maker', Caroline Baker as Molly Parkin's assistant produced a feature on different looks from different manufacturers. The models included Jill Kennington (in purple, left), who looks pretty calm considering the photographer's dog became understandably overexcited during the session and bit her. Photographs by Duffy.

First girl: wool dress on the hanger by Wallis, 6½ gns. Hand-knotted real Asian hair wig by the Ginger Group Wiggery, £30. Martex bath towels at Robinson & Cleaver, £3 7s 6d. Suede boots by Terry de Havilland, 7 gns. Sponges at Boots, 6s 6d each. Second girl: wool dress with scarf by Wallis, 4½ gns. Toothbrushes by Wisdom, 1s 8d, and Halex, 1s 6d. Enamel mug by Goods & Chattels, 7s 6d. Bourjois soap at Woolworth. Nailbrush from a selection at Boots. Third girl: check coat with velvet collar, by Nale Junior of Paris especially for Wallis, 17 gns, and skinny-rib sweater, £1 19s 6d, also at Wallis. Nylon tights by Bear Brand, 19s 11d. On her shoulder: ribbed stockings by Morley, 7s 11d, dyed with Dylon, 1s 3d a pot. She holds Sugar 'n Spice lipstick by Dorothy Gray, 10s 6d. Large compact by Victor Wagner, £1 11s 6d. Shoes by Carel, 8 gns. Suede sling-back shoes by Saxone, £2 19s 11d. Herringbone stockings by Morley, 12s 11d. On the floor: Everwear candlewick bedspread, £4 7s 6d at Robinson & Cleaver

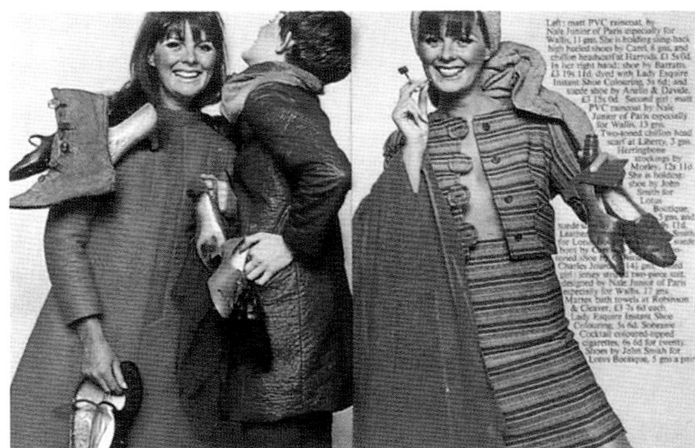

1967

Sunday CITIZEN

Next Sunday: Your farewell voice in the Citizen!

AFTER SIX DAYS IT'S OVER

By DONALD CULLIMORE

Mighty military deeds in the desert.

DAILY EXPRESS

Marianne Faithfull breaks down as Mick Jagger gets three months

Cornered bandit shoots man dead

STONES GO TO JAIL

Naughty boys end up inside.

The pop album becomes pop opera.

The year

Labour devalued the pound; Harold Wilson tried to tell an incredulous nation that 'the pound in your pocket' would not be affected. Francis Chichester completed his solo voyage around the world, the *Queen Mary* made her last voyage to New York, the *QE2* was launched, the *Torrey Canyon* spilled its oil off the Cornish coast, and Donald Campbell was killed on Coniston Water trying to break the world speed record. The Scots went crazy when Celtic beat Inter Milan in the European Cup Final. Driving home from the pub became more hazardous as the breathalyser was introduced. Abortion and sex between consenting homosexuals were legalised in Britain. Elvis Presley finally got married. Desmond Morris's *The Naked Ape* was published, and Professor Christian Barnard performed the first heart transplant operation in South Africa. Muhammed Ali lost his world heavyweight title outside the ring for refusing to fight in Vietnam. The Nigerian civil war started. Israel swept all before it in the Six Days War, while *Fiddler on the Roof* took the West End by storm. The first colour TV transmissions were introduced for BBC2's Wimbledon coverage and, finally admitting that Radio Luxembourg and the new crop of pirate radio stations had a point, the BBC introduced Radio One. San Francisco seized the pop centre stage by reinventing love and mixing it with flower power; Scott McKenzie had a big hit with *San Francisco*. The Beatles responded with *All You Need Is Love* and released their *Sergeant Pepper's Lonely Hearts Club Band* album. The Rolling Stones were arrested on drug charges. Warren Beatty and Faye Dunaway raised the appeal of the anti-hero to new heights in *Bonnie and Clyde*, and Che Guevara's heroic status was assured when he was killed by the CIA in Bolivia.

Right
November 1967
Wool-knit clothes. Photograph by Clive Arrowsmith.

TURN WHITE

The most flattering thing to wear with a tan is white. The mistake too many women make in the summer is not buying enough of it because it shows the dirt more than any other colour and twice as soon. What's more, all these 'brighter than white' slogans can give us a mental block about wearing it in case ours isn't. Solid colours or busy patterns are much easier to take care of—they can be worn several times without self consciousness. Because of this, white clothes might be kept for special occasions only. The disaster here is that you can find yourself most needing your white at the very time it's being laundered or dry-cleaned. The answer is to buy all white. A complete wardrobe in a colour that suits you is obvious logic anyway. Too many women experiment for too long and then wonder why nothing goes with anything - least of all themselves. Before buying anything, make sure of instructions for its care; it's stupid only to buy clothes that have to be expensively dry-cleaned, just as silly to have to wash and iron everything. A good mixture gives you the best of both worlds and, with some organisation, always something clean to wear. This year there are some super white clothes, from towelling beach wear and crisp cotton coats, suits and trousers to feminine bloomer dresses and party clothes. White fur remains one of the most effective scene-stealers for arrivals and exits (as any starlet worth her salt will confirm) and now at last white shoes have lost their Minnie Mouse/Olive Oyle image. They are available in a wide variety of good styles and leathers—patent, pearlised and the softest of kid. Don't be over-concerned if your feet look longer in them—their effect on brown legs is an unbeatable compensation. The same applies to the fear that white makes one look larger: larger than life certainly, but that's good—so why worry? Just get on with it. Stockists of the clothes featured appear on page 130.

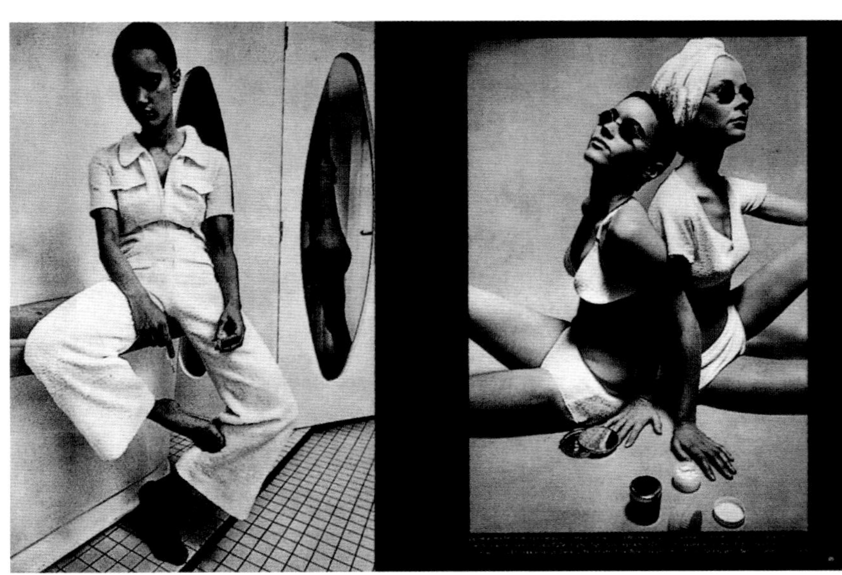

May 1967
'Turn white' fashion feature. Photographs by Jeanloup Sieff.

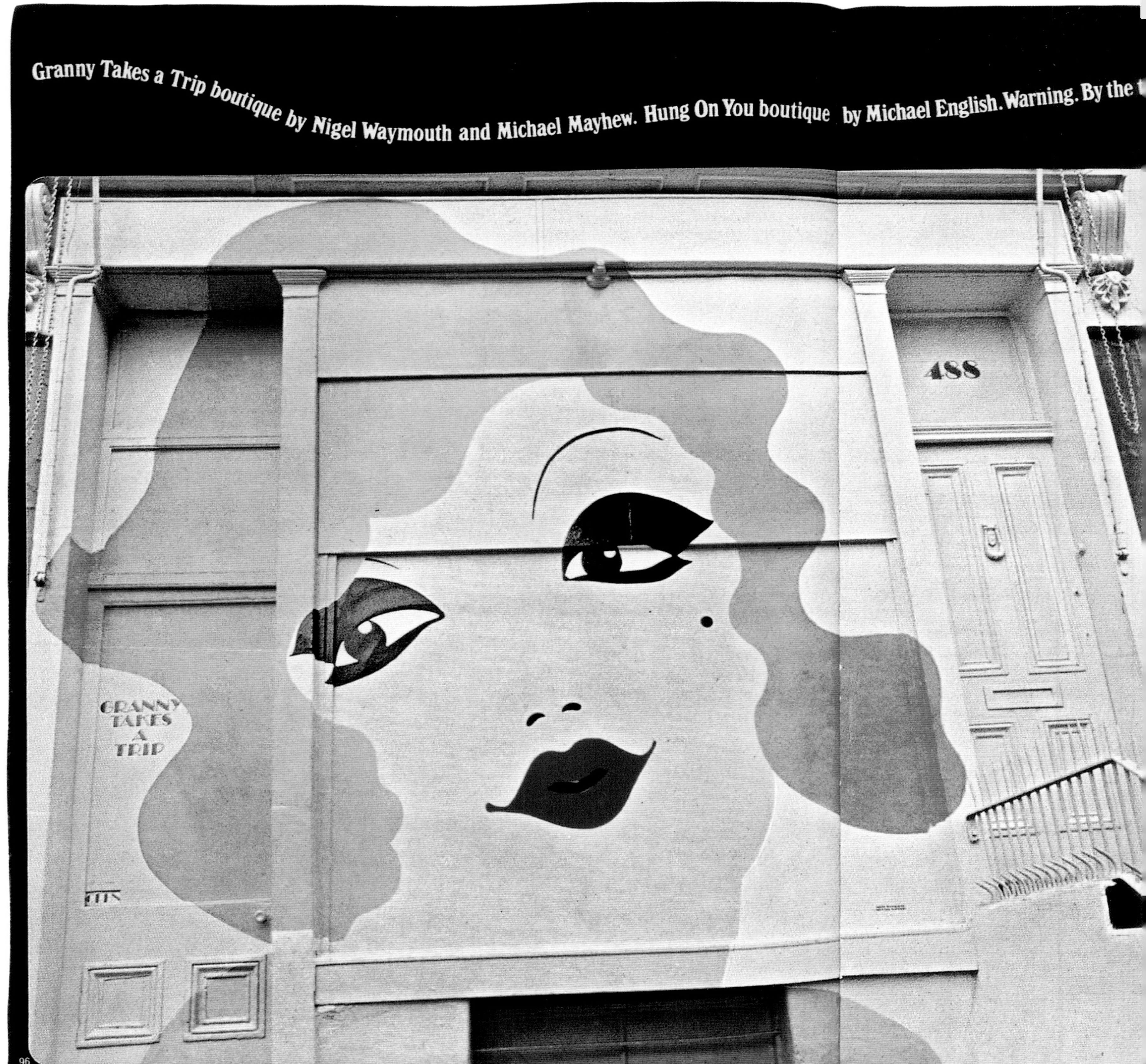
Granny Takes a Trip boutique by Nigel Waymouth and Michael Mayhew. Hung On You boutique by Michael English. Warning. By the
488
GRANNY TAKES A TRIP
96

April 1967
The famous boutiques of the King's Road were constantly being redesigned. Photographs and typography by Harri Peccinotti.

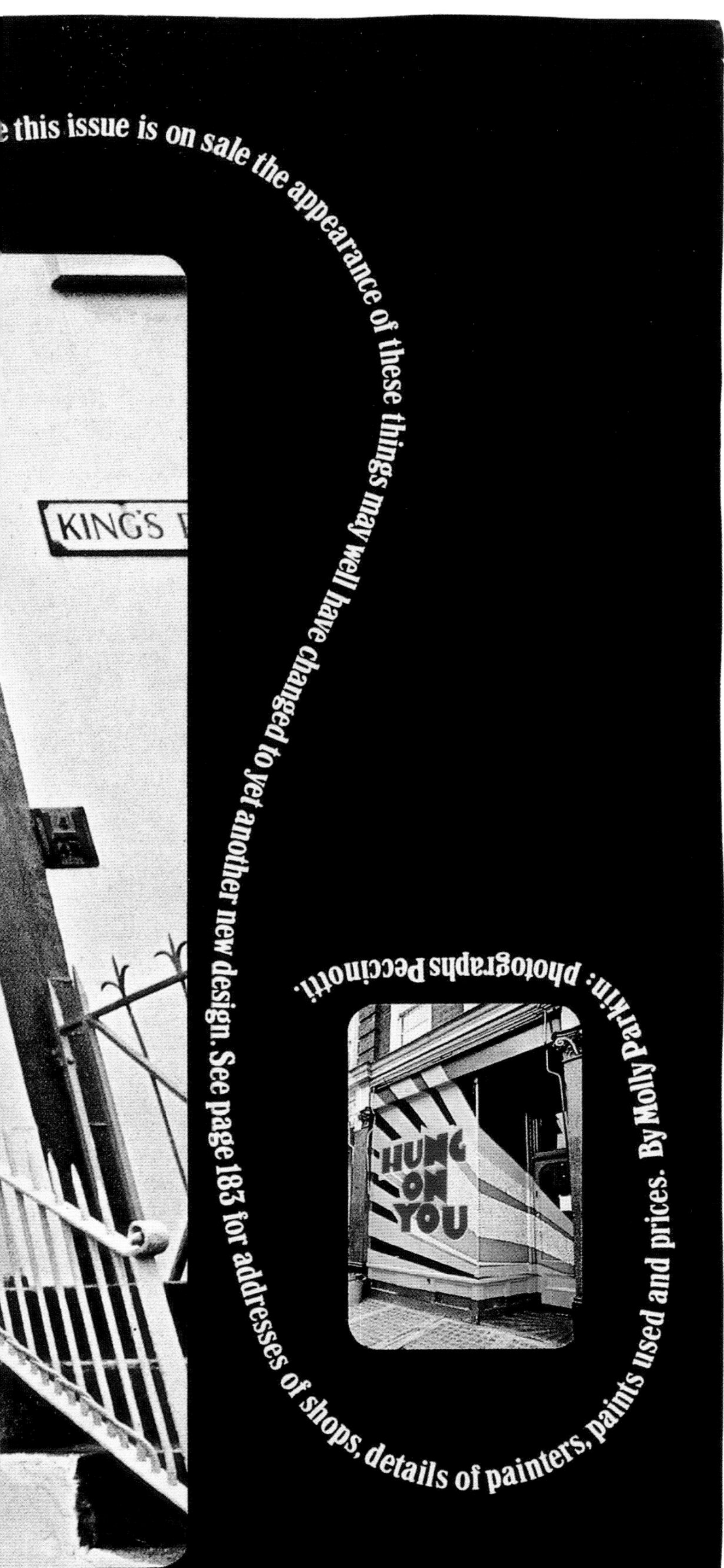

…this issue is on sale the appearance of these things may well have changed to yet another new design. See page 183 for addresses of shops, details of painters, paints used and prices. By Molly Parkin: photographs Peccinotti.
KING'S
HUNG ON YOU

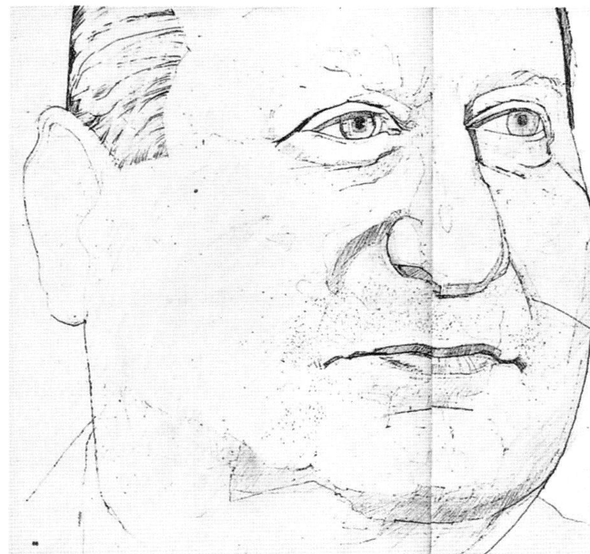

Once upon a time there was a rich theatre merchant called Lew Grade, and a pillar of the establishment called Norman Collins. ITV brought them together and their child was called ATV… Robert Ottaway continues our saga of the telly giants, and no cracks about who's better or worse, or richer or poorer, or who the hell is Mrs Thursday anyway?

February 1967
Britain's giants of television – portrait of Lew Grade by Barry Fantoni.

May 1967
An early illustration by Roger Law on special coloured stock used for Len Deighton's story 'An inexpensive place to die'.

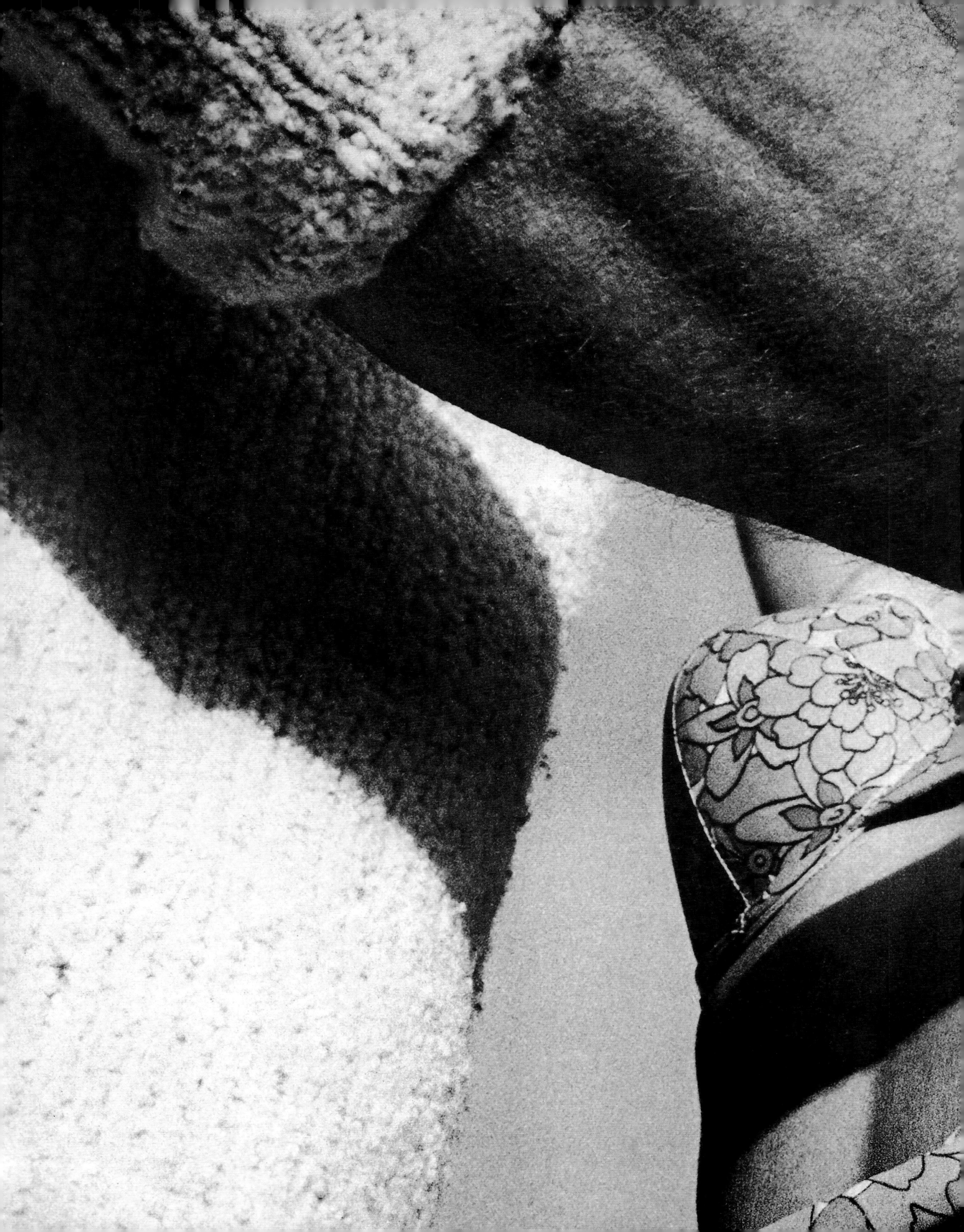

Right and far right
December 1967
Display your wealth and success, travel in furs (twenty years before the Eighties catchphrase: 'If you've got it flaunt it'). Photographs by Hans Feurer.

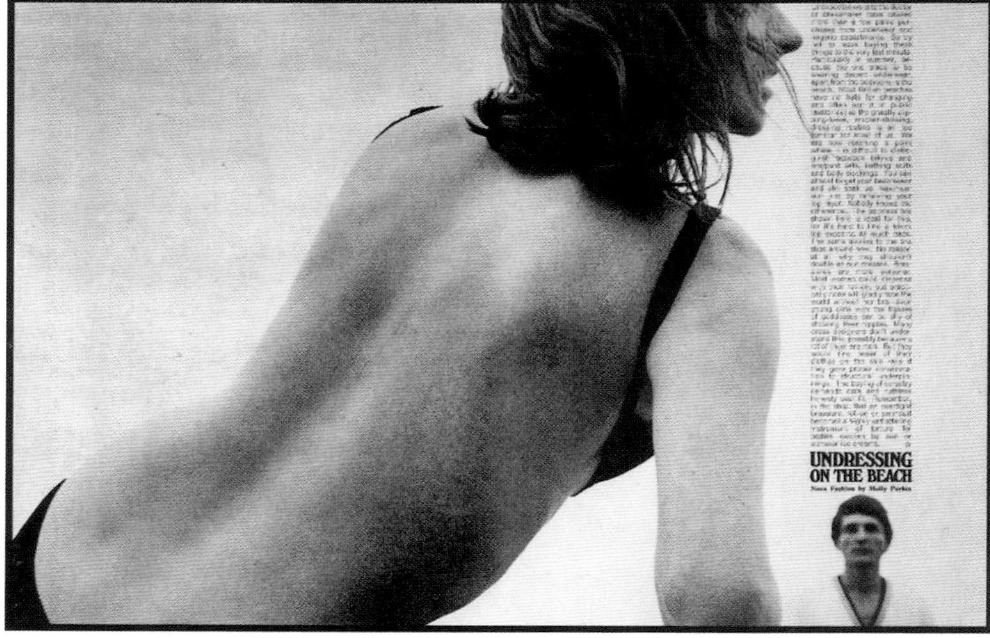

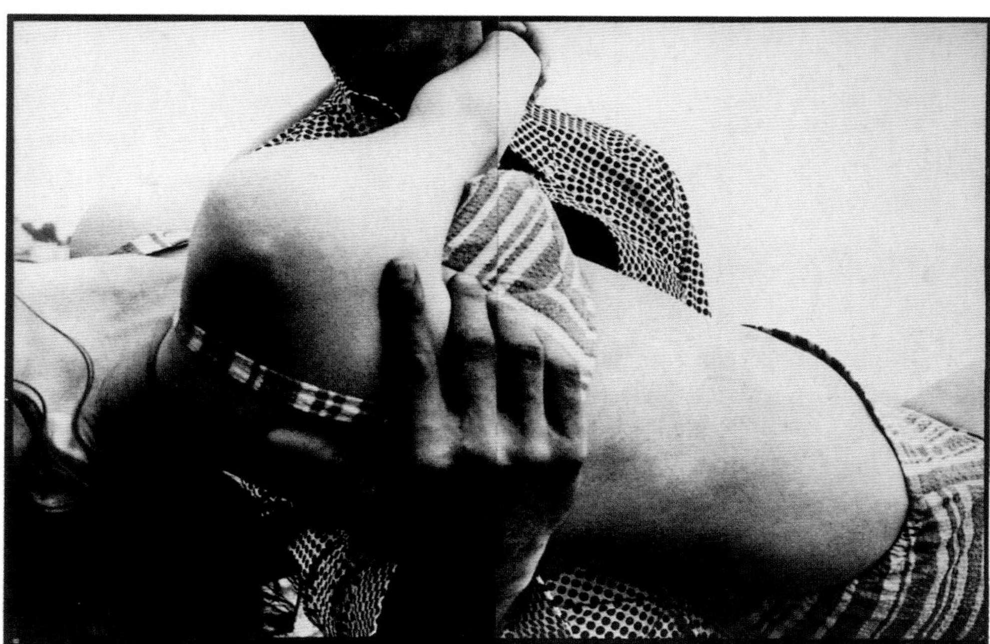

Previous page and left
June 1967
Molly Parkin's swimwear feature 'Undressing on the beach.' The photographer's name was shamefully unrecorded.

1968

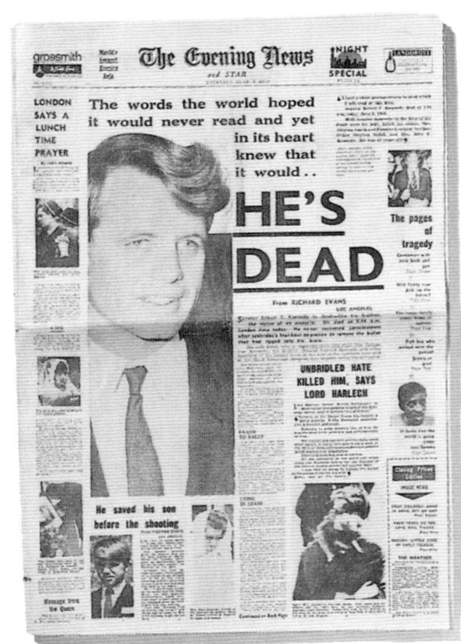

The Evening News and STAR

NIGHT SPECIAL

LONDON SAYS A LUNCH TIME PRAYER

The words the world hoped it would never read and yet in its heart knew that it would . .

HE'S DEAD

From RICHARD EVANS

UNBRIDLED HATE KILLED HIM, SAYS LORD HARLECH

He saved his son before the shooting

The pages of tragedy

The second Kennedy boy to go like that.

Evening Standard

WEST END FINAL

THE RAPE OF FREE PRAGUE

'Heavy fighting' near Castle

Eye witness stories

Parliament recalled by Wilson

Czechs asked us to come, says Russia

Communism was still the great bully.

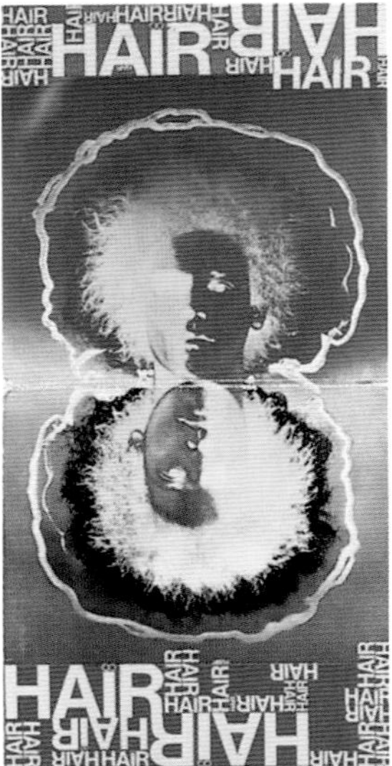

No clothes, lots of Hair on Broadway.

The year

Bobby Kennedy was assassinated. Martin Luther King was assassinated. Alexander Dubcek's Prague Spring withered back into bleak winter as the Soviets invaded Czechoslovakia. The 'troubles' in Northern Ireland began with riots in Londonderry (Derry in Catholic parlance). Enoch Powell made his 'Rivers of Blood' speech on race in Britain. In London's Grosvenor Square anti-Vietnam War demonstrators clashed with police, and student riots moved Paris to the edge of anarchy. Politics and protest even crept into sport with black power salutes from the rostrum at the Mexico Olympics, where David Hemery won Britain's sole athletics gold in the 400 metres hurdles. British football continued on a roll with Manchester United (Charlton, Best, Law *et al*) beating Benfica to lift the European Cup. Graham Hill drove his BRM to win the Formula One championship. John Updike's *Couples* was published. Naked bodies were seen for the first time on Broadway in *Hair*, and a naked Jane Fonda was seen by the world in *Barbarella*. Also at the cinema *The Graduate* propelled Dustin Hoffman to stardom and Lindsey Anderson's *If* showed it like it was in English public schools. On TV *Rowan and Martin's Laugh-in* introduced a scatty, giggling Goldie Hawn. Progressive rock was in the ascendant with rough stuff such as Jimi Hendrix's *All Along The Watchtower* and Joe Cocker's *A Little Help From My Friends*. The Beatles' *Hey Jude* was kept from reaching No 1 by their protegée Mary Hopkin's *Those Were The Days*. London Bridge was sold to an American oil company to be re-erected over the Colorado River. And Richard Nixon won the presidential elections in the USA.

Right
March 1968
Flower power brought the handmade look into fashion. Feature by Brigid Keenan. Photographs by Duffy.

May 1968
Photographer Don Last.
Art director Derek Birdsall.
Beauty editor Brigid Keenan.
The spotty eye make-up originated with Courrèges.

SPOTS
BEFORE THE
EYES
Nova beauty by Brigid Keenan
Face warfare overleaf
DUFFY

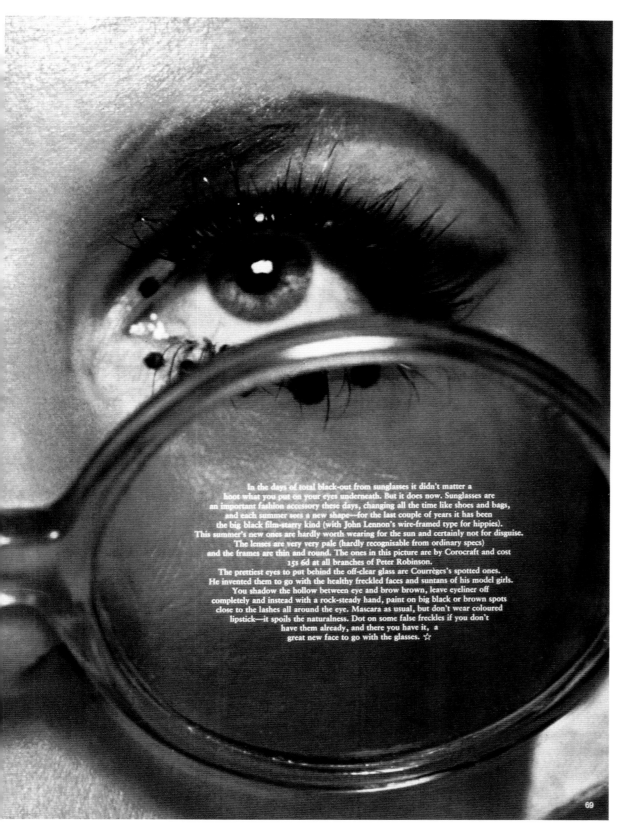

In the days of total black-out from sunglasses it didn't matter a hoot what you put on your eyes underneath. But it does now. Sunglasses are an important fashion accessory these days, changing all the time like shoes and bags, and each summer sees a new shape—for the last couple of years it has been the big black film-starry kind (with John Lennon's wire-framed type for hippies). This summer's new ones are hardly worth wearing for the sun and certainly not for disguise. The lenses are very very pale (hardly recognisable from ordinary specs) and the frames are thin and round. The ones in this picture are by Corocraft and cost 15s 6d at all branches of Peter Robinson.
The prettiest eyes to put behind the off-clear glass are Courrèges's spotted ones. He invented them to go with the healthy freckled faces and suntans of his model girls. You shadow the hollow between eye and brow brown, leave eyeliner off completely and instead with a rock-steady hand, paint on big black or brown spots close to the lashes all around the eye. Mascara as usual, but don't wear coloured lipstick—it spoils the naturalness. Dot on some false freckles if you don't have them already, and there you have it, a great new face to go with the glasses. ☆

69

WHAT PARIS COULD DO FOR THE QUEEN

THE QUEEN AS SHE IS

THE QUEEN AS SHE COULD BE

WHAT PARIS COULD DO FOR THE QUEEN

July 1968
A feature by Brigid Keenan on what Paris could do for the Queen, with art direction by Derek Birdsall. Courrèges agreed to dress a model with the same measurements as Her Majesty (gleaned from Madame Tussauds). Carita did the make-up and Alexandre the hair. The pictures were retouched in New York and promptly impounded by the British customs on their return. They were finally released only with further retouching to lower the hemline and the sanction of Buckingham Palace.

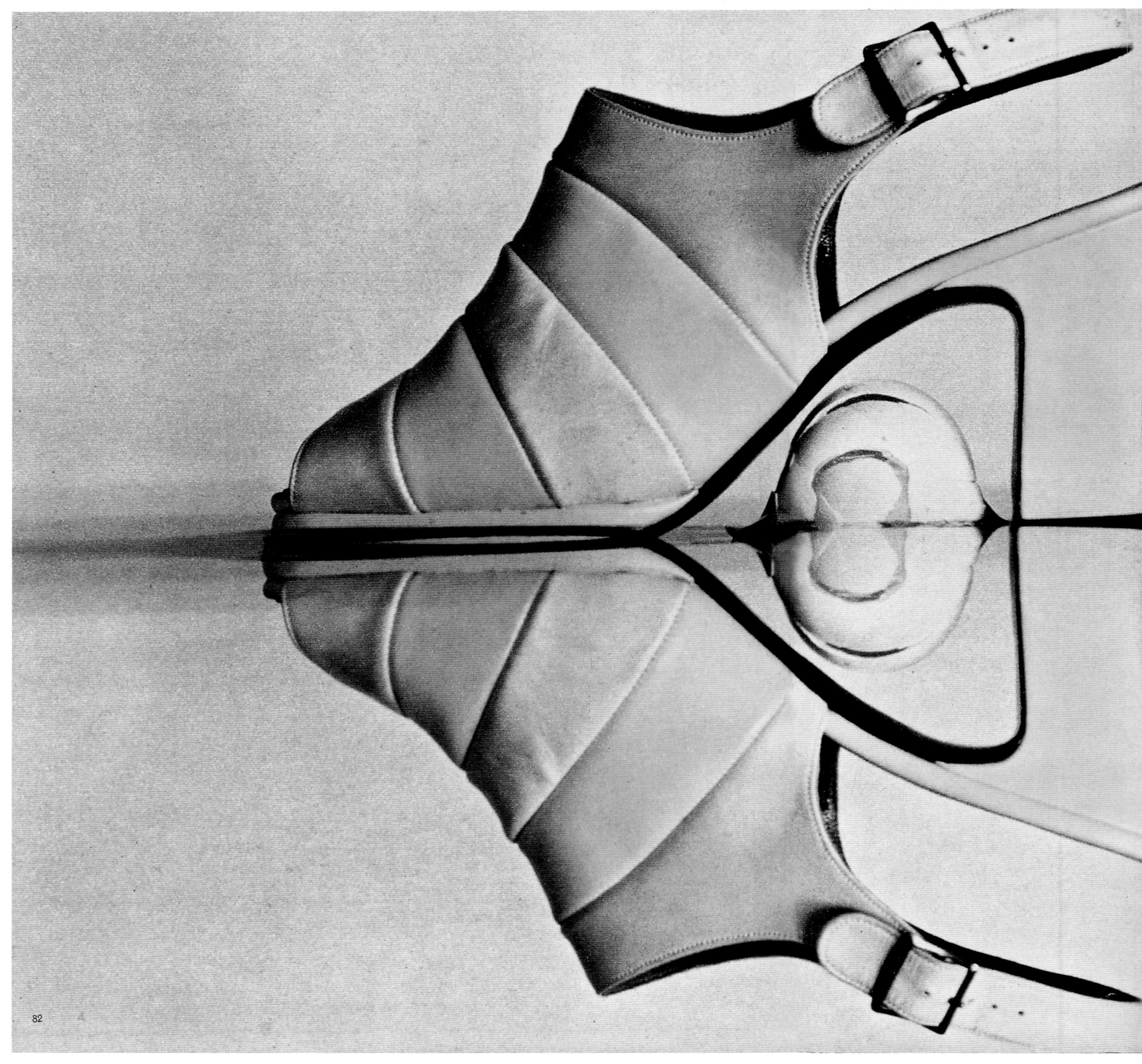
82

'IN THE OLD DAYS THEY USED TO PUT GREASE ON YOUR TEMPLES AND IT TOOK THREE NURSES TO HOLD YOU DOWN'

by Irma Kurtz

Nowadays, though, they give you anaesthetic before the electric-shock treatment. Methods are more sophisticated, even if conditions are still sometimes revealed as barbaric. For most of us, however, the world of the mentally ill—good and bad, old and new—remains not just an unknown territory but one deliberately ignored, shunned with a revulsion that springs from the depths. Mental illness still carries a shame and stigma inherited from the dark ages. Still, despite the advances, the popularisation of medical knowledge and psychiatric theory, despite the advertising by mental-health charities, a mother can tell her troubled child not to write home from a psychiatric hospital.

It is an attitude we can ill afford. One in eight Britons will at some time be treated for mental disorder. Such people occupy forty-seven per cent of our hospital beds. Others will suffer unaided, and perhaps undetected, for the dividing line is narrow and not clearly marked. There are those who come and go across it. Irma Kurtz stayed at Severall's Hospital, Colchester, for several days, believed by all but the superintendent to be a patient. The borderline of reason, she saw, is not a Bedlam. It is an area many of us might be nearer to than we care to think.

October 1968
Illustration by Adrian George for an article by Irma Kurtz on methods for the mentally ill.

March 1968
Illustration by Bob Gill for 'Two returns to Manhattan', by New York City exile Irma Kurtz.

by Caroline Baker

The latest in shoe designs, which for so long have been elegant, boring and unadventurous, now come from Moya Bowler. Here is one that is part of her summer collection of twelve named after the signs of the zodiac, made in soft plain, pearlised, patent leather or suede. On their own they look frighteningly clumpy but when worn they are very flattering. Some have platform soles, high chunky heels; all are very comfortable. You may have difficulty deciding which pair you want as they come in so many different colours; and you may have difficulty finding them as most shoe shops seem to think we won't buy them. At the moment the complete range can be seen at Chic of Hampstead N W 3, Ronald Keith in Oxford Street, London W 1, and Elliston & Cavell in Oxford. The shoe here is the Aries, 7 gns.

83

April 1968
Footwear fashion. Photograph by Barry Kaplan.

Chapter 3

Stairway to heaven 1969-1972

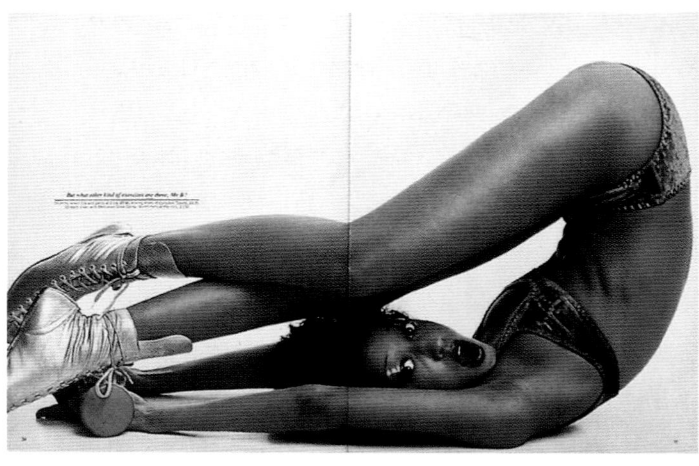

February 1972
Hans Feurer's photography made the point in a feature called 'Meanwhile, exploitation can be fun',

Britain had changed much in *Nova*'s first four years; the Sixties did not end up swinging. By 1969 the transformation from clean-cut optimism to shaggy escapism was complete. The war in Vietnam, the presumptions of politicians, seedy power struggles in the work-place and a slow down in the heady growth of personal wealth had changed attitudes. Although technology did deliver men to the Moon in 1969 it had not changed ordinary lives as had been promised. People shunned their institutional leaders and turned to folk heroes for inspiration.

The huge gatherings at Woodstock in 1969 and its British equivalent on the Isle of Wight in 1970 were more than pop festivals. They were almost religious celebrations of a belief in something new, something better – a revolutionary alternative in attitudes. 'Peace' and 'love' may have been watchwords of the movement but it was more to do with the utter rejection of an establishment that was seen to have failed, and its replacement with a purer, apolitical ethos. These ideas were fed by the theatre, cinema and art. But musicians more than anyone became the figureheads. Their freedom from the past, their artistry and originality, their sheer cheek as well as their lifestyles and clothes seemed to embody the ideal. As ill-defined and irrational as this ideal undoubtedly was, millions in Britain, across Europe and the USA subscribed to it.

Nova had a broad and intuitive grasp of these feelings and it was one of the only magazines that was able to serve them while still managing to maintain its attraction to mainstream advertisers and readers. Now much more than a women's magazine, pictures and articles touched the real life of the country as well as its aspirations and fantasies. *Nova* had the knack of catching the mood of the young and not so young – not only with its visual hijinks but also its free-wheeling editorial approach.

In May 1969 Dennis Hackett finally left the editor's chair and a duo arrived from the *Sunday Times Magazine* to take over *Nova*'s helm: Peter Crookston became the new editor and

David Hillman the art director. Crookston, who had been the *Sunday Times Magazine's* features editor, had ideas of creating a kind of hip *New Yorker*, with long features and plenty of text-only pages. Hillman wanted to add more visual pace and variety to the whole magazine, giving greater overall coherency to what had already been established as the *Nova* look. The two aims were not always compatible, and inevitably their early issues had much of the *Sunday Times Magazine* about them. In December 1970 Gillian Cooke became editor. More in tune with *Nova*'s special mix of style and editorial breadth, she saw the magazine enter what was for many its greatest period. As circulation climbed and confidence grew, design became more sophisticated and art direction more daring than ever.

The fashion scene was now iconoclastic. In 1970 the fashion houses tried to foist the 'midi' mid-calf length hemline on to a public not ready to look old all of a sudden. Instead people turned to the past for their own ideas – giving new life to old clothes found in the attic. Boutiques such as Biba, which offered the affordable alternative to couture, led the new look with darker, faded colours and materials reminiscent of the twenties and thirties. As the sun-drenched look also became popular the bikini became briefer and briefer. To much spluttering as well as delight, St Tropez women took the next logical step and reduced their tops to nothing.

By 1971 the establishment fashion system had been broken. Following and not leading for once, designers frantically offered 'anything-goes': minis, midis, hot pants, ankle-length overcoats. Saint Laurent came to the rescue of women bored with the choice of mini or midi and introduced flared trousers cut tight around the hips. The look evolved into the characteristic figure-hugging, bright coloured dandiness of the Seventies. Satin was used for shirts, trousers and jackets. Diamante and bright plastic jewellery abounded. And of course the notorious platform shoes and boots arrived. It all culminated in the climax of the 'Unisex' look, as men and women dressed more and more alike.

Nova tracked these changes with panache, and also added its own vision that had nothing to do with fashion houses, manufacturers or advertisers. What appeared in the magazine was as often as not completely original. The inspiration and street sense of the art director, fashion editor and photographers produced avant-garde styles which were highly influential. A number of fashion ideas were heralded months, even years, before they caught on; army clothes and North African styles were just two examples. Unlike any other magazine *Nova* wasn't only reporting, it was creating.

The editorial team had stabilized from the comings and goings of the early days. There was a feeling that they were doing something important, something they believed in, and proved to be stubborn when confronted with any interference from a conservative management who did not share their vision. (The 'Heath's wife' affair in March 1972 (see page 149) was a case in point.) By then the art director had become second only in influence to the editor, and in October 1971 David Hillman took on the additional role of deputy editor. He widened the visual artistry that had been applied so successfully to fashion and style to give greater emphasis to other articles, stories and regular features. Further illustrious talent was enlisted: amongst others, photographers Terence Donovan, Helmut Newton, Tony Evans and Sarah Moon and illustrators Celestino Valenti, Mike McInnerney and Jean-Paul Goude. Hillman also brought back Harri Peccinotti, who produced some of his most memorable photographs for the magazine – characteristic close-ups that were classic *Nova*.

But at IPC attitudes towards the magazine were beginning to change, with a decline in respect for *Nova*'s peculiar strengths. Management became more interested in the magazine's appeal to advertisers than anything else. It was perhaps this, coupled with the devastation of the economy and the consequent retrenchment of national attitudes, that began to eat away at *Nova*'s spirit as the Seventies progressed and the phenomenon of the Sixties became a thing of the past.

1969

Monty Python even made walks funny.

A man from Earth stepped on to the Moon.

Daily Mirror

'I have ceased to be President of France. My functions will come to an end at midday'

DE GAULLE SAYS: I QUIT

Non!..The verdict of the nation

The two voters

Moi, je suis fini.

The year

The world glued itself to the TV to watch Man's first step on to another world as *Apollo 11* took Neil Armstrong and Buzz Aldrin to land on the Moon. As the Sixties came to an end John Lennon decided that being in bed with Yoko Ono was better than being with the Beatles, who bade farewell with *Get Back*. Half of America seemed to go on a pilgrimage to the Woodstock Festival. *Je T'Aime, Moi Non Plus*, which had Jane Birkin heavy breathing on record with Serge Gainsbourg, was banned by the BBC and thereby reached No 1. Marvin Gaye produced one of Tamla's greatest, *I Heard It Through The Grapevine*, and the Rolling Stones released their memorable *Honky Tonk Women*. The Anglo-French Concorde made its maiden flight, and de Gaulle resigned the French Presidency. British troops were sent to Northern Ireland. The voting age was reduced from 21 to 18. Tony Jacklin won the British Open Golf Championship. *Midnight Cowboy* confirmed Dustin Hoffman's cinematic versatility; the other Fonda kid, Peter, had his moment in *Easy Rider*. *Monty Python's Flying Circus* proved that British humour, BBC-style, was alive and kicking. Squaring warmth if not modesty with the mini skirt, girls began to wear tights instead of stockings.

Right
August 1969
The gypsy look had been introduced by Christian Dior in January. Photograph by Jonvelle.

The smartest woman in Paris last January was the gypsy outside the Plaza Hotel

Nova fashion by Brigid Keenan/Photographs by Jonvelle

Coming out of the Dior show last winter, saturated with his new Gypsy Look, some of us were astounded to see across the road a woman already wearing it. There she was, only seconds after the Collection, in the full bit. Being short-sighted I tore across the road for a closer look at this marvel of chic, to discover that it *was* a gypsy – selling lucky heather or something outside the Plaza. It seems we were lucky to see a gypsy in gypsy clothes – photographers coming back from the Carmargue tell gloomily of gypsies driving modern American cars, of caravans air conditioned, of the clothes being modern and rather dull. But who wants to be bothered with the unromantic facts. Gypsy clothes (pre-Dior) didn't come ready made – and this is their charm for us now. Like magpies gypsies would simply collect bright bits and pieces that they fancied (new as well as secondhand) and put them all together. The only rules they followed were that skirts must be long and full (gypsies were modest about their legs) and *décolletages* could be as low as they liked (they were not modest about their cleavages). Albane, an actress in Paris who is half gypsy herself, chose and wears the clothes here. Stockists on page 88

Coin necklaces to be wound around the head or neck by Corocraft from £2, at London Docks from £6, Imogen from £4, Deliss from £8. Secondhand shawls embroidered and fringed from Chelsea Antique Market, Kensington Antique Supermarket, Imogen, Deliss, from £4

56

Left

August 1969

Fashion feature – the headline was inspired by the real gypsy spotted outside the Plaza in Paris the day Dior had unveiled his gypsy look for the summer. Photographs by Jonvelle.

A woman and man in their forties. They sit with coffee.

MAN: I'm talking about that time by the river.
WOMAN: What time?
MAN: The first time. On the bridge. Starting on the bridge.
Pause
WOMAN: I can't remember.
MAN: On the bridge. We stopped and looked down at the river. It was night. There were lamps lit on the towpath. We were alone. We looked up the river. I put my hand on the small of your waist. Don't you remember? I put my hand under your coat.
Pause
WOMAN: Was it winter?
MAN: Of course it was winter. It was when we met. It was our first walk. You must remember that.
WOMAN: I remember walking. I remember walking with you.
MAN: The first time? Our first walk?
WOMAN: Yes, of course I remember that.
Pause
WOMAN: We walked down a road into a field, through some railings. We walked to a corner of the field and then we stood by the railings.
MAN: No. It was on the bridge that we stopped.
Pause
WOMAN: That was someone else.
MAN: Rubbish.
WOMAN: That was another girl.
MAN: It was years ago. You've forgotten.
Pause
MAN: I remember the light on the water.
WOMAN: You took my face in your hands, standing by the railings. You were very gentle, you were very caring. You cared. Your eyes searched my face. I wondered who you were. I wondered what you thought. I wondered what you would do.
MAN: You agree we met at a party. You agree with that?
WOMAN: What was that?
MAN: What?
WOMAN: I thought I heard a child crying.
MAN: There was no sound.
WOMAN: I thought it was a child, crying, waking up.
MAN: The house is silent.
Pause
It's very late. We're sitting here. We should be in bed. I have to be up early. I have things to do. Why do you argue?
WOMAN: I don't. I'm not. I'm willing to go to bed. I have things to do. I have to be up in the morning.
Pause
MAN: A man called Doughty gave the party. You knew him. I had met him. I knew his wife. I met you there. You were standing by the window. I smiled at you, and to my surprise you smiled back. You liked me. I was amazed. You found me attractive. Later you told me. You liked my eyes.
WOMAN: You liked mine.
Pause
WOMAN: You touched my hand. You asked me who I was, and what I was, and whether I was aware that you were touching my hand, that your fingers were touching mine, that your fingers were moving up and down between mine.
MAN: No. We stopped on a bridge. I stood behind you. I put my hand under your coat, on to your waist. You felt my hand on you.
Pause
WOMAN: We had been to a party. Given by the Doughtys. You had known his wife. She looked at you dearly, as if to say you were her dear. She seemed to love you. I didn't. I didn't know you. They had a lovely house. By a river. I went to collect my coat, leaving you waiting for me. You had offered to escort me. I thought you were quite courtly, quite courteous, pleasantly mannered, quite caring. I slipped my coat on and looked out of the window, knowing you were waiting. I looked down over the garden to the river, and saw the lamplight on the water. Then I joined you and we walked down the road through railings into a field, must have been some kind of park. Later we found your car. You drove me.
Pause
MAN: I touched your breasts.
WOMAN: Where?
MAN: On the bridge. I felt your breasts.
WOMAN: Really?
MAN: Standing behind you.
WOMAN: I wondered whether you would, whether you wanted to, whether you would.
MAN: Yes.
WOMAN: I wondered how you would go about it, whether you wanted to, sufficiently.
MAN: I put my hands under your sweater, I undid your brassière, I felt your breasts.
WOMAN: Another night perhaps. Another girl.
MAN: You don't remember my fingers on your skin?
WOMAN: Were they in your hands? My breasts? Fully in your hands?
MAN: You don't remember my hands on your skin?
Pause
WOMAN: Standing behind me?
MAN: Yes.
WOMAN: But my back was against railings. I felt the railings . . . behind me. You were facing me. I was looking into your eyes. My coat was closed. It was cold.
MAN: I undid your coat.
WOMAN: It was very late. Chilly.
MAN: And then we left the bridge and we walked down the towpath and we came to a rubbish-dump.
WOMAN: And you had me and you told me you had fallen in love with me, and you said you would take care of me always, and you told me my voice and my eyes, my thighs, my breasts, were incomparable, and that you would adore me always.
MAN: Yes I did.
WOMAN: And you do adore me always.
MAN: Yes I do.
WOMAN: And then we had children and we sat and talked and you remembered women on bridges and towpaths and rubbish-dumps.
MAN: And you remembered your bottom against railings and men holding your hands and men looking into your eyes.
WOMEN: And talking to me softly.
MAN: And your soft voice. Talking to them softly at night.
WOMAN: And they said I will adore you always.
MAN: Saying I will adore you always ●

2: NIGHT
by Harold Pinter

66

67

August 1969

Three mini-plays on love were run together in one issue: Alun Owen's *Norma*, Harold Pinter's *Night*, with illustration by Gilbert Stone, and *Black and Silver* by Michael Frayn.

September 1969
American doyenne Diane Arbus came to England to shoot the article 'Get to know your local rocker' by Peter Martin.

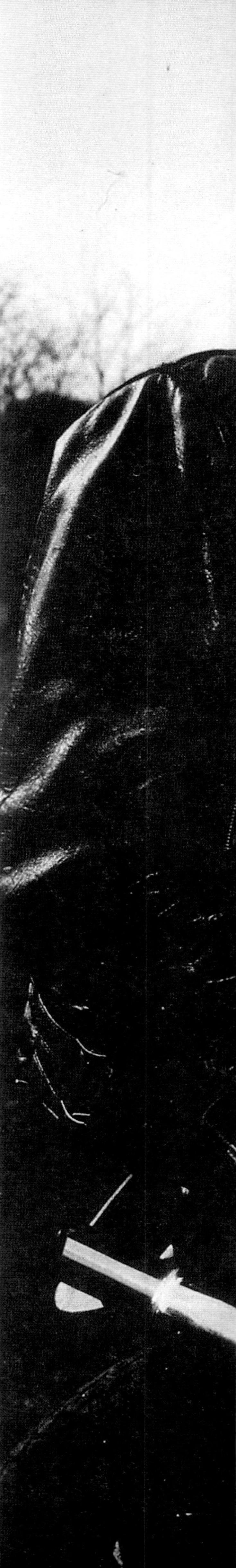

TRIUMPH
DAYGO
M C
59

Right
May/June 1969
While still at the *Sunday Times Magazine*, David Hillman designed the swimwear feature 'Languorous lady' working with Giacobetti, whose shots for the Pirelli calendar had caused a bit of a splash.

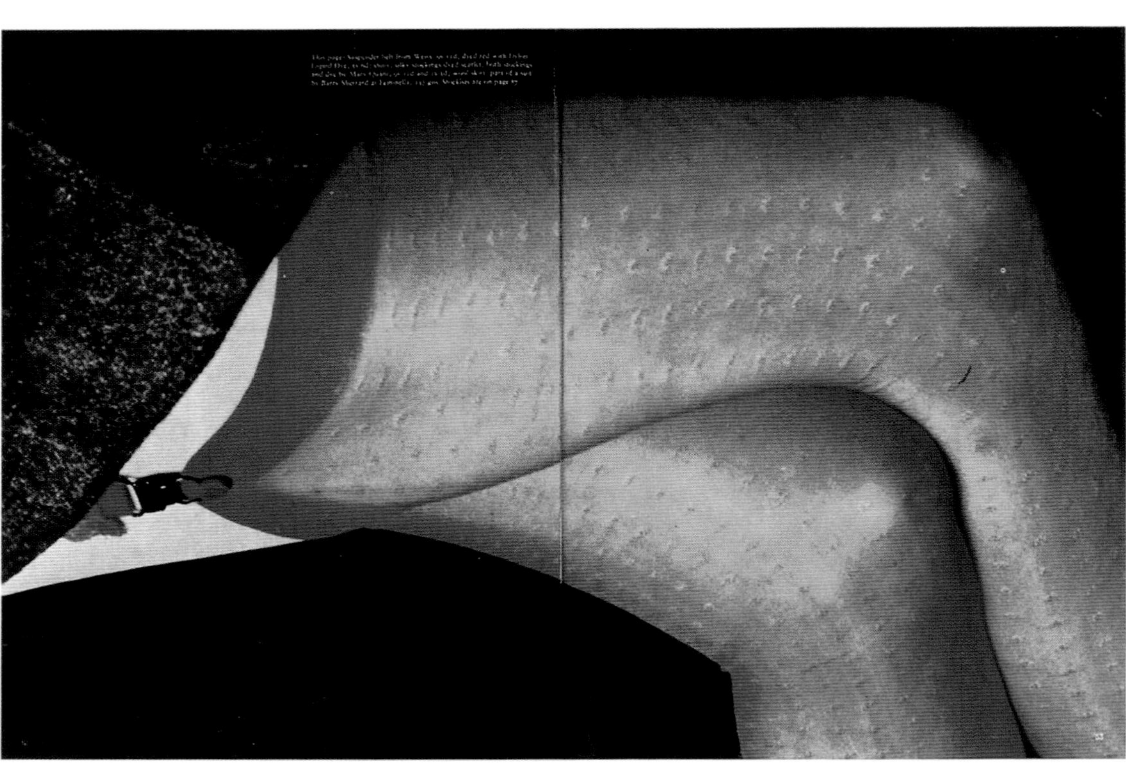

January 1969
Advice to skimpy dressers not to try to hide it. Harri Peccinotti's pictures, Derek Birdsall's art direction.

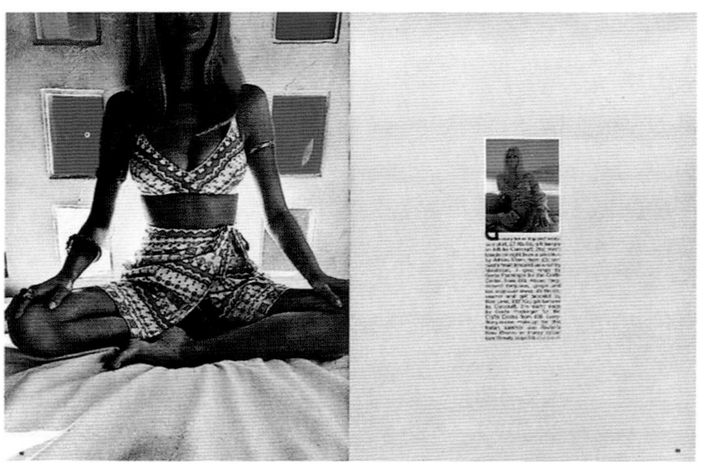

April 1969
Veronica Wade prints inspired by India and shot in India; one of the last features with both photography and layout by Harri Peccinotti.

90

Above: lace-up shorts suit by Lizzie Carr, £6 19s 6d. Far left: swimsuit by Jersea, £4; chain at Anschel, 11 gns. Left: swimsuit by Ian Batten, 5 gns; Corfam wristlet by Paris House, £1 5s. Right: boiler suit by Jersea, £7 5s; Mongolian lamb waistcoat by Femina Furs, 25 gns; velour hat by Richer, £2 19s 6d; shoulderbag by Xanthe Leather, £4 7s 6d; Corfam wristlet by Paris House, £1 5s. Waterproof Mascaramatic by Helena Rubinstein, 15s; lipgloss by Mary Quant, 7s 6d; suntan lotion Halsport by Lancôme, £1 10s 3d. Stockists, page 167

88

Far left: bikini by Baltrik, £4; chain at Anschel, 11 gns
Left: lace-up dress by Lizzie Carr, 7 gns

November 1969
Photographer David Montgomery had established a dispassionate style in his work for the *Sunday Times*. He was invited to adopt a more intimate approach for *Nova*. The article by Peter Martin profiled a skinhead, and began: 'The most important thing about Georgie is his boots'.

August 1969
David Montgomery's photographs for 'The blind train comes on Tuesday', and article on Lourdes by Robert Hughes.

1970

'Who are these guys?'

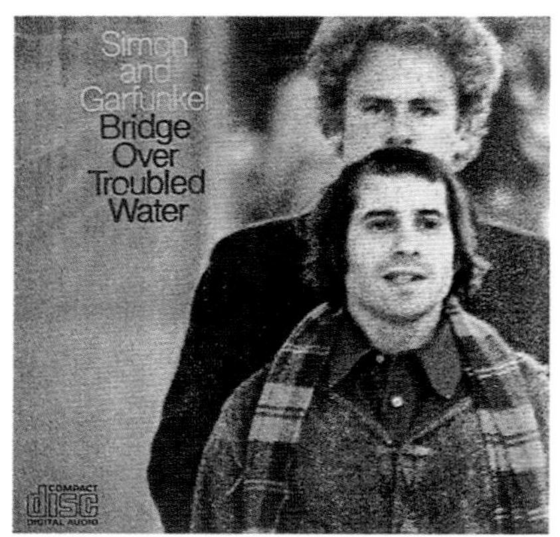

Simon and Garfunkel's greatest.

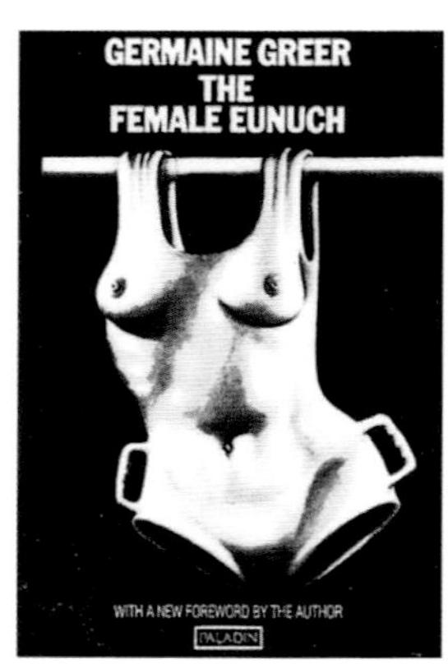

Feminism came into sharper focus.

The year

The Tories won the general election and Edward Heath became Prime Minister. He soon became embroiled in a dock strike and called a state of emergency – the first round of an extraordinary series of battles with the unions. Oil was discovered in the North Sea. Charles de Gaulle died. Things got even worse in South-east Asia as the war spilled over into Cambodia. Nijinsky carried Lester Pigott to win the Derby. The Boeing Jumbo jet made its first flight. National Guardsmen fired into a student anti-Vietnam War demo at Kent State University, killing five. Charles Manson led the horrific ritualised slaughter of Sharon Tate at the Californian home of Roman Polanski. Movie heroes Paul Newman and Robert Redford came together in the smash hit *Butch Cassidy and the Sundance Kid*; *M*A*S*H* and Mick Jagger in *Ned Kelly* were also good box office. The Tamla Motown stable held sway in the charts with stars such as Stevie Wonder; ten-year-old Michael Jackson appeared on the scene as the Jackson Five became teenybopper favourites. Simon and Garfunkel's enormous *Bridge Over Troubled Water* hit No 1. The publication of Germaine Greer's *The Female Eunuch* ignited smouldering feminism; in the USA women began to show how liberated they were by burning their bras.

Right
June 1970
'A touch of Tahiti' introduced sarongs to wear on the beach. Photograph by Hans Feurer.

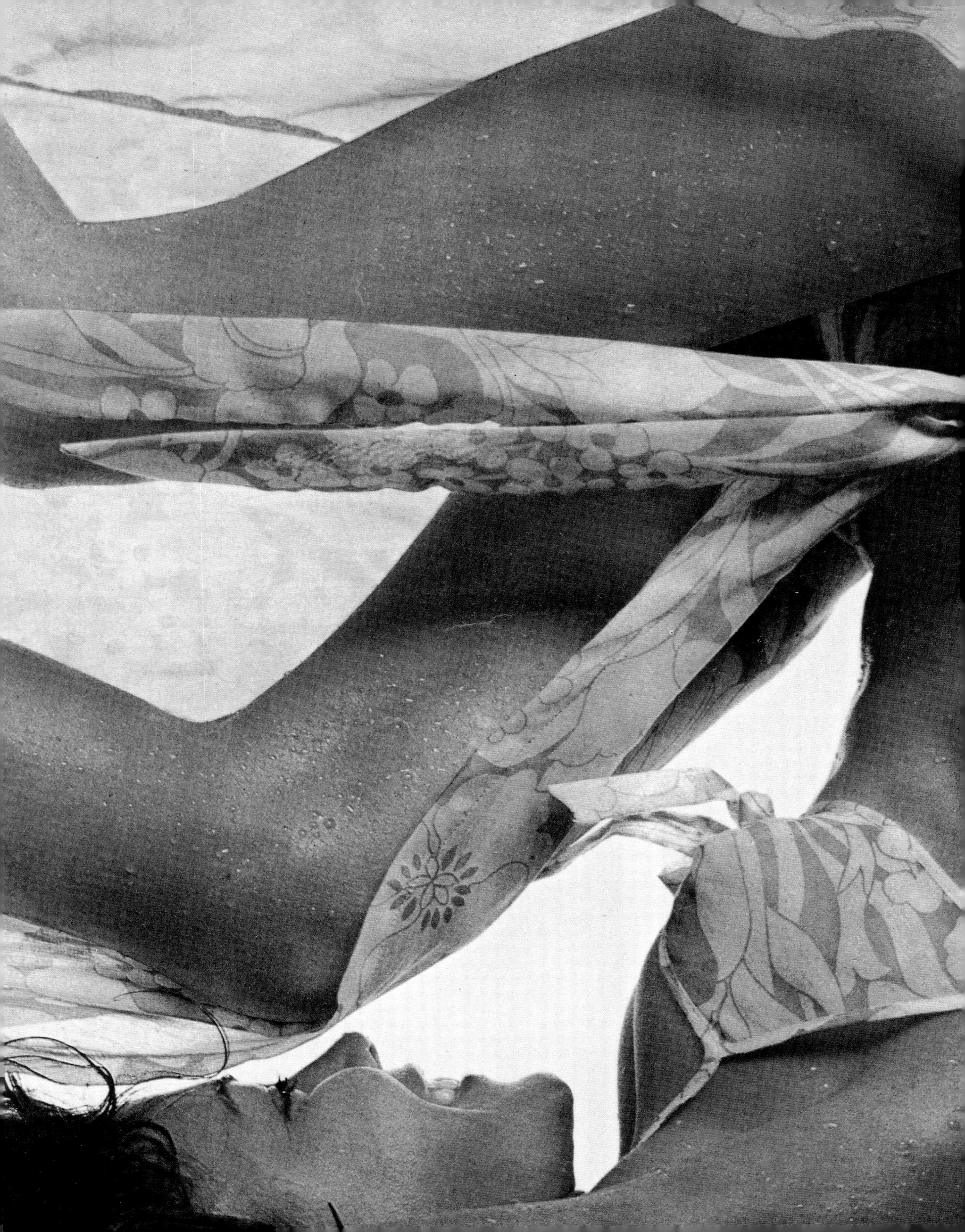

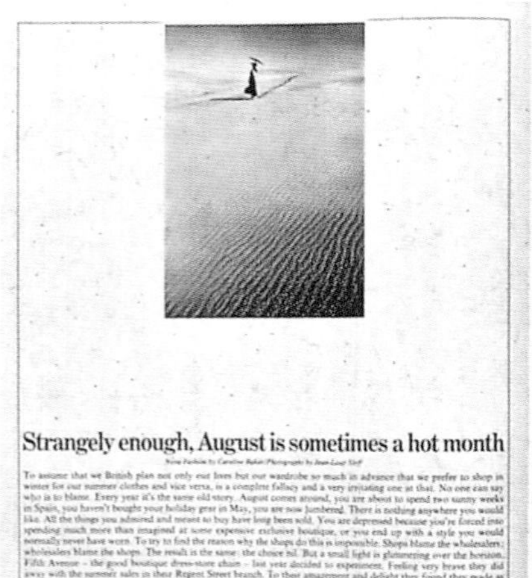

Strangely enough, August is sometimes a hot month

New Fashion by Caroline Baker/Photographs by Jean-Loup Sieff

To assume that we British plan not only our lives but our wardrobe so much in advance that we prefer to shop in winter for our summer clothes and vice versa, is a complete fallacy and a very irritating one at that. No one can say who is to blame. Every year it's the same old story. August comes around, you are about to spend two sunny weeks in Spain, you haven't bought your holiday gear in May, you are now lumbered. There is nothing anywhere you would like. All the things you admired and meant to buy have long been sold. You are depressed because you're forced into spending much more than imagined at some expensive exclusive boutique, or you end up with a style you would normally never have worn. To try to find the reason why the shops do this is impossible. Shops blame the wholesalers; wholesalers blame the shops. The result is the same: the choice nil. But a small light is glimmering over the horizon. Fifth Avenue – the good boutique dress-store chain – last year decided to experiment. Feeling very brave they did away with the summer sales in their Regent Street branch. To their amazement and delight they found they made as much, if not more, profit for the July sales period than they had previously done. Now they are doing away with sales completely in the London area. (Although they admit that in the provinces they still make a profit during sale time.) Not only have they done away with the sales, they realize that most shoppers aren't buying clothes months in advance of the seasons – proof that we are not all as organized as someone would like us to be. So now they are selling summer clothes, both light and heavier, right the way through to the first signs of autumn, as well as always carrying a very small amount of summer things right through winter for the richer cruise-customer. Of course, the same will apply to any winter goods. Let's hope that other shops will follow their lead so we can get some sense into shopping.

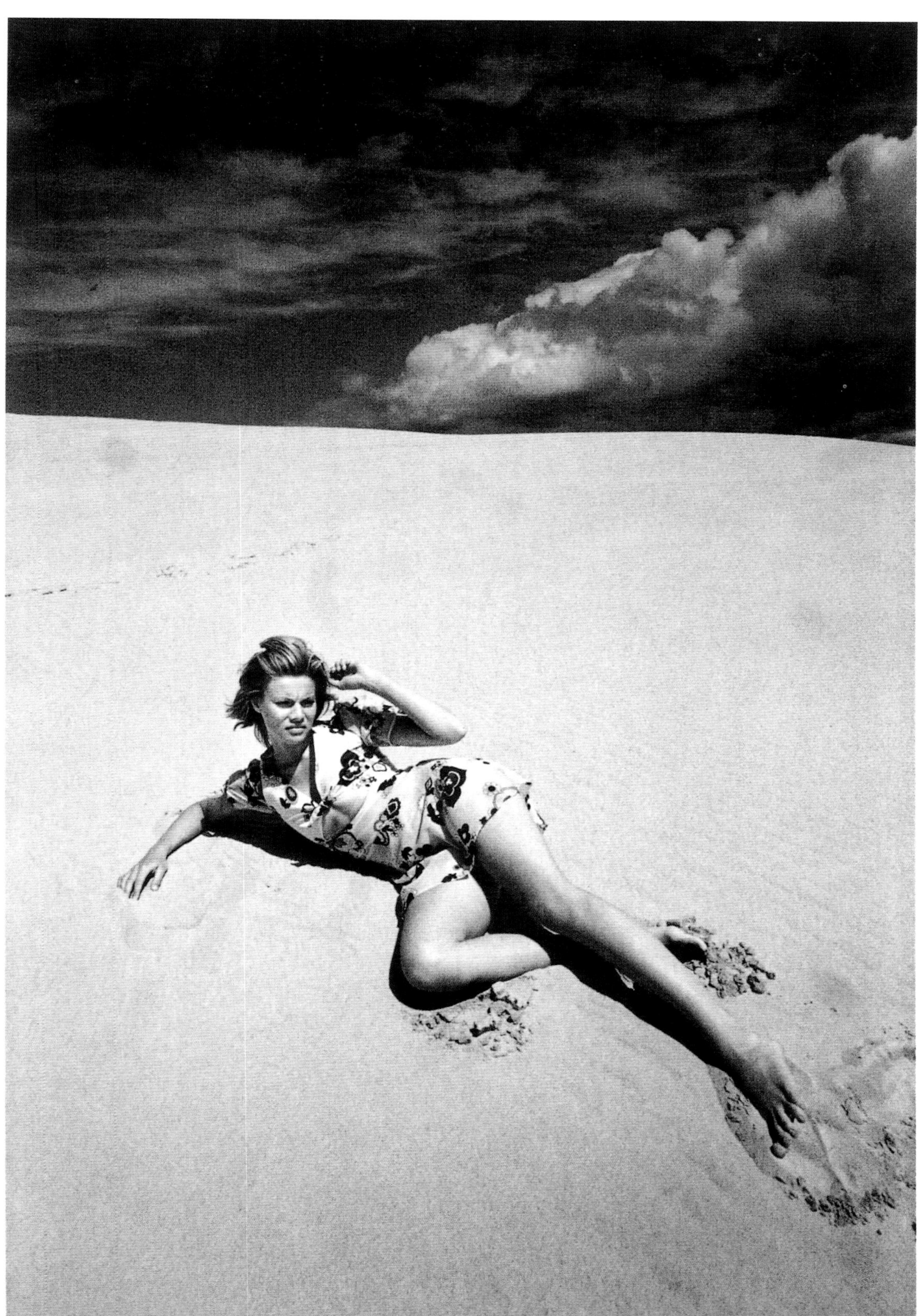

August 1970
Fashion editor Caroline Baker's feature on the difficulties of finding summer clothes in August. Photographs by Jeanloup Sieff.

January 1970
Peter Blake's painting of a black man with a white woman caused the issue to be banned in South Africa. Norman Lewis's short story 'A little rain off the new moon' was actually set in the Caribbean.

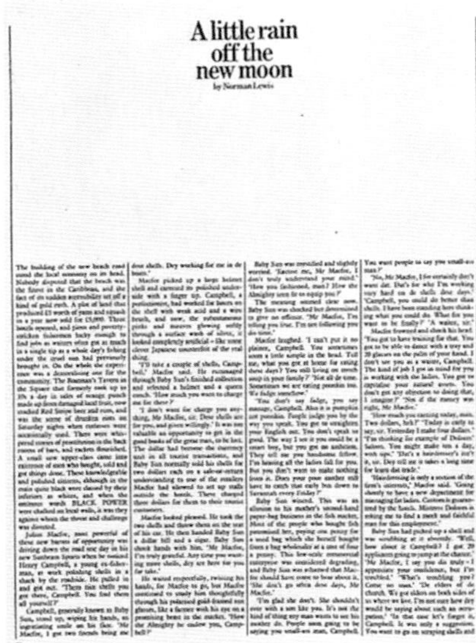
A little rain off the new moon
by Norman Lewis

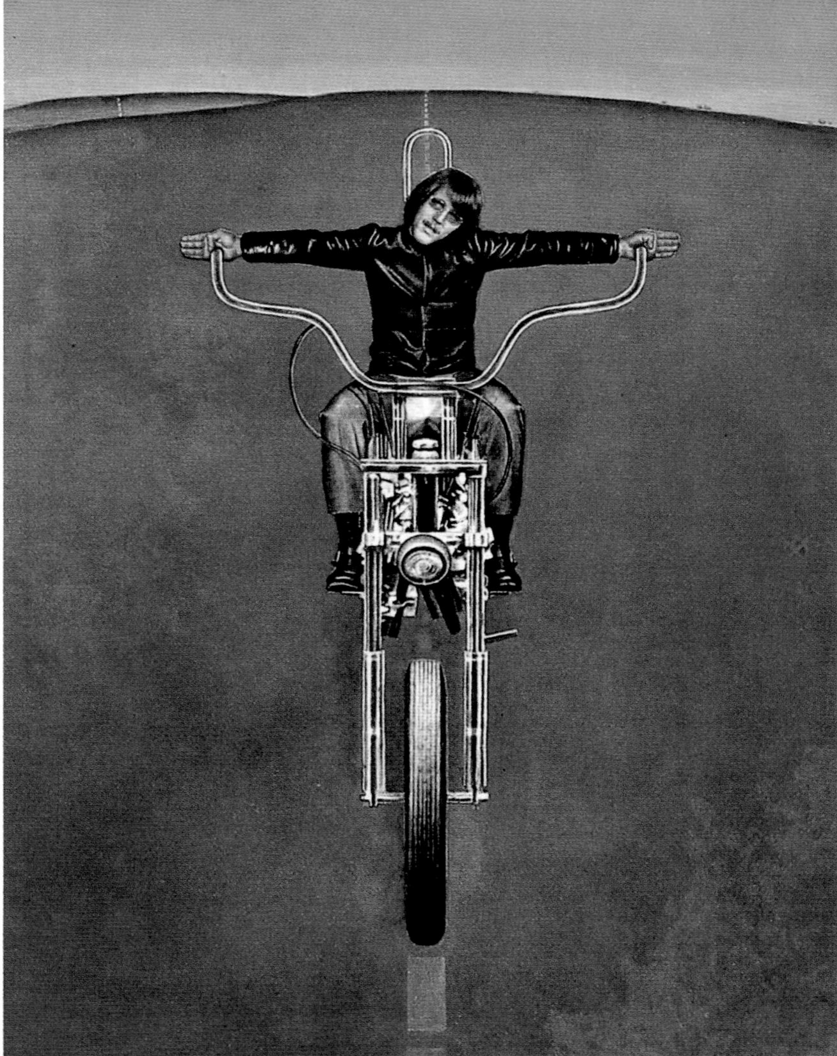

February 1970
Jean-Paul Goude's first work for *Nova* illustrated a Pauline Peters interview with Peter Fonda whose *Easy Rider* film was on release.

March 1970
Peter Blake's painting for an article on George Formby, as remembered by Alan Randall, Formby's uncanny voice-reincarnation.

George Formby
1937

GEORGE FORMBY

1970

September 1970
Jean-Paul Goude's illustration for 'America's gift to the bottoms of the world', a feature on Levi's. The Design and Art Direction Association rather curiously gave the picture its 1971 silver award – for photography.

AMERICA'S GIFT TO THE BOTTOMS OF THE WORLD

Back in the late fifties queuing for Levi's was about the only way you'd get a pair in this country. Partly because they were American and everything American was glamorous and admired in those days; partly because of actor James Dean, who was [illegible] and wore jeans so consistently that they might have been growing on his legs. [illegible] was far exceeding supply. 'You'd find a shop that was expecting a shipment, write the date they were due in your diary and then travel for miles to be first [illegible]. Levi's – the real ones – were like gold dust. You'd go round to someone's house just to look at them. [illegible] To this kind of connoisseur, then and now, a pair of Levi's is perfect and shouldn't be tampered with. They must be worn in – a process sometimes taking up to six years – until you have exactly the right amount of sun bleach and threads bare. If the Levi's wear out in the meantime you may patch them – but only with another pair of Levi's. You could cut off the bottoms if you had genuinely worn them out but some of the other things people do to Levi's nowadays – well, it's sacrilege.' Levi's must be the only garments that successfully fit in with all sorts of 'uniform'.

[illegible] Brigid Keenan/Illustration by Jean-Paul Goude

[illegible] -ically, distinctive clothes associated with one [illegible] group would be abhorred by another but skinheads wear Levi's; [illegible] wear them; surfers and beachboys wear them; hippies [illegible] them and all the while people outside any group at all are wearing [illegible] cut off, tie-dyed to look like camouflage, made to flare with coloured [illegible], braided with braid or fringe, studded, patched, new, worn-in or worn out. Maybe the only people who are not wearing Levi's are the original aficionados. They are outraged because Levi-Strauss are bringing fashion into the Levi business, making them flared and in fabrics apart from denim. [illegible] it is no longer possible to buy a pair of Levi's [illegible] tips (rumour has it that button-ups – which are [illegible] Levi's – are all going to Vietnam) and it's killing the connoisseurs. For these reasons original Levi's are something of collectors' items these days. Photographer Steve Hiett, who owns a particularly covetously well-worn pair, is always being offered money for them – the highest bid so far being £15. Button-up Levi's must be the only contemporary clothing worth more secondhand than new.

Above and overleaf
February 1970
Tantalization, or how to double your circulation at a stroke. The three consecutive spreads were printed back-to-back so you had to buy two copies to make up the complete picture. It was actually shot as three frames by Hans Feurer.

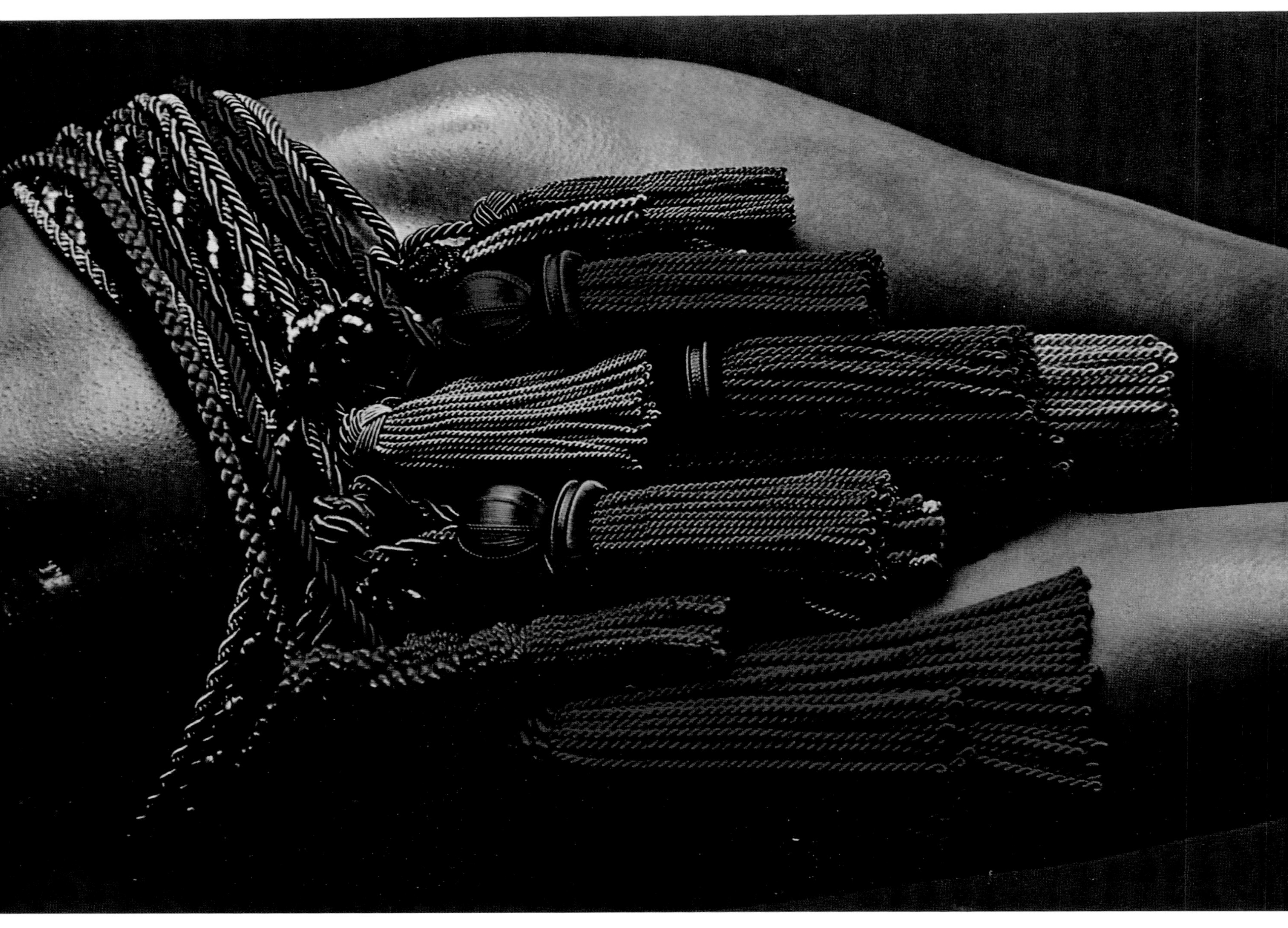

Left
June 1970
Edda Köchl's illustration for 'Summer food' by Caroline Conran.

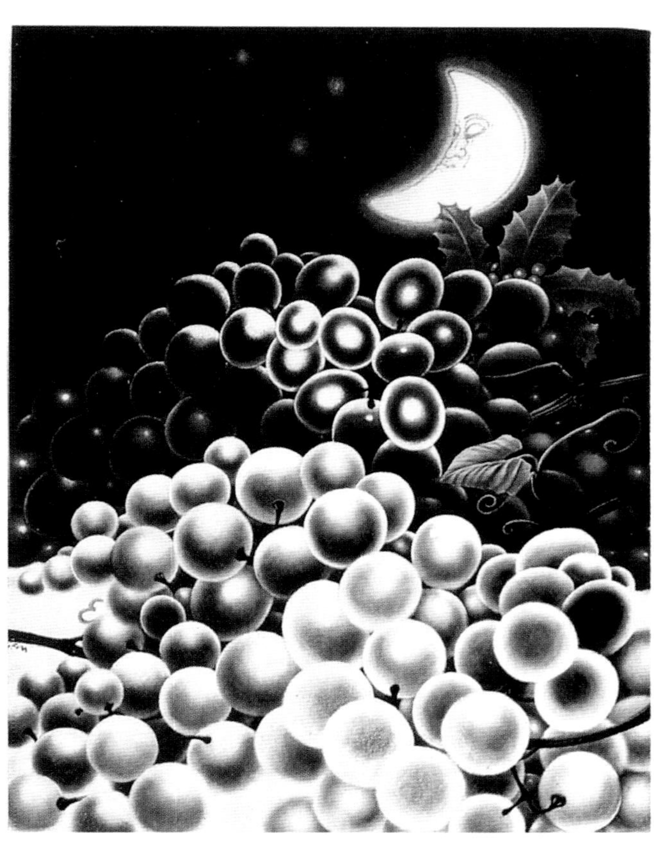

Nova Cookery
by Caroline Conran

Party-giving guaranteed to lead to party-going

Illustration by Alain Le Foll

CHILLI CON CARNE

Serves 12

BOEUF EN DAUBE A LA PROVENCALLE

Serves 12

BRAISED DUCK WITH APPLES

WINE JELLY

Serves 12

FROSTED GRAPES

December 1970
Caroline Conran's food column with illustration by Alain Le Foil.

January 1970
Words in their own right: a spread of pure Plantin by David Hillman continued the short story by Norman Lewis shown on page 102.

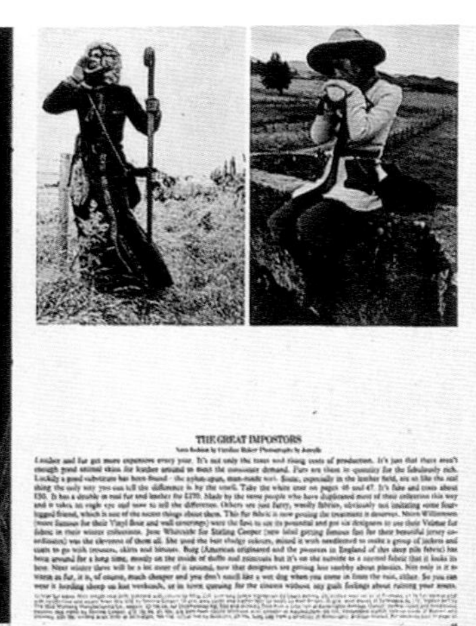

THE GREAT IMPOSTORS

Top
January 1970
One of Jonvelle's photographs for a fake-fur fashion feature by Caroline Baker.

Above
March 1970
Clothes by British designers photographed by Saul Leiter through 'typically British' windows – found in Brighton.

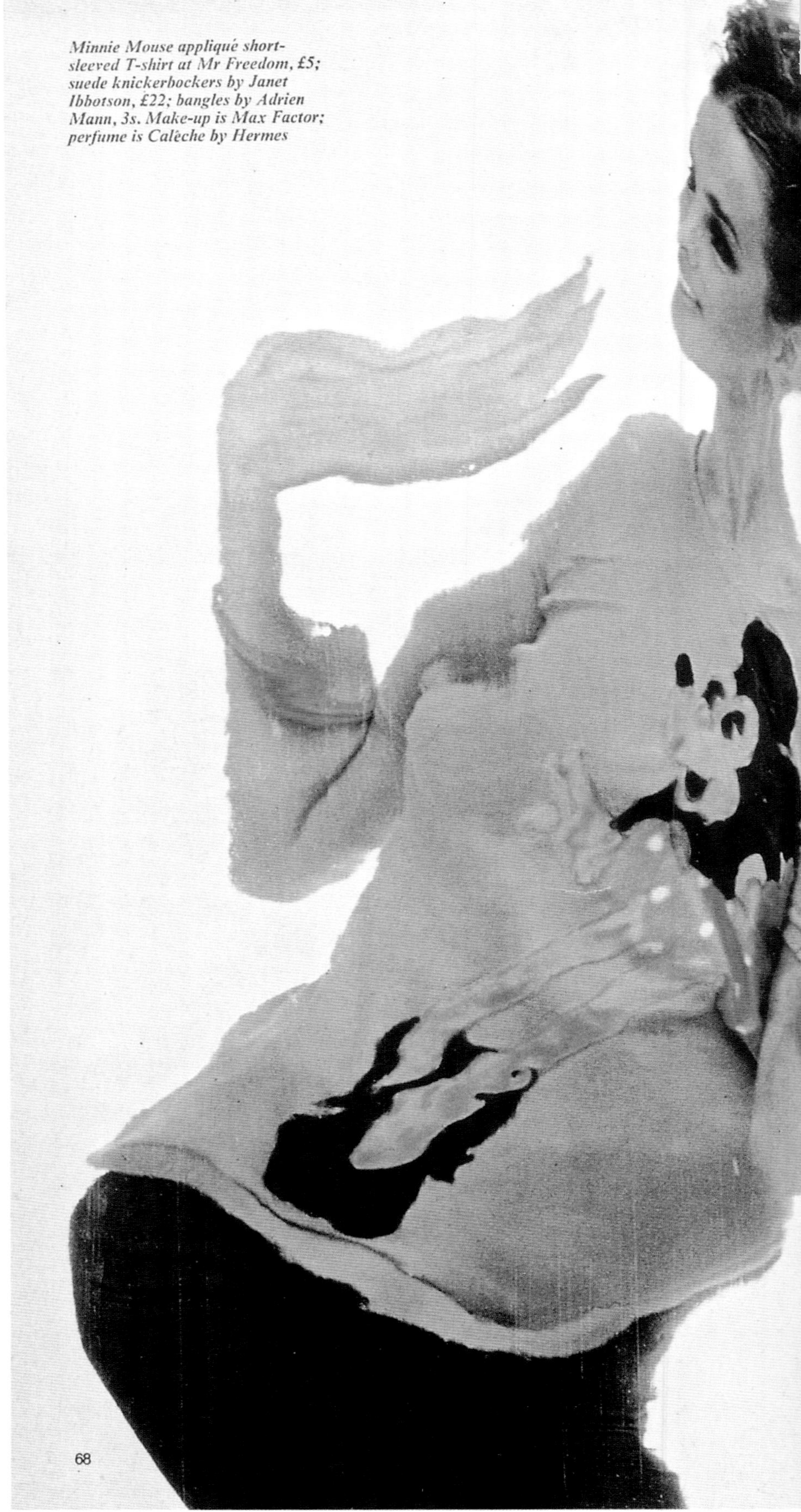

Minnie Mouse appliqué short-sleeved T-shirt at Mr Freedom, £5; suede knickerbockers by Janet Ibbotson, £22; bangles by Adrien Mann, 3s. Make-up is Max Factor; perfume is Calèche by Hermes
68

December 1970
Fancy dressing. The theme: a fairground. The model: Jean Shrimpton in the twilight of her career. The photographer: Hans Feurer. The separate, funny-mirror shots were stripped together at the printers.

YOUNG, SQUARE
AND
BEAUTIFUL

November 1970
Jacqmar silks were brought to a younger market in designs by Zandra Rhodes, Veronica Marsh and Althea McNish. Harri Peccinotti used the same model for each shot and David Hillman put together the montage.

1971

Evening Standard
CITY PRICES
The big switch-over has a smooth start
D-DAY–AND IT'S OFF ON THE DOT!
Fears over Garden plan
Smooth Stock Market switch
Confused? 'It's me, not the customer'
Heated rear window FREE with every new Morris only from Stewart & Ardern

No more 'seven-and-six and half-a-crown make ten bob'.

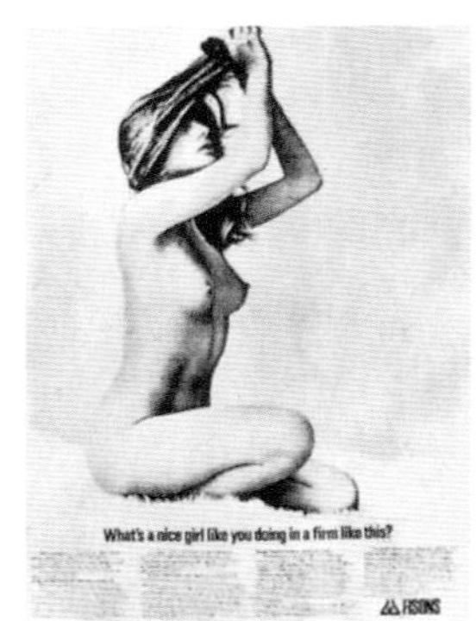

Vivian Neves in *The Times*.

A lot of trouble for the censors.

The year

Rolls-Royce went bust. Pounds, shillings and pence (also known as LSD) gave way to pounds and 'new p's as Britain changed the way it had paid for things since Roman times to a less versatile but simpler decimal system. A certain Education Secretary called Margaret Thatcher abolished free milk at school. The Open University, 'the world's first university of the air', started TV degree course lectures. The civil war in Pakistan ended, making way for the formation of Bangladesh. The first digital watch came on the market. Film makers were in good form with *Sunday Bloody Sunday, Death in Venice* and *The French Connection*, while violence hit new heights in *A Clockwork Orange* and *Straw Dogs*. Reggae entered the mainstream consciousness. Led Zeppelin released their album containing *Stairway To Heaven*, to some the greatest rock track ever recorded. The Tate Gallery put on a major exhibition of Andy Warhol's pop art. The first nude to appear in *The Times* was Vivian Neves in an advertisement for Fisons. Hot pants were introduced as fashion's rather desperate answer to waning interest in the mini and the flop of the midi.

Right
October 1971
The winter athlete look. Photograph by Hans Feurer.

WASHINGTON
GREYS

September 1971
American GIs appeared on television nightly, and army surplus stores provided cheap pickings for battlefield chic, an example of *Nova* pre-empting the fashion scene – the idea didn't catch on until a year or so later. Photographs by Hans Feurer.

October 1971
Trampoline-propelled, mid-air poses – shot by Hans Feurer.

January 1971
Sarah Moon forsook her usual soft-focus, romantic style for a Caroline Baker fashion piece on suits as casual dress, and won the 1972 Design and Art Direction photography gold award. It was the first year that D&AD decided to make two photography gold awards; the other went to Don McCullin for his work in Bengal.

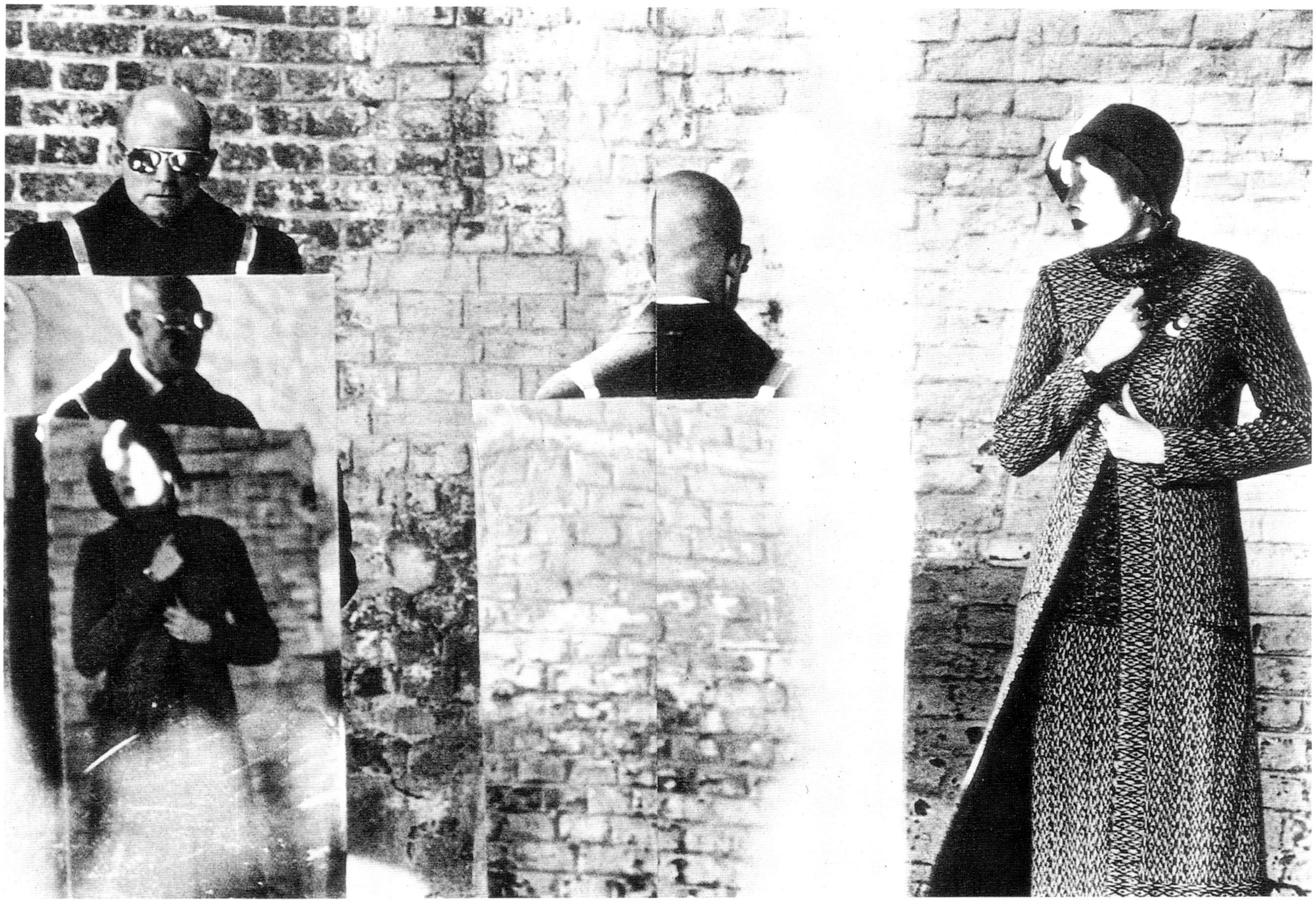

SUITS AREN'T SMART ANY MORE

Stripey wool vest and matching shorts by Lee Bender at Bus Stop, £7.25; multi-striped thigh-length wool socks at Mr Freedom, £2.40

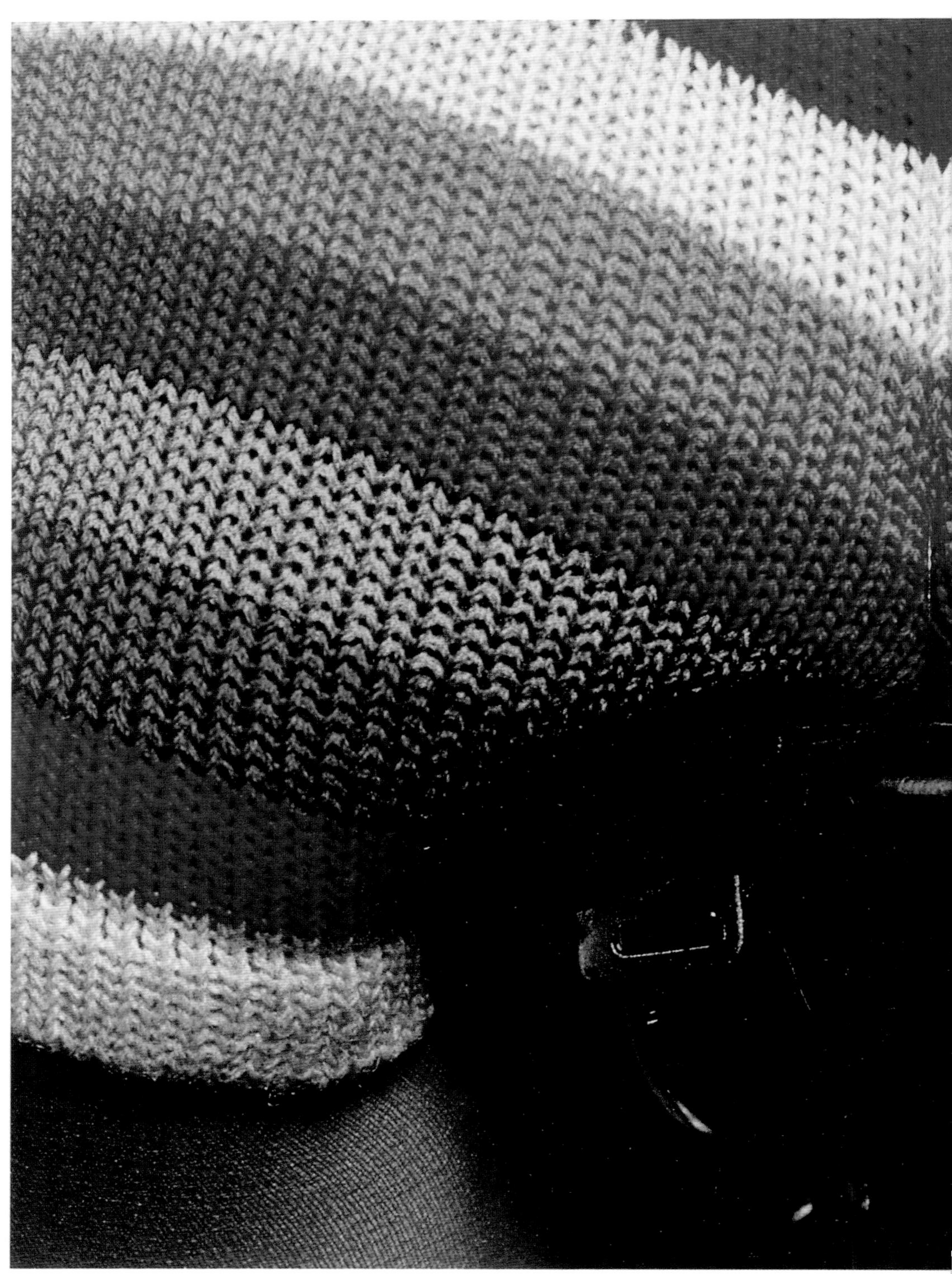

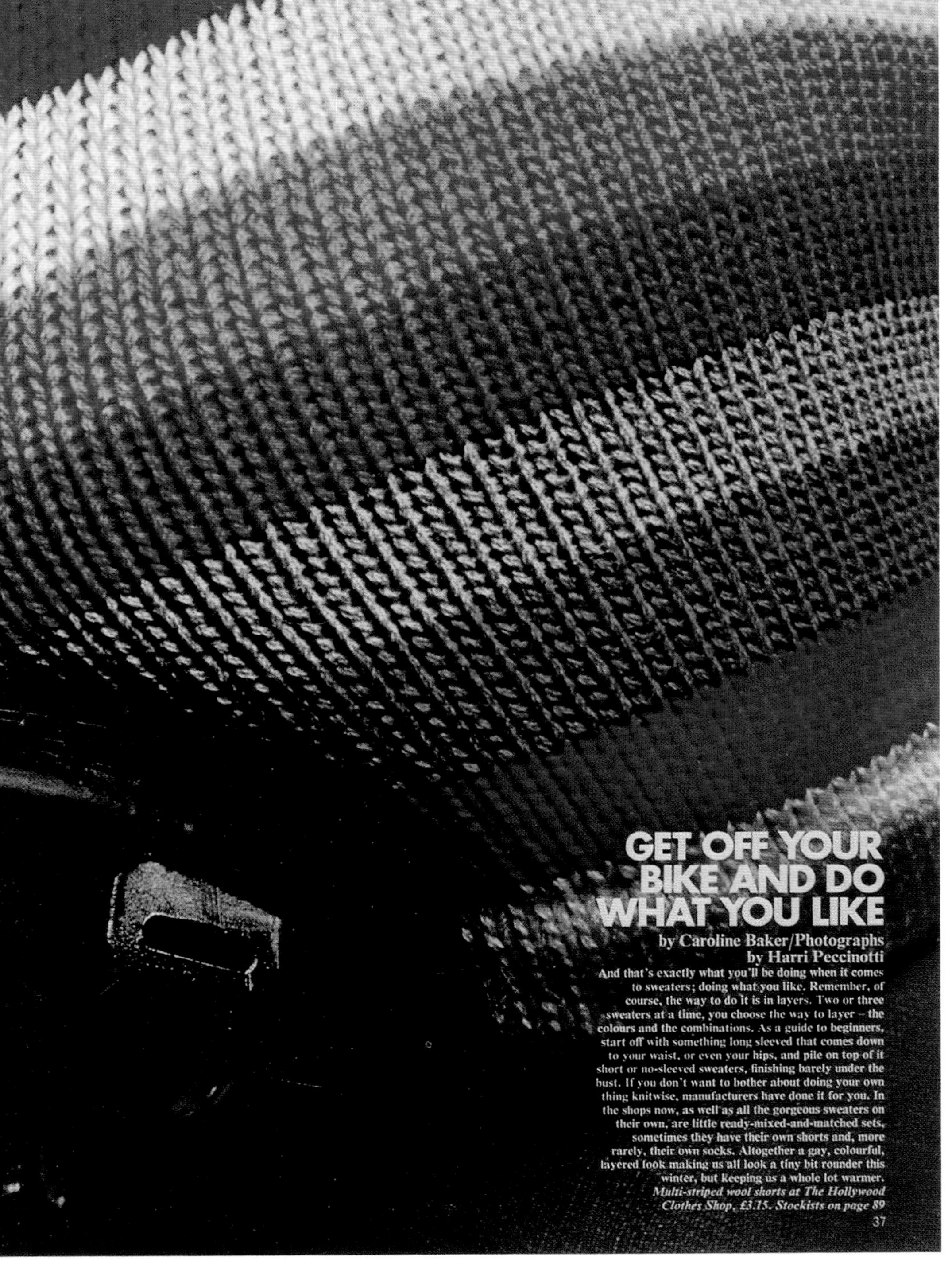

GET OFF YOUR BIKE AND DO WHAT YOU LIKE

by Caroline Baker/Photographs by Harri Peccinotti

And that's exactly what you'll be doing when it comes to sweaters; doing what you like. Remember, of course, the way to do it is in layers. Two or three sweaters at a time, you choose the way to layer – the colours and the combinations. As a guide to beginners, start off with something long sleeved that comes down to your waist, or even your hips, and pile on top of it short or no-sleeved sweaters, finishing barely under the bust. If you don't want to bother about doing your own thing knitwise, manufacturers have done it for you. In the shops now, as well as all the gorgeous sweaters on their own, are little ready-mixed-and-matched sets, sometimes they have their own shorts and, more rarely, their own socks. Altogether a gay, colourful, layered look making us all look a tiny bit rounder this winter, but keeping us a whole lot warmer.

Multi-striped wool shorts at The Hollywood Clothes Shop, £3.15. Stockists on page 89

37

Left and previous page
August 1971
For this feature on wool sweaters and shorts the layouts were drawn out before any photography was attempted. The shoot then carefully followed the plan and the results cut and stripped in for the final montage. David Hillman and Harri Peccinotti were responsible; they both happen to be bike fanatics.

ACCESS TO THE CHILDREN

by William Trevor/Illustration by Edda Köchl

January 1971
Edda Köchl's illustration for William Trevor's article on post-marital strife.

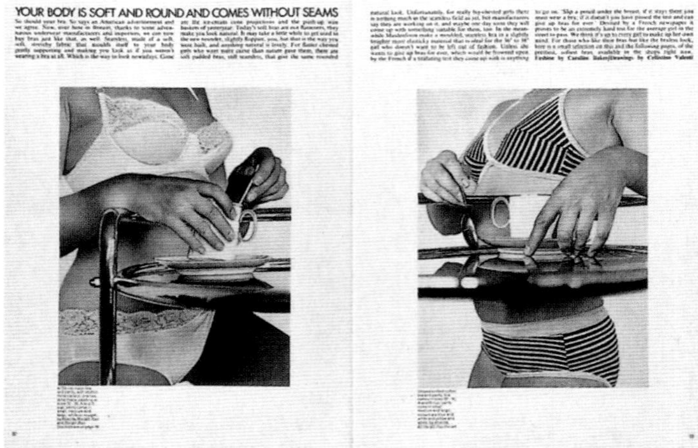

YOUR BODY IS SOFT AND ROUND AND COMES WITHOUT SEAMS

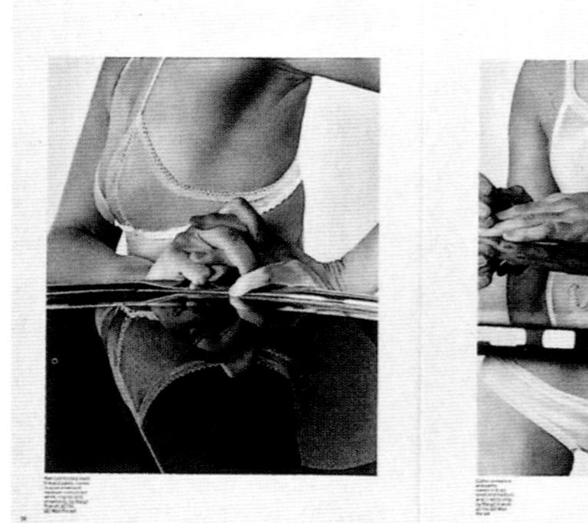

Above and right
February 1971
The cropping looks typical *Nova*, the subjects typical *Nova*, but this is the work not of a photographer but illustrator Celestino Valenti, for a feature on the arrival of soft, seamless bras.

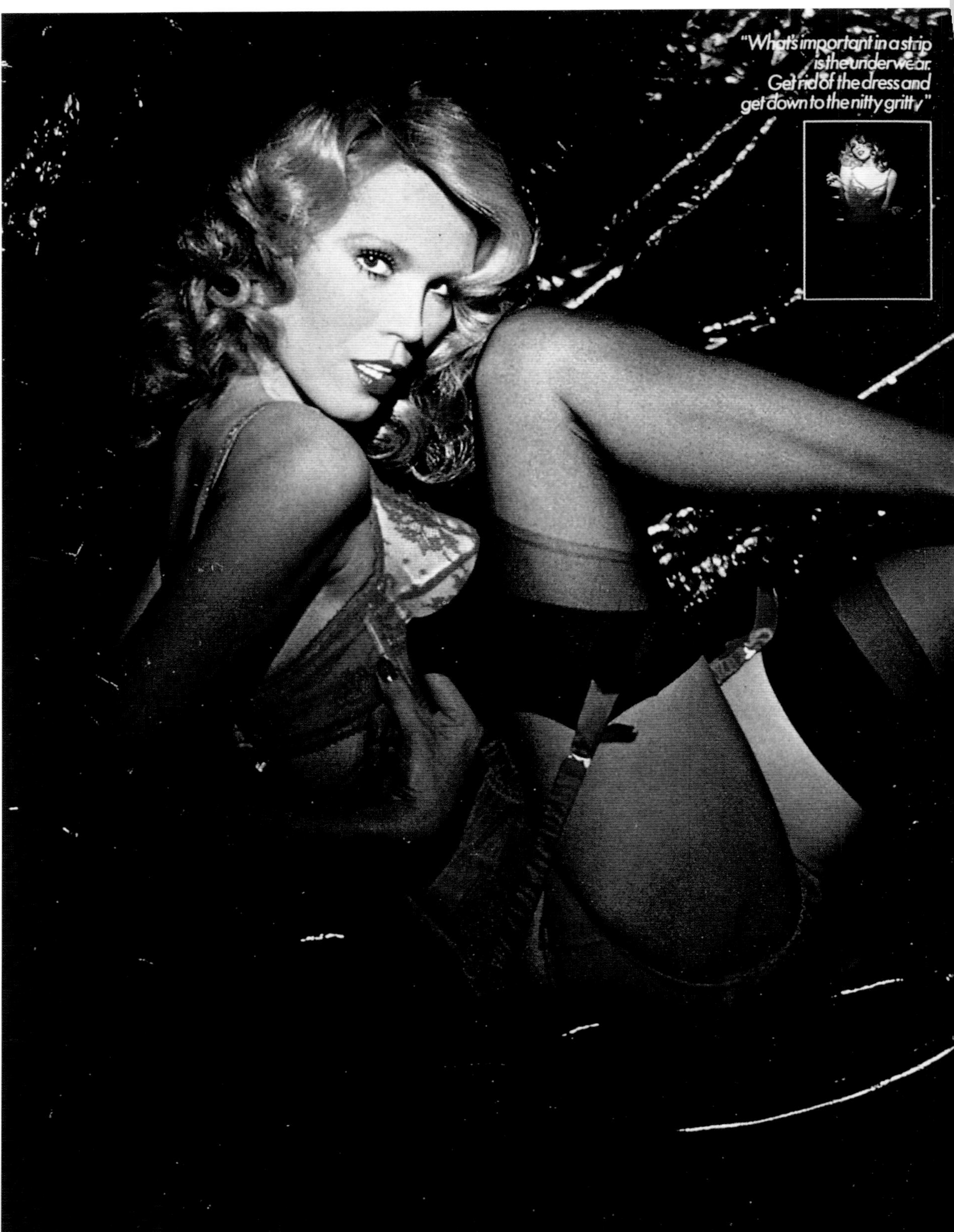

"What's important in a strip is the underwear. Get rid of the dress and get down to the nitty gritty"

May 1971
Duffy photographed the enigmatic Amanda Lear (the clue is buried in her name) demonstrating 'How to undress in front of your man'.

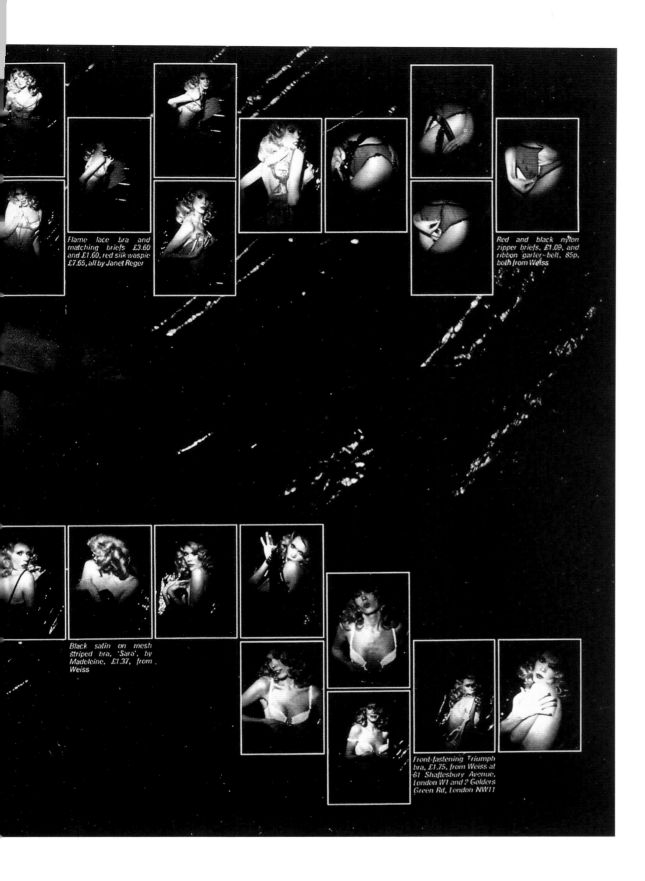

Flame lace bra and matching briefs £3.60 and £1.60, red silk waspie £7.65, all by Janet Reger

Red and black nylon zipper briefs, £1.09, and ribbon garter-belt, 85p, both from Weiss

Black satin on mesh striped bra, 'Sara', by Madeleine, £1.37, from Weiss

Front-fastening Triumph bra, £1.75, from Weiss at 61 Shaftesbury Avenue, London W1 and 2 Golders Green Rd, London NW11

May 1971
Accompanying the piece was a pull-out, do-it-yourself flick book: just cut along the dotted lines and clip it all together for *Nova's* first animated feature.

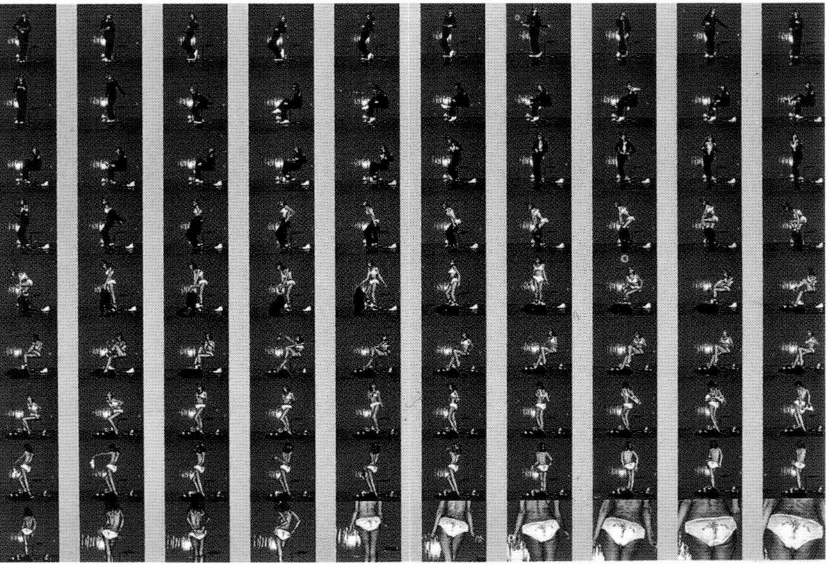

HEY THERE...CHARLIE GIRL

Be a classic. Winter garb has become superbly classic – things like baggy suits that button-up just any-old-how, that have Oxford bags or long shorts or flared hip-hugging skirts to go with them. All in English schoolboy grey, plain or jacquard. Be a comic. Add a giant buttonhole to your lapel or to your soft bowler, wear a bow-tie as a choker, wear gloves all the time, use a walking-stick, paint your eyes sad, wear striped socks and lace-up shoes with rounded toes. Be a proper Charlie.

September 1971
Girls in suits Chaplinesque. Photographs by Sarah Moon.

CAUGHT UNDERWEARS

Above and overleaf
August 1971
Photographer shoot thyself: Helmut Newton appeared in all his shots for a fashion feature on underwear.

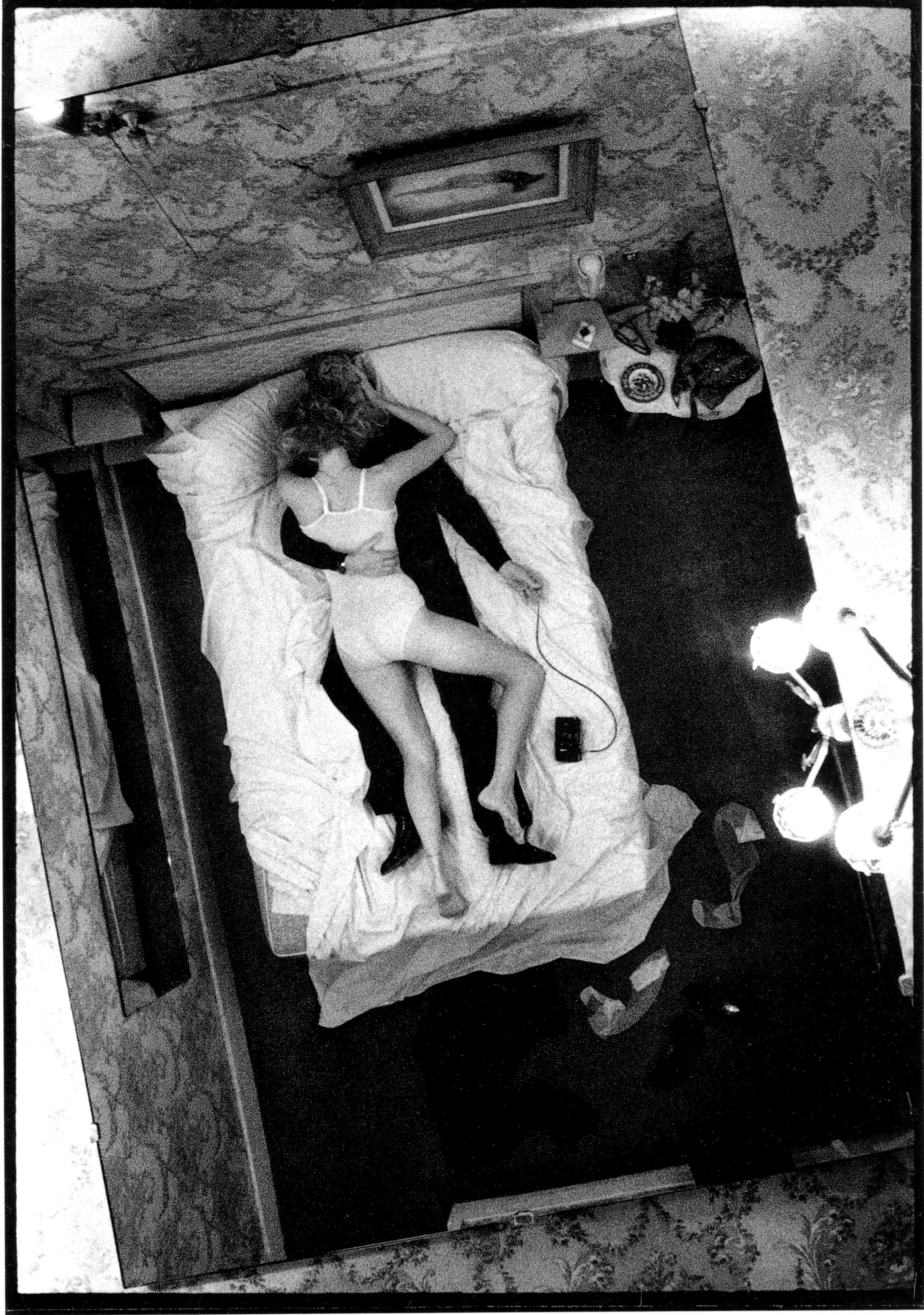

January 1971
Lessons from Peru on keeping warm in winter. Photograph by Jonvelle.

EVERY HOBO SHOULD HAVE ONE

by Caroline Baker
Photographs by Saul Leiter

It warms the cockles of the heart and gladdens the eyes of the beholder, not to mention its owner. It costs rather a lot but, then, why shouldn't it. It is real fur; an expensive investment that needs a lot of thinking about, especially with today's lightning fashion changes. To be on the very safe side buy it very simple, unfussy, no belts or half belts, no buckles no bows, long or extra long for warmth and fashionability. To be very fashionable it must be very square shouldered, jacket shaped, short to the waist, or mini-skirt length, so that it works as a jacket and as a coat. Funky, gaudy colours are allowed as well, but are liable to go out faster than anything else. Fur stoles or scarves, with or without the heads attached, are making a comeback and are much cheaper as there is so much less skin involved. But above all, furs must be worn as casually as clothes are nowadays – looking as if no thought had gone into that nonchalant, put-together style that takes such agonising hours to work out. These furs are strictly from animals not threatened by extinction, as the British Fur Trade Association has agreed not to use skins of any animals in danger of dying out.

Tibetan lamb coat by Fab Furs, approx £200.50; felt hat by Edward Mann, £2; Cover-up tights by Mary Quant, 75p; striped socks from a selection at Fenwick; striped socks (rolled down) at Lonsdale Sports, £1.25; suede ankle boots at Ravel, £4.99; cashmere gloves at W Bill, £1.25. Stockists on page 109

60

December 1971
Lessons from animals on keeping warm in winter. Photograph by Saul Leiter.

Left
October 1971
Illustration by John Holmes for 'A marriage certificate and a bulge turn you into a non-person', an article by Carolyn Faulder. John Holmes's skill with this kind of issue had been demonstrated in his cover for Germaine Greer's *The Female Eunuch*, published the previous year (see page 98).

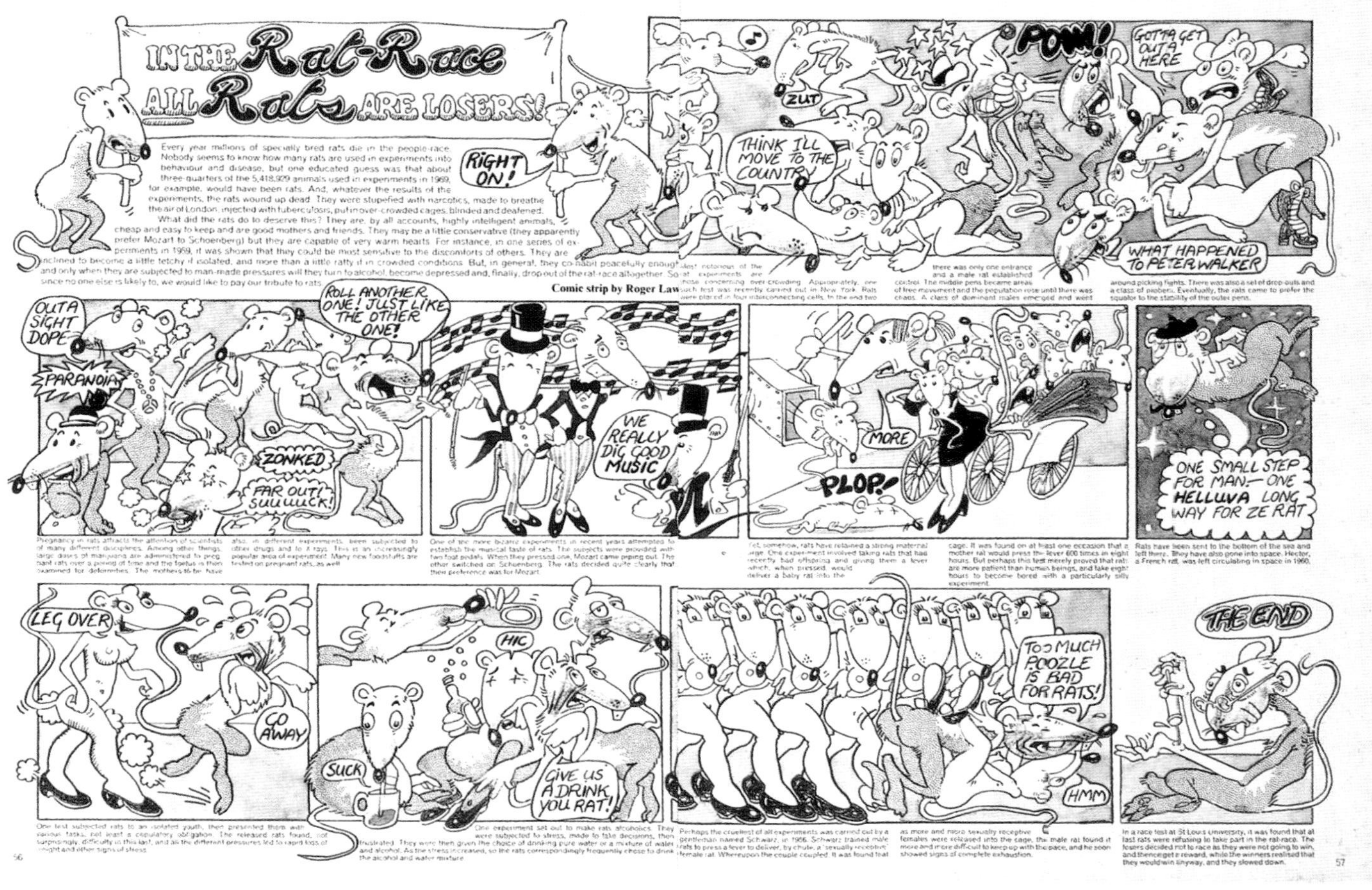

Enoch's Two Letters

by Alan Sillitoe/Illustration by Philippe Weissbecker

Enoch's parents parted in a singular way. He was eight years of age at the time. It happened one morning after he had gone to school, so that he didn't know anything about it till coming home in the evening.

Jack Boden got up as usual at seven o'clock, and his wife, who was Enoch's mother, set a breakfast of bacon and eggs before him. They never said much, and spoke even less on this particular morning, because both were solidly locked in their separate thoughts which, unknown to each other, they were at last intending to act on.

Instead of getting a bus to his foundry, Jack boarded one for the city centre. He sought out a public lavatory where, for the price of a penny, he was able to draw off his overalls, and emerge with them under his arm. They were wrapped in the brown paper which he had put into his pocket before leaving the house, a sly and unobtrusive movement as he called from the scullery: 'So long, love. See you this afternoon.'

Now wearing a reasonable suit, he walked to the railway station. There he met Rene, who had in her two suitcases a few of his possessions that he had fed to her during clandestine meetings over the past fortnight. Having worked in the same factory, they had, as many others who were employed there saw, 'fallen for each other'. Rene wasn't married, so there seemed nothing to stop her going away with him. And Jack's dull toothache of a conscience had, in the six months since knowing her, cured itself at last.

Yet they got on the train to London feeling somewhat alarmed at the step they had taken, though neither liked to say anything in case the other should think they wanted to back out. Hardly a word was spoken the whole way. Rene wondered what her parents would say when they saw she'd gone. Jack thought mostly about Enoch, but he knew he'd be safe enough with his mother, and that she'd bring him up right. He would send her a letter from London to explain that he had gone – in case she hadn't noticed it.

No sooner had Jack left for his normal daylight stint at the foundry than his wife, Edna, attended to Enoch. She watched him eat, standing by the mantelshelf for a good view of him during her stare. He looked up, half out of his sleep, and didn't smile back at her.

She kissed him, pushed sixpence into his pocket, and sent him up the street to school, then went upstairs to decide what things to take with her. It wasn't a hard choice, for though they had plenty of possessions, little of it was movable. So it turned out that two suitcases and a handbag held all she wanted.

There was ample time, and she went downstairs to more tea and a proper breakfast. They'd been married 10 years, and for seven at least she'd had enough. The trouble with Jack was that he'd let nothing worry him. He was so trustworthy and easy-going he got on her nerves. He didn't even seem interested in other women, and the worst thing about such a man was that he hardly ever noticed when you were upset. When he did, he accused you of upsetting him.

There were so many things wrong, that now she was about to leave she couldn't bring them to mind, and this irritated her, and made her think that it had been even worse than it was, rather than the other way round. As a couple they had given up tackling any differences between them by the human method of talking. It was as if the sight of each other struck them dumb. On first meeting, a dozen years ago, they had been unable to say much, which, in their mutual attraction, they had confused with love at first sight. And nowadays they didn't try to talk to each other about the way they felt any more because neither of them thought it would do any good. Having come this far, the only thing left was to act. It wasn't that life was dull exactly, but they had nothing in common. If they had, maybe she could have put up with him, no matter how bad he was.

For a week she'd been trying to write a letter, to be posted from where she was going, but she couldn't get beyond: 'I'm leaving you for good, so stop bothering about me any more. Just look after Enoch, because I've had my bellyful and I'm off.' After re-reading it she put it back and clipped her handbag shut.

Having decided to act after years of thinking about it, she was now uncertain as to what she would do. A sister lived in Hull, so her first plan was to stay there till she found a job and a room. This was something to hang onto, and beyond it she didn't think. She'd just have to act again, and that was that. Once you started there was probably no stopping, she thought, not feeling too good about it now that the time had come.

An hour later she turned the clock to the wall, and walked out of the house for good, safe in knowing that shortly after Enoch came in from school his father would be home to feed him. They had lavished a lot of love on Enoch – she knew that – maybe too much, some of which they should have given to each other but had grown too mean and shy to.

She left the door unlocked so that he could just walk in. He was an intelligent lad, who'd be able to turn on the gas fire if he felt cold. When Mrs Mackley called from her back door to ask if she was going on her holidays, Edna laughed and said she was only off to see Jack's mother at Netherfield, to take some old rags that she needed to cut up and use for rug-clippings.

Top
August 1971
Strip cartoon by Roger Law.

Above
August 1971
Illustration by Philippe Weisbecker for Alan Sillitoe's poignant short story about disappearing parents.

November 1971
Harri Peccinotti sent out into the streets of London offering fivers for the chance to get into *Nova*. Amongst the real pairs are famous fantasy comparisons.

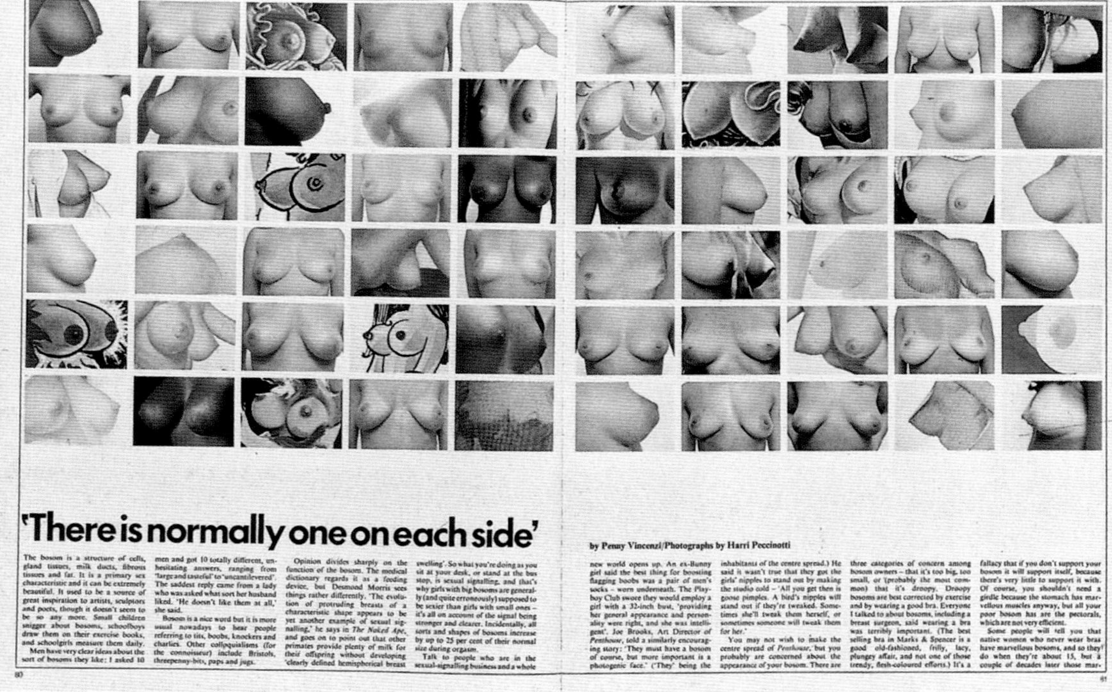

'There is normally one on each side'

by Penny Vincenzi/Photographs by Harri Peccinotti

The bosom is a structure of cells, gland tissues, milk ducts, fibrous tissues and fat. It is a primary sex characteristic and it can be extremely beautiful. It used to be a source of great inspiration to artists, sculptors and poets, though it doesn't seem to be so any more. Small children snigger about bosoms, schoolboys draw them on their exercise books, and schoolgirls measure them daily.

Men have very clear ideas about the sort of bosoms they like: I asked 10 men and got 10 totally different, unhesitating answers, ranging from 'large and tasteful' to 'uncantilevered'. The saddest reply came from a lady who was asked what sort her husband liked. 'He doesn't like them at all,' she said.

Bosom is a nice word but it is more usual nowadays to hear people referring to tits, boobs, knockers and charlies. Other colloquialisms (for the connoisseur) include Bristols, threepenny-bits, paps and jugs.

Opinion divides sharply on the function of the bosom. The medical dictionary regards it as a feeding device, but Desmond Morris sees things rather differently. 'The evolution of protruding breasts of a characteristic shape appears to be yet another example of sexual signalling,' he says in *The Naked Ape*, and goes on to point out that other primates provide plenty of milk for their offspring without developing 'clearly defined hemispherical breast swelling'. So what you're doing as you sit at your desk, or stand at the bus stop, is sexual signalling, and that's why girls with big bosoms are generally (and quite erroneously) supposed to be sexier than girls with small ones – it's all on account of the signal being stronger and clearer. Incidentally, all sorts and shapes of bosoms increase by up to 25 per cent of their normal size during orgasm.

Talk to people who are in the sexual-signalling business and a whole new world opens up. An ex-Bunny girl said the best thing for boosting flagging boobs was a pair of men's socks – worn underneath. The Playboy Club swore they would employ a girl with a 32-inch bust, 'providing her general appearance and personality were right, and she was intelligent'. Joe Brooks, Art Director of *Penthouse*, told a similarly encouraging story: 'They must have a bosom of course, but more important is a photogenic face.' ('They' being the inhabitants of the centre spread.) He said it wasn't true that they got the girls' nipples to stand out by making the studio cold – 'All you get then is goose pimples. A bird's nipples will stand out if they're tweaked. Sometimes she'll tweak them herself, or sometimes someone will tweak them for her.'

You may not wish to make the centre spread of *Penthouse*, but you probably are concerned about the appearance of your bosom. There are three categories of concern among bosom owners – that it's too big, too small, or (probably the most common) that it's droopy. Droopy bosoms are best corrected by exercise and by wearing a good bra. Everyone I talked to about bosoms, including a breast surgeon, said wearing a bra was terribly important. (The best selling bra in Marks & Spencer is a good old-fashioned, frilly, lacy, plungey affair, and not one of those trendy, flesh-coloured efforts.) It's a fallacy that if you don't support your bosom it will support itself, because there's very little to support it with. Of course, you shouldn't need a girdle because the stomach has marvellous muscles anyway, but all your poor bosom has are the pectorals, which are not very efficient.

Some people will tell you that native women who never wear bras have marvellous bosoms, and so they do when they're about 15, but a couple of decades later those mar-

80 91

KEEP YOUR HAIR ON all of it...

From puberty onwards most women spend hours every week shaving, plucking and waxing pubic, facial, leg and underarm hair, believing it – despite it's natural inevitability – to be unhygienic, ugly and unattractive to men. We've established our independence liberated ourselves from our inhibitions about sex and nudity, so perhaps now is a good time to reconsider our attitude to body hair. From her book *Hair*, published this month by Aldous Books Ltd, Wendy Cooper prepared this feature for *Nova*. Photograph by Harri Peccinotti

As a species we have never been in any doubt about the strong link between hair and sexuality. Long before modern understanding of endocrinology revealed the vital role the sex hormones play in triggering the growth of body hair, primitive man had quite simply accepted its obvious connection with sexual maturity. The arrival of facial, axillary and chest hair in the male was a clear sexual signal, and pubic hair in both male and female served also as a sexual cynosure.

In fact, it was probably more. In a sense it baited the trap, for both axillary and pubic hair grow in areas where the skin contains scent glands, whose secretions need exposure to air to develop their full odour. Hair provides a holding surface for this oxidation, which releases a distinctive scent that serves, or at least once served, as a recognition signal and a stimulant to sexual excitement.

Evolution may not be much of a planner, but it is far too good an opportunist not to recognise and favour anything which serves such sexual ends. So, when shrinking forests forced man down from the trees to become a daylight hunter on hot tropical plains and it became necessary for him to shed his heavy primate coat to gain speed, agility and an efficient cooling system, he still retained those special areas of dense hair growth serving purposes that favoured survival.

In the male, hair on the face, together with a good growth of body hair, served yet another purpose as part of the threat display in the struggle for sexual dominance. The well-endowed human male, displaying his strong hair growth, was more likely to frighten off his more scantily equipped rivals, and emerge the victor in any struggle for a mate. In evolutionist jargon such hair growth, because of its link with sexual dominance, is called epigamic hair, and even today, when expensive cars, well-filled wallets and well-cut suits have become in many cultures the contemporary symbols of sexual dominance, there are still some men who can display a growth of epigamic hair that would not disgrace a gorilla.

Clearly, epigamic hair would serve no purpose in the female, who was the prize rather than the protagonist in sexual sorties, so woman was permitted to lose her chest and facial hair, thus highlighting the areas of remaining hair and increasing their sexual significance and attraction.

Of course, in time, the original simple instinctual responses became overlaid by conscious and conditioned beliefs and attitudes. The sexual aura surrounding body hair was transferred, by what the modern analyst would term 'displacement', to apply also to head hair and, together with its apparently magic power to regenerate itself, this made all hair a positive symbol of virility and fertility. As such it was sacrificed throughout the ancient world as a substitute for life itself, and even for chastity. This direct sexual symbolism of hair sacrifice was made most explicit in the rites at the temple of Astarte, Phoenician goddess of fertility, at Byblus. There, at the annual mourning for the dead Adonis, women had the choice of shaving off their hair or prostituting themselves to strangers. The goddess was prepared to accept the sacrifice of chastity or of hair, because both represented fertility.

Deeply rooted in this age-old belief in the sexual power of hair, two parallel myths have emerged. The best known one, that hairiness indicates virility in men, is echoed in the lesser known idea that strong body-

October 1971
The article was from a book by Wendy Cooper called *Hair*, on why women should stop removing it. *Nova*'s publisher became worried by Harri Peccinotti's picture. It was given the 'okay' when it was explained as being an armpit – although in fact...

'As long as it is difficult to recruit sufficient whites to sweep the streets, man the buses, work as hospital orderlies and that sort of thing the blacks will get the jobs that white people won't take...'

(MARCUS LIPTON, M.P. LABOUR)

47

BRIXTON

-the ghetto that Britain built

By Peter Martin/Photographs by Robert Golden

November 1971
Robert Golden's photographs for 'The ghetto that Britain built', an article by Peter Martin on Brixton in south London.

Glad to accept the landlord's law because, in the end, it was the only one that counted

By the year 2000 Britain will probably have a black helot class unless the educational system is radically altered

LET THEM EAT CAKE

Cookery by Caroline Conran
Illustration by Bentley/Farrell/Burnett
Photographed by Bob Croxford

WALNUT MIXER CAKE

BOODLES CLUB CAKE

MARBLE CAKE

QUICK ICING

CHOCOLATE ICING

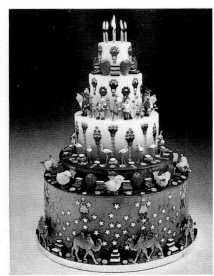

March 1971
Cakes by Caroline Conran, illustration by Bentley/Farrell/Burnett.

April 1971
Illustration by Alan Cracknell for an article on wild flowers used in cooking.

February 1971
Illustration by Gilbert Stone for Maggie Blenkinsop's short story 'It's raining terrible out here'.

Right
September 1971
Tony Evans had the idea for his classic photograph of onions in an onion shaped glass before any article was written. For the idea to become reality he had to convince David Hillman to persuade Caroline Conran to write a piece on pickles. She agreed, eventually.

The trick was achieved using a perspex 'glass' with a plugged opening at the back. Evans didn't actually like the look of real pickling onions – they weren't white enough. So mature spring onions, each one carefully trimmed and peeled, were used instead.

1972

Evening Standard

CITY PRICES

CARNAGE AT MUNICH

Hostages killed after ambush

Do you own a pair of scissors? Then you're on your way to £13,133

Games—on or off?

These were not games they were playing.

Embodiment of superpower confrontation.

When film sex had no hang-ups.

The year

Britain finally signed the Treaty of Rome. Two Israeli athletes and six other hostages died as Arab terrorism visited the Olympic Games in Munich. Idi Amin expelled thousands of Asians from Uganda. In Londonderry British troops opened fire on 'Bloody Sunday', killing thirteen demonstrators. The miners' strike caused power cuts and another state of emergency, culminating in the introduction of the infamous Three-Day Week. The value of the pound sank to an all-time low; interest rates were the highest since before the First World War. Nixon diverted attention from his domestic troubles by visiting Moscow and Peking. The Tutankhamun exhibition opened in London. The first pre-recorded home videos became available, and Clive Sinclair introduced the first pocket calculator. It was Marc Bolan's chart year, also remembered for *American Pie* and *Vincent* from Don Maclean. The West End went strangely religious with *Jesus Christ Superstar* and *Godspell*. John Betjeman became Poet Laureate. Bobby Fischer beat Boris Spassky to become world chess champion. Marlon Brando made *The Godfather* and *Last Tango in Paris* which, so the story goes, did wonders for the sales of butter. And in Paris ex-king Edward VIII died, as the Duke of Windsor.

Right
March 1972
Photograph by Jeanloup Sieff (despite the management's reservations).

March 1972

Peter Howe's photographs for Carolyn Faulder's article on children's rights: 'Make this the year you liberate your child',

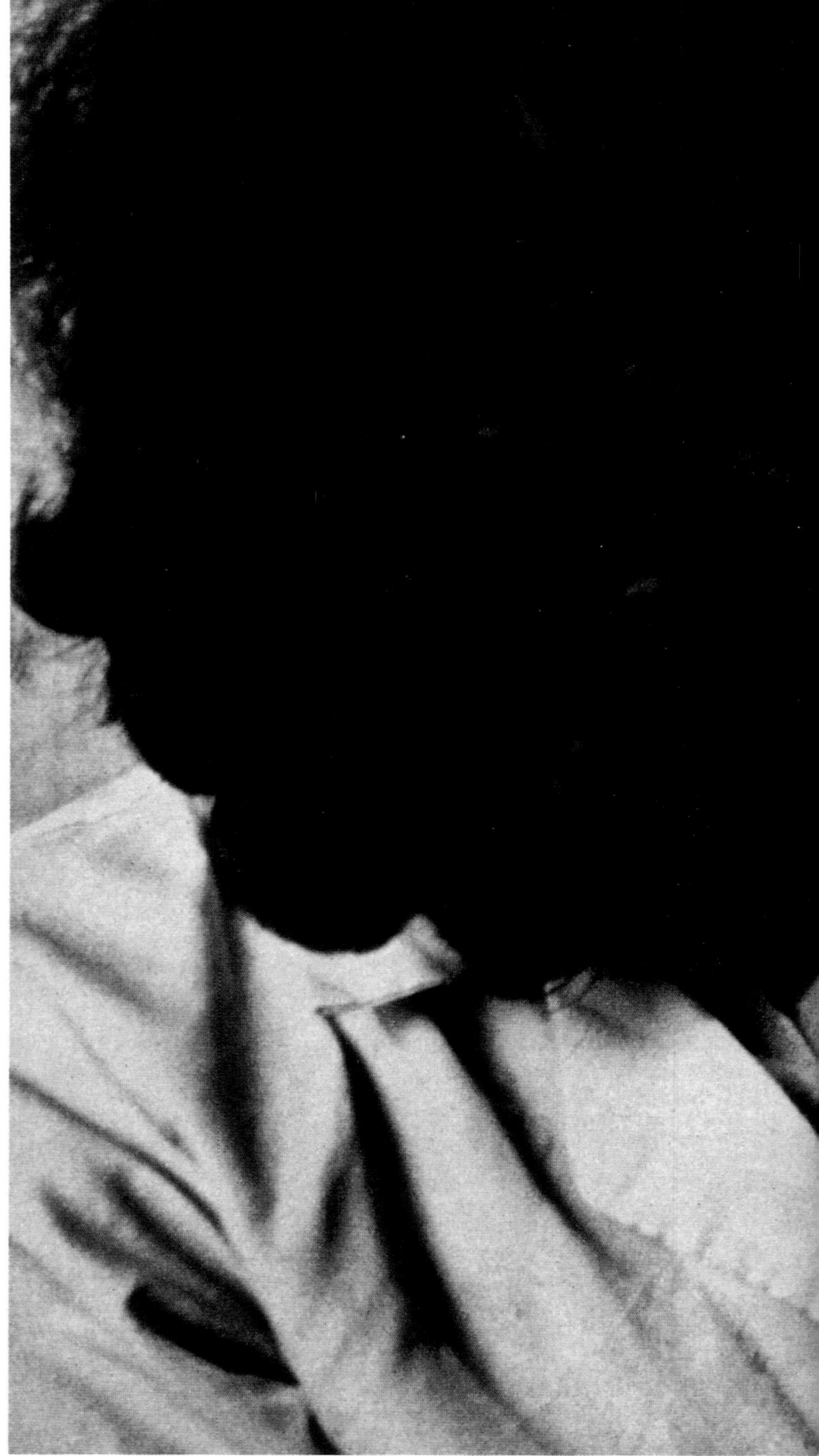

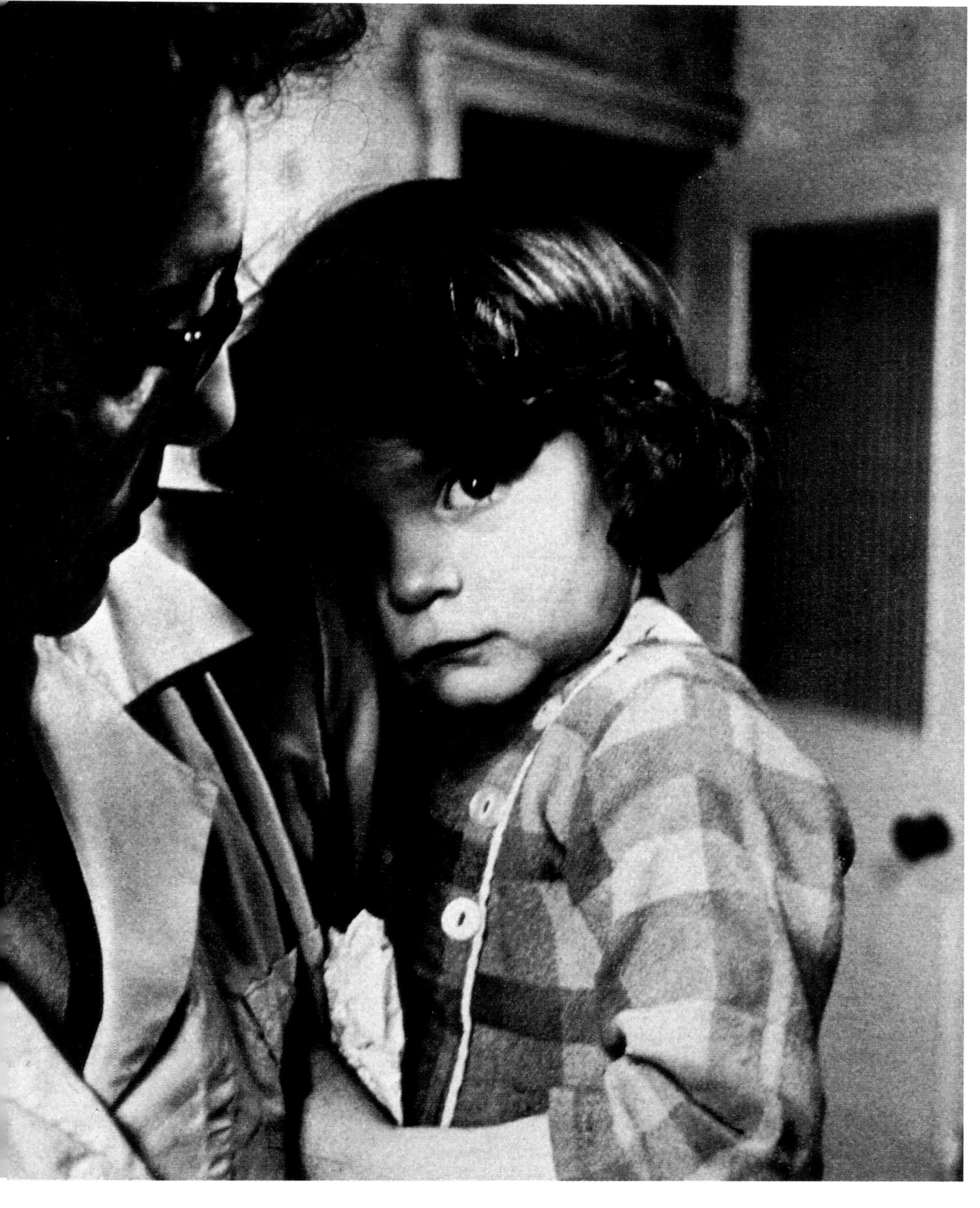

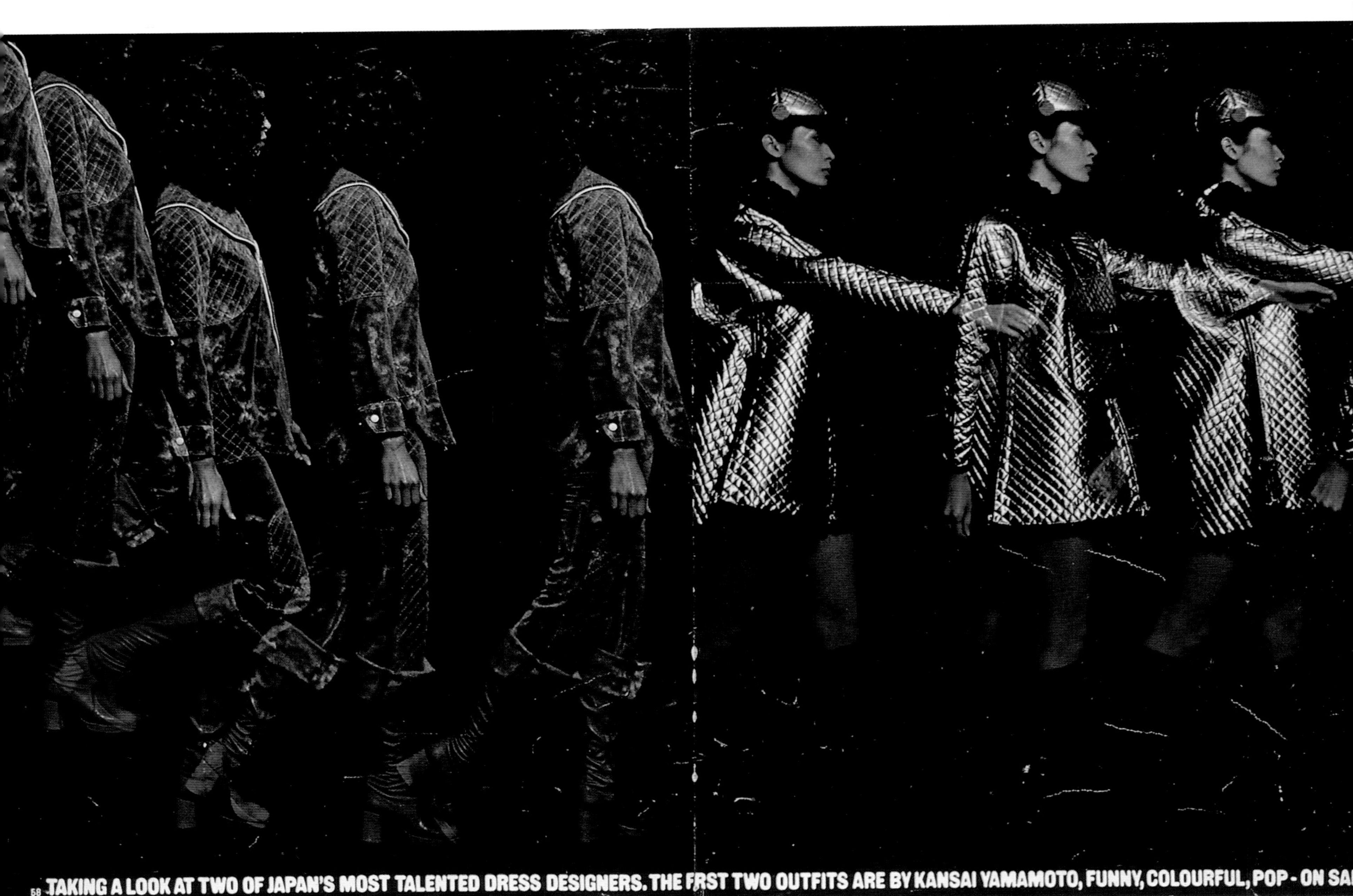
58
TAKING A LOOK AT TWO OF JAPAN'S MOST TALENTED DRESS DESIGNERS. THE FRST TWO OUTFITS ARE BY KANSAI YAMAMOTO, FUNNY, COLOURFUL, POP - ON

HERE AT BOSTON 151 WHO LAUNCHED HIM LAST YEAR. ALL THE REST ARE BY ISSEY MIYAKE, A VERY TALENTED AND ORIGINAL DESIGNER WHO DISLIKES REVIVING OLD

Above and overleaf
April 1972
A trip to Japan by art director David Hillman, photographer Harri Peccinotti and writer Irma Kurtz produced, amongst other things, the idea for a seven-foot frieze on the work of up-and-coming designers Kansai Yamamoto and Issey Miyake. (Once again, you had to buy two copies as the spreads were printed back-to-back.)

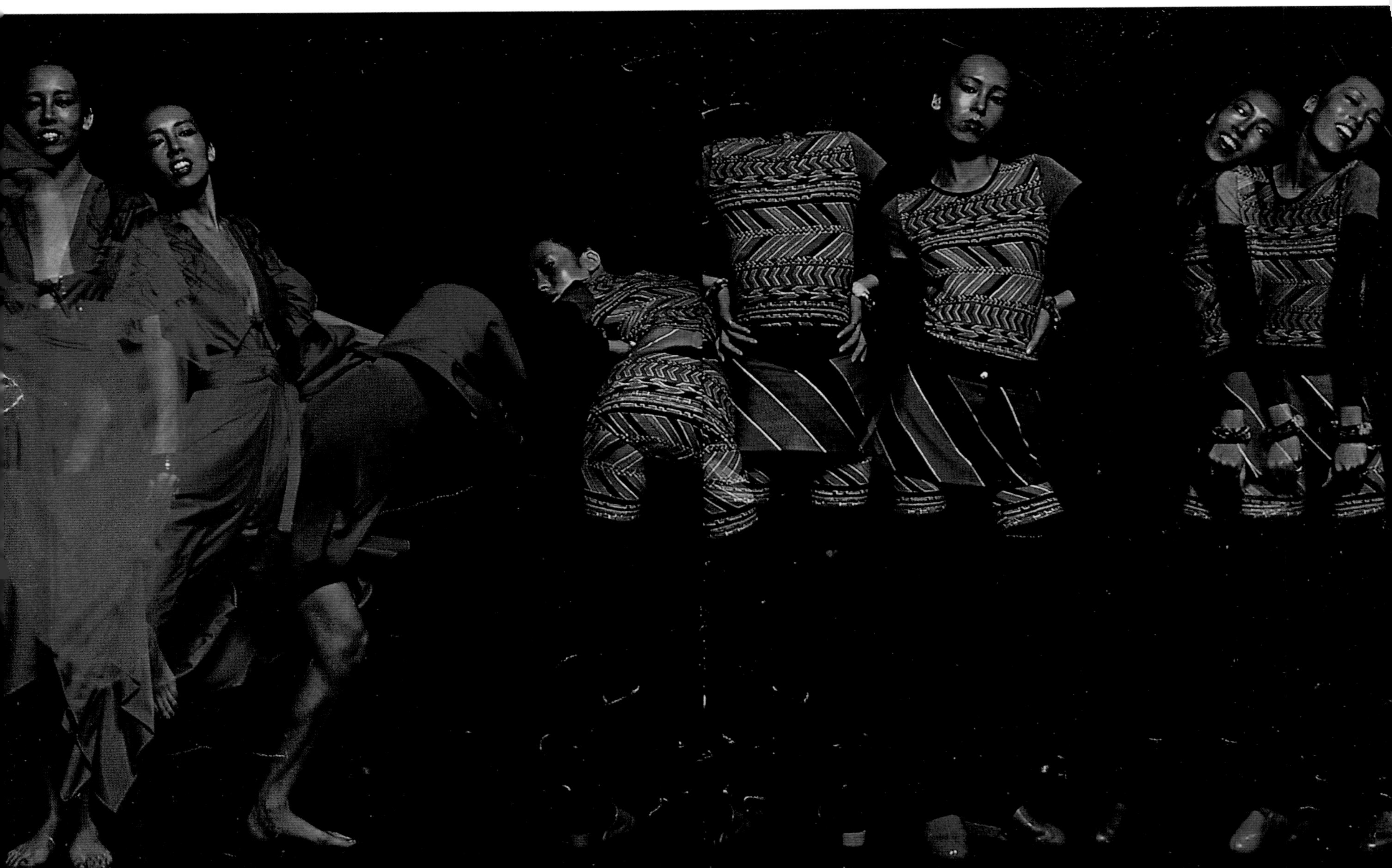
FASHIONS. HE THINKS FROM TOP TO BOTTOM, DESIGNING THE ACCESSORIES, CLOTHES AND UNDIES. SOME OF HIS CLOTHES ARE ON SALE HERE AT ESCALADE. FASHIO

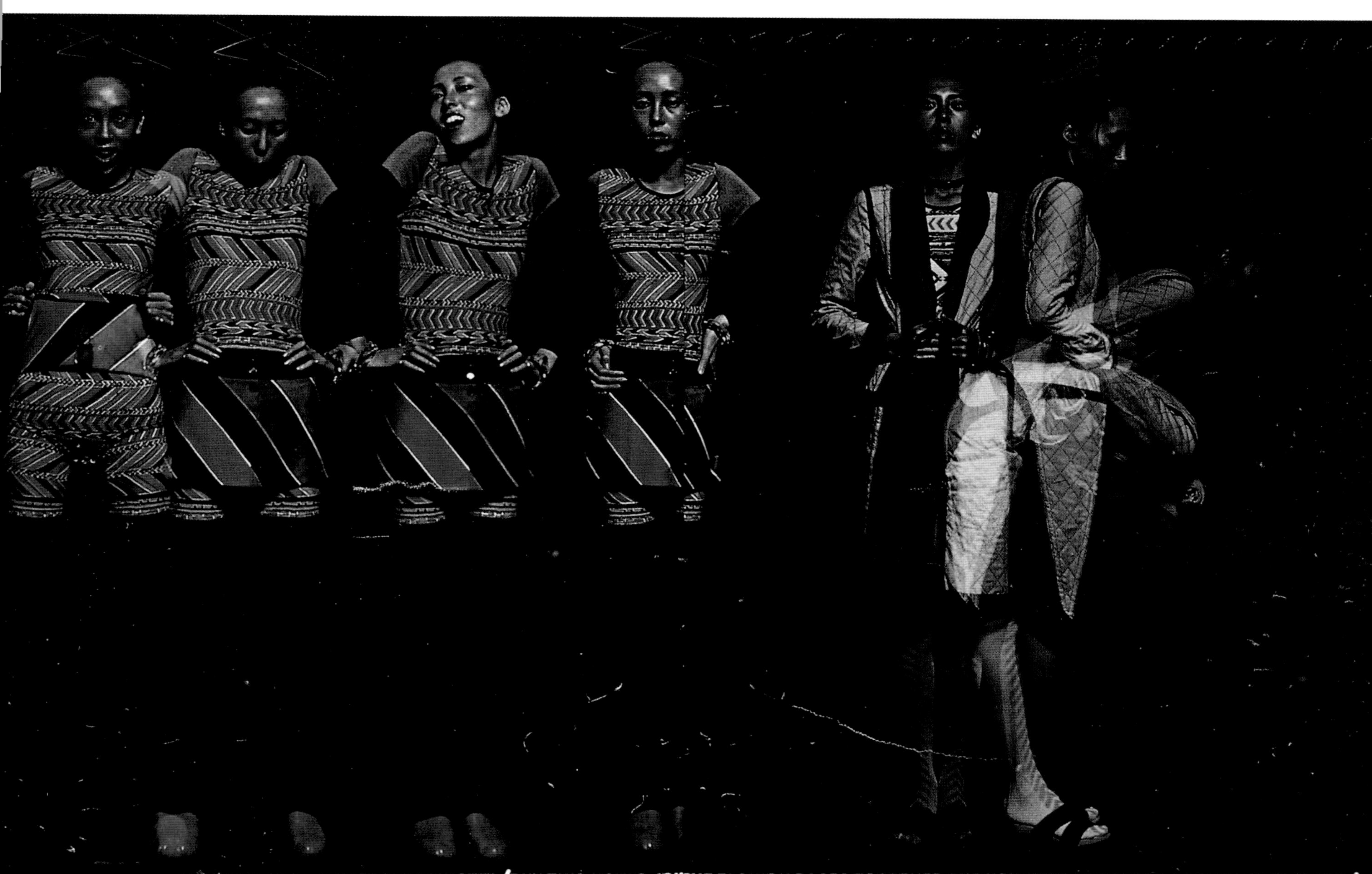
BY CAROLINE BAKER/PHOTOGRAPHS BY HARRI PECCINOTTI. (BUY TWO NOVAS, JOIN THE FASHION PAGES TOGETHER AND YOU HAVE A BEAUTIFUL SEVEN-FOOT FRIEZE.)

Stockists on page 105

May 1972
'Good ghastly taste', a fashion feature by Caroline Baker, showed how to use the gaudy and vulgar with controlled style. Photographs by Harri Peccinotti.

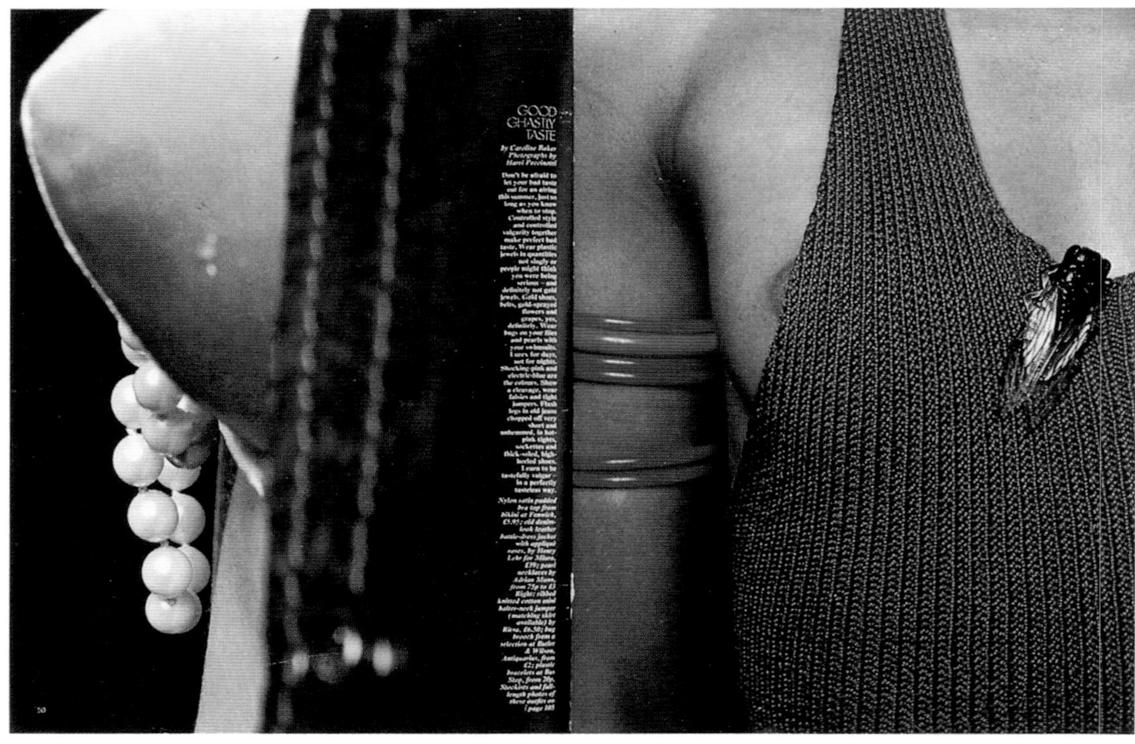

GOOD GHASTLY TASTE

by Caroline Baker
Photographs by Harri Peccinotti

Don't be afraid to let your bad taste out for an airing this summer, just so long as you know when to stop. Controlled style and controlled vulgarity together make perfect bad taste. Wear plastic jewels in quantities not singly or people might think you were being serious – and definitely not gold jewels. Gold shoes, belts, gold-sprayed flowers and grapes, yes, definitely. Wear bugs on your [illegible] and pearls with your swimsuits. Lurex for days, not for nights. Shocking-pink and electric-blue are the colours. Show a cleavage, wear falsies and tight jumpers. Flash legs in old jeans chopped off very short and unhemmed, in hot-pink tights, sockettes and thick-soled, high-heeled shoes. Learn to be tastefully vulgar – in a perfectly tasteless way.

Nylon satin padded bra top from Bikini at Fenwick, £5.95; old denim-look leather battle-dress jacket with appliqué roses, by [illegible], £39; pearl necklaces by Adrian Mann, from 75p to £3. Right: ribbed knitted cotton mini halter-neck jumper (matching skirt available) by [illegible], £6.50; bug brooch from a selection at Butler & Wilson, Antiquaries, from £2; plastic bracelets at Bus Stop, from 30p. Stockists and full-length photos of these outfits on [page 103

The *Nova* that never was

It all happened because *Cosmopolitan* was going to launch the first issue of its UK edition in March. *Nova* staff were keen to upstage the American interloper. A good idea was needed.

And this was it. Edward Heath had been Prime Minister since 1970 and there was still no sign of his ever getting married. What would a dating agency come up with if given the task of finding him a wife?

Heath's details were sent to a well-known computer dating agency under the name of David Jenkins the assistant editor. Four candidates were duly produced and the idea was explained to each of them. One stood head-and-shoulders above the others (she shall remain nameless). She entered into the spirit of the game with a wealth of good ideas of how she would change her man.

The complete issue was printed and about to be distributed when the lady in question dropped her bombshell. She was married. Her husband was in jail in India. She and her daughter were being hunted by police all over Europe for drug smuggling offences – and they were about to give themselves up.

The editor Gillian Cooke told the management and the issue was scrapped. (In fact it was fed to the boilers at Battersea power station, so it did generate some heat.) Hugh Cudlipp, head of IPC, heard about what had gone on and let it be known that he saw the affair as a lost opportunity for both *Nova* and the *Daily Mirror*, not least because of the exposé they could have run on computer dating.

As it happened the woman was cleared of all charges and a number of Scotland Yard detectives ended up with egg on their faces; there were even some resignations, and a book was later published on the affair.

The substitute March issue came out three weeks late. *Cosmopolitan* knew nothing of all this – but they must have wondered at their good fortune, with their first issue having the streets all to itself.

EXCLUSIVE SOUVENIR PICTURES! Meet the bride we found for Ted on page 36

BRITAIN'S GREATEST MAGAZINE MARCH 1972 20p

ARE YOU SURE YOU'RE GOOD IN BED?
SEE PAGE 56

My mother, by Penelope Mortimer
See page 68

LIVING WITH THE MEMORY OF HIS FIRST WIFE!
SEE PAGE 62

SCOOP!

Ted weds

'No more boats' says bride

BY NOVA REPORTER, FEBRUARY 30TH

IN WHAT MUST be the surprise event of the century, Prime Minister Heath was married yesterday in Caxton Hall. The wedding, attended only by close friends, was aptly blessed with glorious spring sunshine.

Despite London's tightest security net ever, the shock news leaked out and women wept in the streets as the happy couple sped to a secret reception. The newly-weds were later spotted leaving Heathrow for a honeymoon in Venice. 'There'll be some changes made,' the bride beamed enigmatically.

March 1972 (unpublished)
The cover was a spoof front page of the *Daily Mirror*. Management pressure to include a line pointing out that it was a 'frolic' was resisted by staff threatening to resign.

'I like giving dinner parties but I'm not inviting all his terrible boating cronies. I'd really mix up our party guests so we'd have a lively evening. Mind you, I'd insist that Ted went on a diet to lose his middle-aged spread, so it wouldn't be much fun for him'

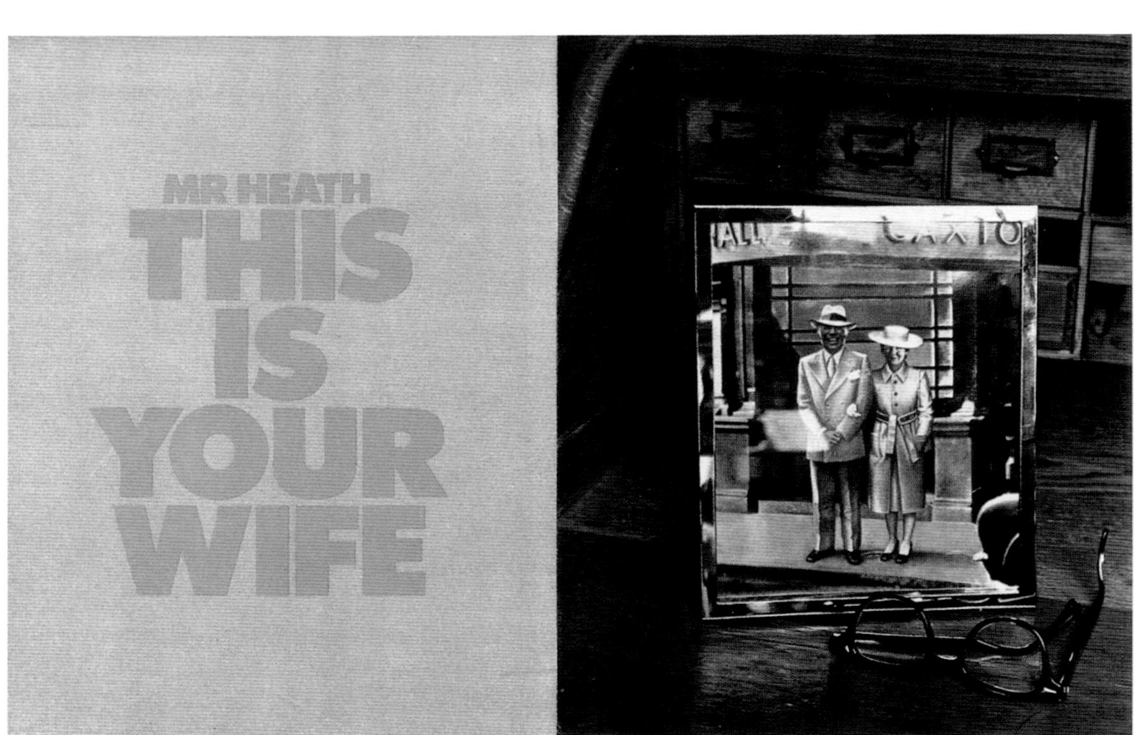
MR HEATH
THIS
IS
YOUR
WIFE

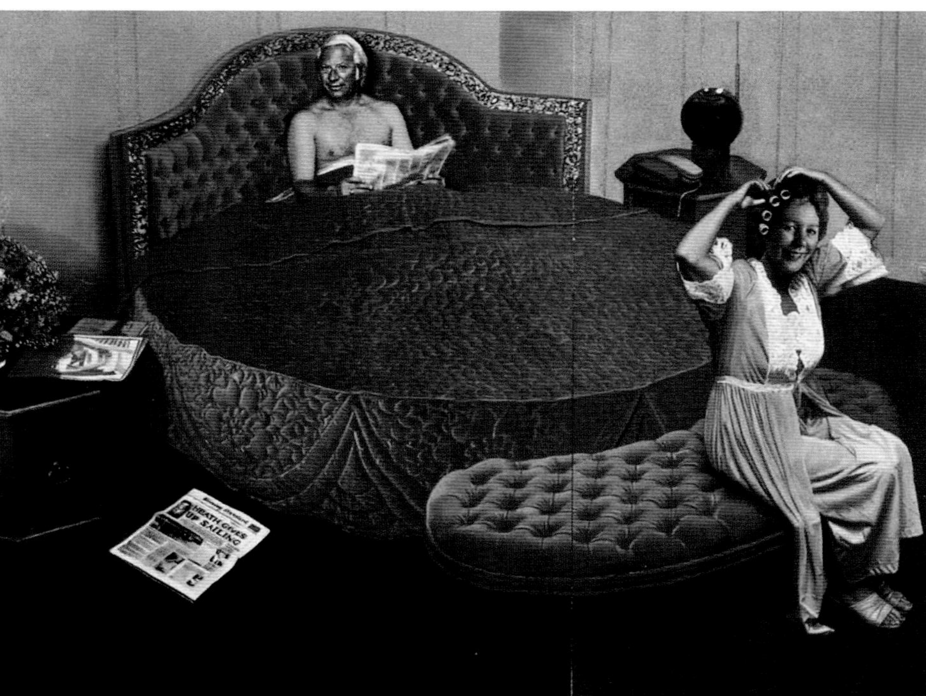

'I've always been early to bed and early to rise and you can't change the habits of a lifetime, so it's lights out at 10.30 and no government work in the bedroom. And another thing . . . I can't stand men who wear pyjamas, it's so old fashioned'

Dinner guests left to right around the table:
Mrs Manson
Lovelace Watkins
Jacquie Onassis
Enoch Powell
Angela Davis
Harold Macmillan
Phyllis Diller
Edward Heath
Bernadette Devlin and Roisin Elizabeth
Patrick Campbell
Bette Davis
Lord George-Brown
Elizabeth Taylor
Jimmy Reid

42

March 1972 (unpublished)
For the Nova that never was (see previous page), illustrator Jean-Paul Goude worked with the Prime Minister's prospective wife on three scenes. The first was the wedding, which was to be at Caxton Hall. The second was how the bedroom at Number 10 would be redesigned. Finally, she drew up a wonderfully mischievous guest list and seating plan for the first dinner party they would throw as a married couple. This had notables such as Enoch Powell sitting next to black activist Angela Davis, and Bernadette Devlin accompanied by her (recently revealed) illegitimate daughter.

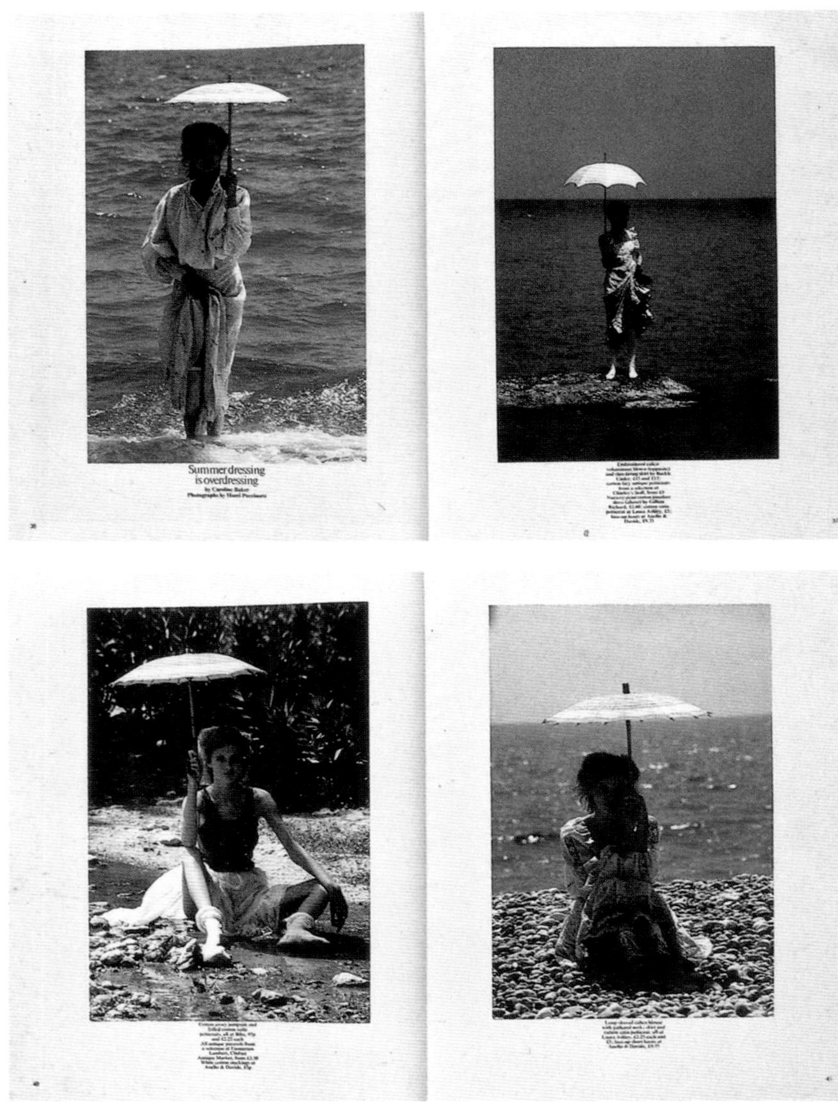

July 1972
Summer dressing. Photographs by Harri Peccinotti.

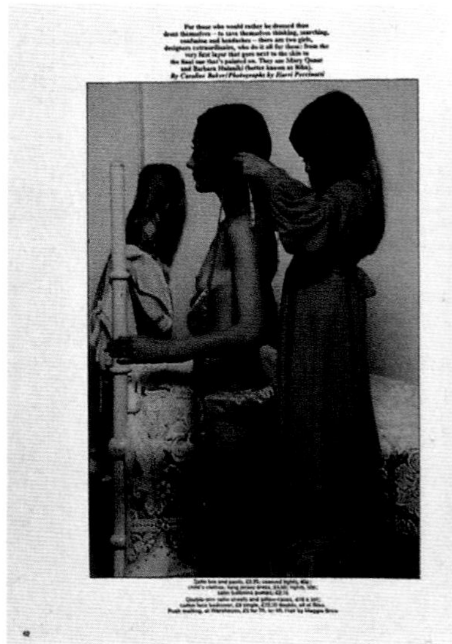

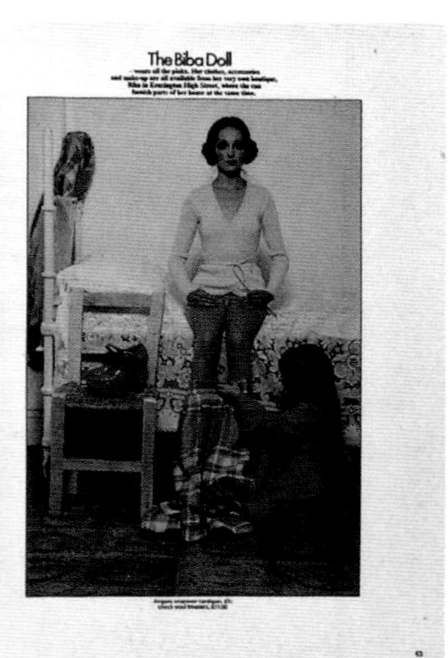

Right and far right
November 1972
The two designers Mary Quant and Biba's Barbara Hulanicki offered everything from underwear to make-up – so you could be a Mary Quant doll or a Biba doll. Photographs by Harri Peccinotti.

78

albert's war

by Anne Merrill/Illustration by Edda Kochl

Albert spent the summer of 1944 slicing sandwiches. It was the last year of the war. The Japanese were being driven out of Malaya, American tanks were rumbling into Europe and Private Albert Simmons was slicing bread in Brentwood, Essex.

Years earlier he had been evacuated to the country with a label tied to his gas-mask and he forgot about bombs and sirens. But at 18 he was sent back to London and found there was still a war going on. He was tested and measured, issued with boots and a gun and a scratchy uniform, then driven to an Army camp in Brentwood where he was to live in a tent with a soldier called Barlow. They sliced bread.

The tent wasn't too bad. Albert was easily pleased. He had been slicing bread for the past three months, at night, sleeping whenever he could on piles of warm crumbs and lying sleepless in his tent all day while the real soldiers strutted up and down outside. Six nights a week slicing bread with Barlow who played *The Lily of Laguna* on his squeeze-box and had once been court-martialled.

Albert thought this would go on indefinitely, until the war was over, and he was only dimly aware that the real soldiers were being sent out every day with packets of nicely sliced sandwiches to join troop ships sailing from Newhaven to the coast of France.

He spoke to some of the soldiers before they went. They were as young as he and they themselves were not sure why they were going or if they would have to fight. Barlow seemed very relaxed about it all. He had his own philosophy, and Albert could have it for free, seeing as how they would ship him off to battle soon enough. Barlow had seen action; he had seen plenty of action. But mostly from a distance. He was 31 and still alive, wasn't he? Doing a cushy job like slicing sandwiches instead of crawling through a muddy field in Normandy with a rifle on his back. Been demoted, of course, and served his detention for disobedience but, since he'd prefer a clean prison bed to a muddy field any day, who was complaining?

Barlow's philosophy was based on his own form of passive resistance: don't obey an order unless it is in your direct interest to do so. He explained the underlying logic to Albert. Orders were simply bluff; the threat of punishment could not be carried out in battle, so if you were ordered to run through machine-gun fire and refused you might be punished afterwards for disobeying the order but at least you had survived the bullets.

'There's an old Chinese proverb,' said Barlow; 'better a live beggar than a dead millionaire.' Albert agreed with this sentiment although he vaguely remembered reading stories in which traitors were summarily shot and it was considered better to be a dead hero than a live coward. But perhaps he wouldn't need to make the choice.

The nights went by. While Barlow played the old songs on his squeeze-box, Albert sang. They performed *The Quartermaster's Stores*, *The Orderly's Song*, *There's A Long, Long Trail A-Winding* and *Ave Maria*. Albert was perfectly happy. He enjoyed talking to Barlow who told him about civilian life before the war, when buying and selling scrap metal brought in £30 a week, which he lost every Friday at the greyhound track. Barlow was as philosophical about this as he was about everything. When Albert told him about the drawings he used to do at home, Barlow found a thin pen and some black ink and encouraged Albert to produce sketches of himself surrounded by bread, of Barlow playing the squeeze-box and of the row of tents in the field outside.

Albert sketched away happily until the day he was marked down for a week's training and had to leave Barlow and the bread and start marching up and down with the others, throwing a rifle onto his shoulder and off again, and standing forlornly in a queue waiting to learn how to fire an anti-tank gun, which made an appalling bang and jerked back in his hand, splitting his palm open. His hand was bandaged up and he did no more gun practice for a couple of days. The others laughed at him and Albert knew the trouble was that he *looked* like a soldier – he was short but very muscular – yet he had no talent for it at all. He had the temperament of a thin, bespectacled weakling, but his body was the wrong shape. They joked about that, too. Sometimes as Albert stood in the showers they would strip his towel away and make remarks about a 'heavyweight howitzer' which baffled him completely, not knowing a howitzer from a hand grenade.

He felt out of place amongst the other soldiers and assumed that at the end of the week he would go back to slicing bread, but it was too late. His name and number had passed along the production line and Private A Simmons was ordered to report to the parade ground with all his equipment for departure at 08.30 hours.

And so Albert sailed reluctantly towards France with his kitbag and his rifle, some sheet music Barlow had given him and a book of Chinese proverbs in the pocket of his battle-dress.

It was the end of summer and very hot. Albert was not sick during the crossing but when they arrived in Normandy he felt weak and exhausted. His unit had to reach a château 20 miles inland before nightfall. They marched down straight roads in single file, spaced out because of the shells and away from the verges because of the mines. When they arrived at the château they were to dig slit-trenches and prepare for possible enemy attack in the morning. Albert was horrified. Although the whole situation seemed to indicate that he was supposed to fight, and the issue of hand grenades and field dressings made this almost certain, he could not shake the conviction that bread-slicing was his proper role in this war and that coming to France was not going to alter it.

After a few miles he became demoralised. Marching was tiring because of the heat and the load he had on his back. As well as his personal belongings, blankets, groundsheet, shovel, water-bottle and ammunition, Albert had been given the Piat to carry. Apart from his natural mistrust of weapons, Albert detested the Piat. It was a large, cylindrical, cheap-looking gun for firing shells at tanks; it was heavy, he was not sure how it worked and he didn't know how to carry it. He tried balancing it across his shoulders, but the coarse canvas sling attached to both ends became tangled up with the shovel on his back. He was carrying it in his arms like a baby, shifting it from side to side, when an officer walked briskly down the line, pausing by Albert and the Piat.

'I should sling that, my man,' he said and walked on. It took some time for this blessed order to penetrate Albert's numbed brain. Sling it! What a charitable and unmilitary thing to suggest! He threw it over the next hedge and it disappeared amongst some nettles.

When they arrived at the château it was almost dark and Albert, happy to be relieved of his burden, lay down on the grass and watched the sunset. There was an old church next to the château; it might have been Norman, and Albert could see the graveyard over a low wall. It was very peaceful. Officers and sergeants stood around discussing the disposition of weapons.

'Bren guns by the stable, and the Piat covering the gate. Where's the Piat?'

'The Piat?' Albert said innocently. 'I slung it over a hedge six miles back, you told me to.'

Afterwards, Albert's fellow soldiers said he would have been given the works if he weren't so obviously stupid and the officers fed up with the long march and the heat. He had the devil's luck. Albert was sent back to find the Piat while the others dug trenches and pitched their tents.

He wandered along the quiet road, singing, enjoying the solitude. There was hardly a sign of war here, except for a few bloated cows and horses that lay rotting in the fields. He started looking for the Piat but soon realised that one hedge was much like another and he had little chance of finding it. But he couldn't go back without it. So he climbed into a field and lay on the grass and thought about his fellow soldiers preparing for an enemy attack, and the lost Piat, and the whole absurdity of trying to win a war he had never started. There was someone else in his field. Two men were walking carefully beside the hedge.

'Qu'est que c'est?'

He stood up and shouted, 'British soldier!'

'Tais toi!'

'I'm looking for a Piat,' he said more quietly, 'a round gun, like this; and my unit's down the road waiting for it – you *are* French, aren't you?'

The men smiled and Albert saw that one of them had the Piat slung over his shoulder.

A beautiful plan was forming in

79

Daddy's girl

by Mark Steadman/Illustration by Philippe Weissbecker

'It has to be did,' he said, speaking the words under his breath, as if he were afraid someone would hear him.

First light would come soon, the East was just beginning to turn grey, but the low moon still let him see the black outline of the house – dark now. He had turned out the light in the kitchen when he had come into the yard.

He worried about the lantern, was afraid Frances might see it – though he knew she couldn't see it from their bedroom window. She would have to get up and come into the kitchen. But she might do that. She would have been missing him from the bed all night now, and it might have waked her up and started her looking for him.

He began by actually cutting some pieces of kindling – thinking and planning after it was too late to do any good. He had burned a hole in the sheet with a cigarette. Tomorrow he would tell Frances it had been an accident, while he was talking to Jackie. She wouldn't think anything about it.

He stood the lightwood on end on the stump that he used for a chopping block, splitting off the pieces in long, jagged splinters, trying to make them come off clean. He had a deft touch, but he was nervous now in spite of himself, thinking ahead. He would have to use his left hand and he might blink too.

'It's got to be did,' he said again.

He had trouble getting the position right, at first propping it up over a piece of the lightwood. But it didn't feel steady enough to him, so he put it down on the block itself, curling the other fingers back out of the way, extending them along the sides of the stump.

He held the axe close to the head, not raising it very high because he was afraid that he wouldn't be able to control it. Then he thought that it might not come clean, and he would have to try more than once. He braced the handle of the axe along the inside of his arm, clamping it into his side with his elbow, still thinking he was going to miss. He was afraid that if he thought about it too much he would begin to tremble, that he might falter at the last minute. The main thing was to make it clean – a single stroke. It would be hard enough to explain anyway, but he thought he could manage if he did it clean.

He counted to steady himself. 'One . . . two . . . three . . .'

The blood welled at the end of the stump of the finger, a swollen red bubble, shiny, pumping off big, slow drops. He closed his eyes, holding the wrist tightly in his left hand, squeezing it to staunch the flow of blood and slow the pumping of the bubble. Behind the lids he could see the other eyes, staring at him open and wide in the moon-filled room. He could feel the other hands on his wrist, locked and still. Holding on – the way you would hold on to a spear thrust into your body, not wanting it to move. Able to bear it if it just wouldn't work in the wound. Not even wanting it out, but just wanting it not to move.

He let the bubble drop on to the block, then another, and another. Covering it. Covering the block and the axe head.

'Call Dr Smoaks, Frances,' he said. His face was chalky white and dead-looking, and his eyes seemed to be receding into their sockets, like lead cooling in a mould.

'Good God, Henry. What you done?' said Mrs Sipple.

'Call Dr Smoaks,' he said. 'Then get me a rag or something to tie it up.'

When she left, he took it quickly from the block, still holding the wrist tightly. He went to the pump-house and put it on the shelf where he kept the tools for the pump, laying it in the back where it wouldn't be seen. Then he walked back to the house and sat down on the steps to the back porch, not wanting to drip blood on the floors inside the house. He was sitting there when the sun came up.

Later, in the afternoon, he went back down to the pump-house. He worried about putting it there, thinking he should have left it on the stump. The ants had gotten to it, and he let them take it. He didn't know what to do about it now anyway. Frances hadn't asked. She had been too worried about him for that. The next time he looked it was gone. A rat probably. He had seen one at the pump-house now and then.

And so it ended like that. With the rat taking it away.

'It's a girl.' Dr Smoaks stood in the Sipple kitchen. It was a cold October night and the windows were sweating, running in black streaks on the black panes.

Mr Sipple stood by the table, frowning slightly. 'Well . . .' he said.

'Don't act that way, Henry,' said Dr Smoaks. 'And don't let Frances see you. It takes a real man to blow the balls clean off.'

'First one ought to be a boy,' said Henry, not looking at him.

'First one ought to be what it is,' said Dr Smoaks. 'It ain't for you to say.' 'I was counting on a boy.'

'You ain't got no right to count on nothing,' said Dr Smoaks. 'Now give me one of them cigars and a cup of coffee.' He sat down at the table. Henry pushed the box of King Edwards toward him. Dr Smoaks opened it and took out a cigar. He rolled it around the edge of the flame to get it started even, puffing the smoke up toward the ceiling. Mr Sipple brought the coffee pot from the stove and poured.

'Frances had a hard time, Henry,' said Dr Smoaks, fanning at the blue cloud that enveloped his head.

'She's all right, ain't she?' said Henry. He stood holding the pot in his hard, balled fist.

'Well, but she had a very hard time.' Dr Smoaks took another pull at the cigar, then sipped the coffee, holding the cup in both hands.

'Is she tore?'

'Always tears a little.'

'But is she tore bad?'

'Pretty bad,' said Dr Smoaks, sipping the coffee. 'I want you to stay away from her till I tell you not to.'

'How long?'

'Can't tell exactly. Seven or eight weeks anyways.'

'Well, but she's going to be all right?'

'I think she's going to be all right, but you got to keep away from her. Till I say so.'

The two men sat at the kitchen table drinking coffee and not looking at each other.

'It ain't going to be *that* long,' said Dr Smoaks. 'It was going to be six weeks anyway. It's always six weeks.'

Mr Sipple didn't say anything.

'It could have been worse,' said Dr Smoaks. 'Think about Dero Mullins. Mae nearly died when Annie came last spring. Dero ain't been able to lay a finger on her . . . not nothing else either . . . for . . .,' he counted on his fingers, '. . . six months now. Six months, Henry. You think about that.'

'You sure she's going to be all right?'

'I'm sure. I just don't know how long, is all. I'll tell you what,' said Dr Smoaks, 'if it's got to be longer than seven weeks, I'll get you fixed up with Maggie Poat.'

Mr Sipple looked at him.

'Course you needn't go telling Frances I said that,' he added. 'That's privileged information. I'm *your* doctor too.'

The corners of Mr Sipple's mouth were pulling up in a little smile. 'You think you could maybe arrange that?' he said. 'Pull some strings and fix it up? Maggie ain't bad. You going to fix it so I wouldn't have to stand in line or something?'

'I'm not talking about what I'd do for Maggie. I'm talking about what I'd do for *you*. Maggie's the best there is,' said Dr Smoaks.

'Reckon it's the nigger blood?' said Mr Sipple.

'I wouldn't say so,' said Dr Smoaks, 'though I wouldn't say no either.'

'She's a lot of woman,' said Mr Sipple.

'She's the best there is,' said Dr Smoaks.

'I'd of thought when Netty come it'd of loosened her up too much. Put her out of business.'

'Needn't be,' said Dr Smoaks.

'Netty was a big baby.'

'Don't make no difference,' said Dr Smoaks. He looked at Mr Sipple. 'You ain't worried about Frances that way?' he said.

'Well, no,' said Mr Sipple. 'It crossed my mind.'

'Don't you worry about Frances,' Dr Smoaks said. 'Just stay away from her till I tell you to. You couldn't even tell the difference. It's going to be better than ever. Maybe by Christmas.'

'Is this one big as Netty?'

'Netty was a big baby.'

'How big is this one?'

'Seven and a half I'd say. Just guessing. Seven and a half or seven and three quarters, something like that.'

'She look all right?'

'Ain't none of them look too good just at first. She's all right.'

'Netty is going to be a better looking woman than her ma.'

'Looks ain't all.'

'She's going to have some of the other, too.'

'God damn, Henry, how you think you can tell that? She ain't but five years old.' 'You can tell.'

'Not me,' said Dr Smoaks. 'I can't tell nothing at all. Just looks like a five-year-old girl to me. Little skinny.'

'Look at her face,' said Mr Sipple.

'Freckled,' said Dr Smoaks. He looked at Mr Sipple for a minute without saying anything. 'I didn't know you had the gift of *prophecy*, Henry,' he said. 'I sure as hell didn't know about that. You speak in tongues too?'

Mr Sipple didn't say anything.

'I'm going to have to sit right here until Osie brings that daughter of yours down here and shows it to you. Then you can look at her face, or whatever it is you got to look at to get it straight, and then you can tell me what line of work she's going to follow when she grows up, and whether her wisdom teeth are going to come through or not, and who's going to get her cherry.'

63

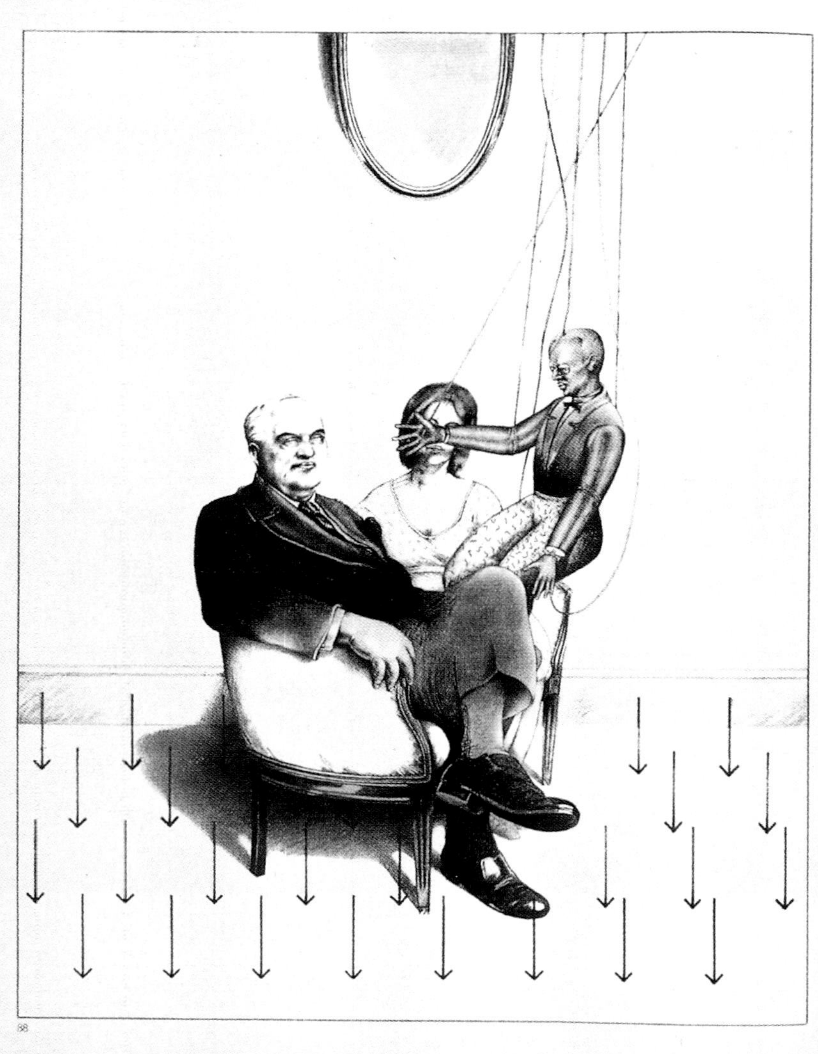

88

Sarah Goodman (wife of Advocate Goodman, as she would be quick to tell you) plotted out her week's activities. She did this at her bedroom desk because it was private, and because she liked its pale pinks and frilled lace lamp-shades. It was only since their house had been sold that each hour of the day had to be accounted for. The Goodmans and their only child Paul had lived in one of those old Johannesburg houses of Parktown, or, as Sarah would have put it – in one of those *distinguished* old Parktown homes – a *Sir* Herbert Baker house, built in the nineteen-twenties. Sarah always smiled when she talked of that house – with that gentle smile she did not know she reserved for the tenderly-remembered dead.

They had left the house five years ago and although the garden still bloomed, and the house thrived with a young family, it had as much life for Sarah, who often passed it, as the cement-coloured tombstone of her mother's grave. Yet she grieved for that house – for its cool spaces, its massive beamed living room with its giant untidy fire-place, for its trees gone anatomical with age.

And now she was confronted with this flat, shapeless, undistinguished – *flat* – too geometric, too pale to accommodate their outsize stinkwood dining-room suite, which, because of its proportions, Sarah regarded as majestic. No, they had only leftovers, and the breakfast-room suite now served the dining room, and the spare-room suite engulfed the marital room. Still, it was a comfortable flat – she could not deny *that* – it had two bathrooms, and Louis still had his study . . . And now that those terrible days of the share-swindle seemed extinct – and they could well afford it – what would be the point of buying another house with Paul grown up? He was a doctor and entitled to a life of his own, as Sarah agreed – besides, his bedroom was the largest in the flat – Sarah had done it up as a study. It was a successful room, leftover furniture notwithstanding.

You could do a lot with leftovers, if you tried hard enough, and made the best of what you had. Look at Whyte, the cook, who unlike her old Esther (of 15 years' service) had not refused to come with them to the flat, even though he had to live in a cell-like room on the top floor, in one of those 'locations in the sky' where women visitors were forbidden and, for that matter, men, too. Sometimes, Sarah thought with an illicit half-shamed smile (who would believe that she could think like this?) Whyte was the most meaningful of all the leftovers of the old house, even more meaningful than the desk she sat at, and the desk was at least 300 years old.

It was almost as if Whyte was part of her most secret inner life: with his little immaculate beard tacked to his polished black face, he had, for Sarah a ridiculous sense of *class* (he claimed that he was descended from an old chief or something like that). He enjoyed a unique sense of dignity and disdain peculiar to the domestic snob. Sarah had noticed that her own sister, Doris, seemed uncomfortable with him – uncomfortable enough to ask after his health. In the old house his fierce rule of his subordinates had gone as if by attachment to his fiercer loyalty to Sarah, and woe betide a servant who drank from a family glass or who forgot to cut the crusts from the bread (you never knew who or what might have touched the bread – oh, he *was* well trained).

Like all good officers, Whyte set a good example, and so enhanced his prestige. He would not so much as touch leftover food without his mistress's permission. Only anger relieved his sullen grim dealings with his fellow servants – now only a wash-girl and a flat-boy who came in every day. With Louis Goodman he was the soul of obsequiousness.

Sarah really believed that she trusted Whyte (the deep-freeze keys were in his keeping) yet when a telegram had come from a distant village informing Whyte of his father's death, Sarah first asked to see the telegram before she gave him the necessary written permission to return home for the funeral. She offered no sympathy. He expected none. 'You are a very good Madam,' he said, when she granted him leave.

Prudence had constrained Sarah to denigrate Whyte whenever the endemic South African servant problem cropped up in company. 'No one but me would put up with him,' she would sigh. 'I should let him go, but you know me –' at this moment she usually paused and smiled weakly – 'I haven't the heart to get rid of him. I have to close my ears to all his cheek.' But lately, protected by new statutes, Sarah altered her habitual comment. She now offered that it was 'terribly hard to get good servants these days,' and that 'Whyte would have to do'.

Whyte had been born in a distant African village and under the new law was permitted only to work for Sarah. If he left her employ, he would be forced to return to his small village where there was no work and much soil erosion. Whyte, like her diamonds or her motor car, belonged to her. Whyte was irrevocably in her name. To pay a servant as little as possible was clever – the ultimate art as far as Sarah was concerned. But she had always been good to Whyte. His children wore Paul's old clothes in their distant village and she did not make him pay.

'None of them appreciate anything you do for them,' was Sarah's maxim, so that whatever she did for Whyte was the result of a lost battle with her principles.

She found safety in suffering: 'Life is hard, Whyte.' Whyte always nodded in sympathetic and sad agreement, 'Yes, Madam. I know Madam. Terrible.'

'They all let you down, you only get kicks for thanks'; it was like an amen at the end of almost every conversation. Her sadness mystified Whyte: 'Madam was well-treated by Master, Master was rich, Paul was a doctor, the servants gave no trouble.' She had all of Whyte's perplexed pity just as she had all of his loyalty. It was her eyes he pitied . . . those eyes which were clamped in a permanent reproach, as if she had been born reproaching the whole world. Whyte had never known why the house had been sold. Perhaps – Sarah wondered now – she should have told him?

She left her desk and crossed to the kitchen, whose sight was sure of solace. The kitchen breathed asepsis and functionalism. Chrome handles ornamented the nullish cream of the walls and the cupboards, the way coffin handles can invoke the look of living furniture. The yellow hanging plastic strips intransigently stained with the death-struggles of flies, like all the impedimenta of the kitchen, suffered a daily washing. Bone-white muslin curtains, heavy with starch, feebly tackled the fan-produced breeze. All the sugars and spices,

THE CHICKEN-MUSHROOM PIE

by Shirley Eskapa/Illustrations by Stewart Mackinnon

89

84

Rosemary said warmly: 'I don't believe you know Nick Skelton?'

She murmured that she didn't and found herself shaking hands with yet another of Rosemary and James's dear friends: a middle-aged man, this one, but impeccably up to date, with side-whiskers and a soft suede jacket, so that his grey hair seemed more like a dandyish affectation than a mark of years passed. He held her hand and, bending down – he was very tall, the way she liked Englishmen to be – he said: 'I didn't quite catch –'

'Sue. Sue Kramer.'

'How do you do, Sue? I have a daughter called Sue.'

She smiled, quickly computing the information, reckoning that his wife was not present – and anyway he didn't look like a married man – that he was probably divorced and that was why he mentioned the daughter so immediately, as a sort of credential – a statement of how things stood . . . '*Oh shut up, you obsessional creature*,' she said to herself, still smiling up at him: '*just because you're divorced yourself you look for other members of the club everywhere . . .*'

He was asking her what part of the States she came from; what she was doing in England; had she known James and Rosemary for long?

'Oh, years,' she said, 'well – 10 years, anyway. Since I was first here on an exchange studentship.' Not wanting to let on that that was more like 16 or 17 years than 10, not wanting him to understand right away that she was thirty-seven. Well, 37 next week, actually. And Rosemary and James hadn't believed it when she mentioned the fact, saying – but perhaps they had just been being kind? – 'Oh go on, you can't be. You look 33 at the very most.'

'Oh but you've forgotten. I *am* nearly 37,' she had insisted, smiling and smiling, for she found that she smiled a lot here in London, freed at one stroke both from the spoilt past and from the menacing future, free as only a foreigner can be free. Here, in London, a city she had always liked and had thought about from time to time with aching nostalgia during the unnumbered years married to Sam Kramer – all those years when not even a child had come to mark the progress of her life – she felt gay again.

It was so long since she had felt gay, and the sensation was so novel that it was intoxicating. She moved about the streets smiling at strangers so that they, disarmed, smiled back at her. She went for long, self-conscious, pointless yet happy walks about the West End, telling herself that, after all, life had given her a second chance and she was still young enough to take it. She daily expected something momentous to happen and, although her visit was now half over and it had not happened yet, the delay only seemed to have sharpened her sense of expectation, her feeling of being wide open to the elements.

What elements? She did not know. She thought of the rain, falling softly that morning beyond the windows of her hotel and then in Regent's Park, and she had loved the rain and had gone walking in it on purpose, but it was not that sort of element she was waiting for. Love? Sex, pain, tenderness, fulfilment . . . ? Any or all of these, she would welcome, she felt.

It was so wonderful to *be* open to such elements again after all those sterile, fighting years. Over at last, all over. And nothing to show for it, not even a child. But if there had been a child it would have been early marred anyway, by its parents' quarrelling, if indeed it had not been from the outset a detestable effigy of Sam in miniature, a monstrous manikin given to rages about trifles and strange fits of sulks that went on for days and always had a different pretext so that you could never hope to pin them down and deal with them once and for all . . . Why, now she might *have* a child, on her own, anybody's child: she had the intoxicating freedom to choose – in theory. Women did have babies at her age, there was no reason why not . . .

He was talking about his job, something to do with television, and she went on smiling at him, gathering that he was so important he would not tell her exactly what he did, for she ought to know. She reflected that years ago this would have worried her – not knowing what he did and fearing to put her foot in it. But one of the few advantages of being nearly 37 was that you were expert enough to keep a conversation going smoothly, steering round awkward corners.

In a moment she would ask him where he lived and then they could talk about how she herself loved London (that never failed with an English person), and then he would probably ask her what her job was and she would explain that, although she was a P.A. in New York, at the moment she was thinking of making a change – that she was really free for

return match

by Gillian Tindall/Illustration by Sue Coe

85

Previous pages
January 1972
Edda Köchl's illustration for a short story by Anne Merrill.
February 1972
Philippe Weisbecker's illustration for a short story by Mark Steadman.
March 1972
Stewart Mackinnon's illustration for a short story by Shirley Eskapa.
June 1972
Sue Coe's illustration for a short story by Gillian Tindall.

February 1972
Ken Martin bet on an Edmund Muskie/John Lindsay Democrat ticket to challenge Nixon (Mr Tightfist) in the 1972 presidential elections. In the event the Democrats went with George McGovern and Sargent Shriver Jr. Illustration by Jean Lagarrigue.

ELECTION '72: In the fight against Mr Tightfist, America must decide who will champion Mr Minority

November 1972
Nova's parody on the Royal Variety Performance had politicians as the stars, including Margaret and the Maisonettes singing *Shame*. The picture was a photographic montage of the Supremes with the heads of Barbara Castle, Shirley Williams and Margaret Thatcher.

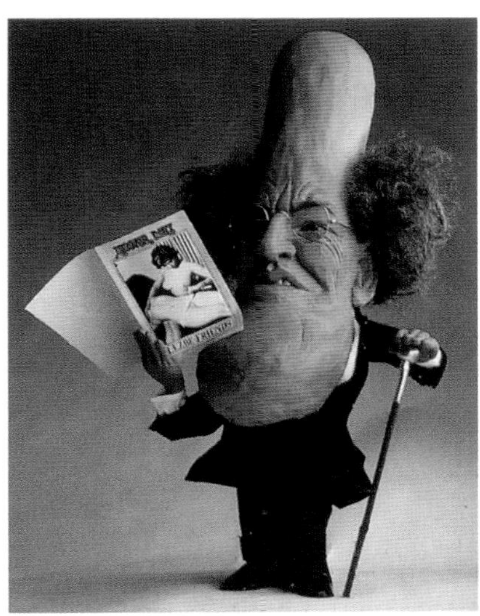

January 1972
Illustration for an article on Lord Longford, who had just published his report on pornography. The metaphor in Roger Law's published version (*top*) is only understood when you see his unpublished version (*bottom*).

May 1972
In an interview profile, Bel Mooney discovered that Margaret Thatcher was a bit of a school ma'am (she was Education Secretary at the time). Michael Rand at the *Sunday Times Magazine* originally commissioned John Holmes's illustration, but decided not to use it. So David Hillman bought it and ran it with the interview.

Overleaf
August 1972
It was Olympics year. The original idea for this feature was to have models running and jumping, shooting and throwing; so the casting specified athletic ability. On location the models proved to be pretty but gauche – obviously not the real thing. Peter Knapp shot them anyway.

To save the idea and add something to it, the transparencies were taken to a television studio and the projected images converted on to a monitor. Fiddling with the colour controls produced some interesting effects and the television images were then re-shot for the final images.

THE HEAVENLY SUITED

September 1972
Terence Donovan's photographs for 'The heavenly suited', a fashion feature by Caroline Baker.

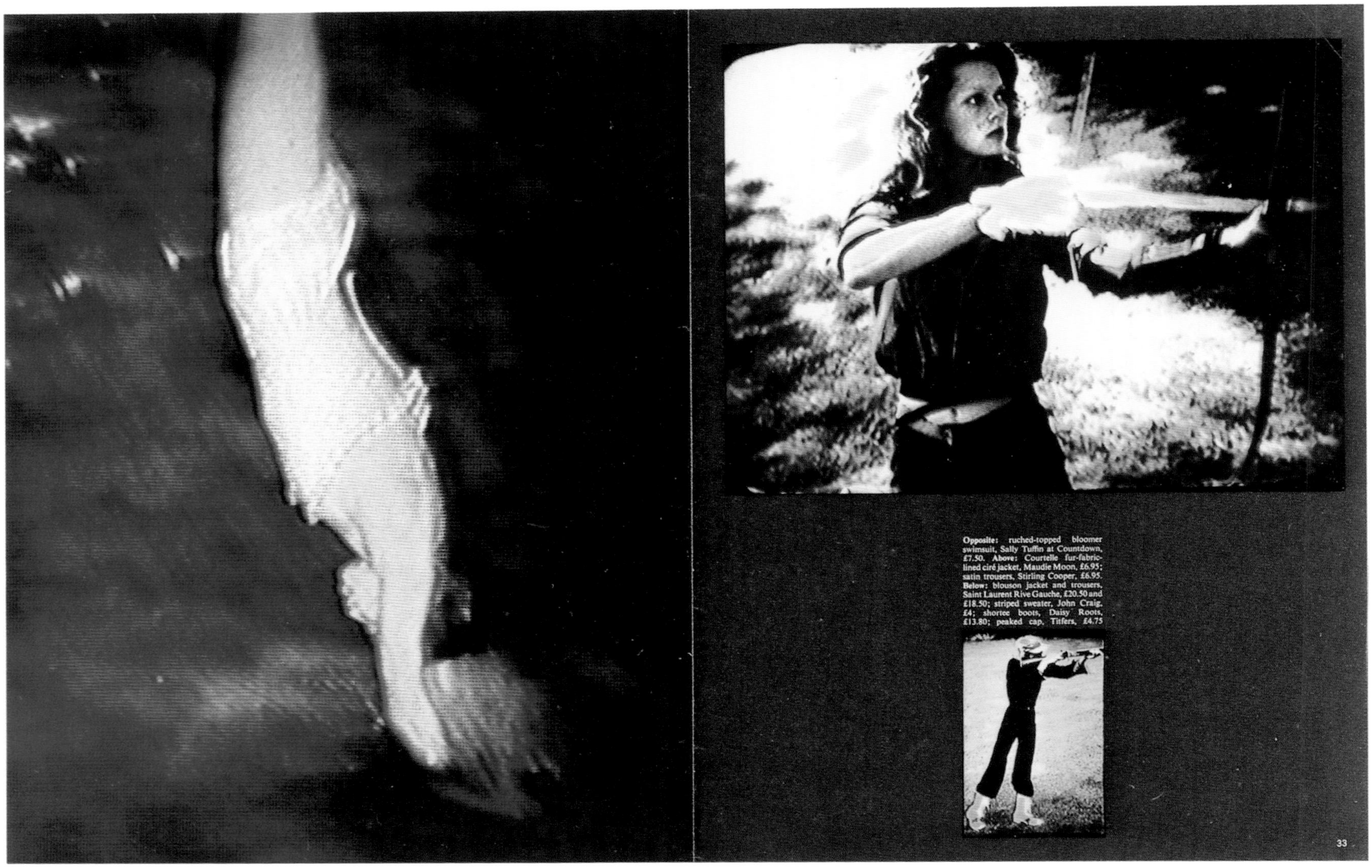

Opposite: ruched-topped bloomer swimsuit, Sally Tuffin at Countdown, £7.50. **Above:** Courtelle fur-fabric-lined ciré jacket, Maudie Moon, £6.95; satin trousers, Stirling Cooper, £6.95. **Below:** blouson jacket and trousers, Saint Laurent Rive Gauche, £20.50 and £18.50; striped sweater, John Craig, £4; shortee boots, Daisy Roots, £13.80; peaked cap, Titfers, £4.75

33

Top: Lurex halter top and shorts, Ritva, £7.50 and £9 to order; socks, Beatrice Bellini Handknits, £5; running shoes, Derber, £4.99. **Above, centre and left:** halter singlets and two-tone T-shirts, Pamla Jim for Marshall Lester, 95p and £1.25; striped singlet and long-sleeved T-shirt, Biba, 75p and £1.40; athletic shorts, Umbro, 74p; socks, Mary Quant, 79p and Echo, 80p; running shoes, Derber, £4.99, Lonsdale Sports, £3.25; fabric numbers, Hamley's, 15p

35

This page: long-sleeved T-shirt under halter singlet, Pamla Jim for Marshall Lester, £1.25 and 95p; athletic shorts, Bukta, 89p; tights, Mary Quant, 75p; striped socks, Echo, 90p; number, Hamley's, 15p. **Opposite:** dolman-sleeved zip-up cardigan, Lee Bender at Bus Stop, £2.50; athletic shorts, Bukta, 89p; tights, Mary Quant, 75p; leg warmers, Anello & Davide, £2.50; running shoes, Lonsdale Sports, £3.25

36

Above: knit shorts, £9, short-sleeved sweaters, £14.50, mini skirts, £15.50, cap-sleeved sweaters, £13.15, leg warmers, £2.50, all by Ritva; tights, Mary Quant, 75p; keds, Dunlop, £1.25. **Right:** satin top and shorts suit, Karen Kranc for Seasons, £6.75, £2.50; long-sleeved cotton T-shirts, Pamla Jim for Marshall Lester, £1.25; satin shorts, Boutique at Simpson, £5.50; tights, Mary Quant, 75p; striped socks, Echo, 80p; baseball boots, Daisy Roots, £12.50; fabric numbers, Hamley's, 15p *Archery equipment by Lillywhites; hockey equipment by Lillywhites and Lonsdale Sports. Television effects by Audio + Video Rentals, Whitfield Street, London W1. Stockists on page 85*

38

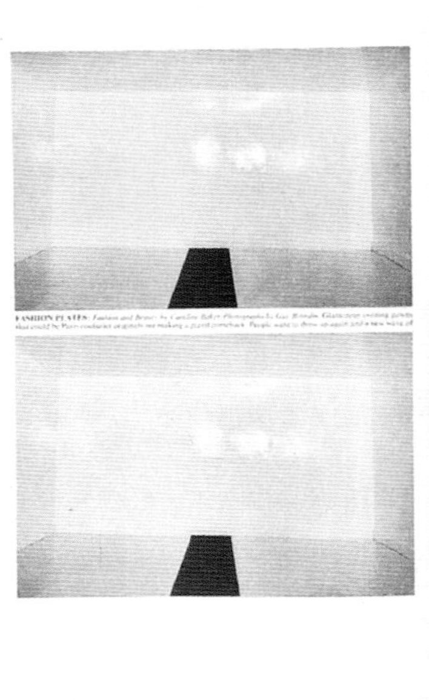

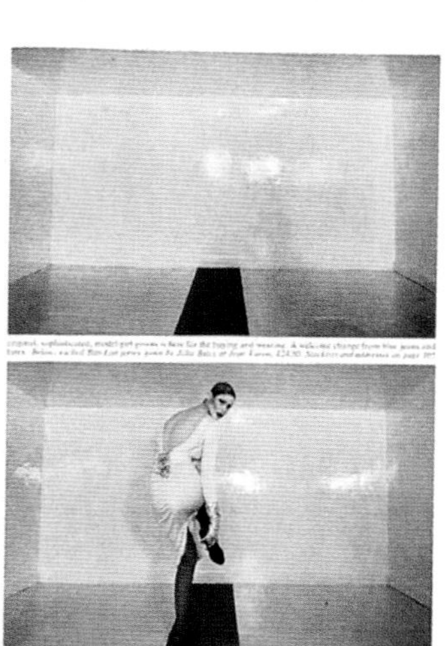

December 1972
Countering the pervasive lurex and jeans that were the dominating style, this feature on elegance was photographed by Guy Bourdin, in the manner of the pre-war fashion plate.

Nothing new has happened to swimwear for many summers. Colours and fabrics mark the fashion changes. The shapes stay the same. For a swimsuit is a swimsuit is a swimsuit – be it a one piece, a two piece, a half piece. And the shops are full of them. Lovely little things in super prints and colours. And that's where the problems begin. They are little, very little indeed. Bikinis especially have got skimpier with every passing permissive year. A year ago a generously endowed size 12 could fit quite neatly into a size 12 swimsuit; today she has to squeeze herself into it and hope that all will stay put when in use. That is to say, if she can get into it at all. And to find a larger size is nigh impossible. The shops have either sold out already or else the buyer never stocked them, since, alas, the majority of today's fashion-conscious ladies slim themselves down to the smaller sizes. Then there are the others – 'them', the unspeakable, unwearable, unsightly 'them', made by the British swimwear manufacturers especially for the fuller figure. And just one look at them is enough to put the fattiest, with good taste, off swimming and beaches for ever. The shapes are okay, for a swimsuit is a swimsuit is a swimsuit, but why couldn't the manufacturers leave the voluptuous out of the swirls and violets and stretch-nylon crunchy fabrics? Why can't they just make large swimsuits in plain and simple colours, stripes, dots and *nice* flower patterns? Meanwhile, until they all realise that the fuller figures sometimes have very good fashionable taste, all that's left – apart from eating less – is to search among the rails of tiny inviting little bikinis and swimsuits in the hope of finding one that will do up. Stockists and manufacturers' addresses on page 82

THREE FOR GOOD MEASURE

By Caroline Baker
Drawings by Celestino Valenti

July 1972
Swimwear.
Illustration by
Celestino Valenti.

Meanwhile, of course, exploitation can be fun

by Caroline Baker
Photographs: Hans Feurer

The sex war wouldn't have lasted so long if some of it, let's admit it, hadn't had its jollier moments. Alberto Vargas, whose work continues to appear extensively in *Playboy* magazine, is a painter who depicts the camp, but consummate, glamour of the vamping woman. It was *Playboy's* idea to add the coyly aggressive joke-line. We are glad to pay tribute to Vargas, who at least has kept us laughing at exploitation. In the meantime, if you're still in the fray, we'll also tell you where to buy the underwear...

Make-up by Barbara Daly; hair by Didier of Jean Louis David, 47, Rue Pierre Charron, Paris; stockists on page 70

Oh yes . . . your health, too, Mr Bottomley

Cover-up tights by Mary Quant, 75p; shoes at Chelsea Cobbler, £15

32

The lady wore black. She looked a million dollars. Anyone could tell she had class, dignity. She was safe in black - everyone is. Black is beautiful. By Caroline Baker / Photographs by Bob Richardson
DAILY NEWS
COPS, FBI FOIL

January 1972
Bleak and sombre in New York City, for a feature on black clothes modelled by Anjelica Huston. Photographs by Bob Richardson.

Long distance?
Depends how I feel
Satin and lace bra and matching French knickers, by Janet Reger, £3.70 each
33

February 1972
Hans Feurer parodied the *Playboy* artist Alberto Vargas for the article 'Who's exploiting who?'.

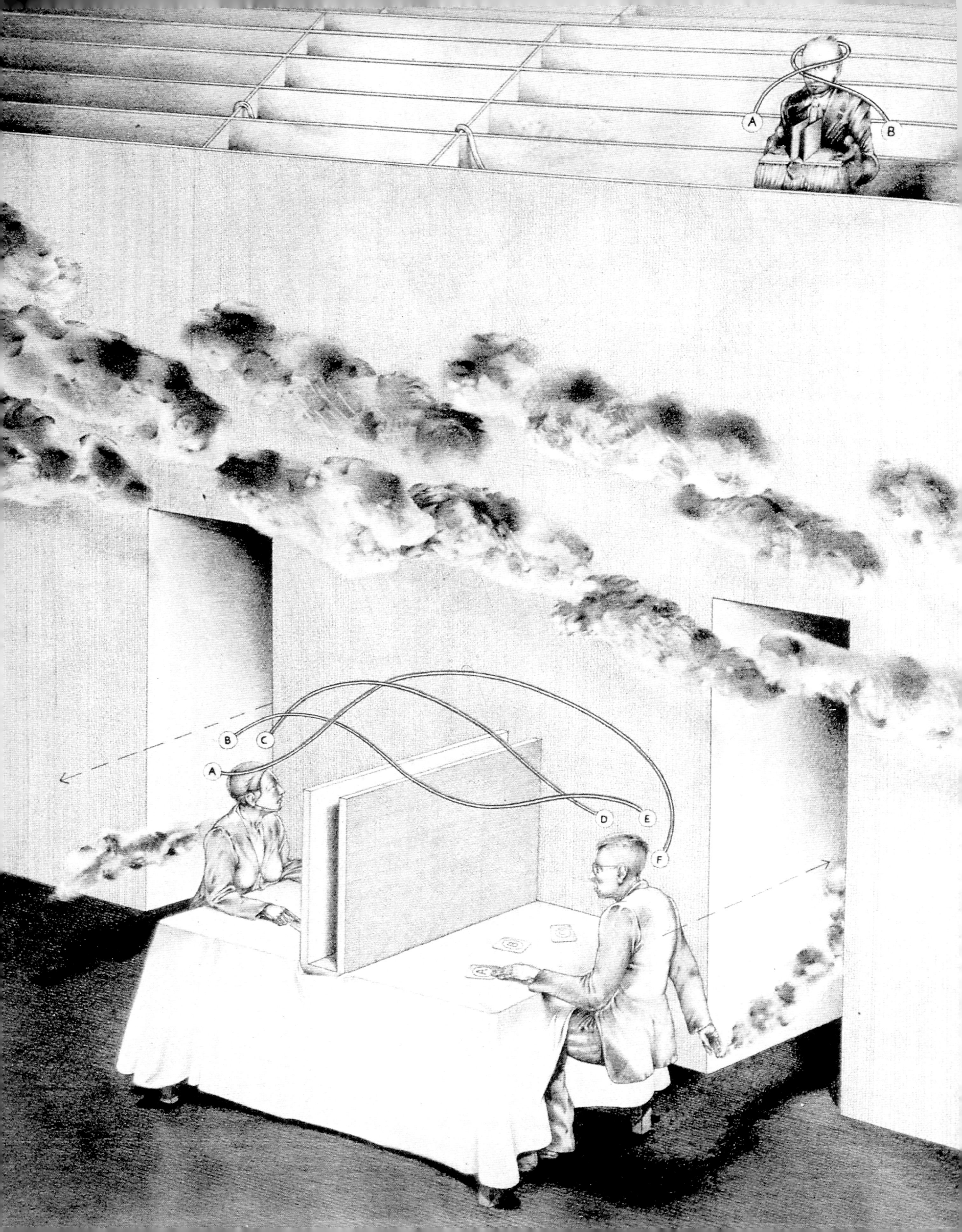
A
B
B
C
A
D
E
F

Left
August 1972
Illustration by Stewart Mackinnon for an article on the supernatural by Paul Pickering.

FEAR

by Sallie Bingham/Illustration by Stewart Mackinnon

IMPOTENCE IS A CRY FOR HELP

But are you there when he calls?

by Catherine Storr/Illustration by Mike McInnerney

Top
July 1972
Illustration by Stewart Mackinnon for a short story by Sallie Bingham.

Above
February 1972
A sensitive subject, sensitively illustrated by Mike McInnerney.

Chapter 3

Candle in the wind 1973-1975

May 1974
The theme of the whole issue was 'blue'. Harri Peccinotti shot acetate jersey swimsuits bathing in blue plastic.

If the Sixties phenomenon really started in 1963, then it surely ended in 1974. The reasons were essentially economic and financial. In Britain, the confrontations between the government and the unions, triggered by the well-meaning but ill-advised 1972 Industrial Relations Act, produced a series of devastating strikes in the strategic industries. The docks, the railways, the coal mines were all hit, and between 1970 and 1974 more working days were lost through strikes than in any period since the war. The debilitation was compounded by the eruption of conflict in the Middle East that sent shockwaves around the world as the Arab oil-producing states supported their brother belligerents by practically doubling the price of crude in 1973.

By November 1973 there was not enough fuel to sustain the working life of the country and a state of emergency was imposed requiring lighting in shops, offices, restaurants and other public places to be cut by half. Although this did much for romantic candlelit dinners, the economy was starving. By Christmas industry was required to work only three days a week to cut its energy consumption. Bitterness and confusion reigned, as well as exasperation with an establishment that didn't seem to know what it was doing. (Tellingly, industry produced just as much in a three-day week as it had in five days.) There just wasn't any money around to provide the time and scope for life's more ethereal indulgences. Thinking, believing, creating were subordinated to an overriding desire to make money and survive.

Despite the gloom *Nova* entered the final period of its life at full throttle; the momentum of the previous period carried it through 1973 as if nothing much was wrong. A keener political edge became apparent with more broad social comment and more lampooning of politicians and the establishment figures who were so obviously messing things up. Visually *Nova* maintained its highly regarded formula, using its cast of great photographers and adding some new names such as Rolph Gobits, Deborah Turbeville and Phil Sayer.

As ever, the fashion scene reflected the mood. The blond-vampire looks and hard-edged haughtiness of David Bowie caricatured the new kind of visual tenseness that was taking over. Flared trousers persisted until the middle of the decade; clogs and platforms gave way to more delicate shoe designs. But it was the return of casual clothes with narrow straight-cut jeans, T-shirts and blouson jackets that led fashion away from the fine, figure-hugging colourful fabrics of the early Seventies into the affected modesty and earnestness of blue-collar chic. Army dressing and ethnic clothes, which had both been predicted by *Nova* months, even years before, began to catch on.

Nostalgia, one of the sure signs of recession, brought a touch of the Fifties back with longer gathered skirts. Some incurable optimists even followed Debbie Harry into mini skirts in a yearning for the happiness of the Sixties. By the summer of 1974 an escapist romantic feeling began to emerge. The layered look with longer overlapping clothes led to a big and baggy profile, the complete opposite of ten years earlier. The spirit of the Sixties was dying and with it the Sixties way of dressing. Around the corner was the return of the peculiarly British phenomenon of class style: bovver boys were beginning to crop their hair and appear half-dressed with plain vests and exposed braces – eventually leading to the punk's mohicans and chains – while the more well-to-do went for out-of-town clothes culminating in the scarves and green wellies of the Sloanes. Fashion had begun a new period of development that was to continue well into the Eighties. But by then *Nova* was no longer there.

By 1974 the writing was on the editor's wall. For a start, that bustling part of London around Covent Garden that had supported so many late nights and early mornings of *Nova* staff became an empty shell when the old fruit-and-veg market closed and moved to a nice, clean, modern environment near Vauxhall. With it went much of the fun of being in the office.

Then *Nova* was hit by soaring paper prices and had to reduce its size in May 1974. Inflation reached a crippling 30 per cent in 1975, and in May that year another cut in size reduced the once gloriously large format into little more than a pamphlet.

Nova disappeared into nothing after the last issue in October 1975. The final vestiges of joy and vitality on which the magazine thrived had gone out of the nation's life. With the decreasing size of its canvas *Nova* seemed to lose authority and lose its way. Advertisers deserted the magazine and it became unsustainable. Significantly, it was the time when advertisements themselves were beginning to challenge editorial design and photography in quality, impact and entertainment. When *Nova* had started, advertising art was years behind. It had caught up, and advertisers were having more say in the running of the media.

The publishing ethos had changed; publishers were required to publish to make money, not make money to publish. Experimentation was out; risk was too risky. Magazines that were primarily purveyors of ideas, entertainment, style and esoteric information became transmuted into, or swallowed by, magazines published primarily as purveyors of profit. The legacy is still with us. Just like the modern motorcar, all that there is now is a well-researched and dreary uniformity, which sells. *Nova*'s owners had increasingly treated it as part of its clutch of women's magazines with a particular 'market niche'. Such thinking was anathema to a magazine that had flourished on freedom and the very fact that it wasn't subject to business definitions; it had begun and had continued by creating its own.

In the circumstances, *Nova* had to go. Perhaps it outstayed its welcome by a year. Unprofitability had become the greatest sin. To continue with it in the new context of the post-Sixties era would have been to create a parody. But *Nova* was always original, never derivative – even of itself. So, like a film star saved from any decline into mediocrity by dying young, *Nova* can simply be remembered for its greatness, which is fixed in time.

1973

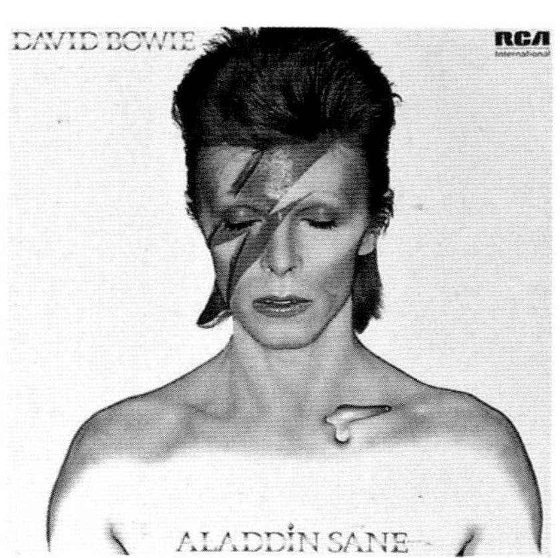

The man from outer space.

NEWS DIGEST

British-Saudi oil deal report 'speculative'

THE SUNDAY TIMES

Heath firm on three-day working

Spanish union leaders jailed

Oil cuts force airlines to use explosive fuel

Let's stop working so hard and save the economy.

THE Sun

Sir Alec Douglas Boob

Blue film sinks ship men

TANKS SAIL INTO EGYPT

Rafts ferry massive Israeli force over the canal

IAIN WALKER

Osmond fans given the slip

BIG VOTE MIX-UP

ARE YOU A HIGH-VOLTAGE LOVER? See Page 11

Israel does it to them again.

The year

Britain joined the European Community. Israel and its neighbours resumed hostilities in the Yom Kippur War. The Arabs responded by doubling the price of oil and, with the miners also on strike, Britain hit the buffers as it ran out of fuel. Edward Heath issued petrol ration books, although they were never used. The Sydney Opera House and New York's World Trade Centre opened. Red Rum won the first of his three Grand Nationals, and Princess Anne married her horse-riding hero Captain Mark Phillips. The Watergate Senate hearings started; Spiro Agnew resigned the vice-presidency after bribery charges. The Cod War broke out in the North Atlantic with Icelandic tugs firing carrots at the Royal Navy. Osmond-mania had the teenies screaming again, Gary Glitter introduced Glam Rock, Bryan Ferry appeared on the scene with Roxy Music, but the pop year belonged to David Bowie. A vintage year on the stage had *The Rocky Horror Show*, Peter Shaffer's *Equus*, Alan Bennett's *Habeas Corpus* and Alan Ayckbourn's *Norman Conquests* trilogy. Kurt Vonnegut's *Breakfast of Champions* and Norman Mailer's *Marilyn*, a biography of Monroe, were published. Jacob Bronowski's *Ascent of Man* was the outstanding TV documentary. The Newman/Redford double act had another movie smash with *The Sting* and Woody Allen came out with *The Sleeper*. VAT was introduced in place of Purchase Tax. Capital punishment was abolished in Britain.

Right
June 1973
The H-line – waist moving towards hips and hems towards the calf – photographed by Terence Donovan.

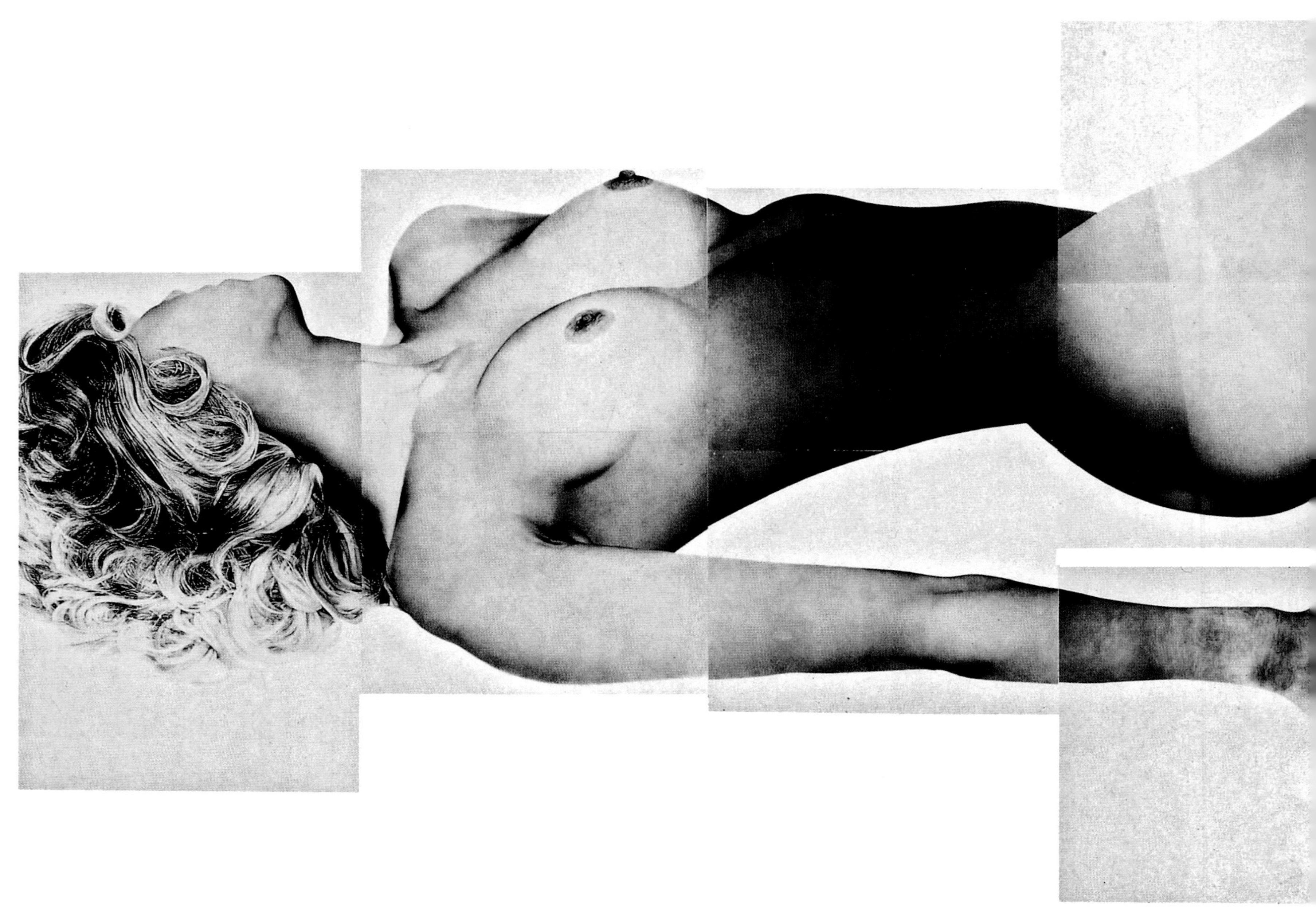

Above
October 1973
The six spreads of Celestino Valenti's *magnum opus*, which made up a fourteen-foot nude when placed together. When *Nova* had done this sort of thing before you had to buy two copies to make up the complete picture. For this you only had to buy one copy (times were hard), as each spread was backed by a beauty plan pertaining to the part of the body shown, together with a year's fitness programme compiled by Pat Baikie.
Overleaf
The assignment had already taken months and its publication put back more than once. Still the illustrator told David Hillman that he considered only the arm and hand to be really finished.

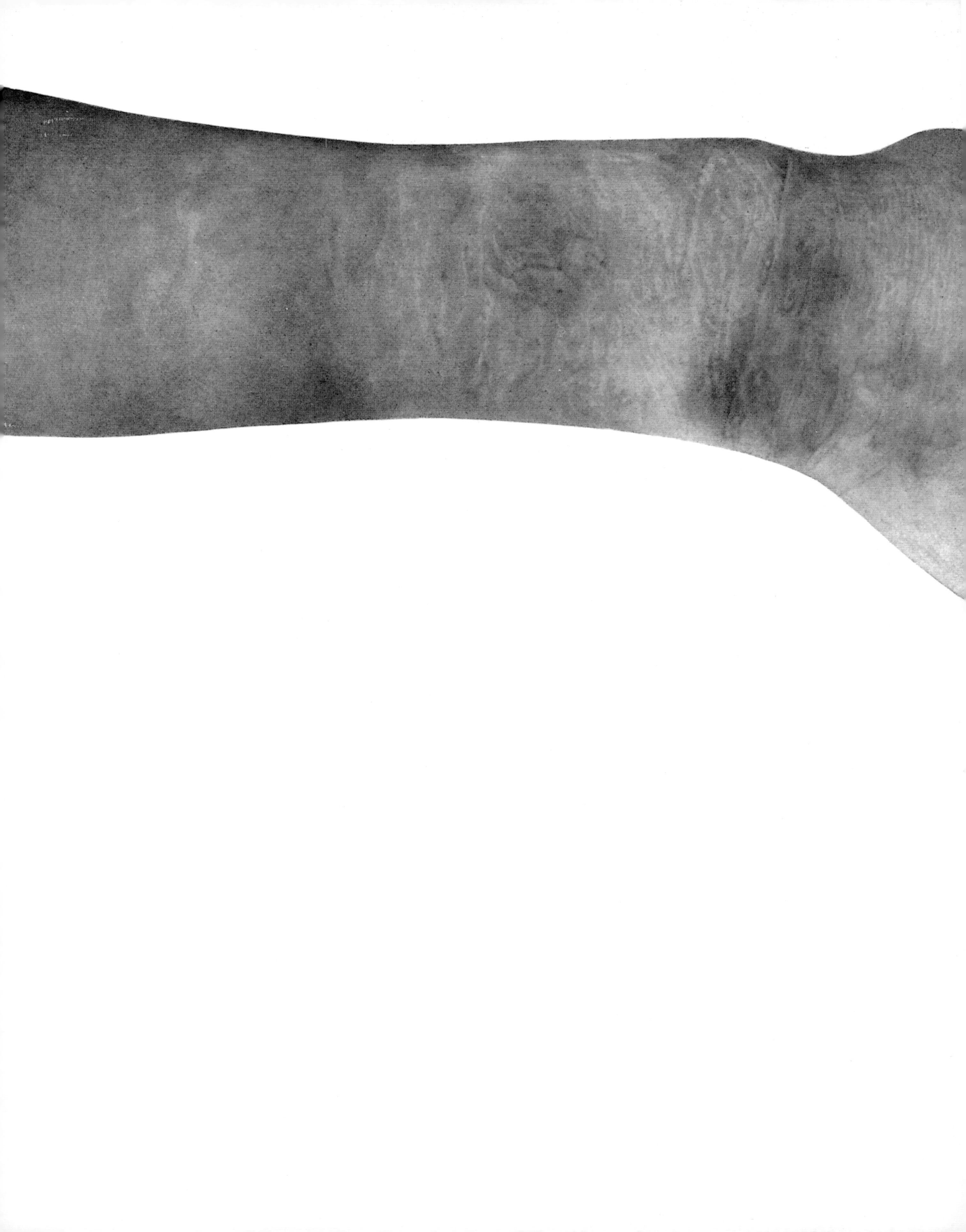

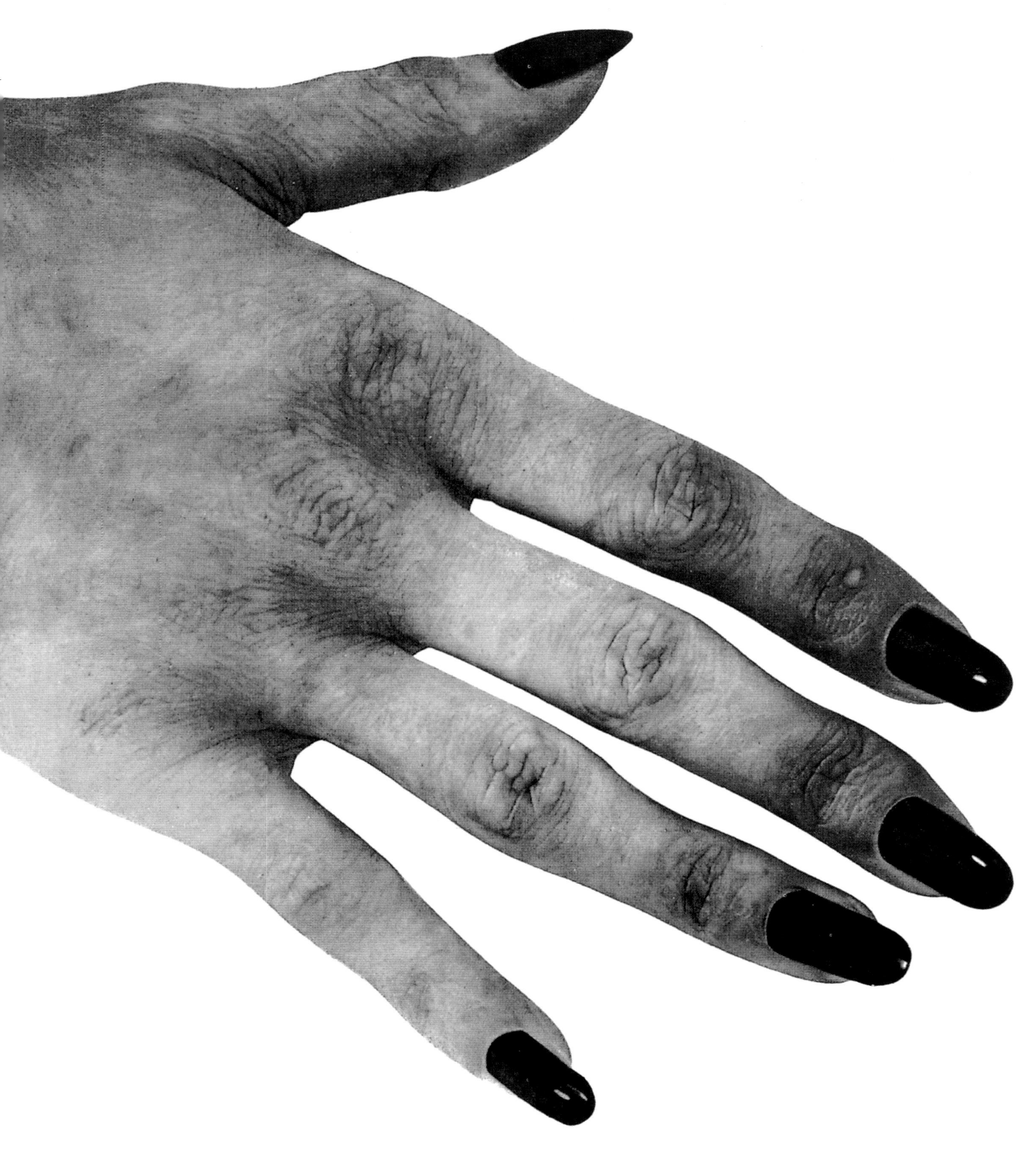

SHEER CLEAR OF THE SHOWERS

by Caroline Baker/ Photographs by Helmut Newton

Plastic fabrics more used to bathrooms than people go into the making of these amazing raincoats. Intended to be worn over normal outfits so that the beauty of them all shows through, they are guaranteed to add some fun to the wetness of British drizzle.

Batwing blouson jackets, calf-length wrap-round skirt (opposite) and airman's trousers (left) by Swanky Modes, £6.50 each; bag by Manydeed for Swanky Modes, £9; child's umbrella at toy shops; nothing-but-a-brim straw hat at Browns, £8; clear sandals at City Lights Studio, £32 to order; accordion plastic headscarf at departmental stores. Stockists on page 97

49

Trenchcoat (opposite) with petal-leaf collar, and 'A' line raincoat (left) with 'debris' sealed in pockets by Swanky Modes, £8 each; child's umbrella at toy shops; clear sandals at City Lights Studio, £32 to order; roomy bag by Manydeed for Swanky Modes, £9; Liqua-creme Freshly Peach with Liqua-frost Burgundy lipsticks and Premier Rose nail polish by Charles of the Ritz, 72p and £1; hair by Frederic of Mod's Hair

August 1973
Helmut Newton's photographs for a feature on plastic waterproofs. The narrow border captions were typical *Nova*.

Opposite: silk print frock by Cacharel, £25; antique kid gloves at Universal Witness, from £4; suede bag by Chelsea Cobbler, £14.95; straw beret by Karl Lagerfeld for Chloe at Browns, £15 to order; swizzle-stick by Calber, 550 francs; veiling at Paul Craig, from 10p per yard; pearl choker by Ciro Pearls, £2.75; Gold Glitter Eye Shadow by Innoxa, 40p; Softly Beige Foundation by Elizabeth Arden, £1.66. **This page:** striped waist-coat at City Lights Studio, £9.50; satin straight skirt by Froks at Che Guevara, £8.95; stockings by Christian Dior, 55p; black pearls by Ciro Pearls, £6; Red Hot Chili lips by Helene Rubinstein, 96p; Brightest Red nails by Max Factor, 35p. Hair by Frederic of Med's Hair; perfume, Norell, £8.15 for 1oz

59

This page: silk costume and bangle by Yves Saint Laurent at Rive Gauche, £95 and from £5.50; straw beret by Karl Lagerfeld for Chloe at Browns, £15 to order; hat trimmings at Paul Craig; ivory and silver jewellery by Fabrice at ZigZag, from £4 to £50. **Opposite left:** three-piece gaberdine costume by City Lights Studio, £33.50; beret by Karl Lagerfeld for Chloe at Browns, £15 to order; gold-starred bangles and rings by Fabrice at ZigZag, £100 and £7; all other jewellery from a selection at Butler & Wilson; **right:** nun's-veiling costume by Janice Wainwright, £29.50; antique gloves at Essenses; straw hat by Jean Charles Brosseau at Browns, £6; veiling and camelias from Paul Craig, from 10p per yard and 10p each

56

April 1973
A feature on the classic cut. Photographs by Helmut Newton.

Right
July 1973
A survey of London's ethnic provisioners. Photographs by Don Silverstein.

January 1973
Don Silverstein's six-page 'where are they now?' gallery included such old-time favourites as Geraldo, Ruby Murray and Yana. Tommy Farr (left), the Welsh heavyweight boxer and one of the few to go the distance with world champion Joe Louis, was working as an agent for the United Paint Co. Ben Warris, partner to Jimmy Jewell in the famous fifties comedy act, was still treading the boards in the resorts and northern towns of England.

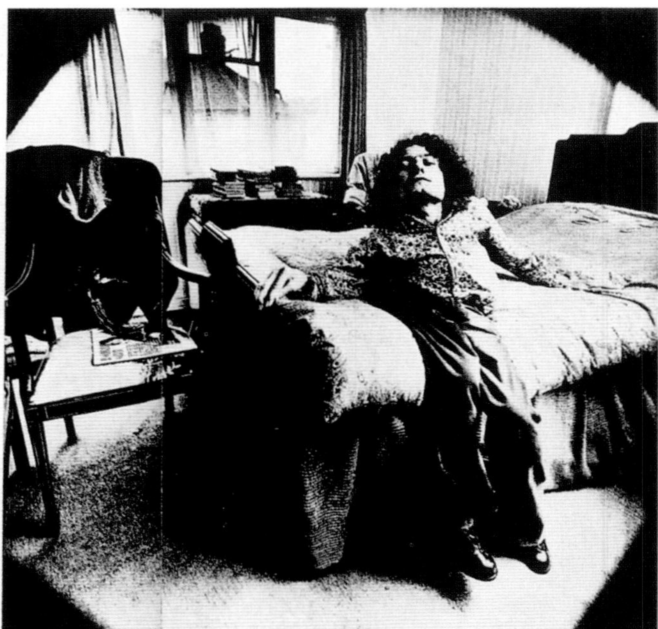

FRAGMENTS OF AN AUTOBIOGRAPHY

by Anthony Maurice Miller/Photograph by Donald Silverstein

January 1973
The brave and touching story of a young writer who had been crippled by polio since he was two and was totally dependent on his family for everything. Photograph of Anthony Maurice Miller by Don Silverstein.

SHOPS WITH A FOREIGN FLAVOUR

photographs by
Donald Silverstein

Okra, pak choi, yams, worsht, zampone, man yeun ling – what they are, where to find them, who sells them and how to make them into bollito misto or cholent. *Nova* goes shopping and talks to the shopkeepers who are changing the British diet

Cohen Hyman, 46 Wentworth Street, London E1

Cohen's kosher butchers is a small family business, in the heart of Petticoat Lane, owned by Mr Mark Cohen and run by him and his son, Sydney, and his wife, Rosie. Sydney's 10-year-old daughter, Rochelle, also in white overalls, sits on a bench under a row of giant meat hooks, watching the television on the other side of the shop. Her father is dressing chickens in the back room; her grandfather is stocking the window with shin of beef and Bloom's frankfurters.

'That's my granddaughter, Rochelle,' says Mr Cohen straightaway. 'Isn't she a lovely girl? She's named after my late mother-in-law, who was a wonderful butcher. And Rochelle wants to be a butcher too, don't you?' Rochelle grins and looks a bit uncertain.

'We don't give her dolls and toys, we give her knives and choppers,' shouts Sydney from the back – and the whole conversation becomes a double-talk act between Mr Cohen and his son.

'The whole family's in the business,' says Mr Cohen Senior. 'All in separate shops of their own.'

Actually it looks as if the whole family is in the same shop in Wentworth street – all in photographs hung on the walls between huge hunks of meat and upside-down chickens.

'That's my sister,' Mr Cohen explains, pointing to a very brown photo of a typically posed Edwardian family. 'My brothers are butchers, my sisters married butchers, my wife came from butchers. Let me show you my wedding photo' – and he pulls it out from among the ledgers, order books and accounts. 'I may look an old geyser now, but my wife, Rosie, bless 'er, she still looks young. You should see Sydney's wife, too, she's very pretty. And up there' – pointing to the photos among the carcasses again – 'that's my mother and father on their wedding day. Isn't he a handsome man? He came over from Russia about 74 years ago and worked in a butcher's shop here for two-and-sixpence a week, from three in the morning till 12 at night.' (Sydney coughs loudly.) 'Gradually he saved a little money out of that and he set up his own little business here; right here on these premises. When I left school I came into the business and we worked very hard and built it up. We're serving the grandchildren of some of our original customers now.'

Mr Cohen is obviously as happy working here with the help of his son, as he was working in the shop with his own father – and his pride in his family is matched only by his pride in the meat he sells.

Next to the ageing photographs hangs his licence to trade as a Retail Kosher butcher, issued by the London Board of Sechita.

'So, what makes me different from an ordinary butcher? What makes a difference is this: We have to observe the Jewish dietary laws and sell kosher meat according to our . . . according to our ecclesiastical authorities, Sid?'

'According to our laws,' comes the reply from the back.

'. . . According to our laws,' finishes Mr Cohen in agreement. 'We're only allowed to sell English meat, meat killed here, supervised by our ecclesiastical authorities' – he's determined to get it in. 'They examine the animal after slaughter – ritual slaughter, that's what makes the difference – and see that it conforms to our laws. Then the housewife has to kosher it herself, too, of course. She has to put it in water for half an hour, to wash the blood out; put it on the draining board so the water runs away, and then salt it and leave it for an hour. Then she washes the salt off and cooks it. Isn't that right, Sid?'

Sydney comes through from the back wiping his hands and launches out into a full explanation of the origin of these laws: 'It all goes back to the time when the Jews were in the hot desert . . .' but his father cuts him off hurriedly . . . 'No, no, we're not supposed to know all that. We're only supposed to know what our ecclesiastical authorities tell us. And if *they* say it's all right, it's all right.'

'It means we can't buy in Smithfield, of course,' says Sydney on his way back to his chickens, 'only from our wholesale kosher markets, so it's like all restricted trades, it costs just a little bit more, but not much. Basic economics,' he shrugs.

'And it means we're inspected regularly,' Mr Cohen senior adds. 'You won't find no pork and no rabbits here; and no hindquarter meat, only forequarter.'

'Nothing from behind the tenth bone,' Sydney chips in with the theory again.

'Of course, we supply the majority of our meat to our Jewish customers, but we have a lot of non-Jewish customers, too, people who come in in their lunch hour because they know it's English meat and it's good quality. They cook our meat in their own way, not a Jewish way, and it tastes just the same. It only tastes different if it's cooked in *our* way; cooked in traditional Jewish recipes passed down from mother to child.

'Orthodox Jews aren't allowed to cook on the Sabbath, so they make *cholent*, which is prepared and placed in the oven on Friday, with a very small light kept on, and taken out on Saturday. That *is* a traditional dish. They use a fattier meat – don't they Sid?'

'Top rib,' shouts Sid.

'. . . and put it in a dish with beans and . . . dumplings, Sid?'

'Yes.'

'. . . and dumplings; and potatoes; and . . . marrow bones, Sid?'

'Er, yes.'

'. . . and marrow bones. And you put it all in the pot, and layer it with *lochen* (that's vermicelli) pudding, and just salt and pepper, and cover it.'

'It's the sort of dish you have and then go back to bed,' Sid laughs. 'Why? Because you can't move afterwards.'

'You start the meal with chopped liver, then *lochen* and chicken soup – Jewish people love poultry. I don't say everybody has that on the Sabbath, mind – but the real orthodox do.

'Any liver will do for the chopped liver – ox, calves or chicken. But it has to be placed in water, then drained, then salted and grilled. Then you put it in a bowl with some onions, cut in very small pieces, and a couple of hardboiled eggs and some melted chicken fat – and chop it all up fine.

'Pickled beef, of course, we sell a lot of that too. It's delicious served with potato pancakes. You just grate the potato with some onion, mix it with egg, season it, and fry it in small pancakes.

'Then we sell the salamis, the Viennas – *worsht* – they're like boloneys, you boil them, and Frankfurters, all from Bloom's. You know, in my opinion, Bloom's is the finest restaurant in England. It is.'

His enthusiasm for Bloom's is quickly diverted by the entry of a customer, a young Jewish woman.

'Mrs Daniels, how are you dear? Did you like what we sent you? See Sydney's daughter? What can we do for you? A chicken? What sort of chicken? A roaster or a fowl? Have a fowl for a change, Mrs Daniels. I haven't got a roaster. Try a fowl. No you can't roast it.'

Mr Cohen suddenly remembers that he hasn't explained Jewish law on meat and milk. 'Jewish people can't have milk and meat together. After their meat meal they have to wait six hours before they can have anything with milk in it.'

'One hour,' says Mrs Daniels.

'Three,' says Rochelle.

'No, it's six,' insists Mr Cohen. Mrs Daniels is certain that in Israel she's seen communities where they only wait one hour, and Rochelle is equally certain that Mr Goldberg said three hours. Mr Cohen shouts for Sydney's support . . .

'Six hours isn't it Sydney?' But Sydney's not too sure either.

'Some people don't wait a second – but don't write that,' Mr Cohen murmurs while the argument goes on. 'And some people eat pork – but don't write that either. Well, what are we going to do, Mrs Daniels? I've got a nice piece of liver for you. How about a nice fried liver and onions tonight. Or how about some lamb chops, Mrs Daniels? I've got some lovely little lamb's chops?'

And Mrs Daniels goes out with liver, lamb chops and shin of beef – but no roasting chicken.

64

Parmigiani Figlio Ltd, 36A Old Compton Street, London W1

Among the strip joints, provision stores and multitudinous restaurants of Soho is Parmigiani Figlio Ltd, a modern Italian shop specialising in wines, salamis, cheeses, hams and any shape of pasta you care to mention.

The Parmigiani family came to England round about 1909, when it was 'a big empire with plenty of gold coins on the floors . . . so to speak', and set up the business, which is now run by Mr Parmigiani's sons Angelo and Nino and Nino's son John, and employs upwards of 20 people.

The inside of the shop is a hive of activity, which is not surprising since they also have anorder service throughout the country, and supply the catering trade.

The ceiling is festooned with salami of every shape and size, cheese and confectionery. Italians are not big sweet eaters, but they do sell quite a lot of confectionery at Easter and Christmas time – though it's expensive. 'If an Italian is making a present he wants a really nice box or fancy jar – he doesn't mind paying for something special. The English don't care about the boxes – they look and see how much is inside,' says Angelo Parmigiani.

At the back of the shop, just behind the rows of dried herbs – basil, sweet marjoram, origano and garlic are most widely used in Italian cooking – are the pasta – about 100 different varieties. 'Each one seems to have a different taste, although they are all made of the same ingredients. It's the way the tongue catches them, the texture and how they hold the sauce which gives each one an individual taste – it's just a matter of preference,' explains Mr Parmigiani. Spaghetti should be cooked in masses of salted water, boiled for six to seven minutes, a cup of cold water added to bring it off the boil, strained and then put back in the pan with butter. Serve it with clam and tomato sauce (tomato paste, water, a little olive oil, perhaps some chopped onion) or *pesto Genovese* (one jar is sufficient for a pound of spaghetti, and contains pine kernels, basil, cheese and oil).

Pasta is eaten at least once daily, either with sauce or in soups such as *minestrone* or *minestra* (a broth with a little macaroni and diced vegetables) followed by a meat or fish dish. 'We eat a lot of white meat like veal – Italians are very squeamish and don't like the blood in red meat. That's why lemon is served with most things: to take away the taste of blood,' says Mr Parmigiani. Two of his favourite dishes are *cotoletta alla Milanese* (fried cutlets of veal coated with egg and breadcrumbs – 'the secret is to add a little olive oil to the butter to stop it burning so that it's cooked inside but soft and unburnt outside; served with mashed or boiled potatoes it's delicious') and *bollito misto*. This consists of a mixture of breast of veal, leg of beef and *zampone* (leg of pork stuffed with spices, pepper and minced pork; some ready-cooked brands need cooking for only 15 to 20 minutes, otherwise a couple of hours is necessary. *Cotechino* is the same thing but in sausage form.) *Bollito misto* is served with *salsa verde*, a green sauce made from parsley, olive oil and garlic – 'almost like mint sauce without the mint' says Mr Parmigiani cryptically. *Bollito misto* is also eaten with *mostarda di frutta*, a unique preserve of fruit in syrup flavoured with mustard and garlic.

'We used to eat a lot of little birds (blackbirds, thrushes) but it's going out of fashion now and there was a lot of protest. But we still eat a fair amount of quail, pheasant and guinea fowl.' Meat is always served by itself with vegetables such as spinach – drained, then mixed with butter and pine kernels – or *finocchio alla Parmigiana* – fennel cooked with parmesan cheese and butter – as side dishes.

'I think that cooking develops more in a poorer country. When people have nothing to eat except a few bones and a little meat they have to add a bit of this and that to make it more tasty. That's how the pizza originated, as a poor man's dish. In the hills around Naples they made *mozzarella* cheese from buffalo milk, dough, took a little origano which was growing wild, a few tomatoes, and it's eaten everywhere now. Italian cooking is very simple. We take the raw material and try to extract the full flavour from it.'

Unlike the French, the Italians are not a big cheese-eating nation, but there is still a wide choice: *fontina*, a mild soft cheese melted in fondues; *taleggio*, creamy cheese with a medium strong taste; *stracchino*, mild creamy spread; *mozzarella*, for pizzas or cannelloni; *ricotta*, similar to cottage cheese, used sometimes as a filling for ravioli; *provolone*, a hard cheese which can be strong or mild; *gorgonzola*; *Bel Paese*; and parmesan, fresh and young for the table, hard for cooking. 'The reason parmesan is so expensive is that it takes two to three years to mature, and the processing is very involved. But a genuine parmesan cheese from Parma is really wonderful – like using truffles,' says Mr Parmigiani.

'We do eat quite a lot of hors d'oeuvres too – not every day but on special occasions. Not like the French, who serve only one dish, but a big tray with sardines, olives, hams, anchovies and slices of salami.'

The selection of salami is large and confusing: *Citteno*, a Milanese salami, pork and veal minced with spices and ground pepper; *mortadella*, mixed pork and other meat; *salame di Felino*, pure pork; *casalingo*, pork coarsely ground with pepper; *coppa*, rolled neck of pig with spices; *pancetta*, pig's stomach mixed with pepper; *Toscano*, pork and veal coarsely minced. On the same counter is *bresaola*, dried salt beef which is served with salad, and of course the famous Parma ham which is specially cured by rubbing salt into it: 'It's the particular flow of air in that part of the country that does the trick.' The San Daniele is much milder and not as salty. Next to the hams are the sausages, which can be fried, boiled or grilled: *salamelle*, spiced pork and *luganega*, a long sausage with no spices.

Of the wide choice of Italian wines, chianti is of course one of the most popular. Some Italians in this country, nostalgic for the wine-making tradition at home, have even been known to tread grapes for their own wine over here.

Fruit and coffee finishes off the Italian meal. 'In Italy, when one eats out everyone is a *Signore* (rich man) even when he's really poor. We don't want just one peach, or one orange, but a whole plateful of fruit to eat as much as we like – all goes on the bill at the end, but . . .' Mr Parmigiani smiles and gesticulates expansively. 'And coffee, too, is important. It must have the three C's – *chiaro*, clear, *caldo*, warm; and *carico*, strong.'

Below: Ana Alamo and Paola Guastadini with Italian specialities

Brett's Provisions, 53 South Lambeth Road, London SW8

Clarence Brett came here from Jamaica in 1956; his wife Pamela joined him four years later. They have had their grocery and off-licence store specialising in West Indian food for three years now. 'I get nostalgic for Jamaica sometimes,' Pamela says, 'but I tell you, growing up in Jamaica we were terribly influenced by England. It was the mother country; we celebrated the Queen's birthday, Victoria Day, Empire Day; the one desire was to come to England to see the Queen. I did think it would be a bit brighter and gayer.'

They sell a mixture of ordinary groceries, eggs, tins, cheese, bread and frozen food, plus West Indian vegetables, yams, green bananas, and special West Indian canned food. They buy their vegetables from Brixton Market – 'You can get everything in England now, even callaloo fresh, that is upper-class spinach' – their canned food, dried peas, oil, from an importers, Enco Brothers. The West Indian specialities are mainly bought by other West Indians but some English customers buy the better known vegetables like sweet potatoes and pumpkin.

Mr Brett's favourite meal is yellow yams, steak and green bananas. Nearly all of their vegetables – yams, dashin, green bananas – are cooked like potatoes and used as such. They do not use the oven as much as we do in English cooking; instead everything is cooked on top of the stove, either stewed, fried or pot roast, in aluminium pots.

Pamela's favourite recipes are:

Stew peas and rice: soak four salted pigs' tails for at least two hours; cut them up and cook in water with two cups of dried gango peas for an hour. Add two ounces of butter, a dash of black pepper, a little salt and three cups of rice. Let it boil rapidly for 10 minutes and then simmer until the liquid is absorbed.

Steak: cut steak into cubes, sprinkle with salt and black pepper, stir it well and leave for half an hour to marinate. Then cook in a little water with one sliced large onion, half a tomato (tomatoes are used more for the colouring than for flavour), thyme and marjoram and simmer for half an hour or until tender. Serve this with boiled yellow yams and green bananas.

Ackee and salt fish: pour boiling water on the salt cod cutlets; then strain, skin and bone them. Strain the ackees (tinned ones are preserved in brine) and pour on boiling water. Put corn oil in a pan and add a sliced large onion and a hot red pepper. Cook till soft, then add flaked cod fish and ackees and stir it all together.

Seasoned rice: Soak a cupful of dried prawns in boiling water. Put two teaspoons of butter in a pan, and fry a sliced onion, half a tomato, then add the prawns, three cupfuls of water and a cup and a half of rice and cook till the water is absorbed.

Mrs Brett serves mackerel with green bananas, flavouring the fish with onion and garlic. Mutton she cooks very slowly for three hours with a little curry powder, black pepper, onion and salt. Chickens are usually pot roast. She makes special puddings with sweet potatoes or cornmeal as follows:

She peels and grates 1½lb sweet potatoes. She prepares a pint of milk by beating in two eggs, two tablespoons sugar and about ½lb dashin grated in to bind it. Mix it all together and flavour with a drop of vanilla and some grated nutmeg, plus two handfuls of raisins or currants if you like. Slowly mix them together well. Put into a greased cake tin, with paper on the bottom, and cook in a 400°/Reg. 6 oven for an hour and a half. If you use cornmeal, use 1lb and add to the same milk mixture. But be careful not to get the mixture too thick. These are used as snacks.

Pumpkin is, of course, made into pumpkin pie and plantin (large yellow bananas) are usually fried for breakfast or sweet snacks. Dried vegetable specialities are gango peas and beans; they take about two hours to cook, and are used in soups and stews. Finally, there are all sorts of tinned vegetables, to be used as substitutes for fresh vegetables, including callaloo (a kind of spinach), okra (ladies' fingers), ackees (cooked with salt fish, which is also sold in West Indian stores), breadfruit, Congo peas and yellow yams.

68

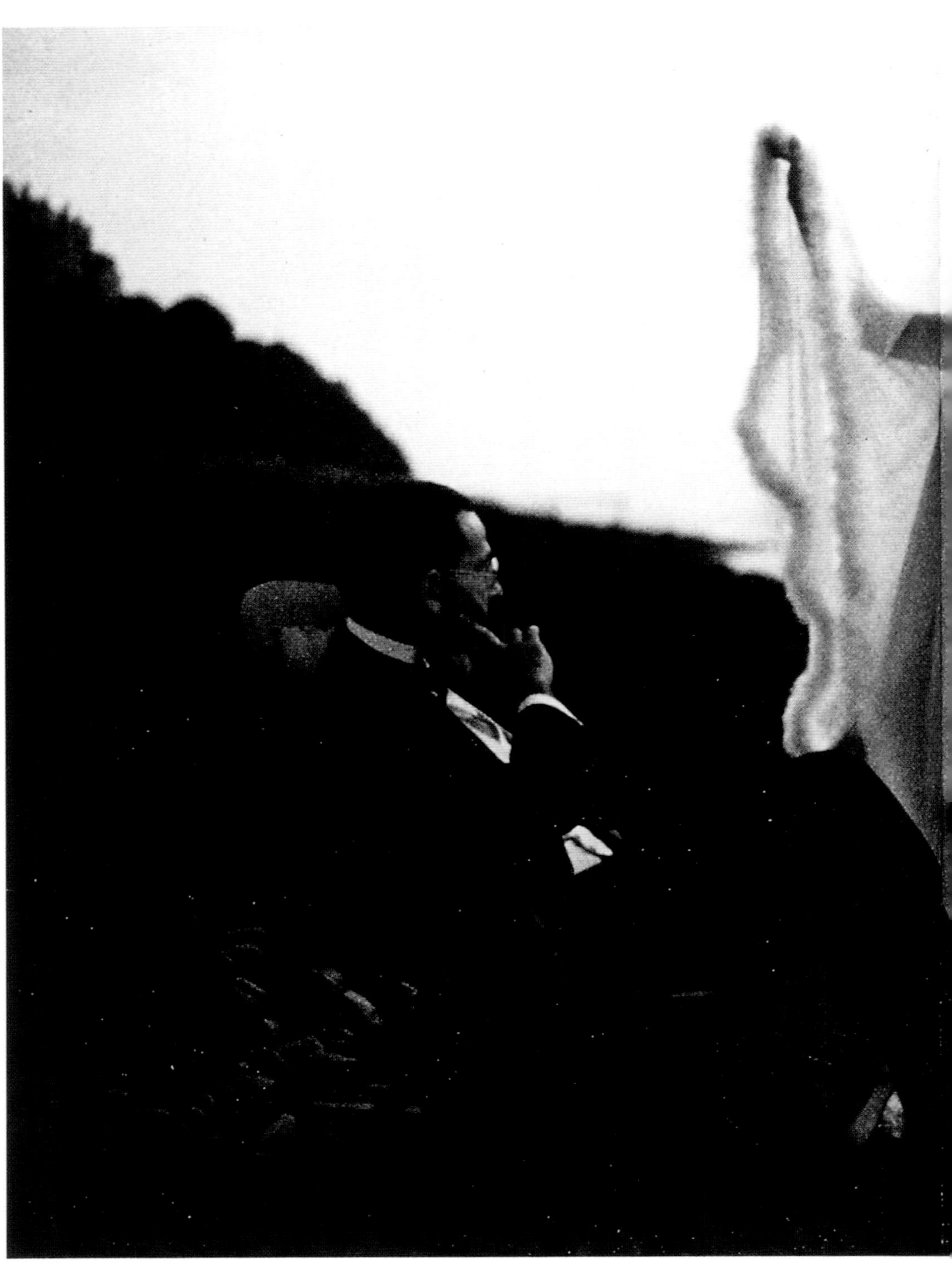

December 1973
Deborah Turbeville's photographs for a feature on evening gowns.

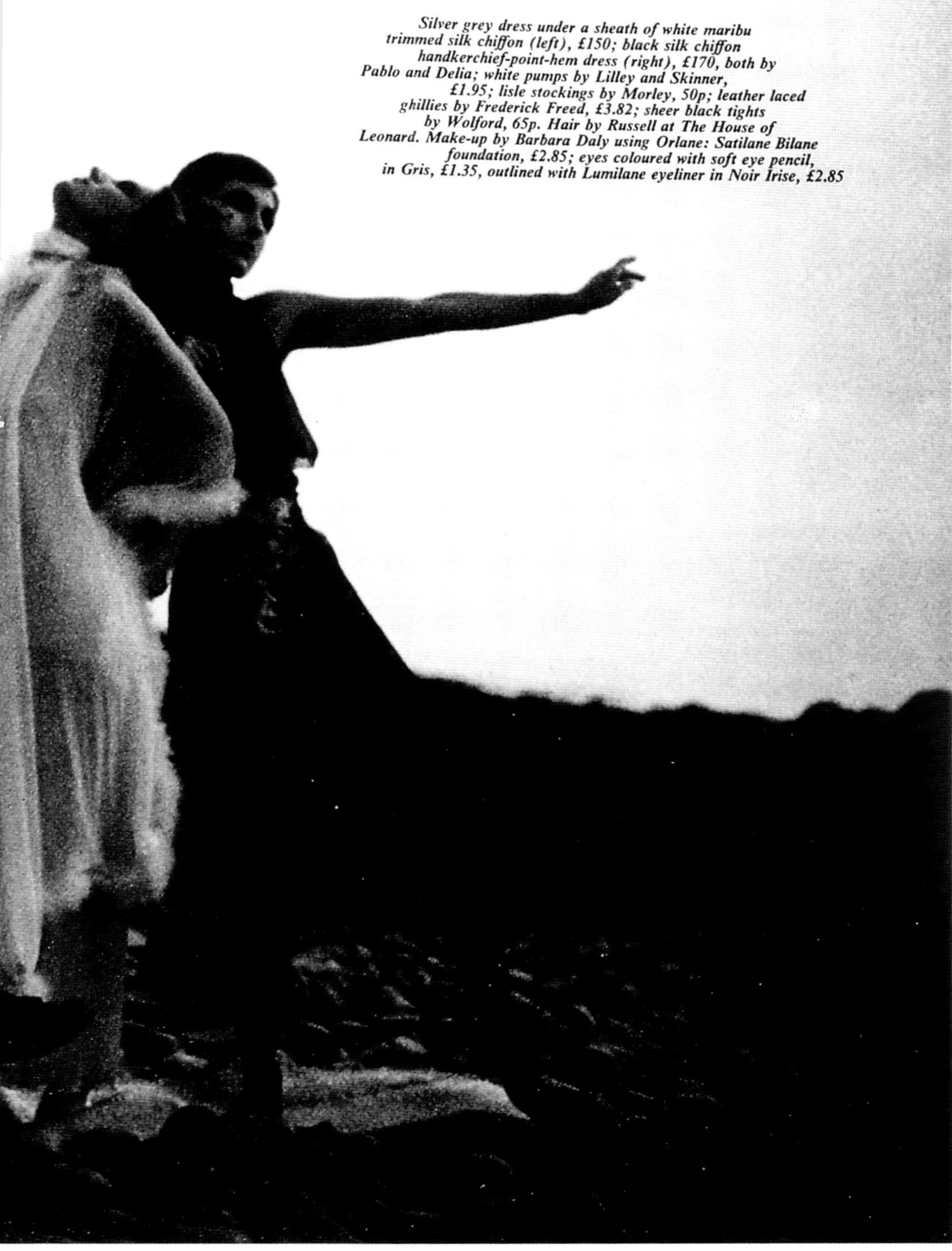
Silver grey dress under a sheath of white maribu trimmed silk chiffon (left), £150; black silk chiffon handkerchief-point-hem dress (right), £170, both by Pablo and Delia; white pumps by Lilley and Skinner, £1.95; lisle stockings by Morley, 50p; leather laced ghillies by Frederick Freed, £3.82; sheer black tights by Wolford, 65p. Hair by Russell at The House of Leonard. Make-up by Barbara Daly using Orlane: Satilane Bilane foundation, £2.85; eyes coloured with soft eye pencil, in Gris, £1.35, outlined with Lumilane eyeliner in Noir Irise, £2.85

A TOUCH OF BALLET CLASS

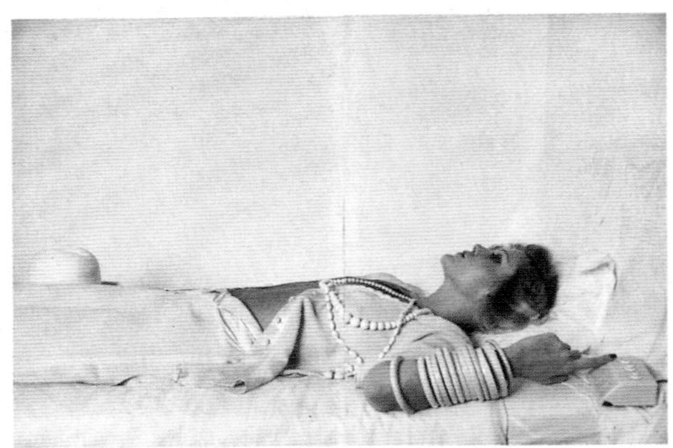

May 1973
Soft and flowing, fast and loose – shot by Harri Peccinotti when he travelled to the Brazilian Grand Prix with the Yardley-McLaren team.

January 1973
Harri Peccinotti's photographs in Morocco for 'The Chic of Araby', Caroline Baker's feature on the eastern look (all clothes available in London).

STOCK MARKET
Lagarrigue
Minding his own business Jim Slater's declared aim is to create the biggest investment bank in the world–which shouldn't take him very long. *by Russell Mil*
70

May 1973
Jean Lagarrigue's illustration for the first spread of Russell Miller's profile of Jim Slater, who was on his first high as the City's golden boy. His Slater Walker investment house could do no wrong. Eventually the enterprise went bust and Slater had to start again.

April 1973
Stewart Mackinnon's illustration for Susan Hill's short story 'Halloran's child'.

September 1973
Jean Lagarrigue's illustration for Melvyn Bragg's short story 'Rough trade'.

October 1973
Edda Köchl's illustration for Anne Merrill's short story 'The private life of Ifor Tombs'.

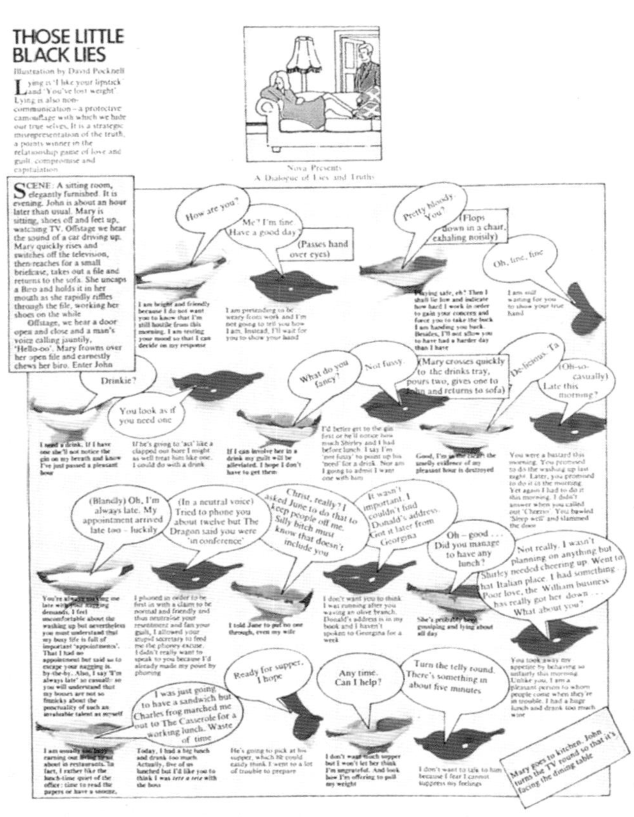

THOSE LITTLE BLACK LIES

Illustration by David Pocknell

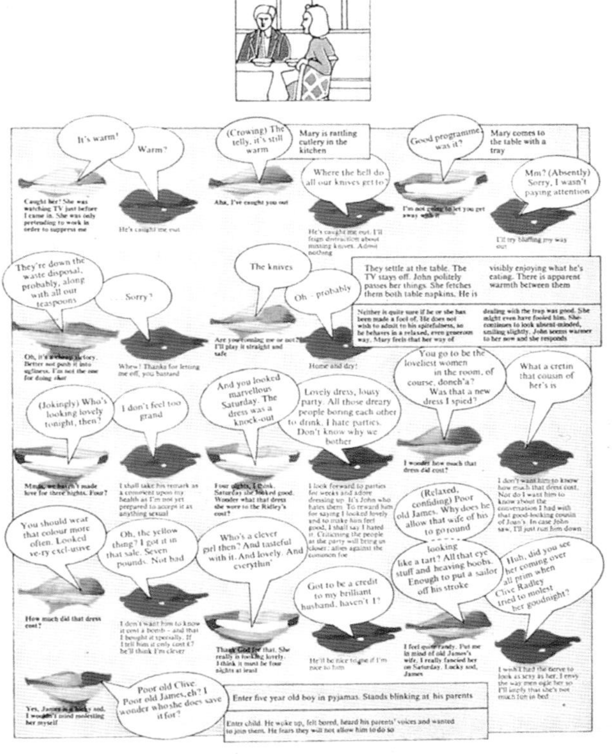

May 1973
The original article on the differences between what we say and what we mean was over ten thousand words long and almost impossible to illustrate. David Hillman thought it could all be reduced to a running illustration. He commissioned David Pocknell to do it, and gave him two days. Every pair of lips was hand drawn and all the type had to be fitted exactly. As the messenger arrived to take it to the printers in Italy Hillman was still pasting up the artwork and Pocknell, who ended up in hospital with an ulcer, finishing the lips.

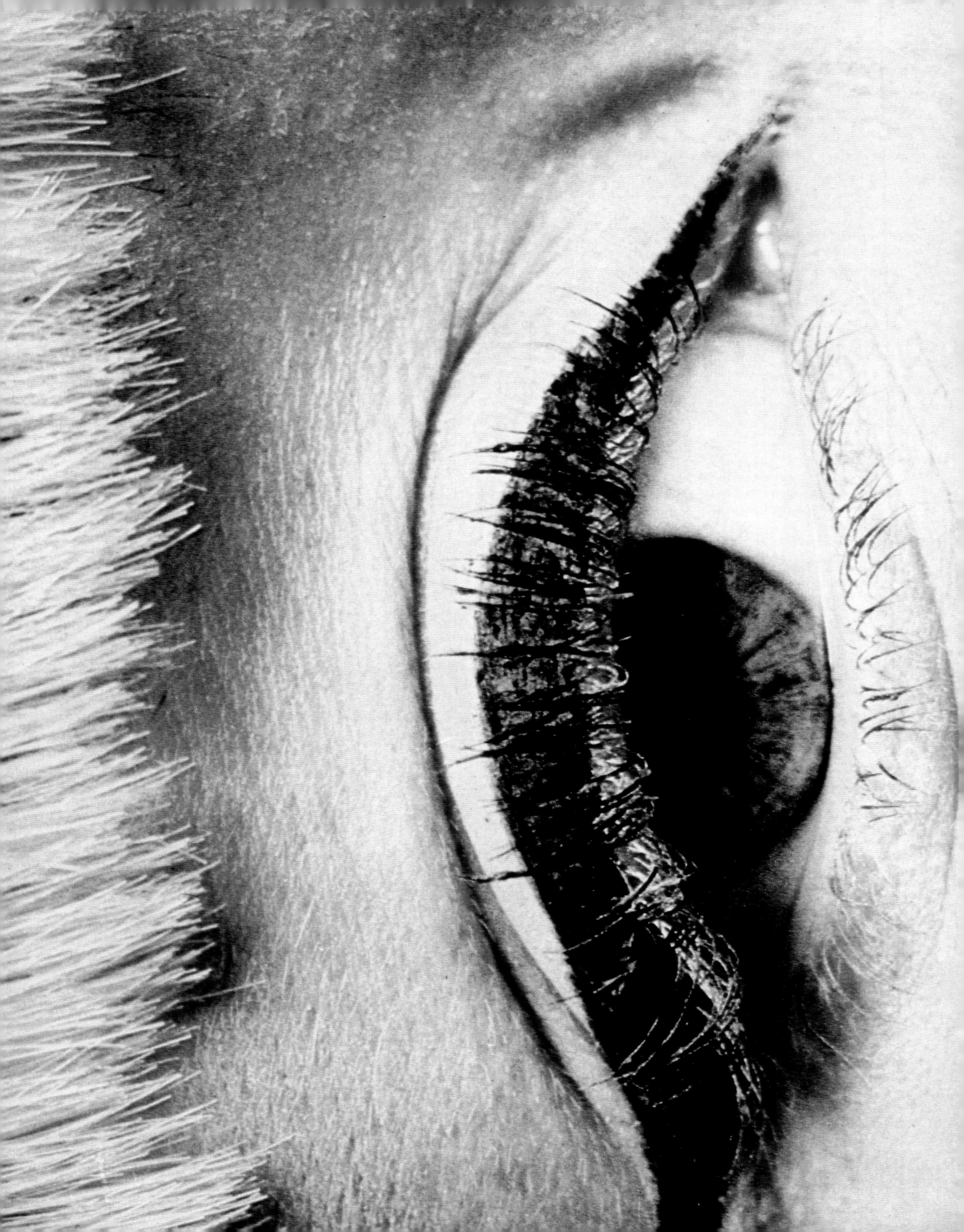

DRAWING THE LINE...

all along the eyelid and beyond with an upward tick. Meaning eyeliner is coming back into fashion, putting the finishing touch to the Fifties feeling running through clothes this spring. Already seen on the leading fashion models, who start more fads these days than anyone else. It takes a deft and steady hand; models recommend the cake eyeliner—lasts longer and doesn't flake so soon. Here, brownish-black cake eyeliner by Max Factor, 30p, applied with a Reeves paintbrush. *By Caroline Baker/ Photograph by Harri Peccinotti*

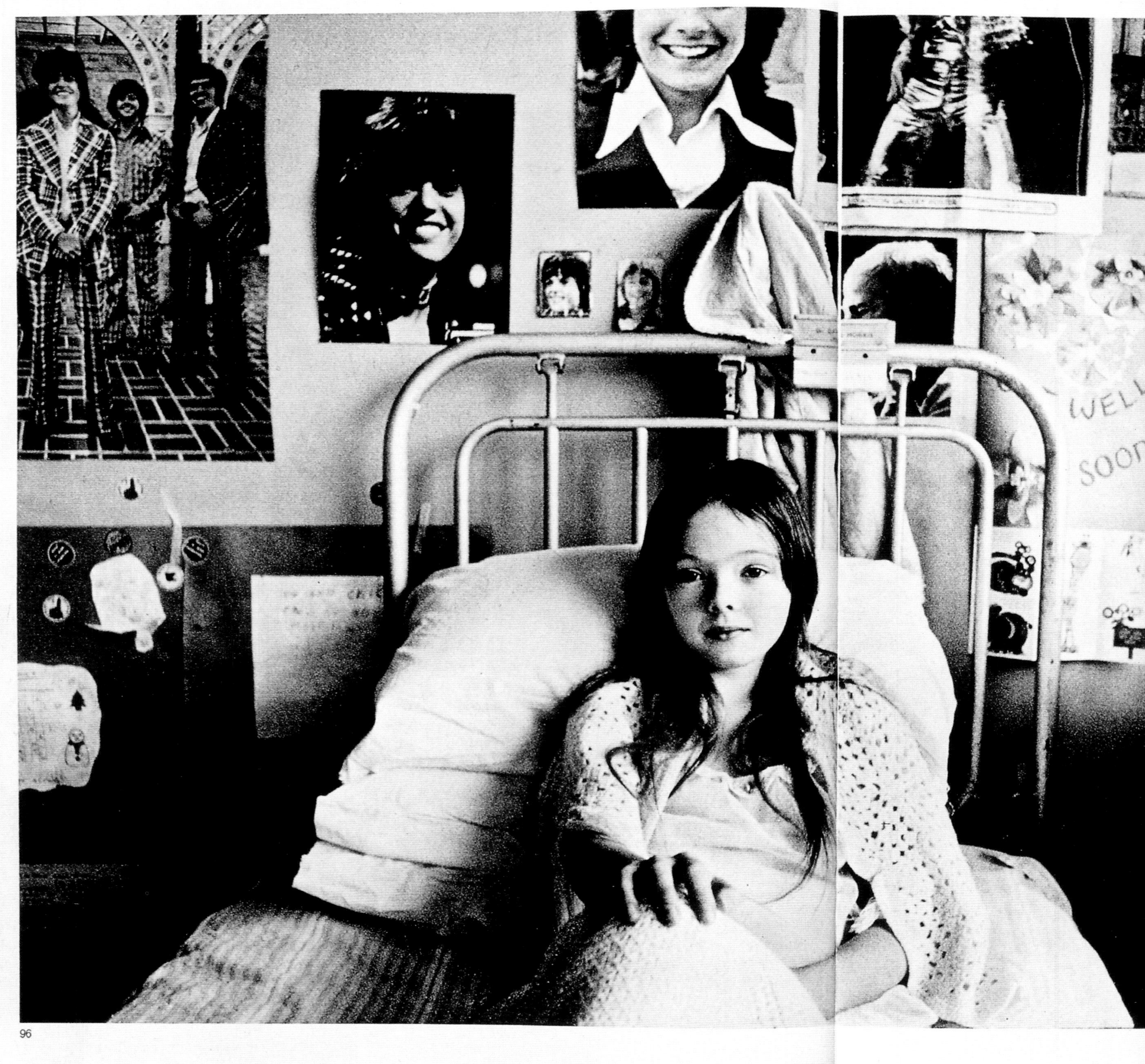

Previous page
March 1973
A feature on eyes by Caroline Baker. Photograph by Harri Peccinotti.

changes in the children's ward...

Some of the most distressing memories of childhood are concerned with spells in hospital, but fortunately medical attitudes are changing. Hospitals are beginning to realise that they have in their care not only the bodies but the minds of their patients. A child needs the emotional reassurance of constant and relaxed visits from his mother and the stimulus and satisfaction of play. He needs, in fact, an environment as close as possible to that of home. Here children talk about their own experiences and *Ruth Inglis* looks at how far the process of humanisation has gone.
Photographs by Peter Howe

'I didn't want to come into hospital because I didn't enjoy it last time, but I've been here eight weeks and this hospital is much nicer. I'm glad I've had the operation because I feel much better now but the tube they put in was irritating me and they kept giving me pain-killers because they thought it hurt. I kept trying to explain that it was only irritating and I didn't want pain-killers but they didn't seem to understand. They always explain what they're doing to me and they told me to ask if I wanted to know anything.

We have school in the morning. It's not really the same as school at home because the work's different and I'm a bit worried I'm falling behind but my school is going to send me some work. Then we have to have a rest for an hour after lunch and you get into trouble if you make a noise – but I get so bored. In the afternoon we go in the playroom and we do painting or we can play with water or plasticine – they have everything in there.

I love Donny Osmond and they let me bring all my pictures in with me to make me feel more at home but even though Mum and Dad come in every day, I still miss them. I do hope Donny Osmond sees this pictur he might write to me.'

Pauline Elcock (aged 11) at Brook Hospital, London

97

May 1973
One six-year-old's opinion of hospital: 'I like the guinea pig because it's like my bunny rabbit at home. I don't like the needle.' The children's comments were followed by Ruth Inglis's article on the better understanding that hospitals were giving to the young. Photographs by Peter Howe.

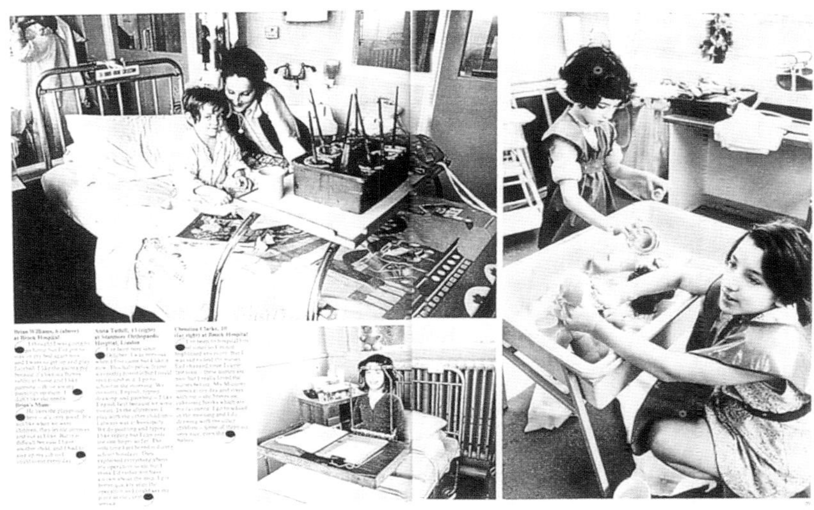

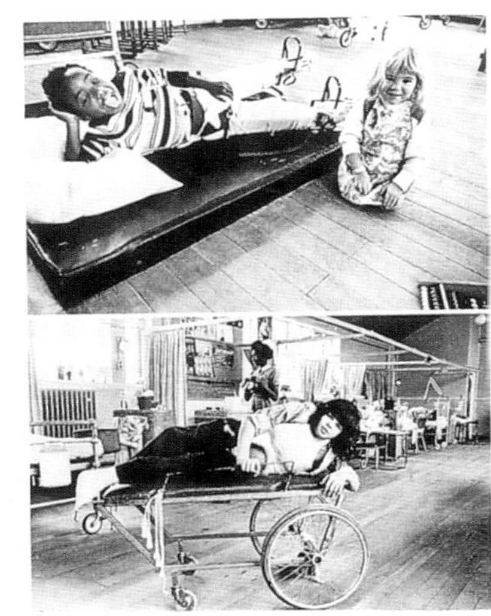

June 1973
An article 'Ma Elsie knows best' by Elaine Grande profiled the ruler of the roost of south London's Clan – three families all living in the same street who had been intermarrying for 60 years. The Clan's thirteen men were regularly in and out of prison: 'We's got two now, but eleven out so we're content. It's when you got only two out that trouble begins.' The deal was absolutely no photographs, not even a visit by an artist. The article was given to Gino D'Achille; he didn't even talk to the writer, and the resulting portrait stunned Grande by its verisimilitude. D'Achille admitted later that he had based it on his own family.

It is said that every alcoholic involves five other people closely connected with him or her and that two of those five will probably need some treatment for mental disturbance as a result of the alcoholic's turbulent and destructive passage through their lives. In this respect the woman alcoholic is a special case. Although the number of professional women with pronounced alcoholic tendencies is rising, the majority of women with a drinking problem are housewives and mothers, and the damage they inflict on their own families is potentially far greater than that of their male counterparts. Here, one woman describes her life as an alcoholic to *Geoffrey Sheridan*; and on page 34 *Rachael Feild* looks at the facts. Illustrations by *Mike McInnerney*

THE WOMAN WHO DRINKS

January 1973
Geoffrey Sheridan talked to a housewife with a problem, and to her husband. Illustration by Mike McInnerney.

November 1973
Roger Law's model celebrated a famous royal engagement.

April 1973
Prue Leith's cookery column started: 'Making a soufflé is child's play.' But not when your husband is meticulous photographer Tony Evans. Each one that Caroline Evans made in the kitchen was rejected when it got to the studio upstairs – either as too light, or too dark but mainly as too low. So they called the gas man in and moved the oven into the studio. They got it right on the nineteenth soufflé.

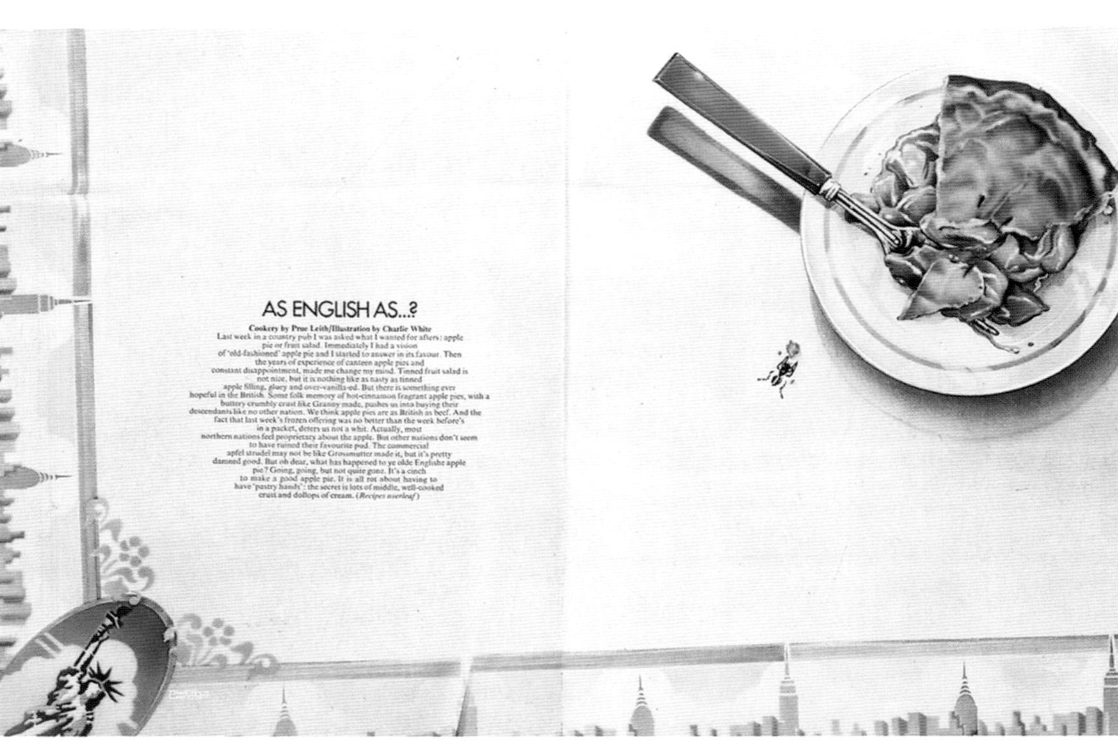

AS ENGLISH AS...?

Cookery by Prue Leith/Illustration by Charlie White

Last week in a country pub I was asked what I wanted for afters: apple pie or fruit salad. Immediately I had a vision of 'old-fashioned' apple pie and I started to answer in its favour. Then the years of experience of canteen apple pies and constant disappointment, made me change my mind. Tinned fruit salad is not nice, but it is nothing like as nasty as tinned apple filling, gluey and over-vanilla-ed. But there is something ever hopeful in the British. Some folk memory of hot-cinnamon fragrant apple pies, with a buttery crumbly crust like Granny made, pushes us into buying their descendants like no other nation. We think apple pies are as British as beef. And the fact that last week's frozen offering was no better than the week before's in a packet, deters us not a whit. Actually, most northern nations feel proprietary about the apple. But other nations don't seem to have ruined their favourite pud. The commercial apfel strudel may not be like Grossmutter made it, but it's pretty damned good. But oh dear, what has happened to ye olde Englishe apple pie? Going, going, but not quite gone. It's a cinch to make a good apple pie. It is all not about having to have 'pastry hands': the secret is lots of middle, well-cooked crust and dollops of cream. *(Recipes overleaf)*

November 1973
Prue Leith's cookery article bemoaned the demise of the real English apple pie. Charlie White II, aptly American, was commissioned for the illustration. It arrived with the fly thoughtfully drawn separately on an acetate overlay – so that David Hillman could use it or not as he liked.

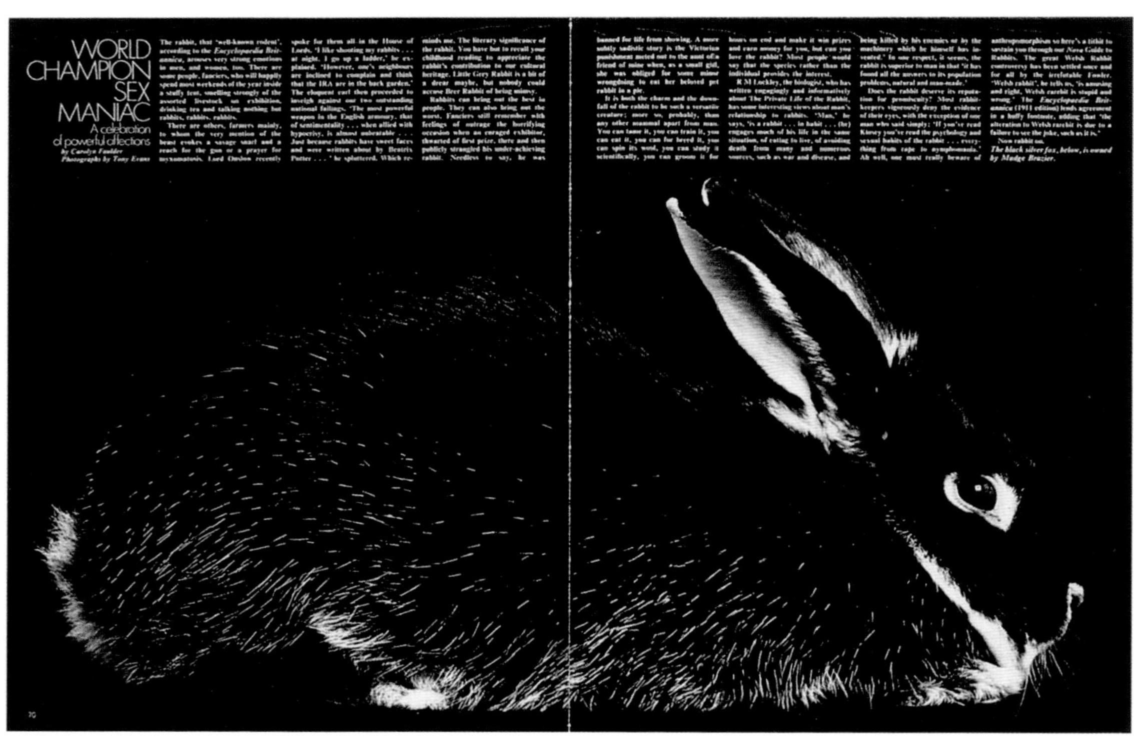

WORLD CHAMPION SEX MANIAC

A celebration of powerful affections

by Carolyn Faulder
Photographs by Tony Evans

The rabbit, that 'well-known rodent', according to the *Encyclopaedia Britannica*, arouses very strong emotions in men, and women, too. There are some people, fanciers, who will happily spend most weekends of the year inside a stuffy tent, smelling strongly of the assorted livestock on exhibition, drinking tea and talking nothing but rabbits, rabbits, rabbits.

There are others, farmers mainly, to whom the very mention of the beast evokes a savage snarl and a reach for the gun or a prayer for myxomatosis. Lord Onslow recently spoke for them all in the House of Lords. 'I like shooting my rabbits . . . at night. I go up a ladder,' he explained. 'However, one's neighbours are inclined to complain and think that the IRA are in the back garden.' The eloquent earl then proceeded to inveigh against our two outstanding national failings. 'The most powerful weapon in the English armoury, that of sentimentality . . . when allied with hypocrisy, is almost unbeatable . . . Just because rabbits have sweet faces and were written about by Beatrix Potter . . .' he spluttered. Which reminds me. The literary significance of the rabbit. You have but to recall your childhood reading to appreciate the rabbit's contribution to our cultural heritage. Little Grey Rabbit is a bit of a drear maybe, but nobody could accuse Brer Rabbit of being mimsy.

Rabbits can bring out the best in people. They can also bring out the worst. Fanciers still remember with feelings of outrage the horrifying occasion when an enraged exhibitor, thwarted of first prize, there and then publicly strangled his under-achieving rabbit. Needless to say, he was banned for life from showing. A more subtly sadistic story is the Victorian punishment meted out to the aunt of a friend of mine when, as a small girl, she was obliged for some minor wrongdoing to eat her beloved pet rabbit in a pie.

It is both the charm and the downfall of the rabbit to be such a versatile creature; more so, probably, than any other mammal apart from man. You can tame it, you can train it, you can eat it, you can for breed it, you can spin its wool, you can study it scientifically, you can groom it for hours on end and make it win prizes and earn money for you, but can you love the rabbit? Most people would say that the species rather than the individual provides the interest.

R M Lockley, the biologist, who has written engagingly and informatively about The Private Life of the Rabbit, has some interesting views about man's relationship to rabbits. 'Man,' he says, 'is a rabbit . . . in habit . . . (he) engages much of his life in the same situation, of eating to live, of avoiding death from many and numerous sources, such as war and disease, and being killed by his enemies or by the machinery which he himself has invented.' In one respect, it seems, the rabbit is superior to man in that 'it has found all the answers to its population problems, natural and man-made.'

Does the rabbit deserve its reputation for promiscuity? Most rabbit-keepers vigorously deny the evidence of their eyes, with the exception of one man who said simply: 'If you've read Kinsey you've read the psychology and sexual habits of the rabbit . . . everything from rape to nymphomania.' Ah well, one must really beware of anthropomorphism so here's a titbit to sustain you through our *Nova* Guide to Rabbits. The great Welsh Rabbit controversy has been settled once and for all by the irrefutable Fowler. 'Welsh rabbit', he tells us, 'is amusing and right. Welsh rarebit is stupid and wrong.' The *Encyclopaedia Britannica* (1911 edition) lends agreement in a huffy footnote, adding that 'the alteration to Welsh rarebit is due to a failure to see the joke, such as it is.'

Now rabbit on.

The black silver fox, below, is owned by Madge Brazier.

November 1973
Profile by Carolyn Faulder.
Photograph by Tony Evans.

FILS
971

1974

The year

Isabel Perón became president of Argentina. Two general elections in Britain were won by Labour, neither convincingly, and inflation hit 20 per cent. The Birmingham pub bomb killed twenty-one people; the IRA also bombed Harrods, Selfridges and Edward Heath's home. Watergate finally forced President Nixon to become the first American President to resign. Emperor Haile Selassie was deposed after ruling Ethiopia since the thirties. Muhammed Ali regained his old heavyweight title from George Foreman. The first disposable razors came on the market. Britain chuckled at Ronnie Barker in *Porridge* on TV. Elton John's *Candle In The Wind* had its first chart success (the second was to be in 1997) and Abba had their first of many with *Waterloo*. Ken Russell's *Tommy* and Mel Brooks's *Blazing Saddles* kept the fun going at the cinema. Newspapers became preoccupied with the curious case of ex-minister John Stonehouse, who disappeared leaving his clothes on a Miami beach, only to resurface in Australia. Lord Lucan went one better and disappeared for good after murder most foul in his home. Alexander Solzhenitsyn was expelled from Russia and collected his Nobel Prize for Literature which had been kept warm for him. The first McDonald's opened in London.

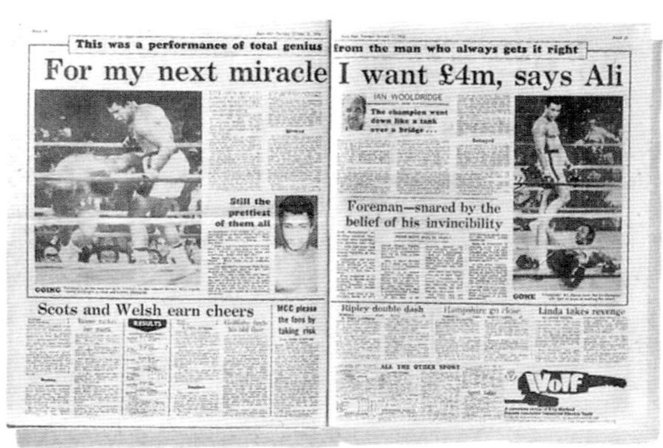

This was a performance of total genius from the man who always gets it right

For my next miracle I want £4m, says Ali

IAN WOOLDRIDGE

Still the prettiest of them all

Foreman—snared by the belief of his invincibility

GOING

GONE

Scots and Welsh earn cheers

MCC please the foes by taking risk

Linda takes revenge

ALL THE OTHER SPORT

Proof that he really was the greatest.

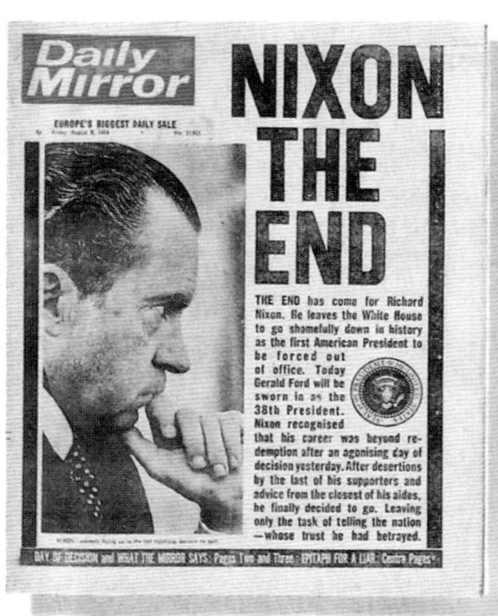

Daily Mirror

EUROPE'S BIGGEST DAILY SALE

NIXON THE END

THE END has come for Richard Nixon. He leaves the White House to go shamefully down in history as the first American President to be forced out of office. Today Gerald Ford will be sworn in as the 38th President. Nixon recognised that his career was beyond redemption after an agonising day of decision yesterday. After desertions by the last of his supporters and advice from the closest of his aides, he finally decided to go. Leaving only the task of telling the nation—whose trust he had betrayed.

DAY OF DECISION and WHAT THE MIRROR SAYS: Pages Two and Three: EPITAPH FOR A LIAR: Centre Pages

What happens if you are caught telling fibs.

THE TIMES

Terrorists' bombs kill at least 17 and injure over 100 in Birmingham

Attacks as IRA man's body is flown from Britain

Bomb a pub in Birmingham and unite Ireland.

Right

September 1974

A picture feature entitled 'Rave on' had Mao bopping with Kosygin, followed by the Shah of Persia with Prince Rainier, Fidel Castro with Willy Brandt and Harold Wilson with Golda Meir in similar vein. The idea was originally commissioned from Jean-Paul Goude for a Levi's ad campaign that never happened. He added to the series especially for *Nova*.

June 1974
Budgets were getting tight and location shoots were cut – even for this outdoor swimwear feature. Photographs (In the studio) by Harri Peccinotti and montage by David Hillman.

Costume piece

By Caroline Baker
Photographs by Harri Peccinotti
Montage by David Hillman
Retouching by John Sinclair

The bathing costume is overtaking the bikini as the seaside thing for water babes. Cut in cotton which doesn't stretch, it holds the body like a corset, giving it curves in all the right places and a shape it hasn't had in a long time

From left to right: *polka-dot bathing costume with a halter collar by Dorothy Perkins, £4.25; rose-and-newspaper-print costume by Miss Mouse, £10.95; geometric-print second-hand bathing suit from an Oxfam shop; leopard-print backless and strappy one-piece by Miss Mouse, £10.95; stamp-print romper top and panties by Miss Mouse, £10.95. All bathing caps by Kleinerts, 49p; waterproof 'Colour On' make-up by Max Factor. Skis by courtesy of Prince's Water Ski Club. Stockists on page 90*

Overleaf
January 1974
The headline puns were getting worse (or better), the theme ideas positively whacky. Suggested by a press story of Communist diplomats enjoying London rather too much, Hans Feurer shot this fantasy of girls in dubious company on a glamorous night on the town. The men were actually all friends of *Nova* and included Harri Peccinotti, Enzo Apicella and David Hillman.

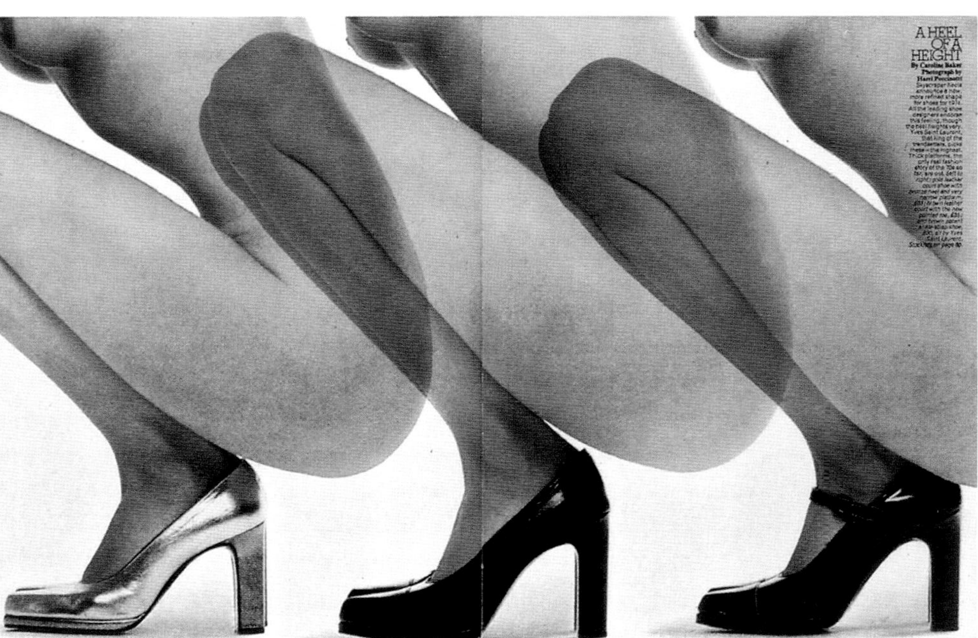

January 1974
Harri Peccinotti's photographs were stripped together for 'A heel of a height', a report on the new season's shoe designs. It was goodbye to platforms, which Caroline Baker described as: 'The only real fashion story of the 70s, so far.'

WE'RE JUST GOOD FUR-RIENDS..

GLAMOROUS evening out for leading ladies of pleasure turns to disaster. Dressed to kill in fashionable furs, Irma and Marie hit the town. Escorted by top diplomats and gold-braided members of foreign armed services they wined and dined at the town's hottest nightspot but finished up in one of the town's coldest – guests of the city police. Our photographer **HANS FEURER** recorded it: fashion editor **CAROLINE BAKER** comments frankly on the fabulous and the false.

DEEP pile leopard fabric coat (left) by Martha Hill, £24; gold lamé gown by Biba, £17.50; chokers and bracelets, silver gilded with gold, by Jones, £16.50, £11; gold button earrings by Christian Dior, £13.75; gold leather bag by Chris Trill for Flight, £17.25; leather gloves by Morley, £4.30; Tendrelle Kleersheer tights by Pretty Polly, 41p; gold strappy sandals by Russell and Bromley, £18.99. Champagne Chapal coney wrap (right) with opossum collar and cuffs by Zandra Rhodes for Austin Garritt, £365; cream Banlon dress by Anne Tyrrell for John Marks, £16.95; gold and ivory necklace and bangle by Christian Dior, £32, £12.35; grey calf envelope by Chris Trill for Flight, £16.50; long beige leather gloves by Morley, £8.25; Tendrelle Kleersheer tights by Pretty Polly, 41p; gold shoes by Russell and Bromley, £18.99. Gentlemen's dress suits to hire from Moss Bros. Photographed outside Grosvenor House, Park Lane; Rolls Royce Silver Shadow by H R Owen of London. *Stockists and addresses: p.80.*

34

FOREST green Chapal coney bolero jacket (left) trimmed in opossum detailed with pink and green velvet bands by Zandra Rhodes for Austin Garritt, £280; black silk Chinese jacket by K Sung, £27.50; black satin quilted trousers by Zandra Rhodes to order from Fortnum and Mason. Black and white zebra fabric wrapover jacket (right), matching skirt and muff and black silk shirt, all by Tsaritsar, £88, £43.45, £15.40, £15.40; entwined bracelets by Yves Saint Laurent, £14.50; leather gloves by Morley, £4.30; boots by Russell and Bromley, £24.99. Photographed at Grosvenor House ballroom.

38

TIGER skin fabric jacket (left) with matching skirt, inset with fake pony skin by Scruffs, £26.50, £15; cream tie-neck blouse by Biba, £6.60; gold dog tag and chain by Andre Bogaert, £25, £6.25; gold bangles by Yves Saint Laurent, £6.60; brown leather clutch bag by Chris Trill for Flight, £17; Tendrelle Kleersheer tights by Pretty Polly, 41p; brown leather boots by Yves Saint Laurent, £56.50. Silver fox fur jacket (right) by Femina Furs, £375; grey tie-neck blouse and wide grey flannel trousers, both by Katherine Hamnett for Tuttabankem, £20, £19.50; leather gloves by Morley, £4.00; navy elastic belt by Mulberry Co., £2.25; gold bangles by Yves Saint Laurent, £6.60. Photographed at Grosvenor House's Red Devil Bar.

DARK mink midi trench coat (left) by Katherine Hamnett for Philip Hockley, £1500; black seamed skirt and grey silk shirt by Katherine Hamnett for Tuttabankem, £14.95, £17; sunglasses by Christian Dior, £15; boots by Yves Saint Laurent, £56.50. Grey and black leopard-print jacket and skirt (right) and long grey fake-raccoon muffler, all by Biba, £13.95, £5, £1[illegible].95; grey silk shirt by Katherine Hamnett for Tuttabankem, £17; sunglasses by Christian Dior, £15; boots by Russell and Bromley, £24.99. Hair by Christopher at Vidal Sassoon. Men's clothing from the Special Offers Dept., Moss Bros. Photographed leaving Grosvenor House, Park Lane

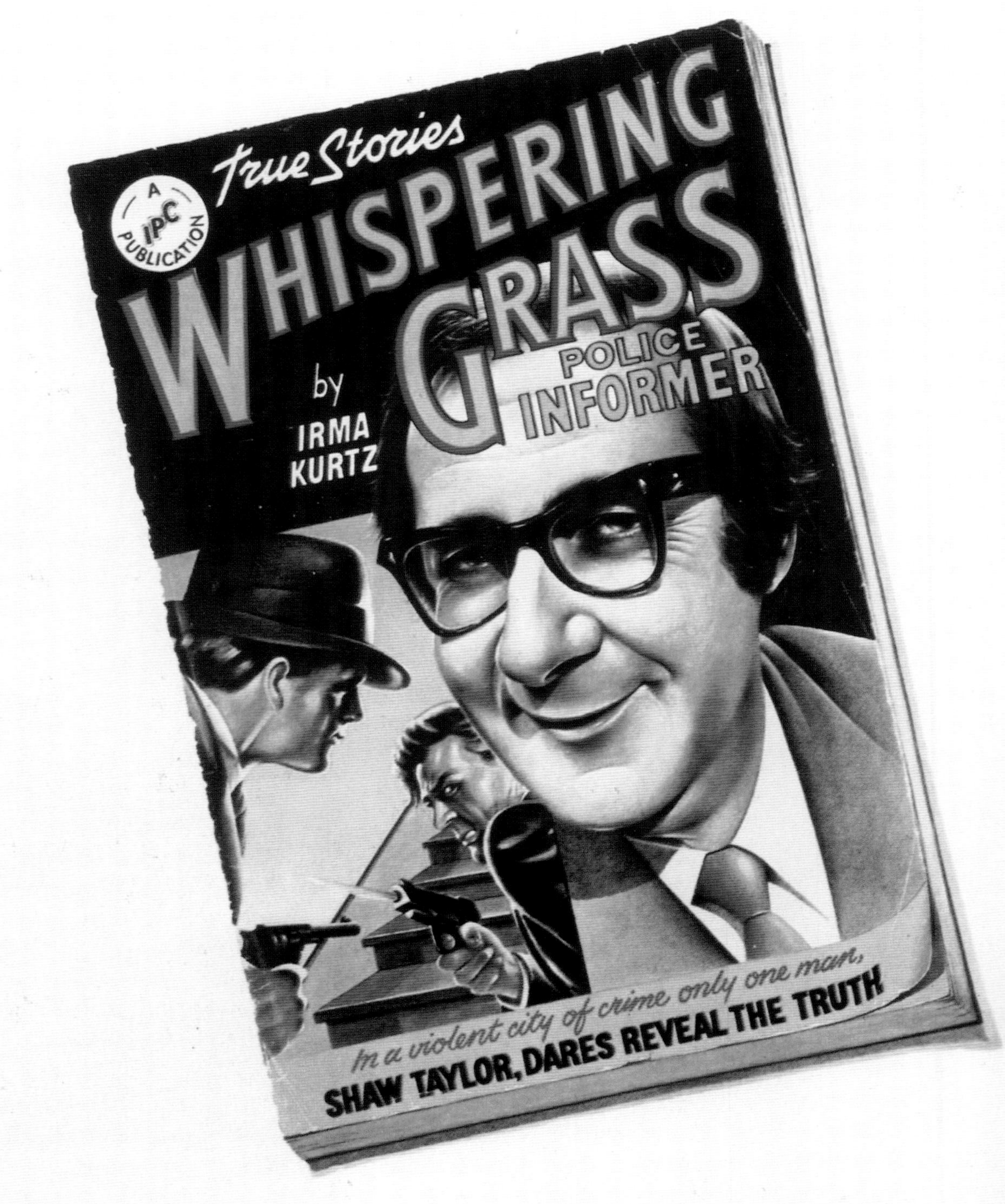

Illustration by John Gorham

February 1974
John Gorham's illustration for a profile by Irma Kurtz of Shaw Taylor, who had made his name with the five-minute, tell-the-police TV show *Police Five*.

WHAT HO, WODEHOUSE

Ruth Inglis shimmers over to Long Island to exchange a civil word with the president of the Drones Club
Illustration by Paul Leith

'I was much too hard up to be a Bertie Wooster'

October 1974
Ruth Inglis interviewed PG Wodehouse on Long Island NY. Illustration by Paul Leith.

COME THE REVOLUTION

as many people believe it must, only one man has the authority, the ability, the popularity to lead it – and win. Jimmy Reid is standing as a Communist in the next general election and could well become the first Communist MP since Willie Gallagher. If he wins he will owe his success as much to his humanity, his driving belief in human rights – the right to work in particular – as to his political ideals. Jimmy Reid talks to John Heilpern about his background, his principles and his hopes for the future.

Photograph by David Reed

March 1974
Jimmy Reid photographed by David Reed. John Heilpern interviewed the charming union convener of the Upper Clyde Shipbuilders who was aiming to be Britain's first Communist MP since the Thirties.

WHISPERING GRASS

HE'S A FINE FIGURE of a fellow, an extrovert, the sort of man who has always fired trust in the fathers of eligible daughters and, wide-eyed, mistaken young girls' mothers for their sisters, the sort of man who gets many slices of home-baked goodies fresh from the oven, dapper, he looks well off but has the common touch. Nobody meeting him for the first time would take him for a professional rat fink. And only someone with a deep understanding of the law-enforcing mind, not all that unlike its opposite, would suspect that his nickname in high circles of crime and punishment, in squalid dockside pubs and in the sunny rooms of New Scotland Yard, is 'Whispering Grass'. Shaw Taylor, the TV sleuth, spearhead of *Police Five* and *Junior Police Five* whose viewing audience every week is probably more than the annual readers of *Sherlock Holmes*, is a man who has found his mission and, even more poignant in the greater scheme of things, an actor who has found a steady job.

'It's more show biz, my job,' said Mr Taylor, 'than copper's business.'

'But if he wanted to,' said a minion from The Yard, 'he could probably be a cop. After more than ten years on *Police Five* he knows quite a considerable amount about police methods,' he said, indicating by the merest shade in his tone that he was only being courteous and even a gifted amateur could never really presume, despite the fantasies of endless detective story writers, to outpace a pro; despite – and this was a slightly unnerving thought – his pretty regular lunches with the Commissioner.

'The Commissioner said to me at lunch the other day,' said Mr Taylor, 'that a policeman only does for money what we should all be doing for free.'

Until that day eleven years ago when ATV found itself with a five-minute hole to fill, nothing would have appeared more unlikely than that Shaw Taylor's career would lead him to The Yard, to lunch with the Commissioner and to policing of the primrose path. He was born and bred in the East End – and did he start one wonders with the hifalutin' monniker he carries or is Shaw Taylor an alias? Do you perhaps remember meeting a small boy, at a guess say forty years ago, who wanted to be an actor and was not called Shaw Taylor?

Young Shaw went to RADA where he learned painfully to rid himself of his impure vowels and to purse his lips around the genteel sounds of a young hopeful's West End diction. His first audition went pretty well except the casting director was awfully sorry, really, but they were looking for someone with a genuine East End accent. His first role, after he had turned down a part in what he was convinced would be a sure-fire flop called *The Mousetrap*, was as a cop. For three years or so he appeared in various Agatha Christie plays – perhaps you saw him once bringing prophetic vigour to the role of a cop or a villain? He's a bigger, better-looking fellow than he appears to be on the box and has a much more lusty sense of humour than his TV spot gives him scope to express.

'There's a lady here from *Nova*,' he said on the phone to a friend at The Yard, 'who wants to know if they can photograph me nude wearing a policeman's helmet. What's that you say? No. But do I want to borrow a truncheon?'

In a particularly enjoyable kind of rep company which toured around and around the Isle of Wight, Mr Taylor met his wife and in due time they produced a son – 'not at all like me. Not an extrovert at all' – who lives with them now in Streatham and expresses mild surprise when his school chums ask him to get his dad's autograph.

UNTIL HE ROCKETED to fame as a police informer, Mr Taylor's career was the steady one to be expected of a man with charisma, the sort of career which depends for its high spots upon television. Like good old Frost – and do you remember seeing that ageing boy with his identikit face? Perhaps in your own living-room? – Mr Taylor fits the screen and the screen fits him: his ebullience, his enthusiasm about crime, might be lost in an auditorium but it is perfectly at home in the shelter of bay windows and not ten paces from a nice cuppa.

He has in fact done a lot of broadcasting in the past and, as might be expected, was a very polished quiz master. As it is with most charismatic public figures, despite his charm in a one-to-one meeting, there seems to be a part of Mr Taylor, the deepest part, which is an absolute secret so that after many meetings with the public figure one feels one has met just that: the public figure. Is there a frightened boy, a Shakespearean actor, a lost commissioner of police, lurking within that well-dressed exterior? Or could it be that deep down inside the public figure there lives a public figure? Have you perhaps noticed anything on your own television screen that would give us a clue

71

DR FRANKENSTEIN'S INSPIRATION

Peter Cushing, king of horror movies, talks to Jane Ennis

Photograph by Rolph Gobits

THE SMALLEST SHOW ON EARTH

Top
September 1974
Peter Cushing, master of the horror movie, interviewed by Jane Ennis. Photograph by Rolph Gobits.

Above
August 1974
Two people and a tent travelled as The Circus Romaine, billed as 'Europe's most compact show'. Liz Gould went to talk to them and Rolph Gobits to photograph them.

July 1974
'Boas are best but pythons will do', profile of a snake dancer by Liz Gould. Photograph by Rolph Gobits.

Right
January 1974
For power cuts and the long winter nights, the Compleat Bedman's pull-out, fold-and-cut guide, designed by John McConnell.

March 1974
John McConnell worked with David Hillman on a fourteen-page *Nova* guide parodying the wartime Ministry of Information (in the guise of the 'Department of Crises') on how to survive the hard times.

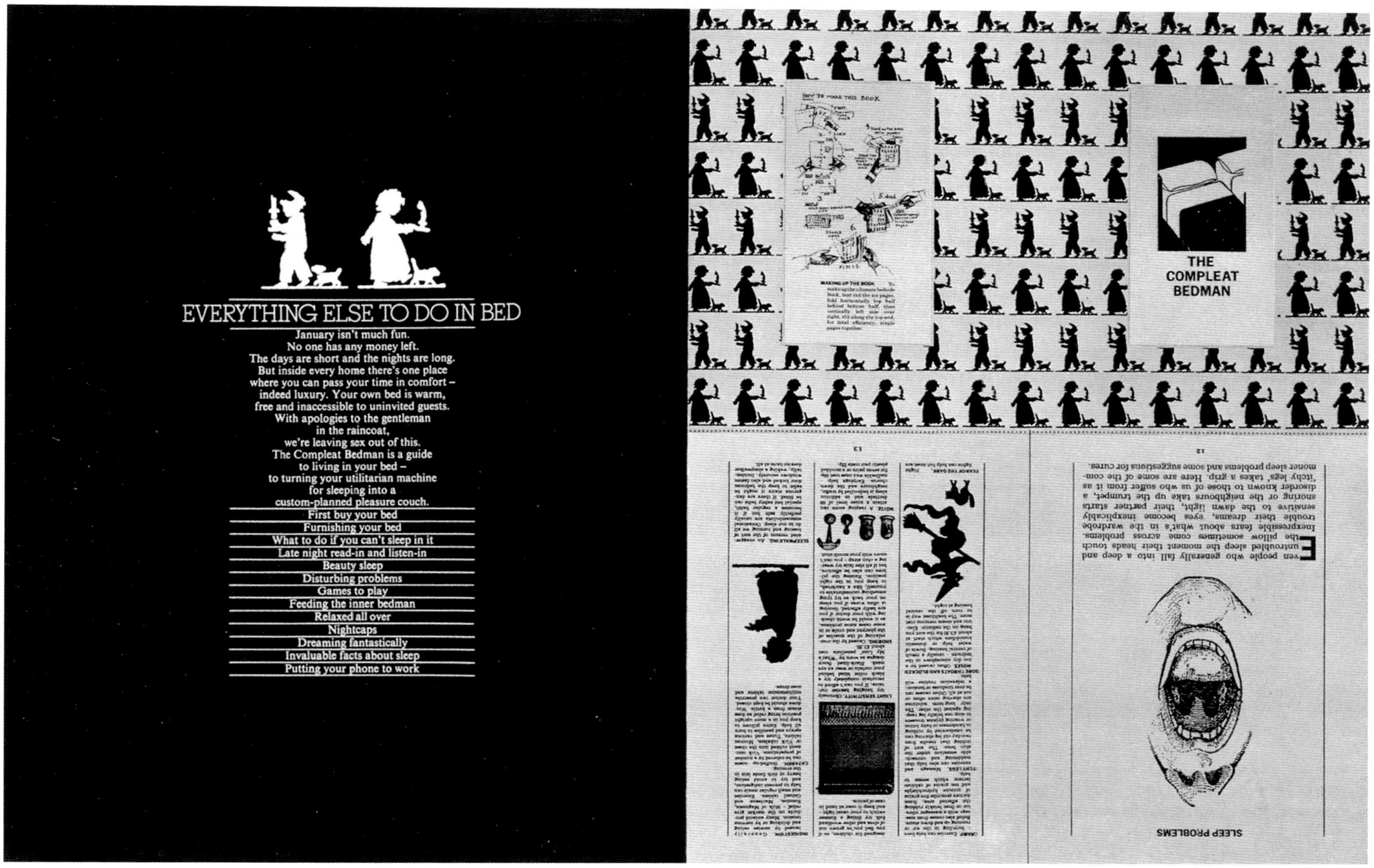

THE COMPLEAT BEDMAN

EVERYTHING ELSE TO DO IN BED

January isn't much fun.
No one has any money left.
The days are short and the nights are long.
But inside every home there's one place
where you can pass your time in comfort –
indeed luxury. Your own bed is warm,
free and inaccessible to uninvited guests.
With apologies to the gentleman
in the raincoat,
we're leaving sex out of this.
The Compleat Bedman is a guide
to living in your bed –
to turning your utilitarian machine
for sleeping into a
custom-planned pleasure couch.

First buy your bed
Furnishing your bed
What to do if you can't sleep in it
Late night read-in and listen-in
Beauty sleep
Disturbing problems
Games to play
Feeding the inner bedman
Relaxed all over
Nightcaps
Dreaming fantastically
Invaluable facts about sleep
Putting your phone to work

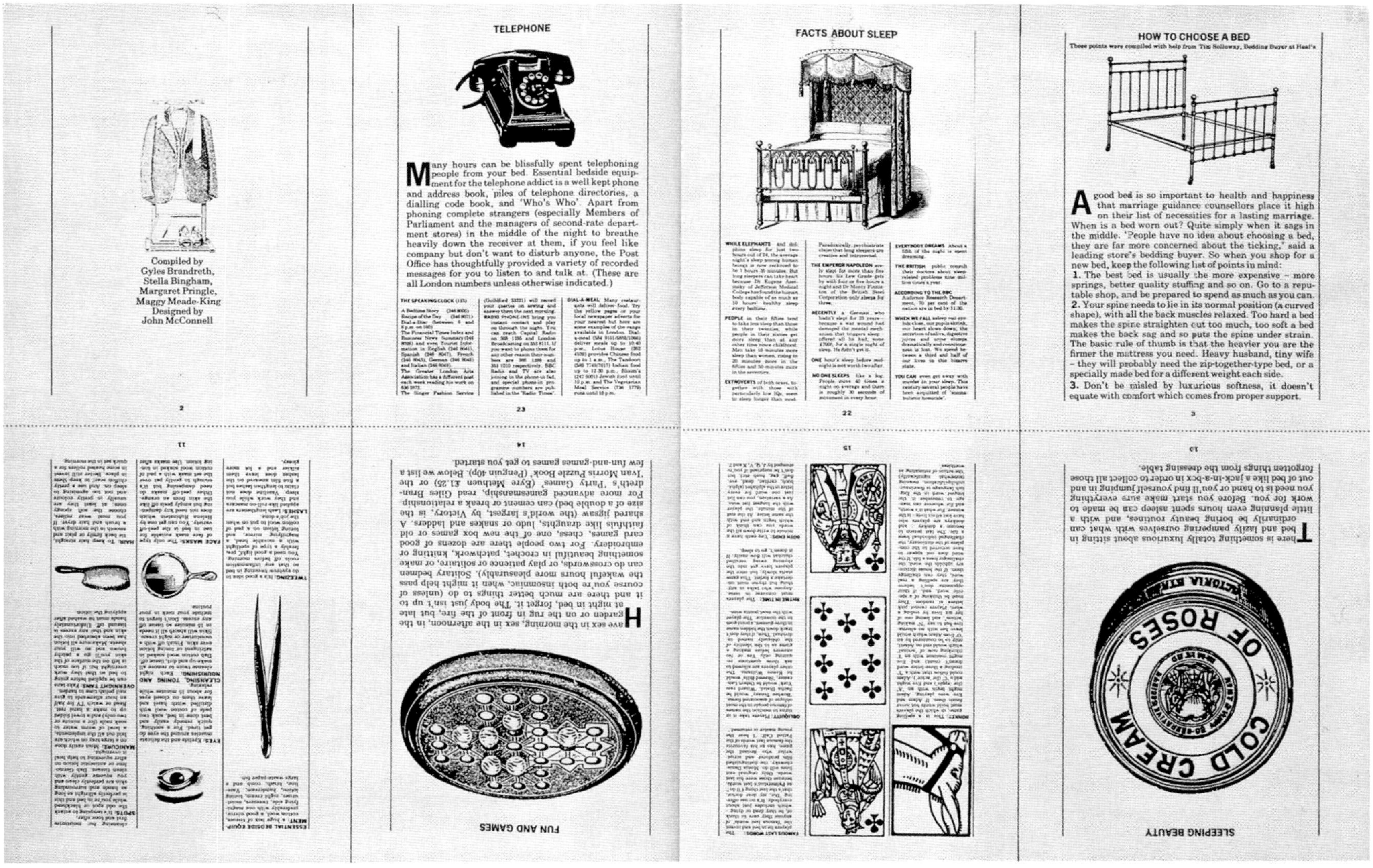

Compiled by
Gyles Brandreth,
Stella Bingham,
Margaret Pringle,
Maggy Meade-King
Designed by
John McConnell

2

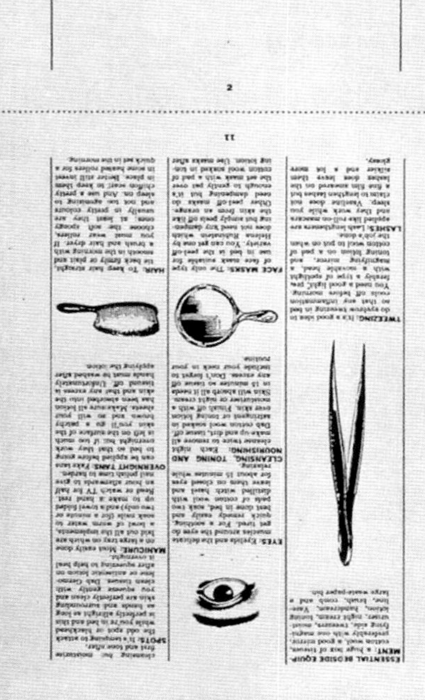

TELEPHONE

Many hours can be blissfully spent telephoning people from your bed. Essential bedside equipment for the telephone addict is a well kept phone and address book, piles of telephone directories, a dialling code book, and 'Who's Who'. Apart from phoning complete strangers (especially Members of Parliament and the managers of second-rate department stores) in the middle of the night to breathe heavily down the receiver at them, if you feel like company but don't want to disturb anyone, the Post Office has thoughtfully provided a variety of recorded messages for you to listen to and talk at. (These are all London numbers unless otherwise indicated.)

23

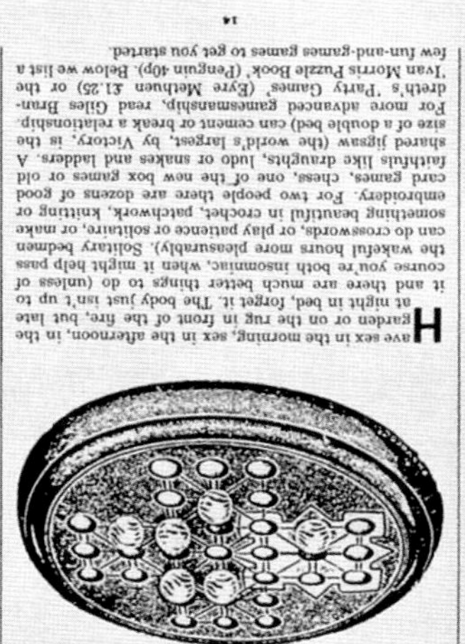

FACTS ABOUT SLEEP

22

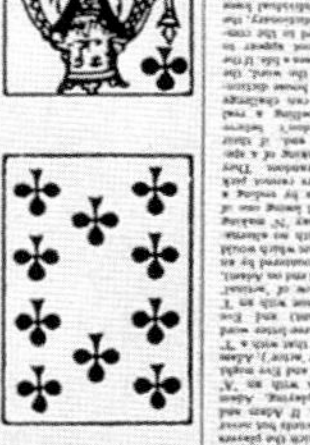

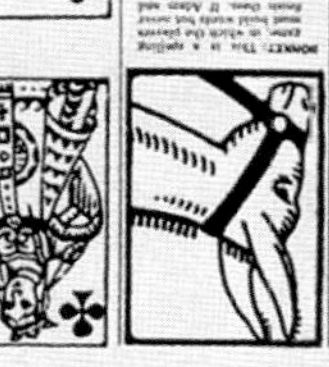

HOW TO CHOOSE A BED

These points were compiled with help from Tim Solloway, Bedding Buyer at Heal's

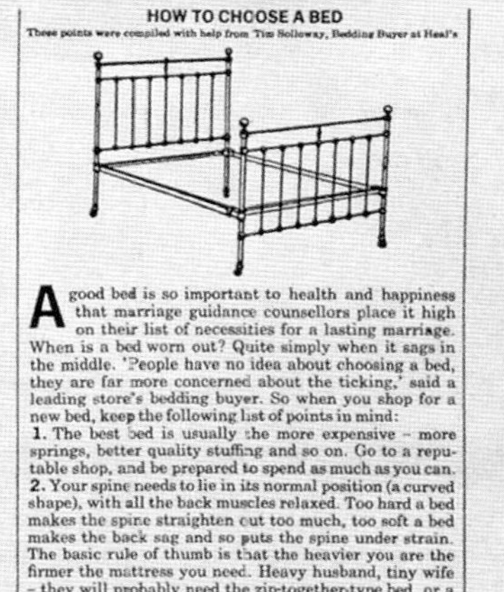

A good bed is so important to health and happiness that marriage guidance counsellors place it high on their list of necessities for a lasting marriage. When is a bed worn out? Quite simply when it sags in the middle. 'People have no idea about choosing a bed, they are far more concerned about the ticking,' said a leading store's bedding buyer. So when you shop for a new bed, keep the following list of points in mind:

1. The best bed is usually the more expensive – more springs, better quality stuffing and so on. Go to a reputable shop, and be prepared to spend as much as you can.
2. Your spine needs to lie in its normal position (a curved shape), with all the back muscles relaxed. Too hard a bed makes the spine straighten out too much, too soft a bed makes the back sag and so puts the spine under strain. The basic rule of thumb is that the heavier you are the firmer the mattress you need. Heavy husband, tiny wife – they will probably need the zip-together-type bed, or a specially made bed for a different weight each side.
3. Don't be misled by luxurious softness, it doesn't equate with comfort which comes from proper support.

3

1975

The man they would call 'The Boss'.

The year

Saigon fell; the war was finally over. In Cambodia Phnom Penh was taken by the Khmer Rouge. Women's rights gained more ground with the Sex Discrimination and Equal Pay Acts, and Margaret Thatcher became leader of the Conservative party. Britain's first referendum confirmed the nation's wish to stay as members of the European Community. The fiendish Rubik's Cube became a craze amongst the underemployed. Dutch Elm Disease killed 6.5 million trees in Britain. The first of Britain's oil from the North Sea came ashore; public money was poured into a severely troubled British Leyland. Inflation peaked at 30 per cent. Arthur Ashe won Wimbledon by lobbing Jimmy Connors. John Cleese became even funnier in *Fawlty Towers*. Jack Nicholson became a star in *One Flew Over The Cuckoo's Nest*, and *Jaws* was Hollywood's big scream offering. Disco music began to take over the pop scene, but Rod Stewart's *Sailing* and Queen's extraordinary *Bohemian Rhapsody* proved there was more to it. Bruce Springsteen's *Born to Run* album started the blue-collar rock wave, sparking another fashion comeback for denim. *Nova* folded.

Jack Nicholson went cuckoo.

Daily Mail

MONEY MAIL TODAY

Frightened, abandoned and waiting for its fate ... that is Saigon as 30 years of war reach a climax with a Dunkirk in the Sky

THE END

Desperate fight to leave

The hugest sigh of relief the world has known.

June 1975
Illustration by Arthur Robins for John Mortimer's article on where to go to make love in the afternoon.

The chill rain, at 9.30 a.m. on this Monday in October, is drifting down. Roy Dearden settles his check trilby more firmly on his head and pushes open the first gate of the terraced street. The rain has splashed his metal-framed glasses and there are tiny flecks of blood from his morning's shave on his white drip-dry collar. A briefcase full of Jehovah's Witnesses literature in his left hand, he has come to announce the end of the world to Thornton Heath.

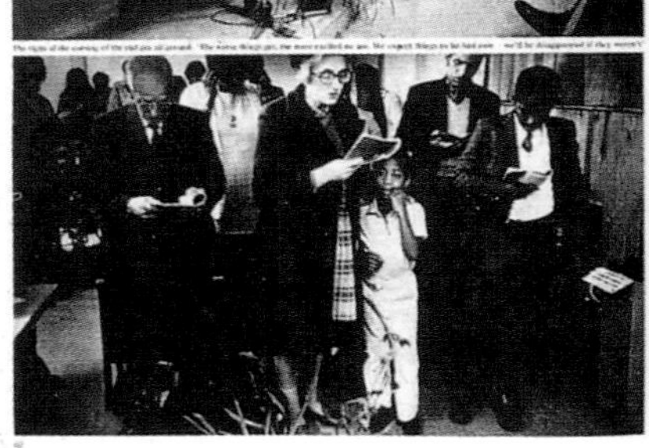

Although the fig tree itself may not
blossom... I will exalt in Jehovah himself.
HAB 3:17,18.

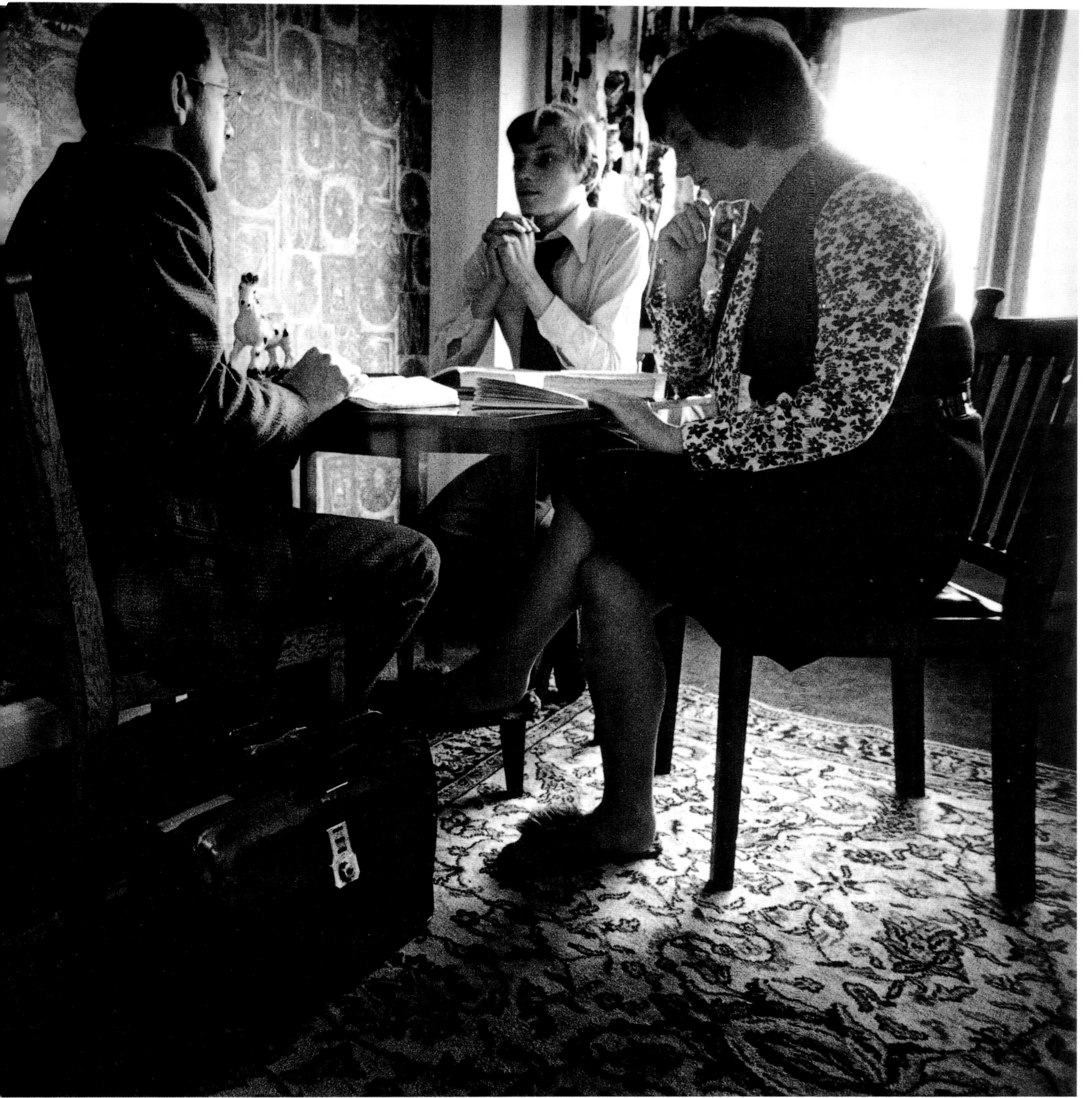

February 1975
Peter Gillman followed Jehovah's Witnesses around town and found them happily waiting for the imminent end of the world. Photographs by Phil Sayer.

January 1975
Sir Frederick Ashton profiled by Pat Barr. Photograph by Rolph Gobits.

NOW YOU SEE THEM NOW YOU DON'T! A ONCE IN A LIFETIME OPPORTUNITY!

MEET THE AMAZING PEFORMING MAGICIANS!

By Pat Barr Photographs Rolph Gobits

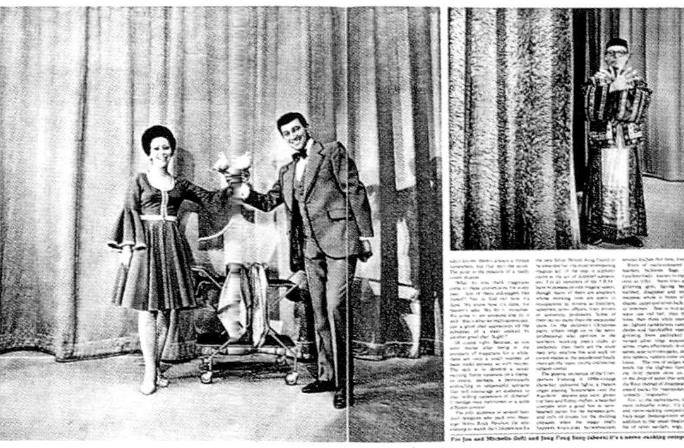

February 1975
Pat Barr visited Britain's annual Magicians' Convention. Photographs by Rolph Gobits.

HOW DOES THE HUMAN RACE?

March 1975
James Hamilton-Paterson interviewed Vienna-born Ivan Illich, author of *Medical Nemesis*, a treatise placing the ills of modern society at the door of technology. Photograph by Peter Howe.

March 1975
Helmut Newton's photographs for Caroline Baker's look at the khaki fashion craze.

KHAKI KOLOURED KRAZE

By Caroline Baker
Photographs by Helmut Newton

Khaki is the biggest fashion craze since blue jeans. Every manufacturer is using it and most designs are inspired by that other group that uses khaki so extensively – the army. The clothes are comfortable, functional and no nonsense. They're not as cheap as army surplus but they fit better and they're classics which will remain wearable for years. When khaki fades from the limelight it reverts to a good shade of earth.

Sage khaki string cotton singlet by Jap at Joseph, £13.95; green khaki cotton wide trousers with buckle fastening, two pleats at waist, and turn-ups, by Marshall Lester, £9.80; webbing belt from a selection of army surplus at Laurence Corner, 60p approx; gold studded leather wristlets from East Street Market, 75p each; 9 carat gold chains and dog-tags from Don Cooper, £38, £22; long white tennis socks from Lonsdale Sports, £1; lace-up leather boots from Olof Daughters, £20.

Hair by Frederic of Mods Hair. Make-up by Clemente of Elizabeth Arden, using their Stop Red lipstick, Sunshine Red nail lacquer, and Creative Colour pencil on eyes and tattoo. Stockists on page 95

60

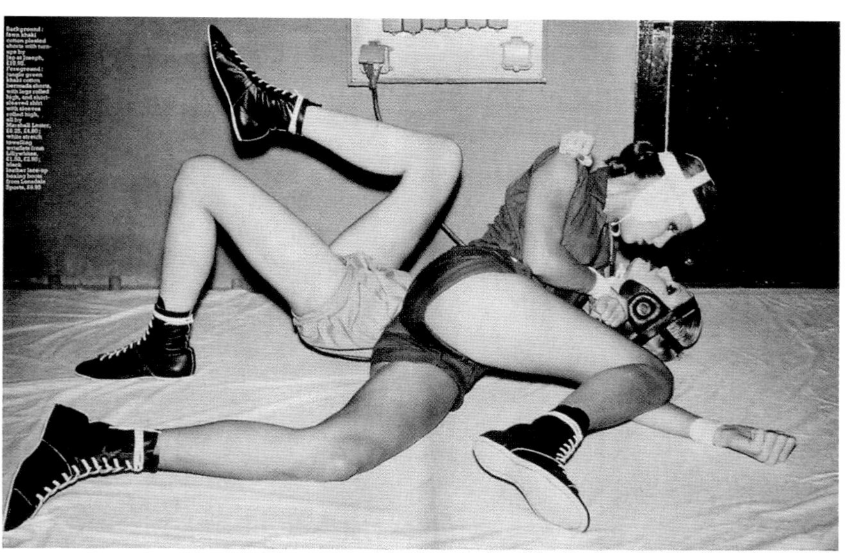

Pick the sport that will do you good and, most important, that you'll like enough to keep up. Illustrations by Arthur Robins

Rugby: very good in terms of heart-lung efficiency but classed as an isometric exercise, which means it involves lots of straining and pushing on muscles which is not good. Is violently competitive, with erratic bursts of activity. Often played in the cold which can increase blood pressure.

Chest expanders: these are good for would-be muscle men or ladies who want to have big busts. If you want to exercise anything more than your arms or shoulders, they aren't worth buying. Can help heart and lung efficiency if you are prepared to put in a great deal of very hard work – however, remember there are pleasanter more dynamic methods.

Running: all right for young and fit. Builds up the leg muscles and heart and lung efficiency. But is not good if very competitive. Difficult to control or regulate, some get too breathless, others not enough.

Dancing: unless very vigorous not strenuous enough to be of much use. Even the quick-step only moves the pulse rate at 110 beats per minute, though Victor Sylvester, at 75, is one of the fittest men in Britain! Jive might be a bit more efficient but the normal disco movement is useless.

32

Keep Fit: they say women mostly do Keep Fit for posture and figure. Good for mobility and flexibility, no good for toning muscles, not sufficiently vigorous for heart-lung efficiency.

Squash: good if you exercise 3 times a week for half an hour, can keep pulse up. Needs initial training. Not good if only played occasionally with too high objectives or if heavy smoker. It's played all year round, fits into office routine, is sociable. But often too competitive to help stress symptoms. Difficult to grade severity of the exercise.

Gymnasium bicycles: good for leg muscles, heart and lung efficiency. Can overstrain yourself unless you regulate the resistance you put on muscles and your speed. Aim at 20 minutes, 3 times a week. Begin slowly, with plenty of rests. Then work up to maximum rate without rests so pulse rate is at peak throughout.

Walking: if it's just the dog, not much use. Too mild to have any effect. Even if you were walking briskly, you would not get your pulse rate above 100 to 110 beats per minute, so unless there are lots of hills and stairs this is well below the target. Good for heart rehabilitation patients. If at least 15 minutes brisk walk twice a day, to and from work, nearer 'training' level.

Swimming: good exercise, uses all muscles. If overweight, water bears weight. Must think how you're swimming, aim for 15 minutes, 3 times a week. Disadvantages: if unfit, breathing pattern in front crawl can put an extra strain on the heart. Cold dips can be bad for blood pressure.

33

Skipping: good for flexibility of shoulders and arm muscles: good for heart and lung efficiency as long as taken seriously and regularly like jogging. But needs to be kept up for 20 minutes, three times a week. Can be too strenuous if not taken slowly at first, as it is mostly used for training very fit athletes. Be careful, if in your late 30s or early 40s, to take plenty of rests to begin with.

Football: good for heart-lung efficiency, keeps pulse rate up (not for players who never move; but it is usually played by the young and fit anyway). Full game and practice session each week required.

Rowing machines: good for trunk, leg and shoulder muscles, though not dynamic. Can be isotonic, meaning there is too much muscle resistance which strains them. And how can you stop it getting boring if you row for 20 minutes three times a week?

Weight lifting: Al Murray, ex national coach, rates this as best exercise if regulated – but only for the already-fit. It exercises all muscles, covers mobility, and you can meditate for relaxation.

Morning exercises: all right if you follow progress charts carefully and keep up for at least 15 minutes daily. But exercise programmes not always thoroughly medically approved. For instance press-ups are often included as part of routines but can be dangerous: if overweight can strain the heart.

34

Golf: almost a non-exercise. Even slows down a normal walking pace. The infrequent violent swing does not improve mobility apart from the shoulder, and is not vigorous enough to improve heart-lung efficiency. It is not relaxing since it is competitive and frustrating. In too cold weather it can raise blood pressure. Indoor golf taken up as exercise by non-golfers is a mistake.

Jogging: unfit would-be joggers should limber up beforehand using free exercises and on-the-spot running. Pace should allow breath for conversation. Ideal for leg muscles, heart and lungs; not good for trunk or flexibility of muscles. Can cause heart attack if taken too fast and if overweight. In cold weather can increase blood pressure. Jog at least three times weekly for 15 minutes; general exercise programme needed as back-up.

Tennis: very good exercise but is seasonal and spasmodic. Better than running etc. because it brings in more mobility exercises in turning, twisting and bending. Uses majority of muscles. If more indoor centres were available it could be the best all-round exercise. You need to play three times a week.

Yoga: not the perfect exercise it is often claimed to be. Exercises muscles, but if taught badly can lead to strained muscles. A system of control, in the West it tends to be taught to people who are already too controlled.

Cycling: good exercise. Uses all the big muscle masses and you're likely to keep it up as it gets you somewhere. All right for the overweight, as weight is carried. Not enough exercise for chest and shoulders. 15–20 minutes a day is enough provided you take in stiff hills or sprint stretches to get the blood rushing.

Left
September 1975
Arthur Robins illustrated a feature on keeping fit, the month before *Nova* passed away.

CREATING A STINK

Cookery by Prue Leith/Illustration by Edda Köchl

THE STUFFING DREAMS ARE MADE OF

By Prue Leith/Illustration by Dan Fern

CLASSIC FORCEMEAT FOR POULTRY OR GAME

SPINACH AND MUSHROOM

RICE, WATERCRESS AND SPRING ONION

APRICOT AND DATE

Top
February 1975
Edda Köchl's illustration for Prue Leith on garlic.

Above
March 1975
Dan Fern's illustration for Prue Leith on stuffings.

June 1975
John Gorham's illustration for Timothy Green's report on gold – what it is, what to do with it, how to make money out of it.

Who did what when

The credits are as recorded in the contents pages of each issue. Only by-lined articles and features are included.

MARCH 1965
Contents
The reading revolution for tots/Anne Scott-James
How I taught my son to read/Dr D.L. Shaw
What's in a label? A guide to quality marks/Elizabeth Gundrey
The Intelligent Woman's Guide to Isms : Humanism/Sir Julian Huxley
Jill Butterfield
A day in the life of Anthony Blond/Llew Gardner
Happy Families 1965/Angela Ince
The Man Who Married a French Wife/short story by Irwin Shaw
Stars of the subtitle circuit/Christopher Booker
British painting in the 1930s/Frank Whitford
Beat and ballad/Kenneth Allsop
Robert Robinson Reviewing
Is there something in it?/Eve Perrick
What is the New Morality?/Monica Furlong
A marriage roundabout/Alma Birk
Doctors and adultery/Brian Inglis
A two-holiday-a-year plan/by Peter and Fiona Carvell
Beauty: Success and Vidal Sassoon/ Elizabeth Williamson
Travel: Tunis before the deluge/James Wellard
Cookery: Syllabub is simple/Elizabeth David
Staff
Editor/Harry Fieldhouse. Assistant editor/Jean Cross. Editorial adviser/Alma Birk. Art editor/Harri Peccinotti. Fashion director/Jill Butterfield. Fashion editor/Penny Vincenzi. Susan Peters. Home & beauty editor/Elizabeth Williamson. Isabel Pearce. Fiction editor/Joy Matthews. Jean Scroggie. Jean Penfold. Michael Wynn-Jones.

APRIL 1965
Contents
We adopted a Chinese orphan/Diana Kareh
Shopping without leaving the home/ Elizabeth Gundrey
The Intelligent Woman's Guide to Isms: Mysticism/Bertrand Russell
How to understand your daily newspaper/ Anthony Lejeune
Mr Bratby settles down/Llew Gardner
Jill Butterfield
A policy for excuses/Jonathan Routh
Sorry I'm late darling, I've been having my hair done/Angela Ince
Total Stranger/short story James Gould Cozzens
Life on the medium wave/John Winton
Jacqueline Kennedy and her year of ordeal/ Gloria Steinem
Beat and ballad/Kenneth Allsop
Robert Robinson Reviewing
Billy Graham and evangelism/Monica Furlong
A case of promiscuity/documentary by Alma Birk
Hallo darling, hallo mate/David Benedictus
I'm a compulsive eater/Sheila Brandon
Beauty: A face in the making/ Elizabeth Williamson
Mexican journey/Laurie Lee
Furnishing: The Bedroom Farce/with Fenella Fielding
Cookery: Potting with the plug-in handmaiden/ Elizabeth David
Staff
Editor/Harry Fieldhouse. Assistant editor/Jean Cross. Editorial adviser/Alma Birk. Art editor/Harri Peccinotti. Fashion director/Jill Butterfield. Fashion editor/Penny Vincenzi. Susan Peters. Home & beauty editor/Elizabeth Williamson. Isabel Pearce. Fiction editor/Joy Matthews. Jean Scroggie. Jean Penfold. Michael Wynn-Jones.

MAY 1965
Contents
A day in the life of a British secretary over there/Willa Petschek
Why the real Mrs. Dales don't keep a diary/Chiquita Sandilands
Something a teenager should be told/Alan Wykes
The Intelligent Woman's Guide to Isms: Logical positivism/A. J. Ayer
The Inquiring Traveller's Digest/Kenneth Westcott-Jones
The British lunch/Angus McGill
At the court of Anne Kerr/Llew Gardner
Jill Butterfield
A man with a head full of dreams/short story by Brian Glanville
The next Big One at the box office/Philip Oakes
Abstracted by Victor Pasmore /Frank Whitford
The war of the Philistines/Arnold Wesker
Folk – the fine and the fake/Kenneth Allsop
Robert Robinson Reviewing
Leisure is for recollecting in tranquility/ Margaret Mead
Who's to blame for old-fashioned houses? Us/José Manser
Parents who reject their children/Alma Birk
Deserving sauces for fish/cookery by Elizabeth David
The long way round to Venice/William Sansom
Programme your make-up by electronics/Elizabeth Williamson
Staff
Editor/Harry Fieldhouse. Assistant editor/Jean Cross. Editorial adviser/Alma Birk. Art editor/Harri Peccinotti. Fashion director/Jill Butterfield. Fashion editor/Penny Vincenzi. Susan Peters. Home & beauty editor/Elizabeth Williamson. Isabel Pearce. Fiction editor/Joy Matthews. Jean Scroggie. Jean Penfold. Michael Wynn-Jones.

JUNE 1965
Contents
Put out more flags/Mollie Barger
What you need to know about space/ Angela Croome
Art: How to buy prints/Frank Whitford
The Inquiring Traveller's Digest: Switzerland/Kenneth Westcott-Jones
The Intelligent Woman's Guide to Isms: Existentialism/Jean-Paul Sartre
Your personality in colour/devised by Dr Ernest Dichter
Auberon Waugh turns private eye
Jill Butterfield
Infidelity: two new stories on an old theme. 1. by Alberto Moravia, 2. by Janice Elliott
Who's afraid of girl graduates?/Gay Firth
The power of Peter Hall/Llew Gardner
The tyranny of the old 78s/Kenneth Allsop
Robert Robinson Reviews
The case of the switched-off husband/Alma Birk
Love: Is this day the beginning of the end? 1. What a bride should wear... and 2. Why the magic isn't likely to last/Ernest van den Haag
Cooking on a skewer/Elizabeth David
What a way to listen/Bryan Magee
For an old-fashioned girl/beauty by Elizabeth Williamson
Staff
Editor/Harry Fieldhouse. Assistant editors/Jean Cross, Jean Scroggie. Editorial adviser/Alma Birk. Art editor/Harri Peccinotti. Felicity Innes. Fashion director/Jill Butterfield. Fashion editor/Penny Vincenzi. Susan Peters. Home & beauty editor/Elizabeth Williamson. Isabel Pearce. Fiction editor/Joy Matthews. Jean Penfold. Michael Wynn-Jones.

JULY 1965
Contents
It only happens to you once/Mary Wolfard
Paint me as I think I am/Peter Carvell
The Intelligent Woman's Guide to Isms: Zen Buddhism/by Arthur Koestler
The Inquiring Traveller's Digest – 3: Italy/Kenneth Westcott-Jones
Hands that do dishes can be as revealing as your face/Winston Clark
Terrifying thoughts on keeping a mistress, 1965/ Jonathan Routh
Jill Butterfield
At the house of a friend/short story by Rosemary Manning
Four who live for racing/Ivor Herbert
The man who knows plenty about you/Llew Gardner
A shotgun wedding – and after/Chiquita Sandilands The sound of fashion/Kenneth Allsop
Robert Robinson Reviews
Jeanne Moreau on morality – her own and other people's/by Richard Grenier
The Teilhard phenomenon/Neville Braybrooke
Return to wild Africa/Juliet Huxley
The luxury of tomatoes/Elizabeth David
Scoring a bull/Roger Pilkington
An outbreak of larceny in the bathroom/Elizabeth Williamson
Staff
Editor/Harry Fieldhouse. Assistant editors/Jean Cross, Jean Scroggie. Editorial adviser/Alma Birk. Art editor/Harri Peccinotti. Felicity Innes. Fashion director/Jill Butterfield. Fashion editor/Penny Vincenzi. Susan Peters. Home & beauty editor/Elizabeth Williamson. Isabel Pearce. Fiction editor/Joy Matthews. Jean Penfold. Michael Wynn-Jones.

AUGUST 1965
Contents
How they took the dread out of summer/Alan Wykes
The Inquiring Traveller's Digest: Spain/Kenneth Westcott-Jones
Get the message?/Angela Ince
Ustinov talking
Jill Butterfield
A woman at the seaside/a new story Edna O'Brien

Love thirty! – are these the best years of your lives?/Jill Pound-Corner
A tourist in Red China/Eve Bracegirdle
The Irrepressible Intellectual –St. John Stevas interviewed by Llew Gardner
Too much harmony/Kenneth Allsop
Robert Robinson Reviews
Argument: Is vocation in decline?/Jonathan Miller
The man for whom progress was a setback/Alma Birk
Beauty: an inside story/Elizabeth Williamson
Authentic sorbets/Elizabeth David
Art: a Corot exhibition/Frank Whitford

Staff

Editor/Harry Fieldhouse. Assistant editors/Jean Cross, Jean Scroggie. Editorial adviser/Alma Birk. Art editor/Harri Peccinotti. Felicity Innes. Fashion director/Jill Butterfield. Fashion editor/Penny Vincenzi. Susan Peters. Home & beauty editor/Elizabeth Williamson. Isabel Pearce. Fiction editor/Joy Matthews. Jean Penfold. Michael Wynn-Jones.

SEPTEMBER 1965

Contents

What Jeeves wouldn't dream of telling about the rich/Christopher Booker
What Jeeves says about himself/Robert Ottaway
Those literary furies/Ruth Inglis
Don't forget the commercials, mum/Lee Langley
Living with a successful husband/Alma Birk
Helping yourself at home/Elizabeth Williamson
Quite often the answer is a lemon/Elizabeth David
The visitor scorpions and women/Roald Dahl
Books, shows/Robert Robinson
Jazz/Kenneth Allsop
Travel: digest of Yugoslavia/Kenneth Westcott-Jones
Back Bite/Frost out of season/David Frost

Staff

Editor/Dennis Hackett. Assistant editors/Kevin D'Arcy, Jean Cross, Jean Scroggie. Editorial adviser/Alma Birk. Art editor/Harri Peccinotti. Felicity Innes. Fashion editor/Penny Vincenzi. Susan Peters. Home & beauty editor/Elizabeth Williamson. Isabel Pearce. Fiction editor/Joy Matthews. Jean Penfold. Michael Wynn-Jones.

OCTOBER 1965

Contents

Childbirth can be fun/Lee Langley, Audrey Whitling
Women behind the men behind the motor show/Jane Gaskell
Bachelors gay/John Wells
Political women/Anna Patrick, Jean Cross
The other woman/Alma Birk
Get to work beautifully on an egg/Elizabeth Williamson
Robots round the house/Elizabeth Gundrey
A promising career/Martha Gellhorn
Reviews: Books by Ruth Inglis/theatre by Robert Robinson/films by Robert Ottaway/jazz by Kenneth Allsop
Travel: Portugal/by Peter Carvell
Back Bite/Steadman

Staff

Editor/Dennis Hackett. Assistant editors/Kevin D'Arcy, Jean Cross, Jean Scroggie. Editorial adviser/Alma Birk. Art editor/Harri Peccinotti. Felicity Innes. Fashion editor/Penny Vincenzi. Susan Peters. Home & beauty editor/Elizabeth Williamson. Isabel Pearce. Fiction editor/Joy Matthews. Jean Penfold. Michael Wynn-Jones.

NOVEMBER 1965

Contents

Fiona and the Baroness Thyssen/Ronald Paul Handyside
Second marriage/Alma Birk
Wives with everything/Llew Gardner
The getaway composer/Robert Ottaway
The making of The Group/Patricia Bosworth
First steps on a nursery slope/Anthony Carson
Money and what to do with it/Russell Taylor
The problems of being good-looking/John Sandilands
Long live the muddied oafs/Pippa Phemister
Early beauty/Elizabeth Williamson
A leaning towards the Latin/George Rosie
Quince, guava, elderflower/Elizabeth David
Led Astray/Dan Jacobson
Reviews: Books by Ruth Inglis/theatre by Michael Wynn-Jones/films by Tom Hutchinson/beat and ballad by Kenneth Allsop
Bite Back/Brigid Brophy

Staff

Editor/Dennis Hackett. Assistant editors/Kevin D'Arcy, Jean Cross, Jean Scroggie. Editorial adviser/Alma Birk. Art editor/Harri Peccinotti. Felicity Innes. Fashion editor/Molly Parkin. Jane Wood. Home & beauty editor/Elizabeth Williamson. Isabel Pearce. Fiction editor/Mary Holland. Jean Penfold. Michael Wynn-Jones.

DECEMBER 1965

Contents

Little women outside/Peta Fordham
Where's Christ this Christmas?/John Wells
Your children's hands/Winston Clark
Why can't we let ourselves go?/Alma Birk
Alfie/Robert Ottaway
The rise and fall of a TV tycoon/Robert Oulahan and William Lambert
Menus to save you cooking your goose/Mary Gilliatt
Coming to the aid of the party/Pamela Vandyke Price
The cheat/Frank O'Connor
Wormwood/Thomas Kinsella
Reviews: Books by Ruth Inglis/theatre by Peter Forber/films by Tom Hutchinson/beat and ballad by Kenneth Allsop
Backbite/John Glashan

Staff

Editor/Dennis Hackett. Assistant editors/Jean Cross, Jean Scroggie. Editorial adviser/Alma Birk. Art editor/Harri Peccinotti. Felicity Innes. Bill Fallover. Fashion editor/Molly Parkin. Jane Wood. Home & beauty editor/Elizabeth Williamson. Isabel Pearce. Fiction editor/Mary Holland. Jean Penfold. Michael Wynn-Jones.

JANUARY 1966

Contents

My breakthrough year/John Glashan
My transitional year/Anthony Carson
Women behind the president/Ruth Inglis
Today a man can stop a mad bull with a button/Alma Birk
The fashion editors/Cherry Farrow
Back to square one/Neville Cardus
Money/Robert Hedley
The honours game/René Lecler
Oranges/Toni del Renzio
Looking-glass war/beauty by Elizabeth Williamson
Shelley would be shocked/Michael Wynn-Jones
Have fun and travel/Penelope Hoare
Holiday/Katherine Ann Porter
Bringing up parents: 1/Eleanor Wintour
Reviews: Books by Ruth Inglis/films by Tom Hutchinson/theatre by Peter Forber/beat and ballad by Kenneth Allsop
Backbite/Heather Ging

Staff

Editor/Dennis Hackett. Assistant editors/Jean Cross, Jean Scroggie. Editorial adviser/Alma Birk. Jean Penfold. Michael Wynn-Jones. Art editor/Harri Peccinotti. Felicity Innes. Bill Fallover. Fashion editor/Molly Parkin. Jane Wood. Home & beauty editor/Elizabeth Williamson. Isabel Pearce. Fiction editor/Mary Holland.

FEBRUARY 1966

Contents

A matter of life and death/Jane Gaskell
Think now, if you were to be murdered, which would be a likely day?/Bill Smithies
Alone with Edward Heath/Mary Holland
Coming shortly, Sharon Tate/Robert Ottaway
Making marriage work/Alma Birk, JP
Divorce/Anne Scott-James
His & hers/Robert Heller
Whatever's happening to men?/Anna Patrick, Simon Raven, John Sandilands
Back to square one/Sid Chaplin
Are you running with me, Jesus?/Malcolm Boyd
Making light of it/Elizabeth Williamson
Soup it up/Mary Wolfard
Maple syrup, Mounties, Mennonites and Montreal/Jean Cross
Anna Lisa's nose/Gina Berrieault
Bringing up parents: 2/Eleanor Wintour
Who cares?/Michael Wynn-Jones
Reviews: Books by Ruth Inglis/films by Tom Hutchinson/theatre by Peter Forber/beat and ballad by Kenneth Allsop
Backbite/Mel Caiman

Staff

Editor/Dennis Hackett. Assistant editors/Jean Cross, Jean Scroggie. Editorial adviser/Alma Birk. Jean Penfold. Michael Wynn-Jones. Art director/Harri Peccinotti. Felicity Innes. Bill Fallover. Fashion editor/Molly Parkin. Jane Wood. Home and beauty editor/Elizabeth Williamson. Isabel Pearce, Fiction editor/Mary Holland.

MARCH 1966

Contents

The buck behind the bunnies/Mary Holland
When the answer is a bottle/Jean Cross
Womansville/Alma Birk
Not just a gentleman/Michael Wynn-Jones
Back to square one/Andrew Sinclair
Lionel shot an arrow into the air/Caryl Brahms
The trouble is to identify, then nurture the tree of knowledge/G T Fowler, John Cohen, Peter Preston
Fashion in fabrics/George Rosie
Made in Japan/Maurice Smith
Hello and goodbye/Elizabeth Williamson
This is your face – at least it is thought that it could be/Elizabeth Williamson
Swine before pearls/George Seddon
Ginger hero/Brian Friel
Bringing up parents: 3/Eleanor Wintour
Who cares?/Ruth Inglis
Reviews: Books by Ruth Inglis/theatre by Peter Forber/films by Tom Hutchinson/ballad and beat by Kenneth Allsop
Backbite/Victoria Glendinning

Staff

Editor/Dennis Hackett. Assistant editors/Jean Cross, Jean Scroggie. Editorial adviser/Alma Birk. Jean Penfold. Michael Wynn-Jones. Art director/Harri Peccinotti. Felicity Innes. Bill Fallover. Fashion editor/Molly Parkin. Jane Wood. Home and beauty editor/Elizabeth Williamson. Isabel Pearce. Fiction editor/Mary Holland.

APRIL 1966

Contents

The Queen at forty/Gabriel Fielding
Her Majesty's Swiss Guard/Ronald Paul Handyside
Women in Ireland – time for another rising?/Llew Gardner
Why do we put up with inefficient doctors?/Bill Smithies
Stella Richman: a woman in charge/Robert Ottaway
Widows/Alma Birk
A child writes/Gillian Wallington
Conscience-keepers against all-comers/Peter Fiddick
Back to square one/Barbara Cartland
Sex remembered, sex observed or sex imagined?/Jane Gaskell
Barely there/beauty by Elizabeth Williamson
Give the veg an edge/Toni del Renzio
Greece/Nigel Walmsley
The snail watcher/Patricia Highsmith
Bringing up parents: 4/Eleanor Wintour
Who cares?/Annette Kobak
Reviews: Books by Ruth Inglis/theatre Peter Forber/films by Tom Hutchinson/ballad and beat by Kenneth Allsop
Backbite/John Heilpern

Staff

Editor/Dennis Hackett. Assistant editor/Jean Cross. Associate editor/Alma Birk. Jean Penfold. Michael Wynn-Jones. Art director/Harri Peccinotti. Felicity Innes. Bill Fallover. Fashion editor/Molly Parkin. Jane Wood. Home and beauty editor/Elizabeth Williamson. Isabel Pearce. Fiction editor/Mary Holland.

MAY 1966

Contents

Vietnam/Brian Moynahan and Harri Peccinotti
Good morning Good morning Good morning/Auberon Waugh
The Don Juan syndrome/Alma Birk
The God-sellers/Michael Wynn-Jones
Oskar Werner, a star who has condescended to make the journey/Robert Ottaway
My pop song/Anthony Carson
Back to square one/Jean Cross
Are the jokers wild?/Dim Pares
A dream of violence among the spires/Dom Moraes
Tickle the palate/Toni del Renzio
Liguian littoral/Christopher Kininmonth
The Brighton Belle/Francis King
Reviews: Books by Ruth Inglis/theatre by Peter Forber/films by Tom Hutchinson/art by Barrie Sturt-Penrose
Backbite/Cressida Lindsay

Staff

Editor/Dennis Hackett. Art Director/Harri Peccinotti. Associate Editor/Alma Birk. Assistants to the editor/Bill Smithies, Michael Wynn-Jones. Assistant editor/Jean Cross. Editorial assistant/Bob Smyth. Art assistants/Felicity Innes, Bill Fallover. Fashion editor/Molly Parkin. Jane Wood. Fiction/Mary Holland. Home and beauty/Elizabeth Williamson. Isabel Pearce. Travel and reviews/Jean Penfold.

JUNE 1966

Contents

Problem for a prince. Nureyev at the crossroads/Patric Walker
Spy. Poet come in from the cold/Ken Wlaschin
S W 3. How high is life in Chelsea?/Michael Wynn-Jones
Love in capital cities. Men of the world by a woman of the world/Irma Kurtz
Bored women are boring women. When (and why) marriage ceases to be enough/Alma Birk
Jimmy Tarbuck. The high priest who is learning the liturgy/John Sandilands
To brown ladies who are not for burning. How not to make an enemy of the sun/beauty by Elizabeth Williamson
Hassan's tower/Margaret Drabble
Bringing up parents : 6/Eleanor Wintour
Reviews: Books by Ruth Inglis/theatre by Peter Farber/films by Tom Hutchinson/art by Barrie Sturt-Penrose
Backbite/Roger Woddis

Staff

Editor/Dennis Hackett. Art director/Harri Peccinotti. Associate editor/Alma Birk. Assistants to the editor/Bill Smithies, Michael Wynn-Jones. Assistant editor/Jean Cross. Editorial assistant/Bob Smyth. Art assistants/Felicity Innes, Bill Fallover. Fashion/Molly Parkin. Jane Wood. Fiction/Mary Holland. Home and beauty/Elizabeth Williamson. Isabel Pearce. Travel and reviews/Jean Penfold.

JULY 1966

Contents

A consumer's guide to the do-it-yourself sex books/David Stafford-Clark
If your husband can't sleep at night, he may be counting management consultants/Robert Ottaway
Confined to a policeman/Llew Gardner
Read faster and remember/Maya and Eric De Leeuw
How I wrote a book?/Anthony Carson
Woman in search/Alma Birk
Starting from cold/Toni del Renzio
Cinderella gone to seed/Molly Parkin
Paint box for a self-portrait/Elizabeth Williamson
You don't have to like Strindberg/Sylvie Nickels
The Nest Builder/V S Pritchard
Reviews: Books by Ruth Inglis/theatre by Peter Farber/films by Tom Hutchinson/art by Barrie Sturt-Penrose
Backbite/Philip Oakes

Staff

Editor/Dennis Hackett. Art director/Harri Peccinotti. Associate editor/Alma Birk. Assistants to the editor/Bill Smithies, Michael Wynn-Jones. Assistant editor/Jean Cross. Editorial assistant/Bob Smyth. Art assistant/Bill Fallover. Fashion/Molly Parkin. Jane Wood. Fiction/Mary Holland. Home and beauty/Elizabeth Williamson. Isabel Pearce. Travel and reviews/Jean Penfold.

AUGUST 1966

Contents

Women who push their luck/Llew Gardner
No mod cons/Michael Wynn-Jones
L S Lowry: a man of his people/Barrie Sturt-Penrose
Sixteenth in succession to the throne of England/David Nathan
Love me, love the bug under my bed/Roger Woddis
Jugglers with emotions/Alma Birk
The Dankworths/Caryl Brahms
Read faster and remember/Manya and Eric De Leeuw
Next time you look in the mirror, read this/beauty by Elizabeth Williamson
Twelve pages to make you think about colour/Molly Parkin
Gelati fit for Neros/Toni del Renzio
On the waves/Harold Brodkey
Reviews: books by Ruth Inglis/theatre by Peter Farber/films by Tom Hutchinson/art by Barrie Sturt-Penrose
Backbite/Tony Gray

Staff

Editor/Dennis Hackett. Art director/Harri

Peccinotti. Associate editor/Alma Birk. Assistants to the editor/Bill Smithies, Michael Wynn-Jones. Assistant editor/Jean Cross. Editorial assistant/Bob Smyth. Art assistant/Bill Fallover. Fashion/Molly Parkin. Jane Wood. Fiction/Mary Holland. Home and beauty/Elizabeth Williamson. Isabel Pearce. Travel and reviews/Jean Penfold

SEPTEMBER 1966
Contents
Read faster and remember/Manya and Eric De Leeuw
Dialogue with a Novice-mistress/Dennis Holman
Eight girls in a hurry/Dam Moraes
Walled-in wives/Ruth Inglis
The best is still to come/Alma Birk
Adding insult to matrimony/Alma Birk
Westward on the book beat/Gabriel Fielding
Poor George, he's got a business conference all next week.../Tony Gray
When you say, darling what a heavenly scent/beauty by Elizabeth Williamson
The art of Klaus Antonio/Nik Cohn
Reviews: books by Ruth Inglis/theatre by Peter Farber/films by Tom Hutchinson/art by Barrie Sturt-Penrose
Backbite/Nancy Nott
Staff
Editor/Dennis Hackett. Art director/Harri Peccinotti. Associate Editor/Alma Birk. Assistants to the editor/Bill Smithies, Michael Wynn-Jones. Editorial assistants/Louise Naintre, Bob Smyth. Art assistant/Bill Fallover. Fashion/Molly Parkin. Jane Wood. Fiction/Jean Cross. Home and beauty/Elizabeth Williamson. Travel and reviews/Jean Penfold.

OCTOBER 1966
Contents
The secret of Ssh.../Robert Ottaway
'Bless me, father, for I have sinned'/Norman Price
The new spinsters/Irma Kurtz
Are Northern women any different?/Alma Birk and Michael Wynn-Jones
It's the first time and she's rather shy/Dom Moraes
Layers of revolt/Alma Birk
Mrs America 1966/Monica Dickens
More words on the North, these you can eat/Marika Hanbury-Tenison
Swings and roundabouts/Molly Parkin
Change your mood with French perfume/beauty by Elizabeth Williamson
The banks are not for breaking/John Izbicki
Goodbye/William Sansom
Staff
Editor/Dennis Hackett. Deputy editor/David Smith. Art director/Harri Peccinotti. Associate editor/Alma Birk. Assistants to the editor/Bill Smithies, Michael Wynn-Jones. Editorial assistants/Louise Naintre, Bob Smyth. Art assistant/Bill Fallover. Fashion & home/Molly Parkin. Jane Wood. Fiction/Jean Cross. Home and beauty/Elizabeth Williamson. Travel and reviews/ Jean Penfold.

NOVEMBER 1966
Contents
Look, your structure's slipping/Richard Lebherz
The lad himself – master of the self-inflicted wound/Robert Ottaway
Married – to a degree/Bob Smyth
To celebrate one good man/Irma Kurtz
A fable/Philip Gardner
If you're an older woman and feeling it.../Elizabeth Dickson
Anne Sexton and her poetry/Ruth Inglis
Are you married to your house or just living with it?/Andrew Duncan
Thought for today/Alma Birk
Two by two to the WMC/Dom Moraes
BBC/Philip Purser
Streets in the sky, heads in the clouds/Mary Gilliat and Tony Gwilliam
Snacks/Marika Hanbury-Tenison
Unfreeze your fifty pounds/Sylvie Nickels
Avec la bébé-sitter/John Updike
Backbite/Angela Coulter
Staff
Editor/Dennis Hackett. Deputy editor/David Smith. Art director/Harri Peccinotti. Associate editor/Alma Birk. Assistants to the editor/Bill Smithies, Michael Wynn-Jones. Editorial assistants/Louise Naintre, Bob Smyth. Art assistants/Bill Fallover, Susan Wade. Fashion & Home/Molly Parkin. Jane Wood. Fiction/Jean Cross. Beauty/Elizabeth Williamson. Terra Nova and reviews/Irma Kurtz. Travel/Jean Penfold.

DECEMBER 1966
Contents
And then John begat the Bible/Irma Kurtz
The season of goodwill, 1945/Langdon Gilkey
The season of goodwill: what a pity it doesn't last longer/Norman Price
The Queen's Christmas message/Auberon Waugh, Ronald Paul Handyside
Women out of line: Ingrid Bjerkås/Paul Neuberg
St Tropez without the bikinis/Peter Foster
Come fly with me/Auberon Waugh
So you think you're well read
ABC/Tom Hutchinson
Beauty ...
And the feast.../Marika Hanbury-Tenison
And pass the rosy wine/Pamela Vandyke Price
Every cripple has his own way of walking/Ann Quin
Backbite/Ruth Inglis
Staff
Editor/Dennis Hackett. Deputy editor/David Smith. Art director/Derek Birdsall. Associate editor/Alma Birk. Assistants to the editor/Bill Smithies, Michael Wynn-Jones. Editorial assistants/Louise Naintre, Bob Smyth. Art assistants/Bill Fallover, Susan Wade. Fashion & home/Molly Parkin. Jane Wood. Fiction/Jean Cross. Beauty/Elizabeth Williamson. Terra Nova and Cool Look/Irma Kurtz. Travel/Jean Penfold.

JANUARY 1967
Contents
Professional women are split personalities?/Sam Ingleby
Sex and the single sexologist/Leslie Farber
Bye-bye blue sky/John Heilpern
The Daughters of the American Revolution/Ruth Inglis
The agony of the self-encounter/ Alma Birk
The Provos/Roy Perrott
Barmaids/Arthur Hopcraft
David Archer, currently wallpaper salesman/Dom Moraes
The economics of a sale/Patricia Rowan
Bread/Michael Wynn-Jones
Let's keep on the light and go to bed/Molly Parkin
Mainstream/Jane Wood
The last night/Norman Mailer
Backbite/by Ronald Handyside
Staff
Editor/Dennis Hackett. Deputy editor/David Smith. Art director/John Blackburn. Associate editor/Alma Birk. Assistants to the editor/Bill Smithies, Michael Wynn-Jones. Editorial assistants/Louise Naintre, Bob Smyth. Art assistants/Bill Fallover, Susan Wade. Fashion and home/Molly Parkin, Jane Wood. Fiction/Jean Cross. Beauty/Elizabeth Williamson. Terra Nova and Cool Look/Irma Kurtz. Travel/Jean Penfold.

FEBRUARY 1967
Contents
Homosexuality/Irma Kurtz
Mary Wilson/Dom Moraes
The far side of Bentine/Tom Hutchinson
The Torah was right/Anthony Brown
Two Valentines: sugar pink but somewhat acid: from him to her/Malcolm Fowler; From her to him/Louise Short
Frozen women/Alma Birk
Theatre of fact/Michael Wynn-Jones
Why don't they eat their words?/Peter Forster
Taka pint every otha day/Vivian Craddock-Williams
ATV/Robert Ottaway
Have you or have you not...£7, 865/Molly Parkin
Have you or have you not...£l/Molly Parkin
Too many Cooks?/Robert Ottaway
Cynosure/Kit Reed
Backbite/by Kenneth Allsop
Staff
Editor/Dennis Hackett. Deputy editor/David Smith. Art director/John Blackburn. Associate Editor/Alma Birk. Assistants to the Editor/Bill Smithies, Michael Wynn-Jones. Editorial assistants/Louise Naintre, Bob Smyth. Art assistants/Bill Fallover, Susan Wade. Fashion and Home/Molly Parkin. Jane Wood. Fiction/Jean Cross. Beauty/Elizabeth Williamson. Terra Nova and Cool Look/Irma Kurtz. Trave/Jean Penfold.

MARCH 1967
Contents
Mong?/Kenneth Allsop
Bells and a bungalow; Tea at Lyons but no sympathy; And Sinfully ever after/by Michael Wynn-Jones; Alma Birk; Ronald Handyside
Is Terence Rattigan the highest paid playwright in the world?/Irma Kurtz
These people are buying their lives/Bill Smithies
Who counts in the county set?/Roy Perrott
Does someone up there love you?/Michael Wynn-Jones
They call you madam, Emmeline (but they take their orders from sir)/Tony Gray
Is nine volts enough to stop your husband alternating?/Alma Birk
Dies irae/Julia O'Faolain
Backcomb/by Irma Kurtz
Staff
Editor/Dennis Hackett. Deputy editor/David Smith. Art director/John Blackburn. Associate editor/Alma Birk. Assistants to the Editor/Bill Smithies, Michael Wynn-Jones. Editorial assistants/Louise Naintre, Bob Smyth. Art assistants/Bill Fallover, Susan Wade. Fashion and Home/Molly Parkin, Jane Wood. Fiction/Jean Cross. Terra Nova and Cool Look/Irma Kurtz. Production and travel/Jean Penfold.

APRIL 1967
Contents
What do you want if you don't need money? Nine young heiresses tell Bob Smyth
Due to the vigilance of the police, a man has been arrested, but is he guilty?/Peter Fiddick
Who's afraid of Brigid Brophy? Don't all shout at once: read this first/Irma Kurtz
The 30,471 sequins were sewn on by hand, while the feet were busy...formation dancing/Arthur Hopcraft
Women on guard. Join the Women's Royal Army Corps – and then what?/Irma Kurtz
Kent Ditton, the last year of a five-year-old/Peter Ditton
Public and private faces. Maurice Edelman talks to Alma Birk
What's between a man and his body? It takes all types to make a Mr Universe/Christopher Matthews
Classics that are always contemporary/Molly Parkin
When in Maratea do as Giuseppina does. Appetising ideas of an Italian cook/Ruth Inglis
Where the gas is. To Ireland with a car/Tony Gray
'A shocking accident' and 'Beauty'/two stories by Graham Greene
Backbite/John Adams – See it my way
Staff
Editor/Dennis Hackett. Deputy editor/Bill Smithies. Art director/John Blackburn. Associate editor/Alma Birk. Assistant to the editor/Michael Wynn-Jones. Editorial assistants/Bob Smyth, Louise Naintre, Carol Ford. Art assistants/Bill Fallover, Susan Wade. Fashion and Home/Molly Parkin, Jane Wood. Fiction/Jean Cross. Terra Nova and Cool Look/Irma Kurtz. Production and travel/Jean Penfold.

MAY 1967
Contents
Why women have babies/Catherine Storr
Good old Frostie/Dom Moraes
Violence: the aura and the fact/Michael Wynn-Jones & Dr Alan Little
Child's play/Ray Green
Do women like each other?/Irma Kurtz
Forty/Alma Birk
Sheila Chichester: living with a gale force/ Ruth Inglis
Backbite/Rosemarie Wittman
Turn white/Fashion by Molly Parkin
Where are all the three-piece suites?/Home by Peter Murray
Chips with everything/Travel by Tony Gray
The girls who didn't listen/Kenneth Allsop
Terra Nova/edited by Irma Kurtz
Cool Look/edited by Ruth Inglis
An expensive place to die/Len Deighton
Staff
Editor/Dennis Hackett. Deputy editor/Bill Smithies. Assistant art director/Bill Fallover. Associate editor/Alma Birk. Assistant to the editor/Michael Wynn-Jones. Production editor/Jean Penfold. Fashion editor/Molly Parkin. Features/Bob Smyth. Production/Louise Naintre, Carol Ford. Art/Susan Wade. Fashion/Jane Wood. Fiction/Jean Cross. Terra Nova/Irma Kurtz. Cool Look/Ruth Inglis.

JUNE 1967
Contents
Here's how things are at Boots and Players/ Bob Smyth
Sex: one law for sons, another for daughters/ Alma Birk
Kennedy: the second assassination/ Paul Breslow
Gore Vidal
Ha, ha, ha, ha! you've nothing to lose but your dignity/Tom Hutchinson
Colour/Home by Peter Murray
Does he hold his nose when you powder?/Beauty by Deborah Thomas
Undressing on the beach/Fashion by Molly Parkin
Allsop/Kenneth Allsop
Backbite/Hugh Pitt
An expensive place to die/Len Deighton
Staff
Editor/Dennis Hackett. Deputy editor/Bill Smithies. Assistant art director/Bill Fallover. Associate editor/Alma Birk. Features editor/Michael Wynn-Jones. Production and travel editor/Jean Penfold. Fashion editor/Molly Parkin. Features/Bob Smyth. Production/Carol Ford. Art/Susan Wade. Fashion/Jane Wood. Fiction/Jean Cross. Terra Nova/Ruth Inglis.

JULY 1967
Contents
Picasso: one of the titans/Barrie Sturt-Penrose
Women who lived with Titans/Ruth Inglis
We never knew that about Australian women/Jan Smith
Home is her mother's prison cell/Bob Smyth
The incredible consequences of being a divorcee/Alma Birk
The Tolleshunt rebellion/Peter Fiddick
That's right, Cathy McGowan/John Sandilands
Switched on for parties/Molly Parkin
Don't cry/Beauty by Deborah Thomas
How many square feet did you have when you last counted/Home by Peter Murray
Allsop/Kenneth Allsop
Staff
Editor/Dennis Hackett. Deputy editor/Bill Smithies. Assistant art director/Bill Fallover. Associate editor/Alma Birk. Features editor/Michael Wynn-Jones. Production and travel editor/Jean Penfold. Fashion editor/Molly Parkin. Features/Bob Smyth. Production/Carol Ford. Art/Susan Wade. Fashion/Jane Wood. Fiction/Jean Cross. Terra Nova/Ruth Inglis.

AUGUST 1967
Contents
Reita Faria awaits you, Miss World/John Sandilands
Why I am angry/Alma Birk
The last eight/Jenny Campbell
How can you call yourself a housewife...?/ Peter Fiddick
Nell Dunn and Jeremy Sandford are always with us/Robert Ottaway
One of God's waiting rooms/Vivian Craddock-Williams
For my son/Dom Moraes
Roast beef and ice cream begin at Calais/ Auberon Waugh
The dictator/Peter Lewis
Far from Paris and all the better for it/Fashion by Molly Parkin
The age of purity/Beauty by Deborah Thomas
Millionaires can afford to sit here/Cookery by Jean Cross
Hannibal lived here/Travel by Dorothy Young
Allsop/Kenneth Allsop
My friend says it's bullet-proof (part 1)/ Penelope Mortimer
Staff
Editor/Dennis Hackett. Deputy editor/Bill Smithies. Assistant art director/Bill Fallover. Associate editor/Alma Birk. Features editor/Michael Wynn-Jones. Production and travel editor/Jean Penfold. Fashion editor/Molly Parkin. Features/Bob Smyth. Production/Carol Ford. Art/Susan Wade. Fashion/Jane Wood. Fiction/Jean Cross. Terra Nova/Ruth Inglis.

SEPTEMBER 1967
Contents
The boy most likely to succeed/Kingsley Martin
This is Vivien Merchant/Peter Lewis
Opt out now? fade out later?/Jan Smith
If the chronology is right.../Elisabeth Woolley
Who's afraid of a couple of ghosts?/Ronald Pavelich Handyside
Denis Hamilton/Ronald Paul Handyside
The common market larder/Vivian Craddock-Williams
Don't just sit there – do something/Alma Birk
If you don't half look good.../Beauty by Deborah

Thomas
Reptiles in season/Fashion by Molly Parkin
Russian passage/Travel by Tony Gray
Allsop/Kenneth Allsop
My friend says it's bullet-proof (part 2)/
Penelope Mortimer
Staff
Editor/Dennis Hackett. Deputy editor/Bill Smithies. Assistant art director/Bill Fallover. Associate editor/Alma Birk. Features editor/Michael Wynn-Jones. Production and travel editor/Jean Penfold. Fashion editor/Molly Parkin. Features/Bob Smyth. Production/Carol Ford. Lindsay Vernon. Art/Susan Wade. Fiction/Jean Cross. Terra Nova/Ruth Inglis.

OCTOBER 1967
Contents
Adam and Eve: where are you now that we need you?/Dom Moraes
The battered baby syndrome/Elisabeth Woolley
The battered mind/Ruth Inglis
Robert Shaw: a dream of father/Tom Hutchinson
God and I/Dom Moraes
A week in the life of Bristow/Frank Dickens
When the French said vive la difference/David Lewis Stein
The compleat hippy/Barry Zaid, Paul Breslow, Peter Laurie and Toni del Renzio
Can you live without David Symonds?/
Peter Lewis
Women in search/Alma Birk
A film princess called Ann Todd/Terence Howitt
Hey remember what we looked like...?/fashion by Caroline Baker
Only the face is changed/beauty by Deborah Thomas
And while you're there, buy me an island/travel by Barrie Sturt-Penrose
Allsop/Kenneth Allsop
'Fenner' and 'A scholar of ancient battlements'/short stories by Morris Lurie
Staff
Editor/Dennis Hackett. Deputy editor/Bill Smithies. Assistant art director/Bill Fallover. Associate editor/Alma Birk. Features editor/Michael Wynn-Jones. Production and travel editor/Jean Penfold. Fashion editor/Caroline Baker. Features/Bob Smyth. Production/Lindsay Vernon. Art/Susan Wade. Fiction/Jean Cross. Terra Nova/Ruth Inglis.

NOVEMBER 1967
Contents
Now Rachel, what was that about Rex again?/John Sandilands
What happened when Bardot met 007/John Sandilands
A life in the night of God and I/Patrick O'Donovan
Madam, if your husband's not an executive you're nothing/Peter Fiddick
'You see, he's been trained to kill'/Dom Moraes You could kill a man with a 31b 13oz mallet/Bob Smyth
HMG's very secret service/Vivian Craddock-Williams
Coronary inquest/Geoffrey McDermott
Poets anonymous/Bob Smyth
Nova questionnaire/Alma Birk
Birmingham brothels: Should disorderly houses be more orderly?/Ray Gosling
Please to remember the fifth of November/Richard Yeend
Guinness is good for them/John Dixon
The shear delight of being gathered in wool/fashion by Caroline Baker
Allsop/Kenneth Allsop
Huggy Bear/David Mercer
Staff
Editor/Dennis Hackett. Deputy editor/Bill Smithies. Assistant art director/Bill Fallover. Associate editor/Alma Birk. Features editor/Michael Wynn-Jones. Production and travel editor/Jean Penfold. Fashion editor/Caroline Baker. Features/Bob Smyth. Production/Lindsay Vernon. Art/Susan Wade. Fiction/Jean Cross. Terra Nova/Ruth Inglis.

DECEMBER 1967
Contents
When the music stops, meditate/Robert Lester
Stop the papers, cancel the milk and switch off the computer/Bob Smyth and Barbara J Williams
Create me a potent image/Crosby, Fletcher, Forbes
God and 1/John Robinson, Bishop of Woolwich
Fiesole fortifies the over-fifties/Ruth Inglis
And was Jerusalem builded here?/Nurit Beretsky
Don't pull your punches/wine by John Higgins
Travel fur/fashion by Caroline Baker
Spend a long night with turkey and oysters/cookery by Patricia Lennard
If the future frightens you, let the present come alive/Christmas presents by Caroline Baker
Allsop/Kenneth Allsop
'A Difficult Age' and 'Wonder Weapon'/short stories by Brian W Aldiss
Staff
Editor/Dennis Hackett. Deputy editor/Bill Smithies. Art director/Bill Fallover. Associate editor/Alma Birk. Features editor/Michael Wynn-Jones. Fashion editor/Caroline Baker. Travel and features/Bob Smyth. Production/Lindsay Vernon, Lynn White. Art/Susan Wade. Fiction/Jean Cross. Terra Nova/Ruth Inglis.

JANUARY 1968
Contents
The Brando you know/john Sandilands
Middle age makes a man think/Philip Oakes
Ten books for Christmas/R P Handyside
She knows about Sandie Shaw/Alma Birk
This is Aldabra. Colour it pink because it belongs to you/Peter Fiddick
A day in the death of Harold Wilson
God and I/Rabbi Louis Jacobs
One half of the bed/Mary Holland
The rise and fall of Palisades/Elisabeth Woolley
Beaks are only human/Arthur Hopcraft
Bea Lillie is no drop-out/Robert Ottaway
We coloured the chair red/home by Molly Parkin
It takes a woman to control the masses/beauty by Caroline Baker
When you get down to your undies/fashion by Caroline Baker
Escape routes '68/travel by Jean Penfold
Allsop/Kenneth Allsop
The Dianas/by Christina Stead
Staff
Editor/Bill Smithies. Art director/Bill Fallover. Associate editor/Alma Birk. Features editor/Michael Wynn-Jones. Fashion editor/Caroline Baker. Production/Lindsay Vernon, Lynn White. Art/Susan Wade. Fiction/Jean Cross.

FEBRUARY 1968
Contents
Mrs John Bull, how do you plead?/Irma Kurtz and Alma Birk
Don't let Lee Marvin scare you/Jane Wilson
The disposal men/Bob Smyth
Good heavens, they're little girls/Russell Miller
Jung and easily Freudened/Jenny Campbell
Le weekend conjugal chez Susan Hampshire/Shirley Flack
Don't just talk about it, get yourself into print/fashion by Caroline Baker
Once I picked a paper poppy/mechanics of home by Molly Parkin
If you weren't last year in Marienbad/Nigel Walmsley
Allsop/Kenneth Allsop
Mrs Beneker/Violet Weingarten
Staff
Editor/Bill Smithies. Art director/Bill Fallover. Associate editor/Alma Birk. Features editor/Michael Wynn-Jones. Fashion editor/Caroline Baker. Production/Lindsay Vernon, Lynn White. Art/Susan Wade. Fiction/Jean Cross.

MARCH 1968
Contents
Why you keep your hands to yourself?/
Peter Fiddick
If it 'appens, it 'appens/Irma Kurtz
Come on Simon, it won't be long now/
John Sandilands
Two returns to Manhattan/Irma Kurtz
The Jennifer Jones Story/Joe Goldberg
Tell the truth? Ask father? Make excuses?/
Alma Birk
After a short illness/Peter Lethsbridge
Don't read this until you are absolutely confident about your wardrobe/Jean Penfold
You haven't a thing to wear and we're coming to take you away/fashion by Caroline Baker
Meanwhile, back on the ranch/embroidery by Brigid Keenan
Ten faces into one will go/beauty by Deborah Thomas
The wall with nine lives/homes by Molly Parkin
Allsop/Kenneth Allsop
Tunc/Lawrence Durrell
Staff
Editor/Bill Smithies. Assistant editor/Peter Fiddick. Features editor/Michael Wynn-Jones. Assistant to the editor/Brigid Keenan. Associate editor/Alma Birk. Fashion editor/Caroline Baker. Production/Lindsay Vernon, Lynn White. Art/Susan Wade. Features/Ian Cotton, Margaret Pringle. Fashion/Maureen Walker. Fiction/Jean Cross.

APRIL 1968
Contents
The logic of see-through/Catherine Storr
The Palomares file/Luisa Isabel Alvarez de Toledo, Duchess of Medina Sidonia
Darling, please talk to me/Shirley Flack
Get Britain off my backside/Lindley Abbatt
How the British mouse keeps the flag flying east of Suez/Ian Cotton
See-through television/Michael Williams
When the sun shines, shine with it/beauty by Brigid Keenan
How to look better than mummy and daddy/fashion by Caroline Baker
Clump, clump/shoes by Caroline Baker
And when the pie was opened...live frogs/cookery by Adrian Bailey
Design for loving/Anthony Carson
Allsop/Kenneth Allsop
The Capitalists/short story by Michael Baldwin
Pages from Cold Point/short story by Paul Bowles
Staff
Editor/Bill Smithies. Assistant editor/Peter Fiddick. Art director/Derek Birdsall. Features editor/Michael Wynn-Jones. Assistant to the editor/Brigid Keenan. Fashion editor/Caroline Baker. Production/Lindsay Vernon, Lynn White. Art/Susan Wade. Features/Ian Cotton. Fashion/Margaret Pringle, Maureen Walker. Fiction/Jean Cross. Contributing Editor/Alma Birk. Entertainments Editor/John Sandilands.

MAY 1968
Contents
'Here women are still a luxury. In England I would be considered a waste'/Brigid Keenan, Princess Pignatelli
'Where the hell do you think you are lady, Fifth Avenue?'/Jurate Kazcikas, Cathy Leroy and Ann Bryan
Nuts in May/John Sandiland
Crumple-horn for King/Vivian Craddock Williams
Where are the women who went to war for freedom?/Alma Birk
Noah's law/Lindley Abbatt
Richard Chamberlain is the fugitive/
Robert Ottaway
So this is what Dr Spock is like as a father/Herbert Spencer
Bringing up Babyhip/Ruth Inglis
Spots before the eyes/beauty by Brigid Keenan
The dinner parties I enjoy most are the ones I give/Denis Curtis
Fashionova/Caroline Baker
When is a mug an ashtray?/Home by Molly Parkin
Allsop/Kenneth Allsop
An outing/Edna O'Brien
Staff
Editor/Bill Smithies. Assistant editor/Peter Fiddick. Art director/Derek Birdsall. Features editor/Michael Wynn-Jones. Assistant to the editor/Brigid Keenan. Fashion Editor/Caroline Baker. Production/Lindsay Vernon, Lynn White. Art/Susan Wade. Fiction/Jean Cross. Features/Ian Cotton. Fashion/Margaret Pringle, Maureen Walker. Travel/Jean Penfold. Contributing editor/Alma Birk. Entertainments Editor/John Sandilands.

JUNE 1968
Contents
'Oh Gahd' said Ava Gardner/John Sandilands
A mother must know something of love/Elizabeth James
The End/Handyside, Cotton, Sandilands, Jones and Palin
Chicago: scheduled to burn this summer/
Paul Breslow
Wickedness is murder in the park/Angus Wolfe Murray and M L Kellmer Pringle
André Malraux: the fire-raiser toes the line/Maurice Edelman
And that leaves the fox/Lindley Abbatt
Go red in the sun/beauty by Brigid Keenan
This summer I am going to wear spots/fashion by Caroline Baker
Sons and lovers/cookery by Denis Curtis
Allsop/Kenneth Allsop
The Public Image/Muriel Spark
Staff
Editor/Bill Smithies. Assistant editor/Peter Fiddick. Art director/Derek Birdsall. Features editor/Michael Wynn-Jones. Assistant to the editor/Brigid Keenan. Fashion editor/Caroline Baker. Production/Lindsay Vernon, Lynn White. Art/Susan Wade. Fiction/Jean Cross. Features/Ian Cotton. Fashion/Margaret Pringle, Maureen Walker. Travel/Jean Penfold. Contributing editor/Alma Birk. Entertainments editor/John Sandilands.

JULY 1968
Contents
What Paris could do for the Queen/Brigid Keenan
My family and I/Patrick Donovan
Do you think you're going to burst?/
Margaret Pringle
The thing about these people is that none of them fly/Brigid Keenan
Meet Meru ius/Anne Batt
If only they smashed pianos in the Olympic Games/Peter Martin
In defence of the Other Woman/Catherine Storr
Good God, it's Julie Andrews/Philip Jenkinson
Stick by the Rock/Travel by Ruth Inglis
Slip into something cool/Cookery by Denis Curtis
Allsop/Kenneth Allsop
A Pyrrhic Victory/Margaret Drabble
Staff
Editor/Dennis Hackett. Assistant editors/Peter Fiddick, Brigid Keenan. Features editor/Michael Wynn-Jones. Features/Margaret Pringle, Ian Cotton. Consultant art director/Derek Birdsall. Art/Susan Wade, Carol Bennett. Fashion editor/Caroline Baker. Fashion assistant/Maureen Walker. Production editor/Bob Smyth. Production/Lindsay Vernon, Lynn White. Contributing editor/Alma Birk. Travel editor/Jean Penfold. Fiction editor/Jean Cross

AUGUST 1968
Contents
Remember bonnie C W?/Michael Wynn-Jones
My family and I/Janice Elliot
Has anyone noticed how glassy-eyed mum's become?/Anne Batt
An extinct bestiary/Kenneth Allsop and Michael Foreman
Please excuse him while he puts his bra on/Russell Miller
I'm quite normal in that way/Arthur Hopcraft
'I used to think I was really ugly' Mick Jagger/Fred Newman
Cranks, castles and casinos/Travel by Arthur Hopcraft
Madam, you just don't know where your wig has been/beauty by Brigid Keenan
A drop of the hard stuff/fashion by Caroline Baker
Before the sun goes down
All you need is a little taste...
...Buy something really vulgar/Brigid Keenan
Cakes, my life!/Cookery by Denis Curtis
Allsop/Kenneth Allsop
The beautiful gun lady/Angela Carter
Couples/John Updike
Staff
Editor/Dennis Hackett. Assistant editors/Peter Fiddick, Brigid Keenan. Features editor/Michael Wynn-Jones. Features/Margaret Pringle, Ian Cotton. Consultant art director/Derek Birdsall. Art/Susan Wade, Carol Bennett. Fashion editor/Caroline Baker. Fashion assistant/Maureen Walker. Production editor/Bob Smyth. Production/Lindsay Vernon, Lynn White. Contributing editor/Alma Birk. Travel editor/Jean Penfold. Fiction editor/Jean Cross.

SEPTEMBER 1968
Contents
Lost/Catherine Storr and Anne Batt
Ustinov/Margaret Pringle
Excerpts from the diaries of the late God/
Anthony Towne
Is Violette Leduc the cannibal or the victim?/
Irma Kurtz
My family and I/Alma Birk
Must be off now got to go to the chiropodist/Judy Froshaug
There are only ten goddam actors in this world. Rod Steiger/Jane Wilson
Mummy never did it like that/Peter Lethbridge
Aprils le déluge/Travel by Barrie Sturt-Penrose
Fashion is dead. Long live clothes/Brigid Keenan
Now you can try a face a d station/Brigid Keenan
Emotional cookery/Denis Curtis
Allsop/Kenneth Allsop

'The favourite' and 'The Sphinx'/Torpor
Staff
Editor/Dennis Hackett. Assistant editors/Peter Fiddick, Brigid Keenan. Features editor/Michael Wynn-Jones. Features/Margaret Pringle, Ian Cotton. Consultant art director/Derek Birdsall. Art/Susan Wade, Carol Bennett. Fashion editor/Caroline Baker. Fashion assistant/Maureen Walker. Production editor/Bob Smyth. Production/Lindsay Vernon, Lynn White. Contributing editor/Alma Birk. Travel editor/Jean Penfold. Fiction editor/Jean Cross.

OCTOBER 1968
Contents
Private faces/Oliver Williams
First get your tycoon.../Shirley Flack
At 63, Henry Fonda has gone bad, and he loves it/John Sandilands
A royal borough's way with the poor: push them out/Jeremy Bugler
When Victoria's dynastic plotting had to stop/Nigel Gosling
In the old days three nurses held you down/Irma Kurtz
My family and I/Philip Oakes
Well just who are the masters now?/Barry Cox
Nassau's nice, but Nice is not nasty/Travel by Jean Penfold
Behind beauty/Beauty by Brigid Keenan
Go West, young woman/Fashion by Caroline Baker
Do the English get the cooking they deserve?/Denis Curtis
Allsop/Kenneth Allsop
I want it now/Kingsley Amis
Cover illustration/Oliver Williams
Staff
Editor/Dennis Hackett. Assistant editors/Peter Fiddick, Brigid Keenan. Features editor/Michael Wynn-Jones. Features/Margaret Pringle, Ian Cotton. Consultant art director/Derek Birdsall. Art/Susan Wade, Carol Bennett. Fashion editor/Caroline Baker. Fashion assistant/Maureen Walker. Production editor/Bob Smyth. Production/Lindsay Vernon, Lynn White. Associate editor/Alma Birk. Show business editor/John Sandilands. Travel editor/Jean Penfold. Fiction editor/Jean Cross.

NOVEMBER 1968
Contents
Is Muggeridge Britain's biggest bore?/Irma Kurtz
Who's zoo in modelling. Veruschka and Nicole/Brigid Keenan
This woman is divorcably clean/Catherine Storr
Birk's Peerage/Alma Birk
'There are a few of Vadim's friends I would love to have babies with'.Jane Fonda's curious menage in St Tropez/John Sandilands
Jean Denton: our girl for the London/Sydney car race/Peter Fiddick
Is America mad? Or just catching up with Las Vegas/John Sandilands
How Mr Updike came to write a very sexy book/Ruth Inglis
Drop in here to drop out Lambeth's shelter for the desperate/Peter Martin
Coming for the rye/Travel in Scotland by Adrian Bailey
'If I don't wear my ear-rings, they think I'm a fellar. The Afro cut/Brigid Keenan
So who needs skis?/Caroline Baker
Are you alone out there?/Cookery by Denis Curtis
Allsop/Kenneth Allsop
The girl from the golden city/short story by Maggie Ross
Cover photograph/Franco Rubartelli
Staff
Editor/Dennis Hackett. Assistant editors/Peter Fiddick, Brigid Keenan, Michael Wynn-Jones. Features/Margaret Pringle, Ian Cotton. Consultant art director/Derek Birdsall. Art/Susan Wade, Carol Bennett. Fashion editor/Caroline Baker. Fashion assistant/Maureen Walker. Production editor/Bob Smyth. Production/Lindsay Vernon, Lynn White. Associate editor/Alma Birk. Show business editor/John Sandilands. Travel editor/Jean Penfold. Fiction editor/Jean Cross.

DECEMBER 1968
Contents
Why children don't understand their parents/Michael Wynn-Jones
Mr and Mrs Barenboim/Maureen Cleave
When, when will his saints go marching in?/Vivian Craddock Williams
'Caroline is the best-dressed bastard in London'/Ian Cotton
A tourist's guide to the flics/Peter Forster
Christmas card/Drawn by Michael Foreman
The shape of things to come/Alma Birk
Mrs Denton will drive 10,000 miles to Sydney/Brigid Keenan
Yours unfaithfully/Ruth Langdon
Meet the fastest gun in the Middle East/Travel in Israel by Kenneth Allsop
Don't be a physical jerk/Brigid Keenan
Light up/fashion by Caroline Baker
Stuffings/Cookery by Denis Curtis
Allsop/Kenneth Allsop
Strictest confidence/Zoe Fairbairns
Cover photograph/Steve Hiett
Running cartoon commentary/Mel Caiman
Staff
Editor/Dennis Hackett. Assistant editors/Peter Fiddick, Brigid Keenan, Michael Wynn-Jones. Features/Margaret Pringle, Ian Cotton. Consultant art director/Derek Birdsall. Art/Susan Wade, Carol Bennett. Fashion editor/Caroline Baker. Fashion assistant/Maureen Walker. Production editor/Bob Smyth. Production/Lindsay Vernon, Lynn White. Associate editor/Alma Birk. Show business editor/John Sandilands. Travel editor/Jean Penfold. Fiction editor/Jean Cross.

JANUARY 1969
Contents
This is Steven Mandell, twenty-four, dead, and trying to buy immortality/Russell Miller
The way they see it in Houston, there are too many foreigners getting good Texan hearts/ Alma Birk
Refrigeration maybe heart transplants yes... but head transplants?/David Tribe
Portrait of a lady and two other ladies/ Margaret Pringle
Is the orgasm really necessary?/Catherine Storr
Now that Beryl Reid is playing a disreputable hard-drinking foulmouthed lesbian, she is likely to win an Oscar/Robert Ottaway
Honi soit qui mal y pense/John Sandilands
Mr Vidal takes pleasure in ambiguity/Arthur Hopcraft
Suffer little children/Peter Martin
Marmalade January 1969/Cookery by Denis Curtis
This is your face/Beauty by Brigid Keenan
What are you trying to hide?/Fashion by Brigid Keenan
A fistful of silver/Caroline Baker
Allsop/Kenneth Allsop
The beastly beatitudes of Balthazar B/J P Donleavy
Staff
Editor/Dennis Hackett. Assistant editors/Peter Fiddick, Brigid Keenan, Michael Wynn-Jones. Features/Margaret Pringle, Ian Cotton. Consultant art director/Derek Birdsall. Art/Sue Wade, Carol Bennett. Fashion editor/Caroline Baker. Fashion assistant/Maureen Walker. Production editor/Bob Smyth. Production/Lindsay Vernon, Lynn White. Associate editor/Alma Birk. Show business editor/John Sandilands. Travel editor/Jean Penfold. Fiction editor/Jean Cross.

FEBRUARY 1969
Contents
Perhaps, madam, we could return to our original arrangement whereby you banked with us/Robert Ottaway
The mind of a fat girl/Anne Batt
Don't tell me you can't remember his name/Ted Simon
Scientists and God/John Wren Lewis
Cecil Beaton is no snob. It's just that he prefers his friends to be glamourous/ Arthur Hopcraft
Peeping Tom is alive and well/Ruth Inglis
Nesters and roosters/Tom Atkins
Is this what we got rid of the Lord Chamberlain for?/Peter Lewis
My family and I/Angus Wolfe Murray
The girls of Girton/Michael Wynn-Jones
Until death do them part/Shirley Flack
Which man will you back in the breakfast revolution?/Peter Fiddick
Writes of spring/Books by Jean Cross
A taste of Spain/Travel by Michael Wynn-Jones
Getting into a lather/Beauty by Brigid Keenan
Living in the streets/Home by Elizabeth Good
Fur ease/Fashion by Caroline Baker
All party cover/Cookery by Denis Curtis
Allsop/Kenneth Allsop
Hush Hush/Naomi May
Cover photograph/Stuart Brown
Staff
Editor/Dennis Hackett. Assistant editors/Peter Fiddick, Brigid Keenan, Michael Wynn-Jones. Features/Margaret Pringle, Peter Martin. Art/Sue Wade, Carol Bennett. Fashion editor/Caroline Baker. Fashion assistant/Maureen Walker. Production editor/Bob Smyth. Production/Lindsay Vernon, Lynn White. Associate editor/Alma Birk. Show business editor/John Sandilands. Travel editor/Jean Penfold. Fiction editor/Jean Cross

MARCH 1969
Contents
In the bag... Yoko Ono/Irma Kurtz
Those people next door/Peter Martin
A short walk on the pampas/Michael Ivens
Destination doubtful – King Constantine and Queen Anne-Marie in exile/Herbert Spencer
Speaking of control, Mr Mailer/Irma Kurtz
Before you gamble on this horse, check for woodworm and dry-rot/Antiques by Barrie Sturt-Penrose
A Sicilian mosaic/Travel by Bob Smyth
...Well, be that as it may.../Fashion by Caroline Baker
Looks delicious darling. Did you buy it yourself?/Cookery by Denis Curtis
You can take it as red/Home by Elizabeth Good
Rags to riches/Moneysworth by Peter Martin
Lord lay scientist – Ritchie-Calder/Profile by Arthur Hopcraft
The Supremes (and friends)/Profile by Margaret Pringle
Randy's syndrome/Fiction by Brian Aldiss
Allsop/Kenneth Allsop
Cover photograph/Ray Green; back view: John Lennon, Apple
Staff
Editor/Dennis Hackett. Assistant editors/Peter Fiddick, Brigid Keenan, Michael Wynn-Jones. Features/Margaret Pringle, Peter Martin. Art/Sue Wade, Carol Bennett. Fashion editor/Caroline Baker. Fashion assistant/Maureen Walker. Production editor/Bob Smyth. Production/Lindsay Vernon, Lynn White. Associate Editor/Alma Birk. Show business editor/John Sandilands. Travel editor/Jean Penfold. Fiction editor/Jean Cross

APRIL 1969
Contents
Brilliant at the character parts he may be.../ John Sandilands
In this paradise pot's legal – but not much fun/ Irma Kurtz
Equal pay now!/Alix Palmer
And these men play gramophone records for money/Arthur Hopcraft
J P Donleavy is fighting.../Peter Martin
'I don't remember anything else for two months – they said it was two months'/Elizabeth Woolley
'Some people say I'm tough, but I'm the kindest man on earth'/Bob Smyth
Mother is a girl's best friend/Alma Birk
Someone must pay the doctor for nothing/Moneysworth by Stella Bingham
This antique business can be most distressing/Antiques by Barrie Sturt-Penrose
The island you've always promised yourself/Travel by Gaia Servadio
This face is waterproof/Beauty by Brigid Keenan
Indian Summer/Fashion by Brigid Keenan
And a long life to all your packages/Home by Elizabeth Good
Easy as pie/Cookery by Denis Curtis
Dr Kronhausen is not on the National Health/Profile by Timeri Murari
Allsop/Kenneth Allsop
The Exterminator/Fiction by Patrick Skene Catling
Cover photograph/Terry O'Neill
Staff
Editor/Dennis Hackett. Assistant editors/Peter Fiddick, Brigid Keenan, Michael Wynn-Jones. Features/Margaret Pringle, Peter Martin. Art/Sue Wade, Carol Bennett. Fashion editor/Caroline Baker. Fashion assistant/Maureen Walker. Production editor/Bob Smyth. Production/Lindsay Vernon, Lynn White. Associate editor/Alma Birk. Show business editor/John Sandilands. Travel editor/Jean Penfold. Fiction editor/Jean Cross.

MAY/JUNE 1969
Contents
Appraisal: Mary McCarthy: George Orwell/A S Byatt: Agony of the middle class liberal/Geoffrey Nicholson: The age of the hard man/Catherine Storr
Get slim luxuriously behind the Golden Door/Brian Moore
Sunglasses without sun/Brigid Keenan
Which rings true?/Brigid Keenan
The rector who roamed Piccadilly.../Michael Williams
Is it true what they're saying about Hampstead?/Peter Way
Fashion: Languorous lady in sea-stretch saga/Caroline Baker, photographs by Giacobetti
Life has not been easy for Miss Dunnage since 1964/Shirley Flack
Lipstick; how much of its price goes on your mouth?/ Beauty by Brigid Keenan
Are the Argylls worth saving?/Arthur Hopcraft
Profile: Mr Matchan, millionaire/Geoffrey Nicholson
Antiques/Barrie Sturt-Penrose
The old man and the seascape/Janet Stewart
How much is a man worth?/Peter Martin
Thunderbolt/Fiction by Frank Tuohy
Support your local playgroup/Brian Jackson
Allsop/Kenneth Allsop
Cover photograph: Jimmy Brown/Susan Wood
Staff
Editor/Peter Crookston. Assistant editors/Brigid Keenan, Michael Wynn-Jones. Features/Margaret Pringle, Peter Martin, Stella Bingham, Carolyn Faulder. Art assistants/Sue Wade, Carol Bennett. Fashion editor/Caroline Baker. Fashion assistant/Maureen Walker. Home editor/Elizabeth Good. Production editor/Bob Smyth. Production/Lynn White. Associate editor/Alma Birk. Literary adviser/A S Byatt. Show business editor/John Sandilands. Fiction editor/Jean Cross.

JUNE/JULY 1969
Contents
Appraisal: Sonia Orwell: Unfair to George/Robert Hughes: What did Sir Kenneth mean by 'Civilisation'?/D A N Jones: Television and violence/Carolyn Faulder
The world's greatest suburb/John Pilger
Fashion: Where's the cardie gone?/Caroline Baker, Photographs by J F Jonvelle
Eyes on plastics/Home by Elizabeth Good
Frailty thy name is woman/Beauty by Brigid Keenan
Profile: Mr Victor Lownes III/Peter Martin
The informers/Rosemary Collins
Fashion: Where do they pick up these strange foreign habits?/Brigid Keenan, photographs by Peter Knapp
Watch it, men – the new boss thinks you may not be tough enough/Nicholas Dromgoole
Perrott's directory of Nu-snob/Roy Perrott
Don't go to pieces on Sunday; do it all on Friday/Cookery by Caroline Conran
Henry Bech takes pot luck/Fiction by John Updike
Watch this face/Portrait by Colin Jones
Montreal/Travel by Barrie Sturt-Penrose
The lure of the bargain square/Richard Usborne
Allsop/Kenneth Allsop
Cover Photograph: Portrait of May Bell/ Peter Blake
Staff
Editor/Peter Crookston. Assistant editors/Brigid Keenan, Michael Wynn-Jones. Features/Margaret Pringle, Peter Martin, Stella Bingham, Carolyn Faulder. Art director/David Hillman. Art assistants/Sue Wade, Carol Bennett. Fashion editor/Caroline Baker. Fashion assistant/Maureen Walker. Home editor/Elizabeth Good. Production/Lynn White. Associate editors/Alma Birk, Irma Kurtz. Literary adviser/A S Byatt. Show business editor/John Sandilands. Fiction editor/Jean Cross

AUGUST 1969
Contents
The sterilised husbands/Shirley Flack and Michael Wynn-Jones
A Pill for men?/Carolyn Faulder
The dancing grannies/Helen Lawrenson
Profile of Lourdes/Robert Hughes/Photographs by David Montgomery
Kew Gardens: best three-pennyworth in London/ John Gale
Love plays/Alun Owen/Harold Pinter/ Michael Frayn

Dr. Hip: adviser to the Underground/
John Sandilands
Appraisal: Education/Ronald Fletcher: Georgette
Heyer AS Byatt: Breastfeeding and nonsense/
Judith Simmonds: Oliver Todd/Michael Wale: Care
of Marie Curie/Carolyn Faulder
Allsop/Kenneth Allsop
Careful with that spray/Beauty by Brigid Keenan
Learn from the gypsies/Fashion by Brigid Keenan
Picnics/Cookery by Caroline Conran
Cover photograph/David Steen

Staff

Editor/Peter Crookston. Assistant editor/Brigid
Keenan. Features/Margaret Pringle, Peter Martin,
Stella Bingham, Carolyn Faulder. Art director/
David Hillman. Art assistant/Carol Rainbird.
Fashion editor/Caroline Baker. Home editor/
Elizabeth Good. Home assistant/Maureen Walker.
Associate editors/Alma Birk, Irma Kurtz. Literary
adviser/A S Byatt. Show business editor/John
Sandilands. Fiction editor/Jean Cross.

SEPTEMBER 1969

Contents

Two women of Vietnam: Mme Ky and Mme
Binh/Brigid Keenan and Carolyn Faulder
Get to know your local Rocker/Peter Martin
Vera Lynn: Heroine of the Burma Reunion/
Pauline Peters
Nostradamus: the Man who could see
Tomorrow/Erika Cheetham
Narcissism/Edward Lucie-Smith
Abortion/Irma Kurtz
Haiti/Norman Lewis
Appraisal: A Few Film Firsts/John Coleman:
Adventures in Greece/Anthony Carson: Henry
Green/Paul Bailey: Konrad Lorenz/Ruth Inglis
The Short Story Classics: Frank Tuohy chooses
Roosya/Ivan Bunin
Antiques: Rings/Barrie Sturt Penrose
Allsop/Kenneth Allsop
Sun Tan/Beauty by Brigid Keenan
London collections/Fashion by Caroline
Baker/Photographs by Hans Feurer
Stamped for the Individual/Home by
Elizabeth Good
They go all the way up to her neck/Fashion
extra by James Wedge
Things we ate last summer/Cookery by
Caroline Conran
Cover photograph/Terence Donovan

Staff

Editor/Peter Crookston. Assistant editor/Brigid
Keenan. Art director/David Hillman. Art
assistant/Carol Rainbird. Features/Margaret
Pringle, Peter Martin, Stella Bingham, Carolyn
Faulder. Fashion editor/Caroline Baker. Home
editor/Elizabeth Good. Home assistant/Maureen
Walker. Associate editors/Alma Birk, Irma Kurtz.
Literary adviser/A S Byatt. Show business
editor/John Sandilands. Fiction editor/
Jean Cross.

OCTOBER 1969

Contents

People who think they look like other
people/Margaret Pringle and Pauline Peters
The Rise and Fall of the Man-made
Millionairess/Irma Kurtz
Words for a Deaf Daughter/Paul West
Portrait of Catherine Freeman/Carl Fischer
The Courtiers/Roy Perrot
Jacqueline Susann/profile by Sara Davidson
Pity the Poor Working Girl/Judith Simmons and
Clive Jenkins
The Picnic/Short story by Jonathan Gathorn-
Hardy
Appraisal: Clive Barnes - the world's most
powerful critic/Michael Wale: What's New
Cineaste?/John Coleman: A View of My
Own/Corinna Adam: Short Story Classic/Paul
Bailey chooses; Behind the Shade/Arthur
Morrison
Antiques/Barrie Sturt-Penrose
Allsop/Kenneth Allsop
Baby Knows Best/Beauty by Brigid Keenan
Crisis-resisting Clothes/Fashion by Caroline
Baker
Affectionate Suppers for Two/Cookery by
Caroline Conran
Cover Photograph/David Montgomery

Staff

Editor/Peter Crookston. Assistant editors/Brigid
Keenan, Joan Chapman, David Jenkins. Art
director/David Hillman. Art assistant/Carol
Rainbird. Features/Margaret Pringle, Peter
Martin, Stella Bingham, Carolyn Faulder. Fashion
editor/Caroline Baker. Sub editor/Deidre Heaton.
Home editor/Elizabeth Good. Home
assistant/Maureen Walker. Literary adviser/A S
Byatt. Associate editors/Alma Birk, Irma Kurtz.
Show business editor/John Sandilands. Fiction
editor/Jean Cross.

NOVEMBER 1969

Contents

Skinheads/Peter Martin, Photographs by David
Montgomery
What's it like, living off women/Carolyn Faulder
Mrs. Morris, sprite, aged 80/Brigid Keenan
Toys in an Artist's Orbit/Edward Lucie-Smith
The Forgotten Fifties/John Mortimer
Life Under the Backlash/Peter Preston
Successful Wives/Alix Colman
By Aer Lingus to the Moon/Anthony Carson
Appraisal: Marcia Haydee/Clement Crisp: Stevie
Smith/by Paul Bailey: Leslie Hurry/Shusha Guppy
Short Story Classics: David Pryce-Jones chooses
Berestechko/Isaac Babel
Prisoners' Wives/C H Ralph
Suzuki – Violin Teacher/Sonia Jackson
Allsop/Kenneth Allsop
Goodbye to the Bra/Fashion Extra by
Brigid Keenan
Make-up for Girls in a Rush/Beauty by
Brigid Keenan
Clothes that Lead a Double Life/Fashion by
Caroline Baker
Charladies/Home by Elizabeth Good
Winter Travel Special: Learning to Ski/John
Sandilands; Winter Sports Resorts/
Roland Huntford
First Catch Your Can/Cookery by Caroline Conran
Cover Photograph/Roger Stowell

Staff

Editor/Peter Crookston. Assistant editors/Brigid
Keenan, Joan Chapman, David Jenkins. Art
director/David Hillman. Art assistant/Carol
Rainbird. Sub editor/Deidre Heaton.
Features/Margaret Pringle, Peter Martin, Stella
Bingham, Carolyn Faulder. Fashion editor/Caroline
Baker. Home editor/Elizabeth Good. Home
assistant/Maureen Walker. Literary adviser/A S
Byatt. Art editor/Edward Lucie Smith. Associate
editor/Alma Birk. Fiction editor/Jean Cross.

DECEMBER 1969

Contents

A Kid's Life in Slum-land/Photographed by
the children who live there/Introduced by
Brigid Keenan
Your Smile Gives You Away/Dr. David Humphries
We're Privileged to Know You...Muriel Belcher,
Olwen Vaughan and Elizabeth Furse/Alix
Coleman, Patrick Campbell and Peter Jenkins
Inside the Nizam of Hyderabad's Junk Room/John
Sandilands
The Girl who Shot Andy Warhol and Mario
Amaya/Mario Amaya
Men Without Women/Peter Martin
Sex Education/Brian Jackson; Alma Birk
introduces Nova questionnaire
Problems of an Agnostic Father/Jonathan Miller
Appraisal: An A to Z of Film Festivals/John
Coleman: A View of My Own/Corinna Adam:
Dublin's Boss/Stan Gebler Davies: Portrait
Painting Lives!/Dr. Roy Strong: Books for
Children/John Rowe Townsend
The Short Story Classics: Pamela Hansford
Johnson chooses The Speciality of the
House/Stanley Ellin
Antiques/Barrie Sturt-Penrose
Allsop/Kenneth Allsop
Clothes to Show off Your Curves/Fashion by
Caroline Baker
Brown Study/Beauty by Brigid Keenan
A Taste of the Cookbooks/Cookery by Caroline
Conran
Cover photograph/Terence Donovan

Staff

Editor/Peter Crookston. Assistant editors/Brigid
Keenan, Joan Chapman, David Jenkins. Art
director/David Hillman. Art assistant/Carol
Rainbird. Sub editor/Deidre Heaton.
Features/Margaret Pringle, Peter Martin, Stella
Bingham, Carolyn Faulder. Fashion
editor/Caroline Baker. Home editor/Elizabeth
Good. Home assistant/Maureen Walker. Literary
adviser/A S Byatt. Art adviser/Edward Lucie-Smith.
Associate editor/Alma Birk. Fiction editor/
Jean Cross.

JANUARY 1970

Contents

The Network Syndrome/Peter Brett (a consultant
psychiatrist) and Brigid Keenan
Lulu/Helen Lawrenson
A Matter of Parliamentary Taste/Margaret Pringle
The Making of a Playmate/Gerry Bryant
The Playmate in Every Woman/Irma Kurtz
Putting on Airs at the Airport/David Jenkins
Mother Teresa/Ann Shearer
Appraisal: Debunking James Bond/Mordecai
Richler: The Short Story Classic: Julian
Mitchell chooses: The Conversion of the Jews
by Philip Roth
Nova Short Story: A Little Rain off the New
Moon/by Norman Lewis
Antiques/Barrie Sturt-Penrose
A View of my Own/Corinna Adam
What 1970 can do for a Woman/Beauty by Brigid
Keenan
Fake Furs: The Great Imposters/Fashion by
Caroline Baker
If your Furniture is too Familiar/Home by
Elizabeth Good
Young Palate Power/Cookery by Carol in Conran
Travel: Form Card for the Sunspots/Carol Wright
Holidays in Home Waters: Ireland/John Gale
Northumberland/David Jenkins
Orkney/Magnus Linklater
Wales/Roy Perrott
Lakeland/Anthony Carson
Big City Culture...In Comfort: Paris/Edward
Lucie-Smith
London/Ian Dunlop
New York/Mario Amaya
Wining Through Burgundy/David Jenkins
Cover photograph/Hans Feurer

Staff

Editor/Peter Crookston. Assistant editors/Brigid
Keenan, Joan Chapman, David Jenkins. Art
director/David Hillman. Art assistant/Carol
Rainbird. Sub editor/Deidre Heaton.
Features/Margaret Pringle, Peter Martin, Stella
Bingham, Carolyn Faulder. Fashion editor/Caroline
Baker. Home editor/Elizabeth Good. Home
assistant/Maureen Walker. Literary adviser/A S
Byatt. Art adviser/Edward Lucie-Smith. Associate
editor/Alma Birk. Fiction editor/Jean Cross.

FEBRUARY 1970

Contents

Span-land Analysed/Elaine Grand
A morning at the Vet's/Pauline Peters
Animals with Money in the Bank/Research by
Margaret Pringle, Stella Bingham
Viva! Viva! (extract from Viva King's
autobiography)/Introduced by Margaret Pringle
To my love .../Valentine customs by Arthur Calder-
Marshall
The Life-style of Peter Fonda/Pauline Peters
Factory Work: why machinery grinds the workers
down/Sara Yeomans
John Cassavetes' new girls/Philippa Pigache
Advertising for Soulmates/Stella Bingham
The Duchess of Medina Sidonia/Nova Profile by
Carolyn Faulder
Sweden: a few myths exploded/Susan Sontag
Appraisal: Moviemakers' Mates/John Coleman;
The Great Poetry War/Julian Mitchell; Mexico's
Hounded Editor/Brian Glanville; Babar's Best
Friend/Carolyn Faulder; The Short Story Classics:
Doris Lessing chooses Paradise of Song/Idries
Shah; Why I'm a Tory/Timothy Raison
A View of My Own/Corinna Adam
Shop window dummies are good
teachers/Fashion Extra by Brigid Keenan
Fashion needs re-thinking: Start here/
Caroline Baker
Secrets of a Royal Mistress/Beauty by
Brigid Keenan
The best in Blinds/Home by Elizabeth Good
Some Like it Hot/Cookery by Caroline Conran
Cover photograph/Hans Feurer

Staff

Editor/Peter Crookston. Assistant editors/Brigid
Keenan, Joan Chapman, David Jenkins. Art
director/David Hillman. Art assistant/Carol
Rainbird. Sub editor/Deidre Sanders.
Features/Margaret Pringle, Peter Martin, Stella
Bingham, Carolyn Faulder. Fashion editor/Caroline
Baker. Home editor/Elizabeth Good. Home
assistant/Maureen Walker. Literary adviser/A S
Byatt. Art adviser/Edward Lucie- Smith. Associate
editor/Alma Birk. Fiction editor/Jean Cross.

MARCH 1970

Contents

How to Package a Prime Minister/Antony Jay.
Realisation/Brian Love, Photography by
Clive Corless
The life-style of the American Ambassador/
Helen Lawrenson
George Formby Lives!/John Gale
Appraisal: Pop-Art's Founder/Mario Amaya;
Monica Dickens/A S Byatt; Why I'll still vote
Labour/Brian Jackson
Nova Short Story: Un Peu Comme Orson
Welles/Elizabeth Troop
A View of My Own/Corinna Adam
The Fifth Columnists/Fashion by Caroline Baker
Slimming Foods don't Slim/Beauty by
Brigid Keenan
Disguises that can Floor You/Home by
Elizabeth Good
Meals a la Carton/Home Extra by Michael Wale
Minitrekking in Morocco/Travel by Margaret Pringle
Cover photograph/Christa Peters

Staff

Editor/Peter Crookston. Assistant editors/Brigid
Keenan, Joan Chapman, David Jenkins. Art
director/David Hillman. Art assistant/Carol
Rainbird. Sub editor/Deidre Sanders.
Features/Margaret Pringle, Peter Martin, Stella
Bingham, Carolyn Faulder. Fashion
editor/Caroline Baker. Home editor/Elizabeth
Good. Home assistant/Maureen Walker. Literary
adviser/A S Byatt. Art adviser/Edward Lucie-
Smith. Associate editor/Alma Birk. Fiction
editor/Jean Cross.

APRIL 1970

Contents

Brigitte Bardot at 35/Brigid Keenan
Your Friendly Neighbourhood Backlash/
Margaret Pringle
Premiere people/Brigid Keenan
Biafra's Cowboy Catholics/Richard Hall
The Empty Room at Number I79/Julia Almond
Big Spenders on the Move/Peter Johnson
Why we're in the Covent Garden Chorus/
Ruth Brandon
Nova Profile: Nicol Williamson/Pauline Peters
The Unloved Ones/Carolyn Faulder
Paul Johnson/David Jenkins
Appraisal: Wolff Olins/Geoffrey Nicholson Home
Movie-makers/John Coleman; Greek
Revolutionary/Cedric Thornberry; The Barbican
Flats/Andrew Downie; Regine Deforges/Ruth
Brandon; David Hockney/Edward Lucie-Smith
Nova Short Story: The Orange Cat/Judith Simmons
How? Nova's new advice service/Mavis Nicholson
A View of My Own/Corinna Adam
Eyes: Woman's Third Dimension/Beauty by
Brigid Keenan
Get Yourself Embroidered/Fashion by Caroline
Baker
Dear Monte/Travel by Anthony Carson
Mail-order Gourmet Food and Time-saving Gadgets/
Novacook Plus by Caroline Conran
Antique Beds/Barrie Sturt-Penrose
Cover photograph/Ghislain Dussart

Staff

Editor/Peter Crookston. Assistant editors/Brigid
Keenan, Joan Chapman, David Jenkins. Art
director/David Hillman. Art assistant/Carol
Rainbird. Sub editor/Deidre Sanders.
Features/Margaret Pringle, Peter Martin, Stella
Bingham, Carolyn Faulder. Fashion editor/Caroline
Baker. Home editor/Elizabeth Good. Home
assistant/Maureen Walker. Literary adviser/A S
Byatt. Art adviser/Edward Lucie-Smith. Associate
editor/Alma Birk. Fiction editor/Jean Cross.

MAY 1970

Contents

School for Stardom/Ann Leslie, Photographs by
Curt Gunther
Last of the Big-time Surgeons/
James Hamilton-Paterson
Doctors: That old black bag has lost its
magic/Ann Shearer
Excuse me, but your tic is showing/David Jenkins
The Pornography of Violence/
Pamela Hansford Johnson
Mary: mean, married and middle-class/
Pauline Peters
The social style of Edmundo Ros/Nova Profile by
Timeri Murari
Hell it was to be young then (extracts from The
Green Leaves of Nottingham)/novel by Pat McGrath
Appraisal Could you live with Buckminster Fuller?/
Kenneth Allsop; Pierre Boulez/Shusha Guppy;
Victorian Death and Heaven/Margaret Pringle;
Antiques: Prints/Barrie Sturt-Penrose;
Pick of the Paperbacks/Christopher Wordsworth;
Two Poems/Sylvia Plath; Your Child and the First
R/Richard Bourne; The worries of F W Woolworth/
Geoffrey Nicholson
How? Advice service/Mavis Nicholson
Tinderbox Green: An everyday saga of estate

living/by Marc and Peter Preston
Women taking the uniformity out of uniforms/Fashion Extra by Brigid Keenan
The Daring Duds of May/Caroline Baker
A Moustache Looks Better on a Man/Beauty by Brigid Keenan
Missing Links in a Chain Store/Home by Elizabeth Good
Blooming Vegetables/Cookery by Caroline Conran
Conran's Chart for All Seasons
Sydney/Nova Travel by John Sandilands
Cover/Peter Knapp

Staff

Editor/Peter Crookston. Assistant editors/Brigid Keenan, Joan Chapman, David Jenkins. Art director/David Hillman. Art assistant/Carol Rainbird. Sub editor/Deidre Sanders. Features/Margaret Pringle, Peter Martin, Stella Bingham, Carolyn Faulder. Fashion editor/Caroline Baker. Home editor/Elizabeth Good. Home assistant/Maureen Walker. Literary adviser/ AS Byatt. Art adviser/Edward Lucie-Smith. Associate editor/Alma Birk. Fiction editor/Jean Cross.

JUNE 1970

Contents

Susan Wilding, Five Husbands Later/Peter Martin
Girl in Number IO/Report by Margaret Pringle and Stella Bingham
Home Truths about Corporation Wives/ Pauline Peters
The Pop Art Pad of Gunther Sachs/ Edward Lucie-Smith
Gimmicks for God/Stella Bingham
One Woman's Fight against Germ Warfare/ Ruth Brandon
Censors Must Go!! John Mortimer
Astra Nova
Appraisal: Cityscape: New York/Michael Wood; Grace Wyndham Goldie/Michael Wale; DDT Hysteria/James Hamilton-Peterson; Tragedies of Married Life/Judith Viorst; Antiques: Chairs/Barrie Sturt-Penrose; Pick of the Paperbacks/Christopher Wordsworth
How?/by Mavis Nicholson
Nova Short Story: Noon/A L Barker
Tinderbox Green/Marc and Peter Preston
A Touch of Tahiti/Fashion by Caroline Baker
The Pretty and the Plain/Beauty by Brigid Keenan
Make-up to Go to Bed In/Beauty Extra by Brigid Keenan
Food for a Hot Summer's Day/Cookery by Caroline Conran
What Men Hate about Home/Home by Mavis Nicholson
Stockists
Cover photograph/Peter Knapp

Staff

Editor/Peter Crookston. Assistant editors/Brigid Keenan, Joan Chapman, David Jenkins. Art director/David Hillman. Art assistant/Carol Rainbird. Sub editor/Deidre Sanders. Features/Margaret Pringle, Peter Martin, Stella Bingham, Carolyn Faulder. Fashion editor/Caroline Baker. Fashion assistant/Pip Newbury. Home editor/Mavis Nicholson. Home assistant/Maureen Walker. Literary adviser and fiction editor/A S Byatt. Art adviser/Edward Lucie-Smith. Associate editor/Alma Birk

JULY 1970

Contents

The Man-trapping World of Helen Gurley Brown/Nora Ephron
Once a Frinton person, always a Frinton person/Stella Bingham/Photography by Colin Jones
The boys who burned themselves/ Carolyn Faulder
Colorado Jim and the vicar's daughter/Pat Barr
Nova Profile: Robert Redford/Helen Lawrenson/ Photographs by Hans Feurer Handbags – what they reveal about you/Margaret Pringle
Getting out of the traffic jam/Terence Bendixson/illustration by Chris Foss
Pornography – and how it degrades Denmark's women/James Hamilton-Paterson
Appraisal: Gyles Brandreth Admits Everything/Magnus Linklater; Child Psychology/Judith Simmons; Dickens: A simpleminded writer of genius/Paul Bailey; Antiques: Georgian Fantasy/Barrie Sturt-Penrose: Pick of the Paperbacks/Christopher Wordsworth: How British Home Stores moved 'up market'/ Geoffrey Nicholson: A View of My Own/Corinna Adam: Poetry/Judith Viorst
Nova Short Story: Jump Out/Paul Winstanley
Tinderbox Green/Marc and Peter Preston
How?/Nova's practical advice column by Mavis Nicholson
In praise of older women/Fashion Extra by Brigid Keenan
Once too divine...now groovy baby/Fashion by Caroline Baker
How to achieve the bosom beautiful/Beauty by Brigid Keenan
Making ice-cream the smooth way/Nova Cookery by Caroline Conran
Luxury food you could live on/Cynthia Kee
A Room of One's Own/Home by Mavis Nicholson
Roughing it in the grand manner/Nova Travel by Neil Bruce
Cover photograph/Hans Feurer

Staff

Editor/Peter Crookston. Assistant editors/Brigid Keenan, Joan Chapman, David Jenkins. Art director/David Hillman. Art assistant/Carol Rainbird. Sub editor/Deidre Sanders. Features/Margaret Pringle, Peter Martin, Stella Bingham, Carolyn Faulder. Fashion editor/Caroline Baker. Home editor/Mavis Nicholson. Home assistant/Maureen Walker. Literary adviser and fiction editor/A S Byatt. Art adviser/Edward Lucie-Smith. Associate editor/Alma Birk.

AUGUST 1970

Contents

A Plea for more Convention/Peter Brett, consultant psychiatrist
Helen's Underground Diary/Helen Lawrenson
Mr Hickey's Young Ladies/David Jenkins
Britain's Witchcraft Boom/Alison Lurie
Sex and the Thirty-Year-Old/Carolyn Faulder
I Remember Life Below Stairs/Pat Barr
The Aborigine Pioneer in Films/Irma Kurtz
Rich Romantic Novelists/Margaret Pringle
What's Happening in London's Parks?/Fay Coventry
Appraisal: Punch and Judy/Penelope Farmer: Eating Outdoors/by Cynthia Kee: Cityscape: Paris/Peter Lennon: Antiques: Stately Homes/Barrie Sturt-Penrose: Pick of the Paperbacks/Christopher Wordsworth
Nova Short Story: One Afternoon/Elizabeth Kimball
Tinderbox Green/Marc and Peter Preston
How?/Nova's practical advice column by Mavis Nicholson
Small Ads Investigated/Beauty by Brigid Keenan
Cool Clothes to Buy Now/Fashion by Caroline Baker
Pregnant can be Beautiful/Fashion and Beauty Extra by Brigid Keenan and Caroline Baker
Summer Party Food/Cooking by Caroline Conran
Looking at London's Tourists/Fashion Extra by Brigid Keenan
Cover photograph/Hans Feurer

Staff

Editor/Peter Crookston. Assistant editors/Brigid Keenan, Joan Chapman, David Jenkins. Art director/David Hillman. Art assistant/Carol Rainbird. Sub editor/Deidre Sanders. Features/Margaret Pringle, Peter Martin, Stella Bingham, Carolyn Faulder. Fashion editor/Caroline Baker. Fashion assistant/Pip Newbery. Home editor/Mavis Nicholson. Home assistant/Maureen Walker. Literary adviser and fiction editor/ AS Byatt. Art adviser/Edward Lucie-Smith. Associate editor/Alma Birk.

SEPTEMBER 1970

Contents

Political Groupies/Sara Davidson
Writers' Notebooks/David Jenkins
Life-styles at Liverpool's Registry Office/ Stella Bingham
Levi's-seat of a nation's fame/Irma Kurtz
Giving Levi's the lived-in look/Brigid Keenan
Pop taste and objets d'ashcan/Kenneth Allsop
Living with gifted children/Paul Pickering
Eddie Cochran – gone but not forgotten/ Peter Martin
Behind the salesgirl's smile.../Pat Barr
The millionaire and his multi-storey monument/by David Jenkins and Peter Martin
Astra Nova/Patric Walker
Appraisal: Collective living in Denmark/Barrie Sturt-Penrose: A View of My Own/Corinna Adam; Tragedies of Married Life: Infidelity: Poem/Judith Viorst; Pick of the Paperbacks/Christopher Wordsworth: Antiques: treasure hunting in Birmingham/Barrie Sturt-Penrose
Nova Short Story: The Journey/Judith Cooke
Tinderbox Green/Marc and Peter Preston
Designers as dressers/Fashion Extra by Brigid Keenan
Casebook of a miracle in make-up/Beauty by Brigid Keenan
Fashion's Entente Cordiale/Fashion by Caroline Baker
Design for a shower/bath room/Home by Mavis Nicholson
Succulent seafood/Cookery by Caroline Conran
The lure of The Scillies/Travel by Anthony Carson
How?/Mavis Nicholson
Cover photograph/Charlotte March

Staff

Editor/Peter Crookston. Assistant editors/Brigid Keenan, Joan Chapman, David Jenkins. Art director/David Hillman. Art assistant/Carol Rainbird. Sub editor/Deidre Sanders. Features/Margaret Pringle, Peter Martin, Stella Bingham, Carolyn Faulder. Fashion editor/Caroline Baker. Fashion assistant/Pip Newbery. Home editor/Mavis Nicholson. Home assistant/Maureen Walker. Literary adviser and fiction editor/A S Byatt. Art adviser/Edward Lucie-Smith. Associate editor/Alma Birk.

OCTOBER 1970

Contents

Robert Ardrey and the population explosion/Antony Jay
Making medicine safer/Ann Shearer
The sound of students/Elaine Grand
Wives and their lovers/Pauline Peters
Germaine Greer on the rights of woman/ Carolyn Faulder
The Napoleon of bigamists/by his daughter, Kathleen Lane
Touchline widows/Peter Martin
Astra Nova/Patric Walker
Nova Short Story: The Elephant Man/Susan Hill
Tinderbox Green/Marc and Peter Preston
How?/Mavis Nicholson
Home discomforts/Mavis Nicholson
The Poor Cook book/Review by Brigid Keenan
War on wrinkles/Beauty by Brigid Keenan
Go gaucho!/Fashion by Caroline Baker
Plump can be pretty/Fashion extra by Brigid Keenan
Winter sports and attendant pleasures/ Nova ski-travel special by John Samuel
Cover photograph/Harri Peccinotti

Staff

Editor/Peter Crookston. Assistant editors/Brigid Keenan, Joan Chapman, David Jenkins. Art director/David Hillman. Art assistant/Carol Rainbird. Sub editor/Deidre Sanders. Features/Margaret Pringle, Peter Martin, Stella Bingham, Carolyn Faulder. Fashion editor/Caroline Baker. Fashion assistant/Pip Newbery. Home editor/Mavis Nicholson. Home assistant/Maureen Walker. Literary adviser and fiction editor/A S Byatt. Art adviser/Edward Lucie-Smith. Associate editor/Alma Birk.

NOVEMBER 1970

Contents

Women as bosses/Harriet Chare
Nervy girl's guide to poise/Dr Peter Driver
Lauren Bacall/Profile by Helen Lawrenson
Being a man isn't easy/Sally Vincent
Garbo's greatest films/Gavin Millar
Hippie pioneers/Sally Vincent
Astra Nova/Patric Walker (Novalis)
Cityscape: London/Seymour Krim
Commentary: Feminine fiction/Judith Cooke
Nova Short Story: Show House/Oliver Pritchett
Travel: Ships and islands in the sun/John Carter
Tinderbox Green/Marc and Peter Preston
How?/by Mavis Nicholson
Yves St Laurent's fan club/Fashion Extra by Caroline Baker
Asian wisdom/Beauty by Brigid Keenan
Designing with children in mind/Home by Mavis Nicholson
Gifts to eat/Cookery by Caroline Conran
Cover photograph/Hans Feurer

Staff

Editor/Peter Crookston. Assistant editors/Brigid Keenan, Joan Chapman, David Jenkins. Art director/David Hillman. Art assistant/Carol Rainbird. Sub editor/Deidre Sanders. Features/Margaret Pringle, Peter Martin, Stella Bingham, Carolyn Faulder. Fashion editor/ Caroline Baker. Fashion assistant/Pip Newbery. Home editor/Mavis Nicholson. Home assistant/ Maureen Walker. Literary adviser and fiction editor/A S Byatt. Art adviser/Edward Lucie-Smith. Associate editor/Alma Birk.

DECEMBER 1970

Contents

Round Britain Theatre/Hilary Macaskill
Elizabeth David/Nova Profile by Harriet Chare
Sexual Jealousy/Sally Vincent
Alarm! Burglars for Christmas/Peter Martin
Primitive painters/Anthony Carson
Space starvation/Joel Richman
Couples living in platonic bliss/Harriet Chare
Astra Nova/Patric Walker
Cityscape: Tel Aviv/Sally Vincent
Nova Short Story: The Diver/V S Pritchett
Tinderbox Green/Marc and Peter Preston
How?/Mavis Nicholson
Choosing toys for children/Maureen Walker
A touch of the Walter Mitty's/Fashion by Caroline Baker
It's fur real/Fashion extra by Caroline Baker
The Gadget game/Beauty by Brigid Keenan
Catering for parties without panic/Cookery by Caroline Conran
Cover photograph/Hans Feurer

Staff

Editor/Gillian Cooke. Assistant editors/Brigid Keenan, Joan Chapman, David Jenkins. Art director/David Hillman. Art assistant/Carol Rainbird. Sub editor/Deidre Sanders. Features/Margaret Pringle, Peter Martin, Stella Bingham, Carolyn Faulder. Fashion editor/Caroline Baker. Fashion assistant/Pip Newbery. Home editor/Mavis Nicholson. Home assistant/Maureen Walker. Literary adviser and fiction editor/A S Byatt. Art adviser/Edward Lucie-Smith. Associate editor/Alma Birk.

JANUARY 1971

Contents

Aphrodisiacs: can certain food and drink give you – or enhance – a super sexual urge?/Report by lain Stewart
The persuasive voices of TV commercials have plenty to say about their jobs/Christopher Matthew
The Palladium – a look behind the scenes at Britain's bastion of the traditional music-hall/Geoffrey Moorhouse
Science and society: can the human race make it to the 21st century?/Robin Clarke and scientists report
Barrie Sturt-Penrose joins the doorstep artists and paints a disturbing picture of how easily we can be hoaxed
Chester Himes, the Harlem negro who, while he was a convict, became a celebrated writer/talks to David Jenkins
Happy marriages face the challenge of the permissive society, but what about challenges thrown up by the partners?/Carolyn Faulder reports
Six new love poems/Robert Graves
Up Front: the column with a keen eye for facts, foibles and fancies/edited by David Jenkins
Nova Short Story: Access to the Children/ William Trevor.
Astra Nova/Patric Walker
How?/Mavis Nicholson answers readers' practical problems
The where and what of hiring/Maureen Walker
How to keep warm/Fashion Extra by Caroline Baker
Suits simply aren't what they used to be/Fashion by Caroline Baker
Keeping young...growing older – for 50 and 15 year olds/Beauty by Brigid Keenan
Put it all in a great big boiling pot/Cookery by Caroline Conran
Cover photograph/Christa Peters

Staff

Editor/Gillian Cooke. Assistant editors/Brigid Keenan, Joan Chapman, David Jenkins. Art director/David Hillman. Assistant/Carol Rainbird. Sub editor/Deidre Sanders. Features/Margaret Pringle, Peter Martin, Stella Bingham, Carolyn Faulder. Fashion editor/Caroline Baker. Fashion assistant/Pip Newbery. Home editor/Mavis Nicholson. Home assistant/Maureen Walker. Fiction editor/Margaret Pringle. Associate editor/Alma Birk.

FEBRUARY 1971

Contents

America's hippies are swinging back to Jesus/Report by Ann Leslie
Patrick Moore, the man who talks about the stars, has himself collected star rating in the process/Profile by John Sandilands
Should fathers be present during childbrith?/Monica Foot talks to a group of men who believe they should
People are often described as a 'man's woman' or as a 'woman's woman'/Carolyn Faulder finds out

just how valid this categorising is
Have the new blocks of council flats demolished the old working-class neighbourliness?/Elaine Grand gets some answers
Guilt – over work, home, friends, foes – but is it really justified?/asks Irma Kurtz
Up Front/edited by David Jenkins
Nova Short Story: Rainin' Terrible Out There/Maggie Blenkinsop
Astra Nova/Patric Walker
Caroline Baker says look out for the little-nothing sweaters of spring
Acne: readers tell how they've battled with this skin scourge/Report by Brigid Keenan
Children reveal some surprising thoughts about their home to Mavis Nicholson
Supper for two can make or break an evening/Cookery by Caroline Conran
How?/Mavis Nicholson answers readers' practical problems
Where to find out whether you're getting the best value for your money/Maureen Walker
Cover photograph/Robert Golden

Staff

Editor/Gillian Cooke. Assistant editors/Joan Chapman, David Jenkins. Art director/David Hillman. Assistant/Carol Rainbird. Sub editor/Sally Lewis. Features/Stella Bingham, Carolyn Faulder, Peter Martin. Fashion editor/Caroline Baker. Assistant/Pip Newbery. Home editor/Mavis Nicholson. Assistant/Maureen Walker. Fiction editor/Margaret Pringle. Contributing editor/Alma Birk.

MARCH 1971

Contents

What happens to the kids who run away to London?/Bel Mooney
Can a woman love two men at once?/Catherine Storr
Old age – a crime against society?/Pat Barr
The Rev. Troy C Perry preaching the right to be a homosexual/Peter Martin
Words of wisdom from Women's Lib literature/Sally Beauman
The invasion of a Saigon hotel by the chewing gum and chocolate army/Irma Kurtz
Readers who also write letters – lots of them/Comment by Irma Kurtz
Astra Nova/Patric Walker
Up Front/edited by David Jenkins
Nova Short Story: Ready to Serve/Oliver Pritchett
By Caroline Baker:
Designers are giving clothes a spring clean
Sing about the blues
Jewellery that looks good enough to eat
Weekend hideaways/Arther Eperon on stolen spring breaks
Sensuous is more than sexy/Beauty by Penny Vincenzi
How?/by Mavis Nicholson
Scented rooms can be so seductive/Maureen Walker
Cooking up less fussy cakes/Caroline Conran
Where the bargains are/Maureen Walker
Cover photograph/Harri Peccinotti

Staff

Editor/Gillian Cooke. Assistant editors/Joan Chapman, David Jenkins. Art director/David Hillman. Assistant/Carol Rainbird. Sub editor/Sally Lewis. Features/Stella Bingham. Carolyn Faulder, Peter Martin. Fashion editor/Caroline Baker. Assistant/Pip Newbery. Home editor/Mavis Nicholson. AssistantMaureen Walker. Fiction editor/Margaret Pringle. Contributing editor/Alma Birk

APRIL 1971

Contents

How to divorce and remain whole/Judith Cooke Simmons
How does the divorced woman with children resume her sex life?/Ann Leslie
Marianne Faithfull's life has been a totter between dreamland and disaster. She talks to Nik Cohn
Medical hypnosis – it can be a lazy man's yoga/says Pat Brown
The Venus Touch, three new poems/Maureen Duffy
The girls who wait outside for Charles Manson/Peter Martin reports
Inside Brazil, where middle-age can be a luxury/James Hamilton-Paterson
Astra Nova/Patric Walker
Up Front/edited by David Jenkins
Nova Short Story; Easy Going Woman/William Trevor
A View of My Own/Sally Vincent By Caroline Baker:
Peasant Thoughts. Thick quilting as light clothing
Skinny, drippy beachwear – proving that fashion is only swim-deep
Beauty – when to slow down on making up/Penny Vincenzi
Through a glass decoratively – painted windows/Mavis Nicholson
The grass roots of cookery – herbs/Caroline Conran
How? Readers' practical problems solved/Mavis Nicholson
Where to get kitted out/Maureen Walker
Cover photograph/Duffy

Staff

Editor/Gillian Cooke. Assistant editor/David Jenkins. Art director/David Hillman. Assistant/Carol Rainbird. Sub editor/Sally Lewis. Features/Stella Bingham, Carolyn Faulder, Peter Martin, Bel Mooney. Fashion editor/Caroline Baker. Assistant/Pip Newbery. Beauty editor/Penny Vincenzi. Home editor/Mavis Nicholson. Assistant/Maureen Walker. Fiction editor/Margaret Pringle. Contributing editor/Alma Birk.

MAY 1971

Contents

Patricia Highsmith cross-examined/Margaret Pringle
Some memories of first love
Roman Polanski talks and talks and talks to Ann Leslie
Can you teach parents to be better parents?/asks Paul Pickering
Wanted – coloured children/Stella Bingham looks at adoption
Convent life – Irma Kurtz spends five days with the Sisterhood
Arrest and arraignment California-style/Mary Ensor
Astra Nova/Patric Walker
Up Front/edited by David Jenkins
Nova Short Story: The Other/Giliian Tindall
A View of My Own/Ann Shearer
How to undress for your husband
Cool natural cottons in Morocco/Caroline Baker
How? Readers' practical problems solved/Mavis Nicholson
Garden statues come indoors/Barrie Sturt-Penrose
Beautfiul blushing men/Penny Vincenzi
The yins and yangs of cookery/Caroline Conran
Holidays à la Club Med/Caroline Baker
Where to volunteer/Maureen Walker
Cover photograph/Duffy

Staff

Editor/Gillian Cooke. Assistant editor/David Jenkins. Art director/David Hillman. Assistant/Carol Rainbird. Production editor/Sally Lewis. Features/Stella Bingham, Carolyn Faulder, Peter Martin, Bel Mooney. Fashion editor/Caroline Baker. Assistant/Pio Newberv. Beauty editor/Penny Vincenzi. Home editor/Janet Fitch. Assistant/Maureen Walker. Fiction editor/Margaret Pringle.

JUNE 1971

Contents

Judith Viorst/interviewed by David Jenkins
Foreigners – for better or for worse/Carolyn Faulder
Who's been prying into your life?/Raymond Palmer investigates
Caterine Milinaire on the gypsy art of Mati Klarwein
Knickers aren't funny at Butlin's any more/Philip Oakes
Doris Day profile/John Sandilands
Under fives need more than mum and telly/Ruth Inglis looks at nursery schools
Motherhood at 15, after all, why not?/Robert Leigh
Astra Nova/Patric Walker
Up Front in New York/edited by David Jenkins
Nova Short Story: Corners/Jonathan Schwartz
A View of My Own/Irma Kurtz
By Caroline Baker:
In a pastoral mood
Bags and blazers, the movie-star look
When she was pink, she was very, very pink .../Beauty by Penny Vincenzi
Salads as they should be/Caroline Conran
Where to go in your lunch hour/Maureen Walker
How? Readers' practical problems solved/Mavis Nicholson
Cover photograph/Max Maxwell

Staff

Editor/Gillian Cooke. Assistant editor/David Jenkins. Art director/David Hillman. Assistant/Carol Rainbird. Production editor/Sally Lewis. Features/Stella Bingham, Carolyn Faulder, Peter Martin, Bel Mooney. Fashion editor/Caroline Baker. Assistant/Pip Newbery. Beauty editor/Penny Vincenzi. Home editor/Janet Fitch. Assistant/Maureen Walker. Fiction editor/Margaret Pringle.

JULY 1971

Contents

The British Museum/Ruth Brandon surveys the relics and talks to some of them
Mrs Bandaranaike/Profile Irma Kurtz
Are custody cases fair on fathers?/Ruth Inglis asks
Where do teachers go from here: the classroom revolution/Bel Mooney
G-golly how schoolgirl comics have changed!/Virginia Ironside
Would a nanny take you on?/Caroline Nicholson
20 years after the blacklist/Kenneth Hurren interviews four Hollywood outlaws
Astra Nova/Patric Walker
Up Front/edited by David Jenkins
Nova Short Story: The Dead End/Colette
A View of My Own/David Jenkins
By Caroline Baker:
Well-dressed soles
After hot pants – cool, collected dresses
Passion wagons/Travel by Arthur Eperon
Beauty is a screwed up face/Penny Vincenzi
Roof-top retreats for city dwellers/Janet Fitch
How to put the brakes on your weight/Penny Vincenzi
Mediterranean ways with vegetables/Caroline Conran
Where to go to market/Maureen Walker
How? Readers' practical problems solved/Mavis Nicholson
Cover/Adrian Flowers

Staff

Editor/Gillian Cooke. Assistant editor/David Jenkins. Art director/David Hillman. Assistant/Carol Rainbird. Production editor/Sally Lewis. Assistant to the editor/Bel Mooney. Sub editor/Jeffrey Mills. Features/Stella Bingham, Carolyn Faulder, Peter Martin. Fashion editor/Caroline Baker. Assistant/Pip Newbery. Beauty editor/Penny Vincenzi. Home editor/Janet Fitch. Assistant/Maureen Walker. Fiction editor/Margaret Pringle.

AUGUST 1971

Contents

PR professionalism, Les Perrin interviewed/Stella Bingham
Pot: Ann Leslie talks to some suburban smokers
Depression: a suitable case for treatment/Lynn Barber
Sex, the church and normality/Paul Pickering
Rat-race losers/Nova cartoon by David Jenkins and Roger Law
Sally Vincent meets Clive Jenkins – the man who radicalised the middle class
Women in trades unions/Stella Bingham
Anthony Carson savours the joys of Olde England
Astra Nova/Patric Walker
Up Front/edited by David Jenkins
Nova short story: Enoch's Two Letters/Alan Sillitoe
Money – a view of my own/Irma Kurtz
By Caroline Baker: Jewellery – a brooched subject
Layering stripey sweaters and shorts
Summer underwear
Painted blinds for picture windows/Janet Fitch
Positive and negative smells/Beauty by Penny Vincenzi
What shall we tell the children about molesters?/Mavis Nicholson
Children in the kitchen/Caroline Conran
How? Readers' practical problems solved/Mavis Nicholson

Staff

Editor/Gillian Cooke, Assistant editor/David Jenkins, Art director/David Hillman, Assistant/Carol Rainbird, Production editor/Sally Lewis, Assistant to the editor/Bel Mooney, Sub editor/Jeffrey Mills, Features/Carolyn Faulder, Stella Bingham, Peter Martin. Fashion editor/Caroline Baker. Assistant/Pip Newbery. Beauty editor/Penny Vincenzi. Home editor/Janet Fitch. Assistant/Maureen Walker. Fiction editor/Margaret Pringle. Contributing editors/Irma Kurtz, Pat Barr, Ann Leslie, Sally Vincent, Ken Martin (New York)

SEPTEMBER 1971

Contents

John Coleman on location with Schlesinger: Filming Bloody Filming
What is the missionaries' role in the cooking-pot of independent Africa?/asks Helen Exley
What do you do if your child is not normal?/Peter Rowlands describes life with his autistic son
Peter Walker – rise of a Superminister
Astra Nova/Patric Walker
Upfront/edited by David Jenkins
The Home – an extract from Penelope Mortimer's new novel
Expatriates – a view of my own/Irma Kurtz
By Caroline Baker:
The army surplus war-game
Classic clothes for proper Charlie girls
Cut up a new face/Beauty by Penny Vincenzi
Living in white open spaces/Janet Fitch
Pack away a pickle or two/Cookery by Caroline Conran
Where to get things fixed/Maureen Walker
Cover photograph/Hans Feurer

Staff

Editor/Gillian Cooke. Assistant editor/David Jenkins. Art director/David Hillman. Assistants/Carol Rainbird, Richard McMillan. Production editor/Sally Lewis. Assistant to the editor/Bel Mooney. Sub editor/Jeffrey Mills. Features/Carolyn Faulder, Stella Bingham, Peter Martin. Fashion editor/Caroline Baker. Assistant/Pip Newbery. Beauty editor/Penny Vincenzi. Home editor/Janet Fitch. Assistant/Maureen Walker. Fiction editor/Margaret Pringle. Contributing editors/Irma Kurtz, Pat Barr, Ann Leslie, Sally Vincent, Ken Martin (New York)

OCTOBER 1971

Contents

If you want to work and breed, what do you do with the children?/asks Carolyn Faulder
Beauty Queens are sort of human, too/Irma Kurtz
Social Security and the unsupported mother/David Jenkins
The snakes and ladders of the sex war. Nova quiz/Jane Deverson and Dr Roger Hobdell
Caroline Nicholson investigates second chances in education for women
Hair is a four-letter word, but should it be unmentionable?/Wendy Cooper
When men were abolished; a look into the future/Irma Kurtz and Peter le Vasseur
As homosexuals see us/Pat Barr
Book page/Joanna Kilmartin
Come softly to my wake/poems by Christy Brown
Astra Nova/Patric Walker
Up Front/edited by David Jenkins
It's a sporting life/Caroline Baker
The right angle on a fashion theorem/Pip Newbery
How? Readers' problems solved/Mavis Nicholson
Where to campaign/Maureen Walker
Cover photograph/Hans Feurer

Staff

Editor/Gillian Cooke. Deputy editor, art director/David Hillman. Assistant editor, features/David Jenkins. Production editor/Sally Lewis. Assistant to the editor/Bel Mooney. Sub editor/Jeffrey Mills. Art assistants/Carol Rainbird, Richard McMillan. Features/Carolyn Faulder, Stella Bingham, Peter Martin. Fashion editor/Caroline Baker. Assistant/Pip Newbery. Beauty editor/Penny Vincenzi. Home editor/Janet Fitch. Assistant/Maureen Walker. Fiction editor/Margaret Pringle. Contributing editors/Irma Kurtz, Pat Barr, Ann Leslie, Sally Vincent, Ken Martin (New York)

NOVEMBER 1971

Contents

Around the world one way with John Sandilands
Profile of Brixton, a British Ghetto/Peter Martin
Ruth Inglis looks into IQ tests and their validity
Monogamy, Sally Vincent probes the one-for-one system
Evangelism and faith healing/Ruth Brandon
Donald Sutherland, actor profile/Peter Martin
Book page/Joanna Kilmartin
Astra Nova/Patric Walker
Up Front/edited by David Jenkins
Feedback/edited by Bel Mooney
Nova short story: Girl, 20/Kingsley Amis
A view of my own/Pat Barr
By Caroline Baker:
Wrap-up fashion, the blanket story
Quick stepping through the sequins and taffeta
Sweaters – a motif for buying
A souped-up variety/Caroline Conran

Where to find a job/Maureen Walker
Staff
Editor/Gillian Cooke. Deputy editor, art Director/David Hillman. Assistant editor, features/David Jenkins. Production editor/Sally Lewis. Assistant to the editor/Bel Mooney. Sub editor/Jeffrey Mills. Art assistants/Carol Rainbird, Richard McMillan. Features/Carolyn Faulder, Stella Bingham, Peter Martin. Fashion editor/Caroline Baker. Assistant/Pip Newbery. Beauty editor/Penny Vincenzi. Home editor/Janet Fitch. Assistant/Maureen Walker. Fiction editor/Margaret Pringle. Contributing editors/Irma Kurtz, Pat Barr, Ann Leslie, Sally Vincent, Ken Martin (New York)

DECEMBER 1971
Contents
Arthur Eperon suivezs the new piste bashers
Clown Smokey can't be a Punch and Judy man without a swazzle/Stella Bingham
It's not a sin to be fat – just bloody unfair/Ann Leslie
Susan Griffin challenges the man-made myths about rape
They're the all-time losers, the New Jersey Reds/Virginia Ironside
Astra Nova/Patric Walker
Up Front/edited by David Jenkins
Feedback/edited by Bel Mooney
Why haven't you written?/Short story by Nadine Gordimer
A view of my own/Catherine Storr
By Caroline Baker:
Fur – the oldest central-heating system in the world
Whites for single sleepers
Choosing toys – kids versus parents?/Janet Fitch asks both
Massage – a second good reason why skin meets skin/Penny Vincenzi
Where....the cracker bang/Maureen Walker
Too many puds spoil the cook/Caroline Conran
Cover/Duffy
Staff
Editor/Gillian Cooke. Deputy editor, art director/David Hillman. Assistant editor, features/David Jenkins. Production editor/Sally Lewis. Assistant to the editor/Bel Mooney. Sub editor/Jeffrey Mills. Art assistants/Carol Rainbird, Richard McMillan. Features/Carolyn Faulder, Stella Bingham, Peter Martin. Fashion editor/Caroline Baker. Assistant/Pip Newbery. Beauty editor/Penny Vincenzi. Home editor/Janet Fitch. Assistant/Maureen Walker. Fiction editor/Margaret Pringle. Contributing editors/Irma Kurtz, Pat Barr, Ann Leslie, Sally Vincent, Ken Martin (New York)

JANUARY 1972
Contents
The panty party – a frolic in suburbia/Carolyn Faulder
Dr Rhodes Boyson Nova profile/Bel Mooney
The facts about AID babies/Jane Ennis
Lord Longford's committee revealed: Gyles Brandreth's private diary
Give me an Old Master any time...Tullah Hanley talks to Peter Martin
Your mind and the matter of illness/Paul Pickering
Barnaby Buildings – no pets, no joy – Ian Cotton looks at flats for the 'homeless'
John Sandilands goes West by Greyhound
Gstaad and I – and a few others/John Kenneth Galbraith
Nova guide: 50 beaches combed/Carol Wright
Astra Nova/Patric Walker
Upfront/edited by David Jenkins
Feedback/edited by Bel Mooney
Albert's War, short story/Anne Merrill
Communicating – a view of my own/Kenneth Allsop
By Caroline Baker:
Casting black looks at fashion
Having your sweater cheesecake – and wearing it
Women's offices updated –Janet Fitch gets 4 designers' plans
Where to send the kids on holiday/Maureen Walker
Cover/Steve Myers
Staff
Editor/Gillian Cooke. Deputy editor, art director/David Hillman. Assistant editor, features/David Jenkins. Production editor/Sally Lewis. Assistant to the editor/Bel Mooney. Sub editor/Jeffrey Mills. Art assistants/Carol Rainbird, Richard McMillan. Features/Carolyn Faulder, Stella Bingham, Peter Martin. Fashion editor/Caroline Baker. Assistant/Pip Newbery. Beauty editor/Penny Vincenzi. Home editor/Janet Fitch. Assistant/Maureen Walker. Fiction editor/Margaret Pringle. Contributing editors/Irma Kurtz, Pat Barr, Ann Leslie, Sally Vincent, Ken Martin (New York)

FEBRUARY 1972
Contents
Masculinity – the inevitable failure to meet its demands: the Men's Liberation Manifesto/David Jenkins
Me sex object, you Jane/Peter Martin
America's presidential election '72 who will stand for Mr Minority?/Ken Martin reports from New York
Ruth Inglis looks in on TV for the under-fives
Impotence – do women even try to understand?/asks Catherine Storr
The joys of younger men – by five older women/interviews by Ann Leslie
Astra Nova/Patric Walker
Upfront/edited by David Jenkins
Books/Joanna Kilmartin
Daddy's girl, short story/Mark Steadman
Chronicle of a cancer case – a view of my own/Kenneth Allsop
By Caroline Baker:
More flesh for exploitation – underwear exploiting whom?
What the designers would have us wear
Take 7 cosmetics and 3 girls and mix/Beauty by Penny Vincenzi
Where to find an aqualung, a parachute, an air balloon, a rifle range.../Maureen Walker
Cover/Hans Feurer
Staff
Editor/Gillian Cooke. Deputy editor, art director/David Hillman. Assistant editor, features/David Jenkins. Production editor/Sally Lewis. Assistant to the editor/Bel Mooney. Sub editor/Jenie Wright. Art assistants/Carol Rainbird, Richard McMillan. Features/Carolyn Faulder, Stella Bingham, Peter Martin. Fashion editor/Caroline Baker. Assistant/Pip Newbery. Beauty editor/Penny Vincenzi. Home editor/Janet Fitch. Assistant/Maureen Walker. Fiction editor/Margaret Pringle. Contributing editors/Irma Kurtz, Pat Barr, Ann Leslie, Sally Vincent, Ken Martin (New York)

MARCH 1972
Contents
Law goes into orbit; space lawyer Cyril Horsford talks to Jane Ennis
'Twas on the good ship Pushkin/ John Sandilands
The rights of children/Carolyn Faulder
Women are not born – transexuals interviewed/Ian Cotton
So who is saying you are good in bed?/asks Peter Martin
Second wives discuss first wives with Pauline Peters
My mother. An evocation/Penelope Mortimer
All you'll ever need to know about motoring. Special Nova supplement/Judith Jackson and Arthur Eperon
Belfast, city of violence with more victims than villains/Patricia Craig
Panorama versus the Church; which medium has the message?/Ian Cotton
Astra Nova/Patric Walker
Up Front/edited by David Jenkins
Feedback/edited by Bel Mooney
The Chicken Mushroom Pie, short story/Shirley Eskapa
Grim fairy tales – a view of my own/Kenneth Allsop
By Caroline Baker:
Living high on nothing but the best
For two pins...
The wall game/Janet Fitch
Strip off to slim down/exercises by Penny Vincenzi
Staff
Editor/Gillian Cooke. Deputy editor, art director/David Hillman. Assistant editor, features/David Jenkins. Production editor/Sally Lewis. Assistant to the editor/Bel Mooney. Sub editor/Jenie Wright. Art assistants/Carol Rainbird, Richard McMillan. Features/Carolyn Faulder, Stella Bingham, Peter Martin. Fashion editor/Caroline Baker. Assistant/Pip Newbery. Beauty editor/Penny Vincenzi. Home editor/Janet Fitch. Assistant/Maureen Walker. Fiction editor/Margaret Pringle. Contributing editors/Irma Kurtz, Pat Barr, Ann Leslie, Sally Vincent, John Heilpern, Ken Martin (New York)

APRIL 1972
Contents
Money - a woman's guide to LSD/Margaret Allen
Choosing the sex of your baby/Jane Ennis
Marriages, for better or for worse?/asks Harriet Barker
Japan – the schizophrenic superstate/Irma Kurtz
The Halle Orchestra – group penance and a cultural shuttle service/Philip Oakes
Astra Nova/Patric Walker
Up Front/edited by David Jenkins
The Robe, short story/Pierre Delattre
Feedback/edited by Bel Mooney
Rabbit Redux/John Updike, an extract, introduced by Auberon Waugh
For 'test drilling' read 'rape' – a view of my own/Kenneth Allsop
By Caroline Baker:
Japanese designers looking to the West
Western designers adapting from the East
Your tummy – beauty starts here/Penny Vincenzi
Where to take a bath/Maureen Walker
Cover/Harri Peccinotti
Staff
Editor/Gillian Cooke. Deputy editor, art director/David Hillman. Assistant editor, features/David Jenkins. Production editor/Sally Lewis. Assistant to the editor/Bel Mooney. Sub editor/Jenie Wright. Art assistants/Carol Rainbird, Richard McMillan. Features/Carolyn Faulder, Stella Bingham, Peter Martin. Fashion editor/Caroline Baker. Assistant/Pip Newbery. Beauty editor/Penny Vincenzi. Home editor/Janet Fitch. Assistant/Maureen Walker. Fiction editor/Margaret Pringle. Contributing Editors/Irma Kurtz, Pat Barr, Ann Leslie, Sally Vincent, John Heilpern, Ken Martin (New York), Jiro Ishikawa (Japan)

MAY 1972
Contents
Genetics: how long can the race be human?/asks Carolyn Faulder
The animals came in tube by tube/Stella Bingham
Gentlefolk-by-the-sea/report by Elaine Grand
You are your memory/says Penelope Mortimer
Cleopatras of the suburbs/Lee Langley records some housewives' fantasies
The tasteful times of Margaret Thatcher/Bel Mooney
Chris Mullin on a slow train to China
Roy Fuller – poet ordinary interviewed by Philip Norman
We're going to the zoo, zoo.../Anthony Carson
Astra Nova/Patrick Walker
Upfront/edited by David Jenkins
Feedback/edited by Bel Mooney
Spring, short story/Rachel Billington
Book freaks – a view of my own/Kenneth Allsop
By Caroline Baker:
A Waitress in Paris: or the ballad of the rag cafe
An acquired bad taste
The sun-light motif/Janet Fitch
Beauty is only a bob/Penny Vincenzi
The fishmonger's fancy/Cookery by Caroline Conran
Where to get take-away food or a cook-at-home cook/Maureen Walker
Cover/Tony Evans
Staff
Editor/Gillian Cooke. Deputy editor, art director/David Hillman. Assistant editor, features/David Jenkins. Production editor/Sally Lewis. Assistant to the editor/Bel Mooney. Sub editor/Jenie Wright. Art assistants/Carol Rainbird, Richard McMillan. Features/Carolyn Faulder, Stella Bingham, Peter Martin. Fashion editor/Caroline Baker. Assistant/Pip Newbery. Beauty editor/Penny Vincenzi. Home editor/Janet Fitch. Assistant/Maureen Walker. Fiction editor/Margaret Pringle. Contributing editors/Irma Kurtz, Pat Barr, Ann Leslie, Sally Vincent, John Heilpern, Ken Martin (New York)

JUNE 1972
Contents
David Jenkins on tour with Frank Zappa
The rules and risks of charter flying/John Carter
When a man is unemployed, what happens to a marriage?/Harriet Baker asks three wives
The Festival of Light – a roar from the silent Majority/Ian Cotton
Spike Milligan, a sort of profile/Betka Zamoyska
Eastfields: one shop, one church, one pub – village life/Pat Barr
Have you ever listened to a child?/asks Leila Berg
Astra Nova/Patric Walker
Up Front/edited by David Jenkins
'Return Match' short story/Gillian Tindall
Feedback/edited by Bel Mooney
A matter of coincidence? a view of my own/Kenneth Allsop
By Caroline Baker:
Act like a lady – if you can't look like one
Colour is a case of common sense/Homes by Janet Fitch
Brown is.../Beauty by Penny Vincenzi
Cold comfort soups/Caroline Conran
Where to complain and get results/Maureen Walker
Staff
Editor/Gillian Cooke. Deputy editor, art director/David Hillman. Assistant editor, features/David Jenkins. Production editor/Sally Lewis. Assistant to the editor/Bel Mooney. Sub editor/Jenie Wright. Art assistants/Carol Rainbird, Richard McMillan. Features/Carolyn Faulder, Stella Bingham, Peter Martin. Fashion editor/Caroline Baker. Assistant/Pip Newbery. Beauty editor/Penny Vincenzi. Home editor/Janet Fitch. Assistant/Maureen Walker. Fiction editor/Margaret Pringle. Contributing Editors/Irma Kurtz, Pat Barr, Ann Leslie, Sally Vincent, John Heilpern, Ken Martin (New York)

JULY 1972
Contents
The awful and awesome lady from Congress – Bella Abzurg/Ken Martin
Few and far away, eccentric hotels/Arthur Eperon
Families behind the barricades: Belfast report from David Jenkins
Hoofing on, Gene Kelly talks to John Sandilancs
Heroic struggles in mouseland/Paul Pickering
The dwindling band of buskers/Colin Duff
Putting your daughter in the stage school/Elaine Grand
Fifty, the unspeakable age/interviews by Sally Vincent
Chronicles from a deserted island/David Jenkins
Astra Nova/Patric Walker
Up Front/edited by David Jenkins
Feedback/edited by Bel Mooney
'Fear', short story/Sallie Bingham
A view of my child/Irma Kurtz
By Caroline Baker:
Overdressed for the summer simmer
A spot of beauty
Swimwear – the full story
The designing Japanese/Janet Fitch
Currying flavour/Caroline Conran
What to do with the children during the summer holidays/Maureen Walker
Staff
Editor/Gillian Cooke. Deputy editor, art director/David Hillman. Assistant editor, features/David Jenkins. Production editor/Sally Lewis. Assistant to the editor/Bel Mooney. Sub editor/Jenie Wright. Art assistants/Carol Rainbird, Richard McMillan. Features/Carolyn Faulder, Stella Bingham, Peter Martin. Fashion and beauty editor/Caroline Baker. Assistant/Pip Newbery. Home editor/Janet Fitch. Assistant/Maureen Walker. Fiction editor/Margaret Pringle. Contributing editors/Irma Kurtz, Pat Barr, Ann Leslie, Sally Vincent, John Heilpern, Ken Martin (New York)

AUGUST 1972
Contents
A normally reliable sauce: report from Dieppe/Arthur Eperon
Kaye Webb of Puffin Books. The landlady of dream island/interviewed by Lesley Garner
The politics of progress/Jackie Gillott
Are we receiving you? Researching the physchic researchers/Paul Pickering
In the Ditch. A brilliant account of tenement living by Buchi Emecheta, an Ibo mother of five, who left a home with four servants in Nigeria and ended up in Pussy Cat Mansions, London
People who dislike their children – and admit it/interviewed by Barbara Anne Taylor
Some of the fun. A gentle tribute to the funfair season/Ian Stokes
The menopause that comes to men/Donald Lehmkuhl
One February morning this year, Clive Adcock came out of Albany Prison having served two years for, amongst other things, breaking into a building. Peter Martin describes his background and first fortnight of freedom. Clive Adcock took the photographs
Astra Nova/Patric Walker

Up Front/edited by David Jenkins
Feedback on consumer groups/Bel Mooney
Nova fiction: Rachel's Island/Sallie Bingham
View of my own. The Olympic farce/
Brian Glanville
By Caroline Baker:
Clothes for your own Olympic Games. A 10-page special event
Put the country back into your home. Rustic delights/Janet Fitch
Pates and pies. A bone-it-yourself section/Caroline Conran
How to lock up. Burglar-baffling/Maureen Walker
Cover photograph/Peter Knapp
Staff
Editor/Gillian Cooke. Deputy editor, art director/David Hillman. Assistant editor, features/David Jenkins. Production editor/Sally Lewis. Assistant to the editor/Bel Mooney. Sub editor/Jenie Wright. Art assistants/Carol Rainbird, Richard McMillan. Features/Carolyn Faulder, Stella Bingham, Peter Martin. Fashion and beauty editor/Caroline Baker. Assistant/Pip Newbery. Home editor/Janet Fitch. Assistant/Maureen Walker. Fiction editor/Margaret Pringle. Contributing editors/Irma Kurtz, Pat Barr, Ann Leslie, Sally Vincent, John Heilpern, Ken Martin (New York)

SEPTEMBER 1972
Contents
In these sceptical days Jewish tradition not only survives but prospers/Irma Kurtz visits an orthodox family
Jews on Judaism/interviewed by Tony Aspler
Chaim Bermant on the Jewish mafia
Can you live with the other woman? Mothers-in law/Carolyn Faulder
The most important opportunity facing educationists is not how to fill the extra year but what to do with the whole five-year curriculum/David Jenkins explores some possible changes
Nova's male pin-up portfolio/photographed by Christa Peters
Foetal medicine: the unborn baby as patient/Ruth Inglis
Helen Lawrenson has been smoking pot on and off for 40 years and thinks it should be legalised
Astra Nova/Patric Walker
Upfront/edited by Peter Martin
Nova fiction: A Talent/Paul Winstanley
Feedback follows up/edited by Bel Mooney
View of my own. Money when the marriage ends/Eva Figes
By Caroline Baker:
Classically clothed
All about hair
Cockles and mussels and shrimps and....Shellfish cooking/Caroline Conran
How to get wired up. Basic electricity/
Maureen Walker
Cover photograph/Tony Evans
Staff
Editor/Gillian Cooke. Deputy editor, art director/David Hillman. Assistant editor, features/David Jenkins. Production editor/Sally Lewis. Sub editor/Jenie Wright. Art assistants/Carol Rainbird, Richard McMillan. Features/Carolyn Faulder, Stella Bingham, Peter Martin. Fashion and beauty editor/Caroline Baker. Assistant/Pip Newbery. Home editor/Janet Fitch. Assistant/Maureen Walker. Fiction editor/Margaret Pringle. Contributing editors/Irma Kurtz,Pat Barr, Ann Leslie, Sally Vincent, John Heilpern, Ken Martin (New York)

OCTOBER 1972
Contents
Jacky Gillott on the politics of ecology
The world-famous, the unique, the incomparable mineral waters of Vittell John Sandilands takes the cure
32 children in every 1000 will leave school unable even to fill in a time-sheet/Paul Pickering reports on the guilt and the shame of illiteracy – and some solutions
Do we give pregnant women the help they deserve?/Carolyn Faulder investigates
Lord Goodman: a man for all seasons/
John Heilpern
The desperately serious world of children's books/Ruth Inglis interviews some unsentimental authors
'Removal men are very special people'. Two of them talk to Virginia Ironside about their work and the people they come across
Astra Nova/Patric Walker
Upfront/edited by Peter Martin
Nova fiction: The Driving Lesson/David Pownall
Feedback on women's groups/Bel Mooney
View of my own. Hollywood myths exploded/Helen Lawrenson
By Caroline Baker:
The antique look for young ladies
New bite at finger-nails
Sweater girls
Pasta cookery/Caroline Conran
How to plumb/Maureen Walker
Cover photograph/Roger Stowell
Staff
Editor/Gillian Cooke. Deputy editor, art director/David Hillman. Assistant editor, features/David Jenkins. Production editor/Sally Lewis. Sub editor/Jenie Wright. Art assistants/Carol Rainbird, Richard McMillan. Features/Carolyn Faulder, Stella Bingham, Peter Martin. Fashion and beauty editor/Caroline Baker. Assistant/Pip Newbery. Home editor/Janet Fitch. Assistant/Maureen Walker. Fiction editor/Margaret Pringle. Contributing editors/Irma Kurtz, Pat Barr, Ann Leslie, Sally Vincent, John Heilpern, Ken Martin (New York)

NOVEMBER 1972
Contents
Some are more equal than others/Jacky Gillott on new union attitudes
Turn on to Jesus. The new interest in Christ and the reaction of the Established Church/investigated by John Heilpern
Husbands who failed to achieve their ambitions/Barbara Anne Taylor interviews three let-down wives
Soppy girls, tomboys, rotters and brave little men. Children in books/Patricia Craig
Parents coping with their children's sexuality/Pauline Peters
Arletty, Comedienne/interviewed by Carolyn Faulder
Austria's Olympic ski team trained in Rumania. Rare ski resorts explored/John Carter
Up Front/edited by Stella Bingham
Nova fiction: Pussy Owl, Superbeast/
Brigid Brophy
Astra Nova/Patric Walker
View of my own. Bi-sexual chic/Helen Lawrenson
By Caroline Baker:
High-soled shoes
All dressed and made up/Biba and Quant
Shelving your problems. Storage/Janet Fitch
Take your pulses/Cookery by Caroline Conran
Staff
Editor/Gillian Cooke. Deputy editor, art director/David Hillman. Assistant editor, features/David Jenkins. Production editor/Sally Lewis. Sub editor/David Paton. Art assistants/Carol Rainbird, Angela Gorgas. Features/Carolyn Faulder, Stella Bingham, Peter Martin. Fashion and beauty editor/Caroline Baker. Assistant/Pip Newbery. Home editor/Janet Fitch. Assistant/Maureen Walker. Fiction editor/Margaret Pringle. Contributing editors/Irma Kurtz, Pat Barr, Ann Leslie, Sally Vincent, John Heilpern, Ken Martin (New York)

DECEMBER 1972
Contents
The politics of the Common Market and the public/Jacky Gillott
Skivvying the High Street hairdressers/Pauline Peters on how to earn £4 a week
The civilised world of radio/Margaret Pringle interviews some familiar names from the original box
Foster homes: to be good they must be very, very good/John Heilpern
An easy death is everyone's ultimate ambition/Peter Martin discovers the fine line between compassion and euthanasia
Tretchikoff, the people's painter/interviewed by Peter Martin
Togetherness can destroy a marriage/
Charlotte Hopson
The church furnishers that has kept up with the times: Vanpoulles/Hilary Macaskill
Cures for the morning after/Catherine Olsen
Astra Nova/Patric Walker
Up Front/editied by David Jenkins
Nova fiction: The Alabaster Necklace/Judy Cooke
View of my own. Learning sexual roles from Santa/Sally Vincent
By Caroline Baker:
Fashion-plate party clothes
Jewellery for real men
Home thoughts for Christmas/Janet Fitch
Inner central heating: pudding cookery/
Caroline Conran
Nova wine supplement/Cyril Ray
Cover photograph/Roger Stowell
Staff
Editor/Gillian Cooke. Deputy editor, art director/David Hillman. Assistant editor, features/David Jenkins. Production editor/Sally Lewis. Sub editor/David Paton. Art assistants/Carol Rainbird, Angela Gorgas. Features/Carolyn Faulder, Stella Bingham, Peter Martin. Fashion and beauty editor/Caroline Baker. Assistant/Pip Newbery. Home editor/Janet Fitch. Assistant/Maureen Walker. Fiction editor/Margaret Pringle. Contributing editors/Irma Kurtz, Pat Barr, Ann Leslie, Sally Vincent, John Heilpern, Ken Martin (New York)

JANUARY 1973
Contents
How impartial is TV news reporting? Political perspectives/Jacky Gillott
The shocking affair of Gabrielle Russier, the French teacher who was hounded to death because of a liaison with her pupil. Nemone Lethbridge discusses the case
Some gleeful moments from the film set of Mistress Pamela/Alex Hamilton
100,000 women are alcoholics/Geoffrey Sheridan and Rachael Field explore their lives
The lonely pioneers of the Open University/
Bel Mooney
One day 20 people came to pay their last respects to an alsatian/Paul Pickering vists a cemetery for pets
Anthony Maurice Miller describes what it's like to be crippled in a society in which normality is all
Children in the air: a survey of the airlines and their guests compiled by Maggy Meade-King and Maureen Walker
Astra Nova/Patric Walker
Up Front/edited by Stella Bingham
View of my own. Providing for the family/
Eva Figes
By Caroline Baker:
Dressing for Arabian days
Sleeping light – duvets/Janet Fitch
The no-diet diet: cookery/Caroline Conran
Cover photograph/Harri Peccinotti
Staff
Editor/Gillian Cooke. Deputy editor, art director/David Hillman. Assistant editor, features/David Jenkins. Production editor/Sally Lewis. Sub editors/David Paton, Anne Boston. Art assistants/Carol Rainbird, Angela Gorgas. Features/Carolyn Faulder, Stella Bingham, Peter Martin, Maggy Meade-King. Fashion and beauty editor/Caroline Baker. Assistant/Pip Newbery. Home editor/Janet Fitch. Assistant/Maureen Walker. Fiction Editor/Margaret Pringle. Contributing editors/Irma Kurtz, Pat Barr, Ann Leslie, Sally Vincent, John Heilpern, Ken Martin (New York)

FEBRUARY 1973
Contents
It would be comforting to think that guerillas, like mini-skirts, are a fad of the times we shall all become bored with/Jacky Gillott
Dream boats/Arthur Eperon looks at ways and means of chartering yachts and cruisers
Ludwig Hahn was allegedly the Commander of Police and of the S.D. in Warsaw in occupied Poland. He is currently on trial in Hamburg/A personal report from Irma Kurtz
Fatherhood as a form of love/Interviews by John Heilpern
The Open Plan revolution in schools/Ruth Inglis
30,000 men have been unemployed for over three years. Life on the long-term dole/
Gerda Cohen
Ken Martin interviews the creator of Snoopy, Lucy, Linus (and blanket), Schroeder, Pigpen and the domitable Charlie Brown
Seasonable thoughts from little Lithuania in Britain/Vicky Weatherby
Bitching at nursery level/Glenda Greene
Astra Nova/Patric Walker
Up Front/edited by David Jenkins
Feedback, consumer action/Maggy Meade-King and Maureen Walker
Nova fiction: An Excellent Thing in a Woman/
A L Barker
View of my own. The deception of Romance/
Bel Mooney
By Caroline Baker:
A classically educated person...
...but woolly minded
Getting your face into shape
Door ways: how to make a perfect entrance/Janet Fitch
Putting a zest into dried fruit/Caroline Conran
Cover photograph/Christa Peters
Staff
Editor/Gillian Cooke. Deputy editor, art director/David Hillman. Assistant editor, features/David Jenkins. Production editor/Sally Lewis. Sub editors/David Paton, Anne Boston. Art assistants/Carol Rainbird, Angela Gorgas. Features/Carolyn Faulder, Stella Bingham, Peter Martin, Maggy Meade-King. Fashion and beauty editor/Caroline Baker. Assistant/Pip Newbery. Home editor/Janet Fitch. Assistant/Maureen Walker. Fiction editor/Margaret Pringle. Contributing editors/Irma Kurtz, Pat Barr, Ann Leslie, Sally Vincent, John Heilpern, Ken Martin (New York)

MARCH 1973
Contents
In search of something fine/David Jenkins accompanies a £30,000 palate round the vineyards of France
Action and passion on the back-lot/Anthony Haden-Guest reports on an epic movie-making venture
Tony Curtis, Superstar, interviewed/
Helen Lawrenson
Is the only child a special case?/asks Ruth Inglis
The odd spire out. Ruskin College/Stella Bingham
Living through breast cancer. The most important 19 pages ever published on this subject/Caroline Nicholson reports on cancer as it affects women today – the screening controversy, treatment and aftercare. Photographs by Henri Elwing
The nicest sort of Roundheads and Cavaliers meet Virginia Ironside
The mellowing of Women's Wear Daily/Cima Star visits the king of the trade journals and its offspring – W
Gloria Emerson reports on her homecoming from Vietnam
Astra Nova/Patric Walker
Upfront/edited by Stella Bingham
Nova fiction: The Deacon/John Updike
View of my own. Coping with nationalised gas/
Eva Figes
By Caroline Baker:
Nostalgia almost up-to-date
Drawing the line again
A touch of style
Something to walk about. Painted floors/
Janet Fitch
Staff
Editor/Gillian Cooke. Deputy editor, art director/David Hillman. Assistant editor, features/David Jenkins. Production editor/Sally Lewis. Sub editors/David Paton, Anne Boston. Art assistants/Carol Rainbird, Angela Gorgas. Features/Carolyn Faulder, Stella Bingham, Peter Martin, Maggy Meade-King, Betka Zamoyska. Fashion and beauty editor/Caroline Baker. Assistant/Pip Newbery. Home editor/Janet Fitch. Assistant/Maureen Walker. Fiction editor/Margaret Pringle. Contributing editors/Irma Kurtz, Pat Barr, Ann Leslie, Sally Vincent, John Heilpern, Ken Martin (New York)

APRIL 1973
Contents
Housing and the everlasting treadmill of rising prices/Anthony Harris
Jottings from haunts of coot and hern/
Margaret Pringle talks to some country writers
Weekend cottages: the pros and cons/
Betty Jerman
Is your child getting the eduction he deserves? How to find out/Brian Jackson
At Tonfanau goodwill is not enough/James Hamilton-Paterson reports from a Ugandan-Asian resettlement camp
Holly Woodlawn: tacky life behind the tinsel/
Ken Martin
Astra Nova/Patric Walker
Up Front/edited by Stella Bingham
Nova fiction: Halloran's Child/Susan Hill
Feedback: consumer action/Maggy Meade-King and Maureen Walker
View of my own. The working woman in fiction/
Penelope Mortimer
By Caroline Baker:
Chic, sleek and sophisticated
Baubles and beads, at market prices
Sitting pretty/Janet Fitch
Pride that comes without a fall. Soufflés/
Prue Leith

Cover photograph/Tony Evans
Staff
Editor/Gillian Cooke. Deputy editor, art director/David Hillman. Assistant editor, features/David Jenkins. Production editor/Sally Lewis. Sub editors/David Paton, Anne Boston. Art assistants/Carol Rainbird, Angela Gorgas. Features/Carolyn Faulder, Stella Bingham, Peter Martin, Maggy Meade-King, Betka Zamoyska. Fashion and beauty editor/Caroline Baker. Assistant/Pip Newbery. Home editor/Janet Fitch. Fiction editor/Margaret Pringle. Contributing editors/Irma Kurtz, Pat Barr, Ann Leslie, Sally Vincent, John Heilpern, Ken Martin (New York)

MAY 1973
Contents
The accent is on fun/Stella Bingham spends an evening with Brown Owl, Tawny Owl and little gnomes and pixies
Political director of popular films with a message: Costa-Gavras/Daniel Yergin
There are always some impediments to the marriage of true minds. Could marriage contracts be the solution?/Carolyn Faulder
The £10,000,000, four-day week, City king from the suburbs. A profile of Jim Slater/Russell Miller
Our Street/Pat Barr revisits the scenes and companions of her childhood
Do you know your sexual appetite? An extract from Free and Female – the Sex life of the Contemporary Woman/Barbara Seaman
Children in hospital/Ruth Inglis
The freedom to grieve is more important than 'putting a good face on it'/Clare Rayner
Astra Nova/Patric Walker
Up Front/edited by Stella Bingham
Nova fiction: Your lover just called/John Updike
Feedback: consumer action/edited by Maggy Meade-King and Betka Zamoyska
View of my own. The hypocrisy of sex eduction/Penelope Mortimer
Loosely fashionable/Caroline Baker
In search of the slim line/Pat Baikie
Your designer and what to do with him/
Janet Fitch
Raw beginnings. Cookery/Prue Leith
Cover photograph/Graham Hughes
Staff
Editor/Gillian Cooke. Deputy editor, art director/David Hillman. Assistant editor, features/David Jenkins. Production editor/Sally Lewis. Sub editors/David Paton, Anne Boston. Art assistants/Carol Rainbird, Angela Gorgas. Features/Carolyn Faulder, Stella Bingham, Peter Martin, Maggy Meade-King, Betka Zamoyska. Fashion and beauty editor/Caroline Baker. Assistant/Pip Newbery. Home editor/Janet Fitch. Fiction editor/Margaret Pringle. Contributing editors/Irma Kurtz, Pat Barr, Ann Leslie, Sally Vincent, John Heilpern, Ken Martin (New York)

JUNE 1973
Contents
Softening up for the show/Eric Clark talks to some warm-up men
Priests talk to Ken Martin, George Armstrong and Peter Watson about their radical, even revolutionary, interpretation of Christianity
Irma Kurtz discusses ways of experiencing birth
Judy Froshaug reports on the latest developments in mechanical childbirth
Jane Ennis explains how genetic counselling can reduce the incidence of inherited defects
Lyn Owen looks at the dangers of playing down post-natal depression
Bel Mooney examines the psychological causes and legal results of baby-snatching
'I was never, never, in my life shy'. A tribute, in quotations, to Sir Noel Coward/compiled by Betka Zamoyska
About 1,000,000 children are so bored by school that they'll do anything to avoid it/Jane Ennis
Ma Elsie, materfamilias extraordinary/
Elaine Grand
Executives get cars: secretaries get paper clips/Eric Clark
Nova supplement on English antique furniture/
Peter Darty
Susan Hill, prize-winning novelist/interviewed by Margaret Pringle
Astra Nova/Patric Walker
Upfront/edited by Stella Bingham
Nova fiction: The View/Alan Sillitoe
Feedback: consumer information/Maggy Meade-King and Betka Zamoyske
View of my own. Images of self/
Penelope Mortimer
By Caroline Baker:
Bathing costumes all of a piece
Drift towards the Twenties
Colour it pastel/Janet Fitch
Holiday health/Carol Wright
Cover photograph/Tony Evans
Staff
Editor/Gillian Cooke. Deputy editor, art director/David Hillman. Assistant editor, features/David Jenkins. Production editor/Sally Lewis. Sub editors/David Paton, Anne Boston. Art assistants/Carol Rainbird, Keith Jones. Features/Carolyn Faulder, Stella Bingham, Peter Martin, Maggy Meade-King, Betka Zamoyska. Fashion and beauty editor/Caroline Baker. Assistant/Pip Newbery. Home editor/Janet Fitch. Fiction editor/Margaret Pringle. Contributing editors/Irma Kurtz, Pat Barr, Ann Leslie, Sally Vincent, John Heilpern, Ken Martin (New York)

JULY 1973
Contents
Sight for sore eyes/Elizabeth Cowley
Lilit Gampel, a self-composed musical prodigy/Joyce Maynard, Photograph by Rod Moyer
What did you do in the war, Mummy?/Pat Barr and Carolyn Faulder, illustrations by Mike Terry, Photographs by Dennis Finn
Middling poor/Elaine Grand, Illustration by Mike McInnerney.
Solitary bliss/Hilary Macaskill
Shops with a foreign flavour/Photographs by Donald Silverstein
The charmless charm of Jacques Tati/Richard Boston, Illustration by David Annersley
Last battle for the beaches/Arthur Eperon, Illustrations by Arthur Robins
Men are comrades, women are rivals/
Mary Stott
Astra Nova/Patric Walker
Up Front/edited by Stella Bingham
Feedback: consumer action/Maggy Meade-King and Betka Zamoyska
Short story: Hitch-hike Ride to Miracleville/
William Wise
View of my own/Penelope Mortimer
If your tan frays at the edges, read on.../Beauty by Pat Baikie, Photograph by Richard Dunkley
A suitable case for packing/Caroline Baker, Photographs by Trevor Sutton
How the west was worn/Fashion by Caroline Baker, Photographs by Harri Peccinotti
All in: knitted swimsuits/Fashion by Caroline Baker, Photographs by Helmut Newton
Headed for style: letterheads/Design by Janet Fitch, Photograph by Tony Evans
More than just a pretty cheesecake/Cookery by Prue Leith, Illustration by Edda Köchl
Cover photograph/Harri Peccinotti
Staff
Editor/Gillian Cooke. Deputy editor, art director/David Hillman. Assistant editor, features/David Jenkins. Production editor/Sally Lewis. Sub editors/David Paton, Anne Boston. Art assistants/Carol Rainbird, Keith Jones. Features/Carolyn Faulder, Stella Bingham, Peter Martin, Maggy Meade-King, Betka Zamoyska. Fashion and beauty editor/Caroline Baker. Beauty consultant/Pat Baikie. Beauty assistant/Pip Newbery. Homes editor/Janet Fitch. Fiction editor/Margaret Pringle. Contributing editors/Irma Kurtz, Pat Barr, Ann Leslie, Sally Vincent, John Heilpern, Ken Martin (New York)

AUGUST 1973
Contents
Memories of a literary festival/Judith Woolf
In the search for self-knowledge, how much of yourself are you prepared to see?/Carolyn Faulder, Photograph by Gary Krueger
Extracts from my autobiography/Omar Khayyam Quraishi, aged 11
In moral danger/Cherry Potter, Photographs by Valerie Santagto
Cleanliness is next to impossible/Peter Martin, Illustration by Josse Goffin
Oh, how we danced/Ann Leslie, Photographs by Peter Howe
Blackpool...A seaside portfolio/Colin Duff
What makes a woman go off sex?/Lyn Owen
Bachelors/Sally Vincent, Illustrations by Charles Raymond
Food for thought/Kevin D'Arcy, Illustration by Mike Terry
Astra Nova/Patric Walker
Up Front/edited by Stella Bingham
Feedback: consumer action/edited by Maggy Meade-King and Betka Zamoyska
Fiction: The Gordian Knot/Margaret Drabble
A view of my own/Peter Martin
Nearly nature's way/Beauty by Caroline Baker, Photographs by Christa Peters
Sheer clear of the showers/Fashion by Caroline Baker, Photographs by Helmut Newton
Topping/Fashion by Caroline Baker, Photographs by Harri Peccinotti
A taste of tapas. Spanish snacks/
Rich Meyerowitz
Cover photograph/Harri Peccinotti
Staff
Editor/Gillian Cooke. Deputy editor, art director/David Hillman. Assistant editor, features/David Jenkins. Production editor/Sally Lewis. Sub editors/David Paton, Anne Boston. Art assistants/Carol Rainbird, Keith Jones. Features/Carolyn Faulder, Stella Bingham, Peter Martin, Maggy Meade-King, Betka Zamoyska. Fashion and beauty editor/Caroline Baker. Beauty consultant/Pat Baikie. Beauty assistant/Pip Newbery. Homes editor/Janet Fitch. Fiction editor/Margaret Pringle. Contributing editors/Irma Kurtz, Pat Barr, Ann Leslie, John Heilpern, Ken Martin (New York)

SEPTEMBER 1973
Contents
'Me name up in lights in the West End! And I have to go home and change the nappies'/John Heilpern, Photographs by Patrick Bergen
A hearty display of glorious beasts/Gordon Burn, Photographs by Peter Howe
Have you lied about your age today?/Susan Sontag, Photography by Harri Peccinotti
Who's been left holding the baby?/Margaret Fishley, Illustrations by Peter Wane.
'Now that we're no longer together I feel free to tell you...'/Ruth Inglis and David Conyers, Illustrations by David Pocknell
Stay as sweet as you are....and you're in dead trouble/James Hamilton-Paterson, Illustrations by Harry Wilson
Do handicapped children handicap families?/Eva Figes
Planning for a rosy future/Anna Coote
Mind and body bending trips. A weekend of yoga/Anne Boston
A round-up of residential short courses/Margaret Fish ley, Illustrations by Mike Terry
Astra Nova/Patric Walker
Up Front/edited by Stella Bingham
Fiction: Rough Trade/Melvyn Bragg, Illustration by Jean Lagarrigue
Feedback: consumer action/Maggy Meade-King and Betka Zamoyska
View of my own/Judith Todd
The gold rush/Jewellery by Caroline Baker, Photograph by Harri Peccinotti
Jumpers for joy/Fashion by Caroline Baker, Photographs by Harri Peccinotti
I dwelt in marble halls/Design by Janet Fitch, Photographs by Tony Evans
Hair today..../Beauty by Pip Newbery, Photographs by Ian Stokes
Barbecue Cookery/Prue Leith, Illustration by Alan Cracknell
Staff
Editor/Gillian Cooke. Deputy editor, art director/David Hillman. Assistant editor, features/David Jenkins. Production editor/Sally Lewis. Sub editors/David Paton, Anne Boston. Art assistants/Carol Rainbird, Keith Jones. Features/Carolyn Faulder, Stella Bingham, Peter Martin, Maggy Meade-King, Betka Zamoyska. Fashion and beauty editor/Caroline Baker. Beauty consultant/Pat Baikie. Beauty assistant/Pip Newbery. Homes editor/Janet Fitch. Fiction editor/Margaret Pringle. Contributing editors/Irma Kurtz, Pat Barr, Ann Leslie, Bel Mooney, John Heilpern, Ken Martin (New York)

OCTOBER 1973
Contents
Nice girls do/Gerda Cohen, Photographs by Colin Curwood
Donovan's dog/Angela Carter, Photograph by Donald Silverstein
Have you room in your heart for lust?/
Gillian Freeman
Is the sauce for the gander sauce for the goose?/Germaine Greer
Something's got to give/Ruth Inglis, Illustrations by Graham Percy
'The diddy-man's Raquel Welch ...'/Elaine Grand, Photographs by Donald Silverstein
The Skomer vole is a unique sub-species, recognisable by the extra projection on its back rear tooth/Mary James, Illustration by Mike Terry.
Back to the grass roots/Richard Mabey and Stella Bingham, Photographs by Tony Evans
Astra Nova/Patric Walker
Up Front/edited by Stella Bingham
Fiction: The private life of Ifor Tombs/Anne Merrill, Illustration by Edda Köchl
Feedback: consumer action/Maggy Meade-King and Betka Zamoyska
View of my own/Alan Coren. Photograph by Geoff Howard
Striking matches/Fashion by Caroline Baker, Photographs by Hans Feurer
Bamboozles/Homes by Janet Fitch, Photographs by Roger Stowell
Beautiful bodywork. Nova's 6-month beauty special/Pat Baikie, Drawings by Celestino Valenti
The skis that please in the high Pyrenees/Travel by Arthur Eperon, Illustration by Arthur Robins
Cover photograph/Donald Silverstein
Staff
Editor/Gillian Cooke. Deputy editor, art director/David Hillman. Assistant editor, features/David Jenkins. Production editor/Sally Lewis. Sub editors/Anne Boston, Gaynor Crawford. Art assistants/Carol Rainbird, Keith Jones. Features/Carolyn Faulder, Stella Bingham, Peter Martin, Maggy Meade-King, Betka Zamoyska. Fashion and beauty editor/Caroline Baker. Beauty consultant/Pat Baikie. Beauty assistant/Pip Newbery. Homes editor/Janet Fitch. Fiction editor/Margaret Pringle. Contributing editors/Irma Kurtz, Pat Barr, Ann Leslie, Bel Mooney, John Heilpern, Ken Martin (New York)

NOVEMBER 1973
Contents
What Mao has done for women/
Emily MacFarquhar
Home thoughts from home/Poems by Alasdair Maclean
Jimmy the song/Anthony Carson, Photograph by Janette Beckman
Patient heal thyself/Dr Clive Wood and Betka Zamoyska, Illustrations by David Pocknell.
House-husbands/Ruth Inglis, Photographs by Aurora Roland
Rabbits, friends, enemies and relations/Carolyn Faulder, Photographs by Tony Evans
Who can make bad sex good?/Carolyn Faulder
A very nice evening indeed/Derek Cooper, Photographs by Peter Howe
Leo Abse; a very public member/John Heilpern, Illustration by Carl Keighley.
Games machines play/Philip Oakes, Illustrations by Peter Brookes
A Miss/Maggy Meade-King.
Inflationary Times/Frances Cairncross and Hamish McRae, Graphics by John McConnell
They're off. A royal occasion/Roger Law
Astra Nova/Patric Walker
Up Front/edited by Stella Bingham
Fiction: Elizabeth Alone/An extract from William Trevor's novel
Feedback: consumer action/edited by Maggy Meade-King and Betka Zamoyska
A View of My Own/Irma Kurtz
A head of the times/Fashion by Caroline Baker, Photographs by Harri Peccinotti
Yokel lady-oo/Tweed fashion by Caroline Baker, Photographs by Saul Leiter
Shady business/Hair colour by Pat Baikie, Photographs by Christa Peters
Buy your leaves/Design by Janet Fitch, Photographs by Roger Stowell
As English as...apple pie/Cookery by Prue Leith, Illustration by Charlie White
Cover photograph/Harri Peccinotti
Staff
Editor/Gillian Cooke. Deputy editor, art director/David Hillman. Assistant editor, features/David Jenkins. Production editor/Sally Lewis. Sub editors/Anne Boston, Gaynor Crawford. Art assistants/Carol Rainbird, Keith Jones. Features/Carolyn Faulder, Stella Bingham, Peter Martin, Maggy Meade-King, Betka Zamoyska. Fashion and beauty editor/Caroline Baker. Beauty consultant/Pat Baikie. Beauty assistant/Pip Newbery. Homes editor/Janet Fitch. Fiction editor/Margaret Pringle. Contributing editors/Irma Kurtz, Pat Barr, Ann Leslie, Bel Mooney, John Heilpern, Ken Martin (New York)

DECEMBER 1973
Contents
Profle of Isaac Hayes/George V. Higgins, American attorney, talks about his block-busting novel
To be...an actor or an extra:
You are what you mustn't eat/Gillian Freeman, Drawings by Harry Wilson.
The world of the weenies/Peter Martin and James Hamilton-Paterson, Photographs by Donald Silverstein
Toys will be toys/Margaret Fishley, Photographs by David Reed
Bores, pedants, slobs/Dr Peter Driver, Illustrations by Roger Coleman
If at first you don't succeed.../Judy Froshaug, Illustrations by Mike McInnerney
Suffer little children's violins/Irma Kurtz
Books at bedtime/Stella Bingham and Nancy Harrison, Photographs by Sally Patch
And please, Father Christmas.../Anna James.
Best book buys for Christmas
Astra Nova/Patric Walker
Up Front/edited by Stella Bingham
Fiction: The stomach/John Cheever
Fiction: Loss and chaos/Olivia Davis, Illustration by Grete Lis
Feedback: consumer action/edited by Maggy Meade-King and Betka Zamoyska
View of my own/Alan Coren
Measure for measure/Derek Cooper
A touch of ballet class/Fashion by Caroline Baker, Photographs by Deborah Turbeville
Keep an eye on you/Beauty by Caroline Baker, Photographs by Harri Peccinotti
Old time favourites/Fashion by Caroline Baker, Photographs by Sarah Moon
Home is where the heat is/Fireplaces by Janet Fitch, Photographs by Rob Matheson
Get you, sweeties/Cookery by Prue Leith, Model by Alan Crackrell, Photograph by Roger Stowell
Cover photograph/Donald Silverstein
Staff
Editor/Gillian Cooke. Deputy editor, art director/David Hillman. Assistant editor, features/David Jenkins. Production editor/Sally Lewis. Sub editors/Anne Boston, Gaynor Crawford. Art assistants/Carol Rainbird, Keith Jones. Features/Carolyn Faulder, Stella Bingham, Maggy Meade-King, Betka Zamoyska. Fashion and beauty editor/Caroline Baker. Beauty consultant/Pat Baikie. Beauty assistant/Pip Newbery. Homes editor/Janet Fitch. Fiction editor/Margaret Pringle. Contributing editors/Irma Kurtz, Pat Barr, Ann Leslie, Bel Mooney, John Heilpern, Ken Martin (New York)

JANUARY 1974
Contents
Fight for life/Carolyn Faulder
Unaccustomed as I am.../Hilary Macaskill
Settlers in the Orkneys/One woman's experience of natural childbirth/Slow bike round Denmark/The plight of black women in South Africa/Disneyland as therapy in a pyschiatric hospital/Rosie Logan – the prisoners' unofficial poet laureate
All about abortion/Carolyn Faulder
Inside everyone there's an electronically controlled, weed selective lawnmower longing to get out/Hilary Macaskill, Photographs by David Reed
Maverick in the mind/John Heilpern, Illustration by Roger Law
How are they teaching your child?/Joyce Robins, Photographs by Reg Wilkins
Rejoice, ye larks and owls/Hilary Rubinstein
Well, if you insist.../Auberon Waugh
One man's clothes/Peter Martin, Photographs by Terence Donovan
24 hours in the life of a British businesswoman/Joseph Wright, Illustration by Jean Lagarrigue
Afterwards/Jenny Wilkes, Photographs by Rosemary Adams
January...February...March/Arthur Eperon. Nova travel calendar of when to go where
We're just good furriends.../Caroline Baker, Photographs by Hans Feurer
Are you sleeping sensually?/Beds by Janet Fitch
Stockists
A heel of a height/Fashion extra by Caroline Baker, Photographs by Harri Peccinotti
Sense of the Orient/Cookery by Prue Leith, Illustration by Mike Cook
Astra Nova/Patric Walker
Up Front/edited by Stella Bingham
Fiction: The Rescue/V S Pritchett
View of my own/Irma Kurtz
Cover photograph/Harri Peccinotti
Staff
Editor/Gillian Cooke. Deputy editor, art director/David Hillman. Features editor/Russell Miller. Production editor/Sally Lewis. Sub editors/Anne Boston, Gaynor Crawford, Lesley Thornton. Art assistants/Carol Rainbird. Features/Carolyn Faulder, Stella Bingham, Maggy Meade-King, Betka Zamoyska. Fashion and beauty editor/Caroline Baker. Beauty consultant/Pat Baikie. Beauty assistant/Pip Newbery. Homes editor/Janet Fitch. Fiction editor/Margaret Pringle. Contributing editors/Irma Kurtz, Pat Barr, Ann Leslie, Bel Mooney, John Heilpern, Ken Martin (New York)

FEBRUARY 1974
Contents
Package kids boom/Arthur Eperon and Betka Zamoyska.
Priestly polemic – Morris West
Why babies are born/Judy Froshaug, Photograph by Donald Silverstein. Contraception up to date/Edited by Stella Bingham, Drawings by John Bavosi
My pill and I/Jane Ennis
The guilt edge between fact and fantasy/Catherine Storr, Illustration by Peter Brookes
'I have spread my dreams under your feet...'/Stella Bingham, Illustration by Arthur Robins
Stone walls do not a prison make/Pat Barr, Photographs by Aurora Roland
Whispering grass, police informer/Irma Kurtz, Illustration by John Gorham
'...to my wedded husband'/Donald Lehmkuhl
'What's wearing a tie got to do with education?'/Pat Barr, Photographs by Peter Howe
At home in the sun/by Arthur Eperon, Illustration by Dave Rowe
A girl's guide to gold/Fashion by Caroline Baker, Photographs by Harri Peccinotti
Hobbies with a fringe on top/handicrafts by Pip Newbery, Photographs by Trevor Sutton
Ahead of hair/Beauty by Caroline Baker, Photographs by Ian Stokes
Rugs with a worldly air/Design by Janet Fitch, Photographs by Harri Peccinotti
Eat up your greens like a good gourmet/ Prue Leith, Illustration by Joyce Tuhill
Astra Nova/Patric Walker
Up Front/edited by Stella Bingham
Fiction: A line of order/Judith Rascoe, Illustration by Howard Pemberton
A view of my own/Russell Miller
Cover photograph/Donald Silverstein
Staff
Editor/Gillian Cooke. Deputy editor, art director/David Hillman. Features editor/Russell Miller. Production editor/Sally Lewis. Sub editors/Anne Boston, Lesley Thornton. Art assistants/Carol Rainbird, Grant Alexander. Features/Carolyn Faulder, Stella Bingham, Maggy Meade-King, Betka Zamoyska. Fashion and beauty editor/Caroline Baker. Beauty consultant/Pat Baikie. Beauty assistant/Pip Newbery. Homes editor/Janet Fitch. Fiction editor/Margaret Pringle. Contributing editors/Irma Kurtz, Pat Barr, Ann Leslie, Bel Mooney, John Heilpern

MARCH 1974
Contents
The man who sugared the Pill/Paul Flattery, Photograph by Shaun Skelly
A mother is someone who learns as she goes/Catherine Storr
Come the revolution .../John Heilpern, Photographs by David Reed
The mechanics of loving/Dr Steven Roles
Doing time/Elaine Grand, Illustration by Mike McInnerney
The life and death of spring/Richard Mabey, Photographs by Tony Evans
Fairytale of New York/William Trevor, Photograph by Pierre Houles
Trim the sails, splice the mainbrace, and stiffen the sinews/Judith Cook, Photographs by Peter Howe
Dressed overall/Fashion by Caroline Baker, Photographs by Terence Donovan
Heart of the family/Home by Janet Fitch and Vivien Hislop, Photographs by Roger Stowell
Slimming on points/Beauty by Pat Baikie, Photographs by Christa Peters
Astra Nova/Patric Walker
Fiction: Did anyone ever ask Beatrice?/Byron Rogers, Illustration by Grete Lis
A view of my own/Irma Kurtz
Cover photograph/Graham Hughes
Staff
Editor/Gillian Cooke. Deputy editor, art director/David Hillman. Features editor/Russell Miller. Production editor/Sally Lewis. Sub editors/Anne Boston, Lesley Thornton. Art assistants/Carol Rainbird, Grant Alexander. Features/Carolyn Faulder, Stella Bingham, Maggy Meade-King, Betka Zamoyska. Fashion and beauty editor/Caroline Baker. Beauty consultant/Pat Baikie. Beauty assistant/Pip Newbery. Homes editor/Janet Fitch. Fiction editor/Margaret Pringle. Contributing editors/Irma Kurtz, Pat Barr, Ann Leslie, Bel Mooney, John Heilpern, David Jenkins

APRIL 1974
Contents
Larry Yaskiel can make you a star/Gordon Burn, Photographs by Robert McFarlane
Suppose you come out of hospital sicker than when you went in.../Eva Figes, Illustrations by Gillian Hills
The USA Enquirer/Ken Martin, Photographs by Aurora Roland
What is a woman?/Sally Vincent
A lot of girls are asking for 'pureplume'/ Ruth Inglis
A second class Christian in Rome/Betty Friedan, Illustration by Mike McInnerney
Cold Turkey/Veronica McNiff, Photographs by Neil Selkirk
Poet without prejudice/Pat Barr, Photograph by Peter Trump
Keep it clean, kids/Jo-an Jenkins and Lynne Alderson,
Forever ensemble/Fashion by Caroline Baker, Photographs by Alice Springs
In need of care and protection/Fashion by Caroline Baker, Photographs by Sarah Moon
How to make the best of tea/Stella Bingham and Maggy Meade-King, Photographs by David Reed
Everlasting flower power, Dried flowers/Janet Fitch, Photographs by Roger Stowell
How to lose a stone, A Nova slimming supplement/compiled by Pip Newbery, Illustrations by Arthur Robins
Astra Nova/Patric Walker
Letters Upfront/edited by Joan Jenkins and Lynne Alderson
Fiction: Who do you think you are?/Malcolm Bradbury, Illustration by Erhard Gottlicher
View of my own/Auberon Waugh
Cover photograph/Alice Springs
Staff
Editor/Gillian Cooke. Deputy editor, art director/David Hillman. Features editor/Russell Miller. Production editor/Sally Lewis, Sub editors/Anne Boston, Lesley Thornton, Art assistants/Carol Rainbird, Grant Alexander, Features/Carolyn Faulder, Stella Bingham, Maggy Meade-King, Betka Zamoyska, Fashion and beauty editor/Caroline Baker, Beauty consultant/Pat Baikie, Beauty assistant/Pip Newbery, Homes editor/Janet Fitch, Fiction editor/Margaret Pringle, Contributing editors/Irma Kurtz, Pat Barr, Ann Leslie, Bel Mooney John Heilpern, David Jenkins

MAY 1974
Contents
How the blues were born/Humphrey Lyttleton
Summertime blues/Penelope Mortimer, Illustration by Mike Terry,
Once in a blue Nova.../Photograph by Tony Evans, Design by Janet Fitch
What's in a blue stocking?/Ruth Brando
Where friends – and others – drop in out of the blue/Irma Kurtz, Photography by Rosemary Adams
Eamonn Andrews, blue eyed boy of the box/Illustrations by John McConnell
Virgin at the blue movies/John Sandilands
True Bluebell/Irma Kurtz
Boys and girls in blue/Maggy Meade-King, Photographs by Peter Howe
How blued-up are you?/Betka Zamoyska
Bolt for the blue, Running away/Carolyn Faulder, Illustrations by Arthur Robins
Blue period/Carolyn Faulder
Blue chip investments/Fashion and beauty by Caroline Baker and Pat Baikie, Photographs by Harri Peccinotti
Blue jean blues/Fashion by Caroline Baker, Photograph by Harri Pecinotti
How to make the best of blue cheese/Sally Lewis, Photographs by Donald Silverstein and Tony Evans
Colour it blue/Design by Janet Fitch, Photographs by Tony Evans
Astra Nova/Patric Walker
Fiction: Beginner's luck/David Pownall, Illustration by Edda Köchl
A view of my own/Patrick Campbell
Cover photograph/Harri Peccinotti
Staff
Editor/Gillian Cooke, Deputy editor, art director/David Hillman, Features editor/Russell Miller, Production editor/Sally Lewis, Sub editors/Anne Boston. Lesley Thornton. Art assistants/Carol Rainbird, Grant Alexander, David Harper. Features/Carolyn Faulder, Stella Bingham,Maggy Meade-King, Betka Zamoyska. Fiction editor/Margaret Pringle. Fashion and beauty editor/Caroline Baker, Beauty consultant/Pat Baikie. Beauty assistant/Pip Newbery. Homes editor/Janet Fitch. Contributing editors/Irma Kurtz, Pat Barr, Ann Leslie, Bel Mooney, John Heilpern, David Jenkins

JUNE 1974
Contents
Astra Nova/Patric Walker
Fiction: Long Distance. An extract from Penelope Mortimer's new novel
A view of my own/Arlene Sobel
It's in print/Fashion by Caroline Baker, Photographs by Guy Bourdin
Show a leg/Beauty by Pat Baikie, Photographs by Harri Peccinotti
Costume Piece/Fashion by Caroline Baker, Photographs by Harri Peccinotti
Self-contained/Cookery by Prue Leith, Photography by Roger Stowell
Letters to his Daughter/Amanda Allsop
A summer season/Photographs by Aurora Roland
Prude Power/Maggy Meade-King, Hilary Macaskill and Betka Zamoyska
All in good time/Judith Froshaug, Photographs by Graham Hughes
'I'm jacking Britain'/Hilary Macaskill, Photographs by Shaun Skelly
Violent playground/Judith Cook
Have you heard the one about Max Wall? He's a brick/Russell Miller, Photographs by Tony Evans
The whiff of the greasepaint, the whimper of the crowd/Anthony Carson
Building castles in the hair/Yvonne Roberts, Photographs by Peter Howe
Poems/Erica Jong
Staff
Editor/Gillian Cooke. Deputy editor, art director/David Hillman. Features editor/Russell Miller. Production editor/Sally Lewis. Sub editors/Anne Boston, Lesley Thornton. Art assistants/Carol Rainbird, Grant Alexander, David Harper. Features/Carolyn Faulder, Stella Bingham, Maggy Meade-King, Betka Zamoyska. Fiction editor/Margaret Pringle. Fashion and beauty editor/Caroline Baker. Beauty consultant/Pat Baikie. Beauty assistant/Pip Newbery. Homes editor/Janet Fitch. Contributing editors/Irma Kurtz, Pat Barr, Ann Leslie, Bel Mooney, John Heilpern, David Jenkins

JULY 1974
Contents
Astra Nova/Patric Walker
Fiction: Kieltys/Susan Hill, Illustration by William Rankin
A view of my own/Irma Kurtz
Lady on the loose/Fashion by Caroline Baker, Photographs by Hans Feurer
How to make the best of a sausage/Sally Lewis, Photograph by Roger Stowell. A guide to make you a connoisseur of katenrauchwurst and saucisson au poivre
Empire built of books/Anne Boston, Photographs by David Reed
Jerry and Charlie can get you most things wholesale/Roger Law, Photography by Dan Wynn
Give us this day our daily dose of hexachlorophene.../James Hamilton-Paterson, Illustration by Edda Köchl , Photographs by Benjamin Lee
Dead or alive/David Jenkins
Portrait of a genius by a genius/Charles James, designer
Who cares about nurses?/Carolyn Faulder, Photographs by Rosemary Adam.
Poem/Maxine Kumin
As flowers go by/Richard Mabey, Drawings by John Gorham

What do they think about us?/Par Barr, Illustrations by Sue Huntley
Boas are best/Liz Gould, Photograph by Rolph Gobits
"Where did I come from?'/Arthur Robins and Peter Mayle
Cover photograph/Han Feurer
Staff
Editor/Gillian Cooke. Deputy editor, art director/David Hillman. Features editor/Russell Miller. Production editor/Sally Lewis. Sub editors/Anne Boston, Lesley Thornton. Art assistants/Carol Rainbird, Grant Alexander, David Harper. Features/Carolyn Faulder, Stella Bingham, Maggy Meade-King, Betka Zamoyska. Fiction editor/Margaret Pringle. Fashion and beauty editor/Caroline Baker. Beauty consultant/Pat Baikie. Beauty assistant/Pip Newbery. Homes editor/Janet Fitch. Contributing editors/Irma Kurtz, Pat Barr, Ann Leslie, Bel Mooney, John Heilpern, David Jenkins

AUGUST 1974
Contents
Astra Nova/Patric Walker
Fiction: Penetrating to the heart of the forest/Angela Carter, Drawing by Mike McInnerney
A view of my own/Bel Mooney
Stitchless/Fashion by Caroline Baker, Photographs by Harri Peccinotti
When the sun shines.../Beauty by Pat Baikie, Illustrations by Mick Brownfield
How to make the best of green leaves. Green salads/Prue Leith and Maggy Meade-King, Illustrations by Agneta Noreth
The day the taxis went to the seaside/Elaine Grand, Photographs by Aurora Roland
Where Britain rests its weary head/Donald Zec, Illustration by Jean Lagarrigue
Father as mother/David Jenkins, Photographs by Gary Kruger
Transplants: are our hearts in it?/Russell Miller, Research by Fiona Grafton, Illustration by John Bavosi, Photographs by Nobby Clark and Phil Sayer
Professor for the real world/David Jenkins, Photograph by Donald Silverstein
'Some of the girls drink so much they pass out...'/Margaret Fishley, Illustrations by George Lacroix
Home truths about violence/Bel Mooney, Illustration by Rita Muhlbauer and Hanno Rink
The smallest show on earth/Liz Gould, Photographs by Rolph Gobits
The IUD – do we really know enough about it?/Carolyn Faulder
Never were there such devoted sisters/Mary James, Photographs by Mike Hardy
Cover photograph/Graham Hughes
Staff
Editor/Gillian Cooke. Deputy editor, art director/David Hillman. Features editor/Russell Miller. Production editor/Sally Lewis. Sub editors/Anne Boston, Lesley Thornton. Art assistants/Carol Rainbird, Grant Alexander. Features/Carolyn Faulder, Stella Bingham, Maggy Meade-King, Betka Zamoyska. Fiction editor/Margaret Pringle. Fashion and beauty editor/Caroline Baker. Beauty consultant/Pat Baikie. Beauty assistant/Pip Newbery. Homes editor/Janet Fitch. Contributing editors/Irma Kurtz, Pat Barr, Ann Leslie, Bel Mooney, John Heilpern, David Jenkins

SEPTEMBER 1974
Contents
Astra Nova/Patric Walker, Illustration by Edda Köchl
All you need to know about pregnancy and work/Maggie Meade-King
Fiction: The going-away clothes/David Pownall, Illustration by Karin Blume
A view of my own/William Trevor
Peasantly/Fashion by Caroline Baker, Photographs by Sarah Moon
Signs of the times, Collecting old clocks/Janet Fitch, Photograph by Roger Stowell
The great British pizza/Cookery by Peter Straub, Photographs by John Ferrara
In one ear and out the other/Fashion and beauty by Caroline Baker and Pat Baikie, Photographs by Ian Stokes
How to liberate your daughter in many uneasy lessons/Marion Meade, Illustration by Arthur Robins
Queen Mother of all Vietnam/Della Denman
Memory is made of...er.../Ruth Inglis, Illustration by Gillian Hills
Do you remember?/Tony Buzan
Rave on?/Illustrations by Jean-Paul Goude
God on whose side?/David Jenkins, Photographs by Peter Howe
Does sex ruin a good friendship?/Carol Dix, Illustrations by Arthur Robins
Dr Frankenstein's inspiration/Jane Ennis, Photograph by Rolph Gobits
You'll be a man, my son/James Hamilton-Paterson, Illustrations, by Peter Brookes
'I feel like some ex-prisoner in an occupied country...'/John Mortimer, Photograph by Donald Silverstein
The artistic integrity of a lesbian vampire/ Arlene Sobel
The unkindest cut of all?/Judy Froshaug
Cover photograph/Harri Peccinotti
Staff
Editor/Gillian Cooke. Deputy editor, art director/David Hillman. Features editor/Russell Miller. Production editor/Sally Lewis. Sub editors/Anne Boston, Lesley Thornton. Art assistants/Carol Rainbird, Grant Alexander. Features/Carolyn Faulder, Stella Bingham, Maggy Meade-King, Betka Zamoyska. Fiction editor/Margaret Pringle. Fashion and beauty editor/Caroline Baker. Beauty consultant/Pat Baikie. Beauty assistant/Pip Newbery. Design editor/Moira McConnell. Design consultant/ Janet Fitch. Contributing editors/Irma Kurtz, Pat Barr, Ann Leslie, Bel Mooney, John Heilpern, David Jenkins

OCTOBER 1974
Contents
Astra Nova/Patric Walker
Fiction: Between buses/Harris Dulany, Illustration by Dan Fern
A view of my own/Irma Kurtz. Is sex over-rated?
Glass plantation/Design by Janet Fitch, Photograph by Tony Evans. Indoor plants grown in an aquarium
The final coat/Fashion by Caroline Baker, Photographs by Roger Stowell
How they brought the good news from Memphis to Newcastle/Stella Bingham, Illustrations by Mike Terry
Checking out/Carolyn Faulder, Photograph by Shaun Skelly
The answer lies in the soil/Stella Bingham, Photographs by Malcolm Robertson
Paternity suits/Liz Gould, Photographs by Peter Howe
Poems/John Pudney
Hold your hand out, naughty boy/Pat Barr
The unacceptable faces of politicians/Margaret Fishley
Ee-aye-addio, Harvey's won t'cup/illustrations by Jean Lagarrigue
Danger – doctors sleepwalking/James Hamilton-Paterson, Illustrations by Candy Amsden
What ho, Wodehouse/Ruth Inglis, Illustration by Paul Leith
Cover photograph/Harri Peccinotti
Staff
Editor/Gillian Cooke. Deputy editor, art director/David Hillman. Features editor/Russell Miller. Production editor/Sally Lewis. Sub editors/Anne Boston, Lesley Thornton. Art assistant/Grant Alexander. Features/Carolyn Faulder, Stella Bingham, Maggy Meade-King, Betka Zamoyska. Fiction editor/Margaret Pringle. Fashion and beauty editor/Caroline Baker. Beauty consultant/Pat Baikie. Beauty assistant/Pip Newbery. Design editor/Moira McConnell. Design consultant/Janet Fitch. Contributing editors/Irma Kurtz, Pat Barr, Ann Leslie, Bel Mooney, John Heilpern, David Jenkins

NOVEMBER 1974
Contents
Astra Nova/by Patric Walker, Illustration by Goffin
All you need to know about caring for elderly parents/Maggy Meade-King
A view of my own/Ann Leslie
Dance, dance, dance little lady/Stella Bingham, Photographs by Geoff Howard
An Englishman's home is.../Colin Bell, Illustration by Mike Terry
Oh God, Alison, I can't stand it a minute longer/Illustrations by Arthur Robins, Photographs by Nobby Clark
The life and soul of a mining village/Pat Barr, Photographs by Jim Arnould
Mrs World/Lesley Garner, Photographs by Roger Stowell
The bitterest emotion of all/Judy Froshaug. Illustrations by Sue Coe-Szilagyi
Moments in time/Andre van Strip
Lest we forget – Nova's salute to the victims of the hunting field/Illustration by Roger Law, Photograph by Terry Jones
What makes Peter Hain a radical Liberal?/ Bel Mooney, Photograph by Peter Howe
Eyes and nays/Beauty by Pat Baikie, Illustrations by Celestino Valenti
Layered on thick/Fashion by Caroline Baker, Photographs by Hans Feurer
Presents by post/Lynne Alderson and Anne Boston
Roots of pleasure/Cookery by Prue Leith, Photograph by Roger Stowell
A breath of wet air/Humidifiers by Lynne Alderson, Illustrations by Ken Lewis
Cover photograph/Hans Feurer
Staff
Editor/Gillian Cooke. Deputy editor, art director/David Hillman. Features editor/Russell Miller. Production editor/Sally Lewis. Sub editors/Anne Boston, Lesley Thornton. Art assistant/Grant Alexander. Features/Carolyn Faulder, Stella Bingham, Maggy Meade-King, Betka Zamoyska. Fiction editor/Margaret Pringle. Fashion and beauty editor/Caroline Baker. Beauty consultant/Pat Baikie. Beauty assistant/Pip Newbery. Design editor/Moira McConnell. Design consultant/Janet Fitch.

Contributing editors/Irma Kurtz, Pat Barr, Ann Leslie, Bel Mooney, John Heilpern, David Jenkins

DECEMBER 1974
Contents
There will be snow and skating on the Thames/Keith Waterhouse
Family Gathering/Pat Barr, Photographs by Peter Howe
I believe in Christmas Father/Hilary Macaskill, Photographs by Donald Silverstein
Christmas fireside fun and games for all the family/Illustration by John Gorham, Graham Percy, Arthur Robins
When I was a child/Elizabeth Taylor
Mrs Lunt/Sir High Walpole
The plum pudding pantomime/Horace Mayhew
Good time dames/Elaine Grand, Photography by Donald Silverstein
Komic Karacter Kwiz/illustration by Mick Brownfield
If I were Father Christmas/Auberon Waugh, Photograph by Donald Silverstein
After all, it is His birthday/Carolyn Faulder
This year we'll do Christmas prop'ly/Patrick Campbell
Astra Nova/Patric Walker, Illustration by Edda Köchl
Christmas wrappings/Fashion by Caroline Baker, Photographs by Donald Silverstein
The groaning board/Prue Leith, Photographs by Roger Stowell
Spirits of the season/Kingsley Amis
My blue haze/George Melly, Photograph by Roger Stowell
Cover painting/Larry Learmonth
Staff
Editor/Gillian Cooke. Deputy editor, art director/David Hillman. Features editor/Russell Miller. Production editor/Sally Lewis. Sub editors/Anne Boston, Lesley Thornton. Art assistant/Grant Alexander. Features/Carolyn Faulder, Stella Bingham, Maggy Meade-King, Betka Zamoyska. Fiction editor/Margaret Pringle. Fashion and beauty editor/Caroline Baker. Beauty consultant/Pat Baikie. Beauty assistant/Pip Newbery. Design editor/Moira McConnell. Design consultant/Janet Fitch. Contributing editors/Irma Kurtz, Pat Barr, Ann Leslie, Bel Mooney, John Heilpern, David Jenkins

JANUARY 1975
Contents
Astra Nova/Patric Walker
Short Story: Office Romances/William Trevor
A view of my own/John Heilpern
What is a housewife?/Ann Oakley and Bel Mooney
Could this be the face of men's lib?/Yvonne Roberts
Poems/Maxine Kumin
Sir Fred Ashton/Profile by Pat Barr
Flash bang wallop. Family photography/Moira McConnell
I'm late, I'm stupid...Irish childhood/William Trevor
Can we stop growing old?/Wendy Cooper
Very nice homes from home. Theatrical landladies/Gordon Burn
Cot deaths investigated/Paulette Pratt
What I'd do if I were in charge/Judith Cook
Stop the car, I want to get out/Carolyn Faulder
Keep on caring. A view of the Salvation Army/Peter Howe
Creating a disturbance/Illustrations by Mike McInnerney
Beauty: Ladies prefer blondes/Pat Baikie
Fashion: Getting into the habit/Caroline Baker
Cookery: Bang on bangers/Prue Leith
Travel: Places in between/Arthur Eperon
Cover photograph/Roger Stowell
Staff
Editor/Gillian Cooke. Deputy editor, art director/David Hillman. Features editor/Russell Miller. Production editor/Sally Lewis. Sub editors/Anne Boston, Lesley Thornton. Art assistants/Grant Alexander, Valerie Burnett. Features/Carolyn Faulder, Stella Bingham, Maggy Meade-King, Pip Newbery. Fiction editor/Margaret Pringle. Fashion and beauty editor/Caroline Baker. Beauty consultant/Pat Baikie. Fashion assistant/Deirdre Hancock. Design editor/Moira McConnell. Design consultant/Janet Fitch. Design assistant/Lynne Alderson. Contributing editors/Irma Kurtz, Pat Barr, Ann Leslie, Bel Mooney, John Heilpern, David Jenkins

FEBRUARY 1975
Contents
Astra Nova/Patric Walker
A view of my own/John Mortimer
Housing special. How best to get a home/Frances Cairncross and Hamish McRae
Earthbound. What are the Court Line pilots doing now?/Frank Branston
Whose class enemy? Joe Gormley interviewed/Andrew Duncan
London street markets/Rosie Logan and Colin Duff
Kid's stuff. Mr Pugh the puppet man/Maggy Meade-King
Jehovah's Witnesses. An investigation/ Peter Gillman
Poem/James Hamilton-Paterson
Not just a pretty pair. Breast feeding/ Judy Froshaug
Now you see them, now you don't. Magicians' convention/Pat Barr
Angela Down. A profile/Wilfred De'Ath
Jo Martin gave up everything to look after her old folk/Elaine Grand
Good time clothes/Pip Newbery
I guess it's fufu for lunch...An extract from 'Black Zion'/ David Jenkins
Fashion: Slithery knittery/Caroline Baker
Beauty: The very pink of perfection/ Caroline Baker
Design: Pots in common/Moira McConnell
Cookery: Creating a stink/Prue Leith
Cover photograph/Graham Hughes
Staff
Editor/Gillian Cooke. Deputy editor, art director/David Hillman. Production editor/Sally Lewis. Sub editors/Anne Boston, Lesley Thornton. Art assistants/Grant Alexander, Valerie Burnett. Features/Carolyn Faulder, Stella Bingham, Maggy Meade-King, Pip Newbery. Fiction editor/Margaret Pringle. Fashion and beauty editor/Caroline Baker. Beauty consultant/Pat Baikie. Fashion assistant/Deirdre Hancock. Design editor/Moira McConnell. Design consultant/Janet Fitch. Design assistant/Lynne Alderson. Contributing editors/ Irma Kurtz, Pat Barr, Ann Leslie, Bel Mooney, John Heilpern, David Jenkins

MARCH 1975
Contents
Astra Nova/Patric Walker
Sally Vincent reads books
All you need to know...about spring cleaning/Lynne Alderson
Short story: A Love Story/Penelope Mortimer
A view of my own/Irma Kurtz
Bottoms are tops. A guide for men who turn you on/Carolyn Faulder
Who needs wrinkles? Hormone replacement therapy/Lyn Owen
Ivan Illich, philosopher, priest, social critic, interviewed/James Hamilton-Paterson
Who am I? : the search for an identity/Catherine Storr; How three women found themselves/Hilary Macaskill; How Lord Clark got to know himself/Pat Barr
Priests in training/Hilary Macaskill

Victoria Station, its passenger jams and staff of hundreds observed/Peter Martin
You can't win 'em all. Boxer Ray Fallone interviewed/Liz Gould
Everyone's got a book in them somewhere. Unpublished writers/Sally Vincent
Please put a penny in. Collecting boxes/ Margaret Pringle
Beauty: Do it yourself diet/Pat Baikie
Design: Fresh as a fake daisy/Moira McConnell
Fashion: T-shirts – to give you all the support you need/by Caroline Baker
Fashion: Khaki kolored kraze/Caroline Baker
Cookery: The stuffing dreams are made of/ Prue Leith
Cover photograph/Harri Peccinotti
Staff
Editor/Gillian Cooke. Deputy editor, art director/David Hillman. Production editor/Sally Lewis. Sub editors/Anne Boston, Lesley Thornton. Art assistants/Grant Alexander, Valerie Burnett. Features/Carolyn Faulder, Stella Bingham, Maggy Meade-King, Pip Newbery. Fiction editor/Margaret Pringle. Fashion and beauty editor/Caroline Baker. Beauty consultant/Pat Baikie. Fashion assistant/Deirdre Hancock. Design editor/Moira McConnell. Design consultant/Janet Fitch. Design assistant/Lynne Alderson. Contributing editors/Irma Kurtz, Pat Barr, Ann Leslie, Bel Mooney, John Heilpern, David Jenkins

APRIL 1975
Contents
Astra Nova/Patric Walker
Sally Vincent reads books
Alan Coren eats out
All you need to know...about exterminating pests/Lynne Alderson
Short story: Babes in Benidorm/Pamela Haines
A view of my own/John Mortimer
Stan Flashman – king of the ticket touts/Barbara Drillsma
Access to the children/Elizabeth Dickson
How to strengthen the inner woman. Martial arts/Georgina David
The Common Market Game/Oliver Pritchett
Drugs and the unborn child/Carolyn Faulder
Busmen's day out at Newbury/Liz Gould
'I haven't been young for some time.' Tennessee Williams talks to Irma Kurtz
One bad day on the Stock Exchange/ Andrew Duncan
Francoise Giroud, Minister for Women's Affairs. Interviewed/Carolyn Faulder
Boys and girls come out to play. Which would they rather be?/Hilary Macaskill
Back to Berlin. Going home/Eva Figes
Shawls: Cross your heart/Caroline Baker
Fashion: Re-cycle your style/Caroline Baker
Mahogany: Wood with a touch of polish/Moira McConnell
Fashion extra: Sodden in the rain/Caroline Baker
Beauty: Plaits grow up/Pat Baikie
Travel: What's on in Europe?/Sally Lewis and Arthur Eperon
Cookery: The answer is a lemon/Prue Leith
Staff
Editor/Gillian Cooke. Art director/David Hillman. Assistant editor/Carolyn Faulder. Sub editors/Anne Boston, Lesley Thornton. Art assistants/Grant Alexander, Valerie Burnett. Features/Stella Bingham, Maggy Meade-King, Pip Newbery. Fiction editor/Margaret Pringle. Fashion and beauty editor/Caroline Baker. Beauty consultant/Pat Baikie. Fashion assistant/Deirdre Hancock. Design editor/Moira McConnell. Design assistant/Lynne Alderson. Contributing editors/Irma Kurtz, Pat Barr, Ann Leslie, Bel Mooney, John Heilpern, David Jenkins

From May 1975 Nova's page size was so reduced that there was no room for by-lines.

MAY 1975
Contents
Irma Kurtz: In my opinion
An extract from John Updike's latest novel
Staff
Editor/Gillian Cooke. Art director/David Hillman. Assistant editor/Carolyn Faulder. Sub editors/Anne Boston, Lesley Thornton. Art assistants/Grant Alexander, Valerie Burnett. Features/Stella Bingham, Maggy Meade-King, Pip Newbery. Fiction editor/Margaret Pringle. Fashion and beauty editor/Caroline Baker. Beauty consultant/Pat Baikie. Fashion assistant/Deirdre Hancock. Design editor/Moira McConnell. Design assistant/Lynne Alderson. Contributing editors/Irma Kurtz, Pat Barr, Ann Leslie, Bel Mooney, John Heilpern, David Jenkins

JUNE 1975
Contents
The Eco-Spasm Report: Alvin Toffler looks to the future
Patric Walker
Irma Kurtz: In my opinion
Staff
Editor/Gillian Cooke. Art director/David Hillman. Assistant editor/Carolyn Faulder. Sub editors/Anne Boston, Lesley Thornton. Art assistants/Grant Alexander, Valerie Burnett. Features/Stella Bingham, Maggy Meade-King, Pip Newbery. Fiction editor/Margaret Pringle. Education/Eileen Totten. Fashion and beauty editor/Caroline Baker. Beauty consultant/Pat Baikie. Fashion assistant/Deirdre Hancock. Design editor/Moira McConnell. Design assistant/Lynne Alderson. Contributing editors/Irma Kurtz, Pat Barr, Ann Leslie, Bel Mooney, John Heilpern, David Jenkins

JULY 1975
Contents
Patric Walker
Irma Kurtz: In my opinion
Staff
Editor/Gillian Cooke. Art director/David Hillman. Assistant editor/Carolyn Faulder. Sub editors/Anne Boston, Lesley Thornton. Art assistants/Grant Alexander, Valerie Burnett. Features/Stella Bingham, Maggy Meade-King, Pip Newbery. Fiction editor/Margaret Pringle. Education/Eileen Totten. Fashion and beauty editor/Caroline Baker. Beauty consultant/Pat Baikie. Fashion assistant/Deirdre Hancock. Design editor/Moira McConnell. Design assistant/ Lynne Alderson. Contributing editors/Irma Kurtz, Pat Barr, Ann Leslie, Bel Mooney, John Heilpern, David Jenkins

AUGUST 1975
Contents
William Rushton demonstrates tie-to-Y-fronts stripping
Patric Walker
Irma Kurtz: In my opinion
Short story: Mrs Silly/William Trevor
Staff
Editor/Gillian Cooke. Art director/David Hillman. Assistant editor/Carolyn Faulder. Sub editors/Anne Boston, Lesley Thornton. Art assistant/Valerie Burnett. Features/Stella Bingham, Maggy Meade-King, Pip Newbery. Fiction editor/Margaret Pringle. Education/Eileen Totten. Fashion and beauty editor/Caroline Baker. Beauty consultant/Pat Baikie. Fashion assistant/Deirdre Hancock. Design editor/Moira McConnell. Design assistant/Lynne Alderson. Contributing editors/Irma Kurtz, Pat Barr, Ann Leslie, Bel Mooney, John Heilpern, David Jenkins

SEPTEMBER 1975
Contents
Patric Walker
Irma Kurtz: In my opinion
Short story: Against Witches/by M K Gilchrist
Staff
Editor/Gillian Cooke. Art director/David Hillman. Assistant editor/Carolyn Faulder. Sub editors/Anne Boston, Lesley Thornton. Art assistant/Valerie Burnett. Features/Stella Bingham, Maggy Meade-King. Fiction editor/Margaret Pringle. Education/Eileen Totten. Fashion and beauty editor/Caroline Baker. Beauty consultant/Pat Baikie. Fashion assistant/Deirdre Hancock. Design editor/Moira McConnell. Design assistant/Lynne Alderson. Contributing editors/Irma Kurtz, Pat Barr, Ann Leslie, Bel Mooney, John Heilpern, David Jenkins

OCTOBER 1975
Contents
Has moderation gone too far?/ asks John Mortimer
Poems/Valerie Grosvenor Myer
Patric Walker
Irma Kurtz: In my opinion
Books: Margaret Drabble
Cover photograph/Roger Stowell
Staff
Editor/Gillian Cooke. Art director/David Hillman. Assistant editor/Carolyn Faulder. Sub editors/Anne Boston, Lesley Thornton. Art assistant/Valerie Burnett. Features/Stella Bingham, Maggy Meade-King. Fiction/Margaret Pringle. Education/Eileen Totten. Fashion and beauty editor/Caroline Baker. Beauty consultant/Pat Baikie. Fashion assistant/Deirdre Hancock. Design editor/Moira McConnell. Design assistant/Lynne Alderson. Contributing editors/Irma Kurtz, Pat Barr, Ann Leslie, Bel Mooney, John Heilpern, David Jenkins.

Index

Page numbers in *italics* refer to illustration captions

A
Abba, 194
Agha, M F, 37
Agnew, Spiro, 170
Aldridge, Alan, 13, *53, 66*
Aldrin, Buzz, 88
Alexandre, *83*
Alfie, 56
Ali, Muhammed, 70, 194
All Along The Watchtower, 80
All You Need Is Love, 70
Allen, Woody, 170
Allsop, Kenneth, 47
American Pie, 140
Amin, Idi, 140
Amis, Kingsley, 36
Anderson, Lindsey, 80
Anne, Princess, 170
Apicella, Enzo, *197*
Arbus, Diane, 13, *92*
Armstrong, Neil, 88
Arrowsmith, Clive, *70*
Ascent of Man (Bronowski), 170
Ashe, Arthur, 206
Ashton, Sir Frederick, *211*
Ayckbourn, Alan, 170

B
Bacon, Francis, 36
Baikie, Pat, *173*
Baker, Caroline, 12, 47, *69, 101, 110, 116, 148, 159, 182, 188, 197, 212*
Barbarella, 80
Bardot, Brigitte, 36
Barger, Mollie, *50*
Barker, Ronnie, 194
Barnard, Dr Christian, 70
Barr, Pat, *211*
Batman, 56
Beach Boys, the, 56
Beard, Peter, *44*
Beatles for Sale, 48
Beatles, The, 6, 37, 48, 56, *56,* 70, 80, 87
Beatty, Warren, 70
Bennett, Alan, 170
Bentley/Farell/Burnett, *138*
Biba, 87, *152*
Biggs, Ronnie, 48
Bill, Max, *44*
Bingham, Salle, *167*
Birdsall, Derek, 11–12, 13, 47, *82, 83, 94*
Birk, Alma, *66*
Birkin, Jane, 87
Bjerkaas, Ingrid, *60*
Black and Silver (Frayn), *91*
Blackburn, John, 13, 47
Blake, George, 56
Blake, Peter, 13, *102*
Blazing Saddles, 194
Blenkinsop, Maggie, *138*
Bohemian Rhapsody, 206
Bolan, Marc, 140
Bonnie and Clyde, 70
Bono, Sonny, 48
Booker, Christopher, 47
Born to Run, 206
Bourdin, Guy, *162*
Bowie, David, 7, 169, 170
Bragg, Melvyn, *185*
Brando, Marlon, 36, 140
Brandt, Willy, *194*
Breakfast of Champions (Vonnegut), 170
Bridge Over Troubled Water, 98
Brodovitch, Alexey, 37, *38*
Bronowski, Jacob, 170
Brooks, Mel, 194
Brooks, Ray, 48
Bulmer, John, *43*
Burroughs, William, 36
Butch Cassidy and the Sundance Kid, 98

C
Caine, Michael, 56
Campbell, Donald, 70
Candid Camera, 50
Candle In The Wind, 194
Cardin, *65*
Carita, *83*
Carter, Gordon, *48*
Castle, Barbara, *157*
Cathy Come Home, 56
Cher, 48
Chichester, Francis, 70
Christie, Julie, 48
Churchill, Sir Winston, 48
Cleese, John, 206
Cleland, T M, 37
Clockwork Orange, A, 112
Cocker, Joe, 80
Coe, Sue, *156*
Connors, Jimmy, 206
Conran, Caroline, *109, 138*
Cooke, Gillian, 12, 13, 87, *149*
Cooper, Wendy, *135*
Cosmopolitan, 12–13, *149*
Couples (Updike), 80
Courrèges, André, 46, *82, 83*
Cracknell, Alan, *138*
Crawford, Michael, 48
Crookston, Peter, 11, 12, 13, 86–7
Cudlipp, Hugh, 7, 8, *149*
Cushing, Peter, *203*

D
D'Achille, Gino , *190*
Daily Mirror, 7, *149*
David, Elizabeth, 8, 47
Davis, Angela, *151*
Davis, Miles, 36
Dean, James, 36
Death in Venice, 112
Deighton, Len, *75*
Devlin, Bernadette, *151*
Dior, Christian, *88, 91*
Donovan, Terence, 13, 87, *159, 170*
Douglas-Holme, Sir, 48
Dr Chivago, 48
Dubcek, Alexander, 80
Duffy, *69, 80, 124*
Dunaway, Faye, 70
Dunne, Nell, 48
Dylan, Bob, 48

E
Easy Rider, 88, *102*
Edward VIII, King, 140
Eleanor Rigby, 56
Elizabeth, II, Queen, *83*
Elle, 37, *43*
Ennis, Jane, *203*
Equus (Shaffer), 170
Eros, 40
Eskapa, Shirley, *156*
Esquire, 37, *38*
Evans, Caroline, *192*
Evans, Tony, 87, *138, 192*

F
Faithfull, Marianne, 48
Fallover, Bill, 13, 47
Fantoni, Barry, *53, 75*
Farr, Tommy, *178*
Faulder, Carolyn, *133, 142, 192*
Fawlty Towers, 206
Female Eunuch, The (Greer), 98, *133*
Fern, Dan, *215*
Ferry, Brian, 170
Feurer, Hans, 13, *78, 86, 98, 105, 110, 112, 115, 165, 197*
Fiddler on the Roof, 70
Fieldhouse, Harry, 7–8, 13, 46, 47
Fischer, Bobby, 140
Flair, 10
Fleckhaus, Willy, 37, *40, 44*
Fletcher, Alan, 12
Foil, Alain Le, *109*
Fonda, Jane, 80
Fonda, Peter, 88, *102*
Fonssagrives, Fernand, *38*
Forbes, Colin, 12
Fordham, Peta, *54*
Foreman, George, 194
Formby, George, *102*
Frayn, Michael, *91*
Freewheelin' Bob Dylan, 48
French Connection, The, 112

G
Gainsbourg, Serge, 87
Gaulle, Charles de, 87, *88,* 98
Gaye, Marvin, 88
George, Adrian, *85*
Geraldo, *178*
Get Back, 88
Ghandi, Indira, 56
Giacobetti, *94*
Gill, Bob, *85*
Gillman, Peter, *209*
Ginzburg, Ralph, *40*
Glitter, Gary, 170
Gobits, Rolph, 168, *203, 211*
Godfather, The, 140
Godspell, 140
Golden, Robert, *136*
Good Vibrations, 56
Gorham, John, *200, 215*
Goude, Jean-Paul, 87, *102, 104, 151, 194*
Gould, Liz, *203*
Grade, Lew, *75*
Graduate, The, 80
Graham, Billy, 48
Grande, Elaine, *190*
Green, Timothy, *215*
Greer, Germaine, 98, *133*
Guardian, 12
Guevara, Che, 70
Gurley, Helen, 12

H
Habeas Corpus (Bennett), 170
Hackett, Dennis, 9, 10, 11, 13, 37, 47, 86
Hair, 80
Hair (Cooper), *135*
Hamilton, David, *43*
Hamilton-Paterson, James, *211*
Harper's Bazaar, 36, 37, *38*
Harry, Debbie, 169
Hattersley Jr., Ralph M, *40*
Hawn, Goldie, 80
Heath, Edward, 48, 98, *149,* 170
Hefner, Hugh, *60*
Heilpern, John, *201*
Hemery, David, 80
Hendrix, Jimi, 80
Hey Jude, 80
Hill, Graham, 80
Hill, Susan, *185*
Hillman, David, 11, 12, 13, 37, *43,* 87, *94, 109, 111, 121, 138, 145, 157, 173, 185, 192, 196, 197, 204*
Hispard, Marc, *43*
Hoffman, Dustin, 80, 88
Holland, Mary, *60*
Holmes, John, *133, 157*

Honky Tonk Women, 88
Hopcraft, Arthur, 9
Hopkins, Mary, 80
Howe, Peter, *142, 189, 211*
Hughes, Robert, *97*
Hulanicki, Barbara, *152*
Huston, Angelica, *165*

I
I Got You Babe, 48
I Heard It Through The Grapevine, 88
If, 80
Illich, Ivan, *211*
Ince, Angela, 8
Inglis, Ruth, *189, 201*
International Publishing Corporation (IPC), 7, 10, 11, 12, 47, 87
Israel, Marvin, *36*

J
Jacklin, Tony, 88
Jackson, Michael, 98
Jagger, Mick, 98
Jaws, 206
Je T'Aime, Moi Non Plus, 88
Jenkins, David, *149*
Jesus Christ Superstar, 140
Jewell, Jimmy, *178*
John, Elton, 194
Jonvelle, *88, 91, 110, 130*

K
Kane, Art, *43*
Kaplan, Barry, *85*
Keenan, Brigid, 9–10, *80, 82, 83*
Kennedy, Bobby, 80, *80*
Kennedy, John F, 36–7
Kennington, Jill, *69*
Kerouac, Jack, 36
King, Cecil Harmsworth, 7, 47
King, Martin Luther, 80
Kinks, the, 48
Kinsella, Thomas, *53*
Knack, The, 48
Knapp, Peter, 37, *43, 159*
Köchl, Edda, *66, 109, 122, 156, 185, 215*
Kosygin, *194*
Kurtz, Irma, 9, 47, *85, 145, 200*

L
Lagarrigue, Jean, *156, 184, 185*
Langley, Lee, *55*
Larkin, Philip, 46
Last, Don, *82*
Last Tango in Paris, 140
Law, Roger, 13, *75, 133, 157, 191*
Lear, Amanda, *124*
Led Zeppelin, 112
Leiter, Saul, *36, 43, 60, 110, 130*
Leith, Paul, *201*
Leith, Prue, *192, 215*
Lennon, John, 88
Lewis, Norman, *102, 109*
Liberman, Alexander, 37
Life, 37
Lindsay, John, *156*
Little Help From My Friends, A, 80
Longford, Lord, *157*
Louis, Joe, *178*
Lubalin, Herb, *40*
Lucan, Lord, *194*

M
Mackinnon, Stewart, *156, 167, 185*
Maclean, Don, 140
Macmillan, Harold, 36, 37
Mailer, Norman, 170
Malcolm X, 48
Man About Town, 43
Manson, Charles, 98
Mao Tse-Tung, *194*
Marilyn (Mailer), 170
Marsh, Veronica, *111*
Martin, Ken, *156*
Martin, Peter, *92, 97, 136*
*M*A*S*H,* 98
Maxwell, Max, *43*
McCall's, 37, *40*
McConnell, John, 12, *204*
McCullin, Don, *116*
McGovern, George, *156*
McInnerney, Mike, 13, 87, *167, 191*
McKenzie, Scott, 70
McNish, Althea, *111*
Medical Nemesis (Illich), *211*
Meir, Golda, *194*
Merrill, Anne, *156, 185*
Midnight Cowboy, 88
Miller, Anthony Maurice, *178*
Miller, Russell, *184*
Minshall, John, *55*
Miyake, Issey, *145*
Monk, Thelonius, 36
Monkees, The, 56
Monroe, Marilyn, 36, *40,* 170
Montgomery, David, *97*
Monty Python's Flying Circus, 88, *88*
Moon, Sarah, 13, 87, *116, 127*
Mooney, Bel, *157*
Moore, Bobby, 56
Morris, Desmond, 70
Mortimer, John, *207*
Murray, Ruby, *178*
Muskie, Edmund, *156*

N
Naked Ape, The (Morris), 70
Ned Kelly, 98
Neves, Vivian, 112, *112*
New Yorker, 12, 87
Newman, Paul, 98, 170
Newnes, George, 7, 10, 46, 47
Newton, Helmut, 13, 87, *127, 176, 177, 212*
Nicholson, Jack, 206, *206*
Night (Pinter), *91*
Nixon, Richard, 80, 140, *156,* 194
Norma (Owen), *91*
Norman Conquests trilogy (Ayckbourn), 170

O
O'Brien, Edna, *53*
One Flew Over The Cuckoo's Nest, 206
Ono, Yoko, 88
Osborne, John, 36
Osmonds, the, 170
Owen, Alun, *91*

P
Parker, Charlie, 36, 47
Parkin, Molly, 9, 12, *46, 60, 65, 66, 78*
Paul, Art, 37
Peccinotti, Harri, *3,* 9, 13, 37, 46, 47, *50, 53, 54, 56, 60, 62, 73,* 87, *94, 111, 121, 134, 135, 145, 148, 152, 168, 182, 188, 196, 197*
Penn, Irving, *39*
Pentagram, 12
Perón, Isabel, 194
Persia, Shah of, *194*
Peters, Christa, 37, *44*
Peters, Pauline, *102*
Phillips, Captain Mark, 170
Pickering, Paul, *167*
Pigott, Lester, 98
Pinter, Harold, *91*
Playboy, 37, *165*
Pocknell, David, *185*
Polanski, Roman, 98
Pollock, Jackson, 36
Porridge, 194
Powell, Enoch, 80, *151*
Practical Mechanics, 10
Presley, Elvis, 36, 70

Q
Quant, Mary, 6, *152*
Queen, 206
Queen, 9, 37, *43,* 47

R
Rabanne, Paco, *46, 65*
Rainier, Prince, *194*
Rand, Michael, 11, 37, *157*
Randall, Alan, *102*
Rave, 10
Redford, Robert, 98, 170
Reed, David, *201*
Reid, Jimmy, *201*
Renzio, Toni del, *60*
Rhodes, Zandra, *111*
Richardson, Bob, *165*
River Deep, Mountain High, 56
Rizzo, Willy, *43*
Robins, Arthur, *207, 215*
Robinson, Robert, 47
Rocky Horror Show, The, 170
Rolling Stones, The, 6, 48, 70, 88
Rolling Stones Volume II, 48
Routh, Jonathan, *50*
Rowan and Martin's Laugh-in, 80
Roxy Music, 170
Russell, Ken, 194

S
Sailing, 206
Saint Laurent, Yves, 87
San Francisco, 70
Sassoon, Vidal, 47
Sayer, Phil, 168, *209*
Selassie, Emperor Haile, 194
Sergeant Pepper's Lonely Hearts Club Band, 70
Shaffer, Peter, 170
Sharif, Omar, 48
Shaw, Sandie, 47, 48
Sheridan, Geoffrey, *191*
Show, 37, *39*
Shrimpton, Jean, *110*
Shriver Jr., Sargent, *156*
Sieff, Jeanloup, *46, 65, 73, 101, 140*
Sillitoe, Alan, *133*
Silverstein, Don, *178*
Simon and Garfunkel, 98, *98*
Sinclair, Clive, 140
Slater, Jim, *184*
Sleeper, The, 170
Smith, Ian, 48
Smithies, Bill, 13
Sokolsky, Mel, *39*
Solzhenitsyn, Alexander, 194
Sound of Music, The, 48
Spassky, Boris, 140
Speight, Johnny, 56
Springfield, Dusty, 47
Springsteen, Bruce, 206, *206*
Stairway To Heaven, 112
Steadman, Mark, *156*
Steadman, Ralph, 9, *53*
Stern, Bert, *40*
Stewart, Rod, 206
Sting, The, 170
Stingray, 48
Stone, Gilbert, *91, 138*
Stonehouse, John, 194
Storch, Otto, 37, *40*
Straw Dogs, 112
Sunday Bloody Sunday, 112
Sunday Times Magazine, 11, 12, 37, 86, 87, *94, 97, 157*
Supremes, The, 48, *157*

T
Tate, Sharon, 98
Tatler, 7–8
Taylor, Shaw, *200*
Thatcher, Margaret, 112, *157*
Those Were The Days, 80
'Till Death Us Do Part, 56
Times, The, 112, *112*
Tindall, Gillian, *156*
Tommy, 194
Town, 37, *43*
Treacy, Eleanor, 37
Trevor, William, *122*
Turbeville, Deborah, 168, *180*
Turner, Ike, 56
Turner, Tina, 56
Tushingham, Rita, 48
Twen, 37, *44*
Twiggy, 56, *56*
Tynan, Kenneth, 48

U
Ungaro, *65*
Up the Junction (Dunne), 48
Updike, John, 80

V
Valenti, Celestino, 13, 87, *122, 164, 173*
Vanity Fair, 37
Vargas, Alberto, *165*
Vincent, 140
Vincenzi, Penny, 8, 12, 47, *48*
Vogue, 37
Vonnegut, Kurt, 170

W
Wade, Veronica, *94*
Walker, Patric, 9, 47
Warhol, Andy, 112
Warris, Ben, *178*
Waterhouse, Keith, 36
Waterloo, 194
Weisbecker, Philippe, *133, 156*
White II, Charlie, *192*
Whiting, Audrey, *55*
Who, The, 48
Williams, Shirley, *157*
Wilson, Harold, 70, *194*
Wodehouse, PG, *201*
Wolf, Henry, 37, *38, 39*
Wolsey, Tom, 37, *43*
Woman's Own, 10
Wykes, Alan, *54*

Y
Yamamoto, Kansai, *145*
Yana, *178*
Yellow Submarine, 56, *56*

David Hillman was *Nova*'s art director from 1969 until it closed in 1975; he was also deputy editor during that time. He had previously been a designer at the *Sunday Times Magazine*. In 1976 he set up his own business and went to Paris to work for *Le Matin*. From 1978 he was a partner of the international design group Pentagram for 29 years, and now runs his own studio. Amongst his best-known work there was the redesign of the *Guardian* in 1987 and of numerous magazines including *New Statesman* and *Society and Design*.

Harri Peccinotti was *Nova*'s first art director – as photographer as well as designer. He had previously worked in advertising before becoming art director of *Flair* and *Vanity Fair*. In the Seventies, he continued to shoot for *Nova* and magazines such as *Vogue*, *Elle* and *Marie Claire* and then moved to Paris, working for *Le Nouvel Observateur* then *Le Matin* and *Rolling Stone*. More recently he has photographed for *Sartoria*, *Cube*, *Playboy*, *Esquire*, *The Gourmand* and *7000 Magazine*. His work has been exhibited in Florence, Rome and Paris.

David Gibbs cut his journalistic teeth in the 1960s at IPC Business Press, which in the IPC firmament was the less glamorous cousin of IPC Magazines, *Nova*'s publisher. He met David Hillman at Pentagram in the 1980s and the two collaborated on a number of books, including this and the bestselling *Century Makers*, a celebration of 20th-century ingenuity. In pursuit of income and happiness as a writer and editor, he has worked for many commercial, academic and institutional clients in print, videos, websites, museums and books, in Britain and around the world.

The authors and publisher would like to acknowledge the following for the illustrations listed by page number.

Page 46
Daily Mirror, Mirror Group Newspapers '86 Ltd
The Freewheelin' Bob Dylan, CBS Records/ Sony Music
The Knack, poster, Vintage Magazine Collection.
Page 56
Vogue, Condé Nast Publications Limited
Daily Mirror, Mirror Group Newspapers '86 Ltd
Yellow Submarine, cartoon, Vintage Magazine Collection.
Page 62
Sunday Citizen, Mirror Group Newspapers '86 Ltd
Daily Express, Express Newspapers Ltd
Sgt Pepper's Lonely Heart's Club Band, Apple Corps Limited.
Page 80
The Evening News, Associated Newspapers/Solo
Evening Standard, Associated Newspapers/Solo
Hair, Polydor Limited.
Page 88
Monty Python's Flying Circus, BBC TV/Vintage Magazine Collection
Man on the Moon, NASA
Daily Mirror, Mirror Group Newspapers '86 Ltd.
Page 98
Butch Cassidy and The Sundance Kid, 20th Century-Fox/Vintage Magazine Collection
Bridge Over Troubled Water, Sony Music
The Female Eunuch, HarperCollins Publishers.
Page 112
Evening Standard, Associated Newspapers/Solo
The Times/Fisons, Times Newspapers Limited
A Clockwork Orange, poster, Vintage Magazine Collection.
Page 140
Evening Standard, Associated Newspapers/Solo
Spassky vs Fischer, Harri Peccinotti
Last Tango in Paris, poster, Vintage Magazine Collection.
Page 170
Aladdin Sane, MainMan SAAG
The Sunday Times, Times Newspapers Limited
The Sun, News Group Newspapers Ltd.
Page 194
Daily Mail, Associated Newspaper Holdings
Daily Mirror, Mirror Group Newspapers '86 Ltd
The Times, Times Newspapers Limited.
Page 198
Born to Run, Sony Music
One Flew Over The Cuckoo's Nest, United Artists/Vintage Magazine Collection
Daily Mail, Associated Newspaper Holdings.

Every effort has been made to trace and acknowledge all copyright holders. The authors and publisher would like to apologise if any omissions have been made.